HARVARD MIDDLE EASTERN MONOGRAPHS

XVIII

REBIRTH OF A NATION

THE ORIGINS AND RISE OF MOROCCAN NATIONALISM, 1912–1944

BY

JOHN P. HALSTEAD

DISTRIBUTED FOR THE

CENTER FOR MIDDLE EASTERN STUDIES

OF HARVARD UNIVERSITY BY

HARVARD UNIVERSITY PRESS

CAMBRIDGE, MASSACHUSETTS

1969

SBN 674-75000-4

Second Printing, 1969

LIBRARY OF CONGRESS CATALOG CARD NUMBER 67-31566

PRINTED IN THE UNITED STATES OF AMERICA

ACKNOWLEDGMENTS

To express my gratitude to those who have helped at various stages of my research is a pleasant duty indeed. I must first thank Robert Hunneman and the Ella Lyman Cabot Fund, the State University of New York, and my own family for making possible two trips to Morocco in 1958–59 and 1963 and providing two summers away from teaching for the uninterrupted cultivation of the muse. Had it not been for that unique North African nationalist, Margaret Pope, the work would have lacked much of its authority, for it was she who introduced me to the inner circles of the nationalist leadership. To many of the nationalists who appear on the pages of this book, but especially to Mohammed Lyazidi, Omar Abdeljalil, Allal al-Fassi, Mohammed Hassan al-Ouezzani, Ibrahim al-Kittani, Ahmed Mekouar and Mohammed Daoud, goes my deep appreciation for their time, patience and confidence, and to the last three named, for placing some of their private papers at my disposal. Interviewing, often a gruelling task, was for me a delight, owing to the grace and candor of these and other men who consented to discuss their views and experiences with me on repeated occasions. To Mohammed al-Fassi, Rector of the University of Morocco, there is a special word of gratitude for his beneficent influence on my career, both in Morocco and during his trips to this country. The late Mehdi ben Barka, apparently assassinated by political rivals somewhere near Paris, conceived an earlier form of the chart of Morocco's three phases of "nationalism" which appears in Figure 1. Abdullah Regragui, Curator of the Bibliothèque Général de Rabat, and his staff, must accept my thanks for their cooperation and for making available to me the facilities and services of their library and archives. Lockwood Library at my university undertook to microfilm the private papers and other materials which have been so helpful to me. Carl Brown, formerly of the Center for Middle Eastern Studies at Harvard, but now at Princeton, has graciously extended his help and advice in more ways than I can mention. For the exacting job of typing, I pay homage to Mrs. Jane Nitterauer and to Mrs. Ellen Shaw, but especially to Mrs. Esther Munshen of our departmental staff who must wonder how many drafts are really necessary. In the case of my mother-in-law, Mrs. Alta T. McClintock, and my good friend, Sheldon Thompson Viele, I must acknowledge fidelity beyond the call of duty, for they undertook the onerous but indispensable task of reading proof at one stage of the manuscript. Most of all, I thank my wife, Susan, for the quiet hours she miraculously provided in a houseful of children, for her patience with my coming late to meals, for ignoring the unfinished household chores, and for the ready cup of coffee and her large servings of understanding.

NOTE ON METHOD AND TRANSLITERATION

Because much of the information about the early years of Moroccan nationalism is lodged in the memories of its dramatis personae or in the scattered private papers which accidentally survived repeated confiscations, I was fortunately able to interview extensively several of the nationalist leaders. This explains such cryptic endnotes as "M.L.2:5," signifying the fifth page of my notes on the second interview with Mohammed Lyazidi. The list of Moroccans interviewed and the dates of each interview appear at the beginning of the Bibliography under the heading "Key to Interviews."

The troublesome problem of transliteration from the Arabic is complicated in North Africa by discrepancies between French and English practice. After a fruitless effort to reconcile the two by some means of standardization, I have resorted to a simplified English transliteration in most cases (e.g., Zawiya instead of Zaouia, Sharifian rather than Chérifien), deviating from this only in two cases: certain Moroccan names which usage has consecrated in the French style (e.g., al-Ouezzani in place of al-Wazzani, or Moulay Hassan rather than Mawlay Hassan) and titles of books or periodicals where French transliteration or North African usage is a matter of public record (e.g., el-Hayat rather than al-Hayat, or ech-Chihab rather than al-Shihab). To indicate the plural of an Arabic word, in most cases I have simply added an "s" to the singular form.

J.P.H.

East Aurora, N.Y.
June 1967

CONTENTS

LIST OF TABLES

LIST OF FIGURES

REBIRTH OF A NATION

THE ORIGINS AND RISE OF MOROCCAN
NATIONALISM, 1912–1944

INTRODUCTION

The *Reconquista* had dealt harshly with the Moors. Their retreat from Granada brought tears to the eyes of Boabdil who turned back to gaze upon the towers of the Alhambra from the foothills of the Alpuxarras at Padul and weep like a woman for what he could not defend like a man.[1] Where once luxuriant hillsides of olives and corn adorned the earth, where once the fountains of the Alhambra delighted the ear, the Inquisition rolled out a chronicle of butchery and obscurantism which destroyed forever the exquisite culture of Moorish Andalusia. The remnants of the persecuted Moriscos fled to Barbary in the early years of the seventeenth century to eke out their generations in indigence, piracy and isolation.

Nor have modern times been less cruel to this beleaguered people. One of the last to relinquish their sovereignty to an expanding Europe, they finally succumbed in 1912. But if the Moors were forcibly ejected from Europe in the seventeenth century and forcibly subjected to it in the twentieth, their later humiliation led to a reconstruction of their national dignity as their earlier had not. Morocco's recent history parallels the Hegelian response which Islamic peoples have typically made to the expansion of Europe: first, the degrading realization of backwardness and the uncritical adoption of Western ways without regard to their applicability to a non-Western society; next, a militant, often military, resistance to Westernization when it is seen to cause the disruption of native society or, even worse, the imposition of alien rule. Ultimately, a kind of synthesis takes place, wherein the more imaginative native leaders mobilize selected ideas and techniques of oriental as well as occidental origin, fashioning the curiosity which we call "colonial nationalism" and which has, indeed, created something resembling nations in the former colonial world. Morocco's response conforms broadly to the general pattern while exhibiting certain unique characteristics of its own (see Figure 1).

Morocco's Westernizing phase, for example, was embryonic.

[1] Stanley Lane-Poole, *The Story of the Moors in Spain* (New York, 1886) p. 267.

FIGURE 1. PHASES OF MOROCCAN OPPOSITION TO EUROPEAN PENETRATION, 1873–1956

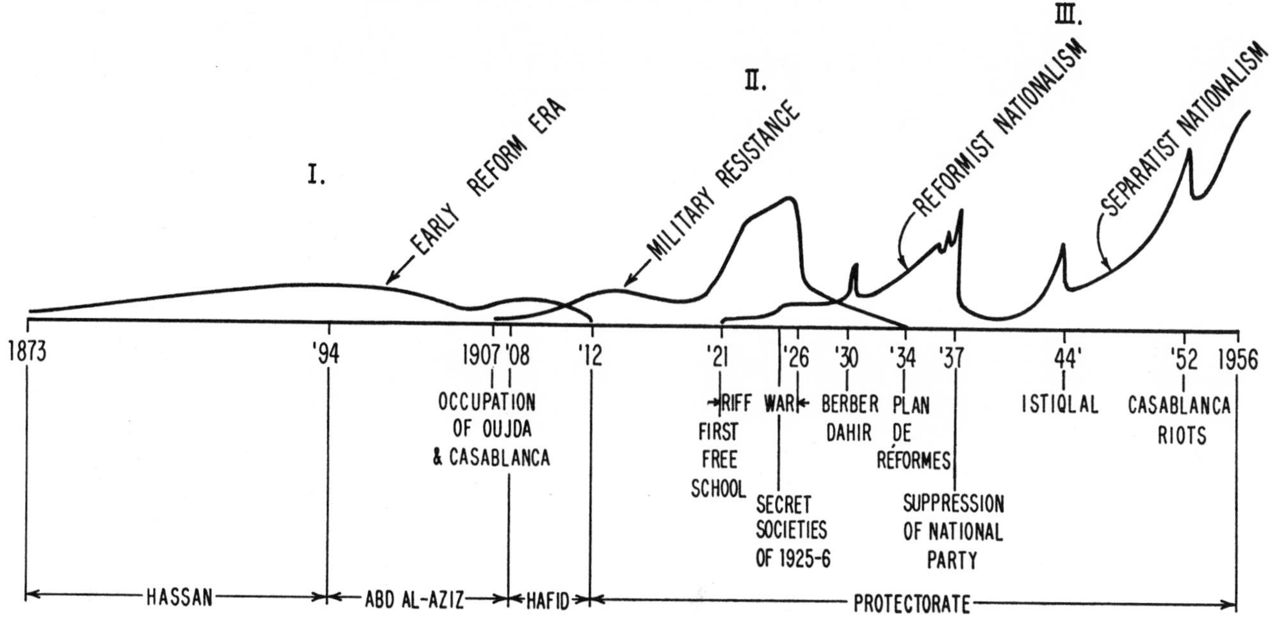

I. EARLY REFORM ERA

II. MILITARY RESISTANCE

III. REFORMIST NATIONALISM / SEPARATIST NATIONALISM

1873   '94   1907 '08   '12   '21   '26   '30   '34   '37   '44'   '52   1956

OCCUPATION OF OUJDA & CASABLANCA

RIFF WAR

FIRST FREE SCHOOL

BERBER DAHIR

PLAN DE RÉFORMES

ISTIQLAL

CASABLANCA RIOTS

SECRET SOCIETIES OF 1925-6

SUPPRESSION OF NATIONAL PARTY

HASSAN — ABD AL-AZIZ — HAFID — PROTECTORATE

The disaster at Isly on August 13, 1844, where a French army of 11,000 mauled a Sharifian force four times its size in one brief morning, jolted her out of her stubborn isolation and, along with the recent trade treaty with Britain, led to a rapid growth in Euro-Moroccan commerce. Morocco's response was a dilute, half-hearted modernization of the army and administration which flickered spasmodically throughout the reigns of Moulay Abd al-Rahman and his two successors. After Moulay Hassan's death in 1894, the anemic modernizing impulse was easily deflected by corrupt courtiers who sought to recover power by indulging the youthful Abd al-Aziz in his obsession for Western gadgetry. And after the death in 1900 of the able Negro vizier, Ba Ahmed ben Moussa, all attempts to pursue a consistent reform policy foundered in the mire of aristocratic preferment and reaction. A last feeble gesture at modernization on the part of an independent Morocco was made in 1908 by a small group of Tangier intellectuals, the editors of the weekly *Lisan al-Maghreb*, who vainly proposed a reform based on the Turkish ("Midhat") Constitution as restored in July of that year. It is doubtful that more than a hundred Moroccans ever read the Tangier draft, and it had no effect whatever on contemporary political conditions.[2] Early

---

[2] The author was unable to locate copies of *Lisan al-Maghreb* while in Morocco, but a detailed summary of the constitutional project will be found in A. Benabdallah, *Les grands courants de la civilisation du Maghreb* (Casablanca, 1958), pp. 135–140.

Phase I. A reform movement which arose in the mid-nineteenth century to stave off European penetration and ended in 1908–12 with the establishment of the protectorate.

Phase II. The military resistance to the French occupation which began in 1907 and ended with the capitulation of the last Berber chieftains in 1934.

Phase III. A reform movement, originally religio-cultural but progressively more political, which began after World War I and continued until independence — this being the "nationalist" movement properly so-called.

The third phase, moreover, is divisible into two parts: the reformist era, 1921–37, which is the chief concern of this book, when the movement was based on the assumption that the French would agree to introduce reforms leading eventually to independence; the separatist era thereafter, when the nationalists came to realize that the French never intended to grant independence.

Note. The author is indebted to Mehdi ben Barka for the original conception of Figure 1 (interview, April 7, 1959), although Mr. Ben Barka was not responsible for later alterations of detail.

Moroccan reformism was a puny thing without defenders at court.

Although hostilities between Moors and Europeans erupted sporadically throughout the nineteenth century, the military phase of Morocco's reaction to European penetration cannot be said to have started until after 1900. It opened with the tribal resistance to the French occupations of Oujda and Casablanca in 1907. Its zenith was reached, not at the moment the protectorate was proclaimed but after World War I when Abd al-Krim nearly drove the Spanish out of the north. But this was "tribal nationalism," which, because of its internal contradictions, had no creative future in the modern world and was finally crushed in Morocco in 1934.

Modern colonial nationalism cannot be discerned in Morocco before 1921, when the future leaders of the country came to realize that neither isolation nor rebellion, but constructive reform of their outmoded society must be their ultimate defense against the French preponderance. Moroccan nationalism began, therefore, as a reformist movement and remained so until World War II. Thereafter, the accumulated frustrations of two decades drove the nationalists into separatism, a transformation proclaimed by the foundation of the Istiqlal (Independence) Party and the riots of January 1944 and which culminated in independence in 1956.

The career of Istiqlal is well documented in works by Rézette, Julien, Ayache, Ashford, Landau and others. How Moroccan nationalism was born, reached maturity and revived a Moorish nation which had once been the glory of the western Mediterranean is a less familiar story and the subject of this book.

How could a people utterly devoid of a sense of nationhood in 1912 become so self-consciously nationalistic only thirty years later, a mere moment in the long history of the Moors? If they were really a "people," why had their revival not occurred earlier? Was their emergence from their long interregnum merely a reaction against French military pressure, as early anti-imperialists professed to think? If so, why had it not taken place a century ago? Or was it to be explained by the subversive doctrines infiltrating from the Middle East which so enraged the colonialists? If so, why had Arab nationalism failed to take hold in Morocco when it did in Egypt? Or was it caused not so much by invasion and subversion as by exportation — the exportation of the European revolution in ideas and technology which Rupert Emerson and others hold to be the fountainhead of the non-West's revolt against the West?

Since it appeared to the author that none of these considerations could be ignored, it seemed proper to examine each of them separately in order to determine to what extent each had shaped the doctrines, the methods and the leadership of Moroccan nationalism. This effort resulted in the chapters of Parts Two and Three of this book. Part Four examines the waxing or waning influence of each of these forces as the nationalist movement matured. Part One sets the scene by explaining how the peculiar circumstances of Morocco's acquisition conditioned France's rights and duties there and defined the bounds within which the reformer-nationalists were obliged to work.

It might be well to mention that in a country like Morocco, tradition colored at every turn the ideas and behavior of the nationalists. Tradition was the climate, other factors the weather which precipitated the storm of nationalism. But while allusions to this climate are occasionally made, the author's purposes do not include its comprehensive analysis, for such would be equivalent to a cultural history of Morocco which others are far better qualified to undertake. Hence, the role of tradition is not so much to be explained as to be recognized when met. A good example is the staunch adherence of Morocco to the monarchy, an institution to which most national movements have been hostile or indifferent, which is explained in part by the unique politico-religious role played by independent Moroccan sultans during centuries when most other Middle Eastern lands were under alien rule. Another example, as Rézette points out, is the peculiar influence which the religious brotherhoods have exercised over Morocco and which could not help but shape the early reformists' societies. The reader may assume that characteristics of Moroccan nationalism unexplained by the weather of the protectorate period are attributable to the climate of tradition.

Nationalism is a frame of mind, or frames of mind, or frames of minds. Hence, this book is a study in ideas — how they grew and moved about, the men who entertained them, and the institutions and movements which embodied them. The dramatis personae will be numerous and variegated: philosophers and agitators from Egypt, Syria, Algeria and Tunisia; colonists from France and their confederates of the Comité du Maroc; French and Spanish soldiers and administrators; diplomats and colonial officers of every major European power; French liberals who espoused the Moroccan cause for altruistic reasons; Socialists and Communists and Fascists who supported the Moroccans often for less than altruistic reasons; the sultans and their functionaries on the local and national scene, here sympathetic, there hostile to the reformist spirit; and finally, the reformers themselves who became nationalists during the three decades encompassed by this book. The latter were mostly younger men, typically of the educated, urban middle class of Fez, Rabat and Salé at the outset, who did not relish the prospect of being assimilated by France, who were offended by subservience and inspired by the example of other peoples, oriental as well as occidental, to believe that Morocco had the right and the capacity to make her own way. Whether they were justified or not is of little interest here. How they justified themselves is the meat of the story.

PART ONE

THE SETTING

I

THE DUAL MANDATE: 1900–1912 [1]

Moulay Hassan ben Mohammed ben Abd al-Rahman (1873–1894) had been the last Moroccan sultan of any real competence. By great effort he had managed to pay off the British loan and the Spanish indemnity of 1861 and to reduce the *bled as-siba* (outer, or unconquered, land) to its smallest dimensions since the days of Ismail, even to the point of subduing the Atlas Mountains and part of the desert. But even Hassan had not been able to prevent the spread of "protection" and other forms of European interference, and under his incurably juvenile successor, Abd al-Aziz, the authority of the Makhzen (Moroccan government) was further dissipated by royal indulgence and by a circle of self-seeking courtiers and foreign adventurers.

Within a year of Hassan's death, the British minister in Tangier could accurately characterize Morocco as a "loose agglomeration of turbulent tribes, corrupt Governors, and general poverty and distress." [2] For the next five years, only the power, tact and financial sagacity of the grand vizier, Ba Ahmed, staved off the inevitable collapse, and upon the death of that much calumniated minister, Morocco succumbed to the fate of a medieval state surviving anachronistically into the twentieth century. At the turn of the century, the question was not whether Morocco would retain her independence, but to which European power she would surrender it.

Aside from the political situation, Morocco was a most desirable prize. She possessed a fertile *tell* (coastal plain) far broader than Algeria's; her forest reserves were extensive; her population was the least dense of the Maghreb ("the West," i.e., North Africa with relation to the rest of the Arab world); her varied climate permitted the cultivation of tropical as well as temperate-zone crops; and her mineral deposits were reputed to be abundant. Accordingly, Morocco promised a virgin market and a plentiful source of raw materials and unoccupied land to an industrial Europe faced with rising competition, protectionism and periodic economic crises.

The two powers chiefly concerned with Morocco's potential were Britain and France. Italy was preoccupied to the east, Portugal had been forced out of the game long ago, and Spain seemed content to cling to its enclave on the coast of the Sahara and its Mediterranean toeholds at Ceuta and Melilla. Germany could claim about 10 per cent of Morocco's foreign trade, but politically its government was indifferent to Morocco until after the events of 1904. At the turn of the century, France accounted for over 30 per cent of the Moroccan trade, but Britain's share, over 40 per cent in 1902–03, had for decades surpassed the French and continued to do so until 1904–05.[3]

Britain's involvement in Morocco was commercial and strategic rather than territorial. As early as 1845, after the Moroccan defeat at Isly at the hands of France, the British consul in Tangier received a dispatch from the Foreign Office stating that "our permanent object must be to exert ourselves to the utmost in assisting to uphold the authority of the Sultan and to arrest every incident which might threaten it with fresh danger."[4] Neither policy nor objectives had changed in the intervening half-century. Britain wanted, if possible, to preserve her lucrative commercial preponderance in Morocco, and even more to secure her control of the Straits by preventing the establishment of a European rival on the southern shore. Downing Street sought above all to keep Morocco from becoming an international incident.

France, however, — or perhaps it is more accurate to say Frenchmen — had cast acquisitive eyes on Morocco since 1830, and advocates of expansion frankly outlined strategies for sub-verting Algeria's neighbor. Such talk gathered momentum after the humiliation of 1871, and especially after Bismarck began to encourage France to seek revenge elsewhere than on the "blue line of the Vosges," but it took the genius of Théophile Delcassé to visualize the proper form and scope of France's restoration to international prestige and to understand Morocco's place in the larger scheme. Delcassé's interest in Morocco was of long standing. As a young journalist for Gambetta's *République Française*, he had been agitating for a Franco-Spanish partition of Morocco as early as 1886,[5] and as undersecretary of state for, then minister of, colonies (1893–95) and foreign minister (1898–1905) he had become convinced that the isolation of Germany and the acquisition of Morocco were both dependent on an understanding with Britain, preferably a military *entente*.

But as of 1900 France could claim no special prerogatives by virtue of which she could intervene in Morocco. It is true that the Treaty of Lalla-Marnia (1845) had given her trading privileges on the eastern frontier and the right to police the border, but in the west her commercial rights, arising from the Convention of Madrid (1880), were shared on a most-favored-nation basis by all the other signatories.[6] Moreover, France had made no overt move against Morocco before 1900, preoccupied as she was with the occupation of the Sudan, but the Fashoda crisis had determined the limits of the Sudanese effort and had furnished an additional incitement to overseas adventure by wounding her national pride.

By 1900 France was ready for a new colonial venture, and it is significant that in that year her policing of the Moroccan-Algerian border became so active that Abd al-Aziz appealed to Queen Victoria to use her good offices to induce the French government to fix the frontier once and for all. Delcassé assured the British ambassador that France had no ulterior motives as regards Morocco, an assurance which was received with gratitude by the young sultan, although one may wonder with how much credence. Jean Jaurès took this occasion to charge that Delcassé had artificially created the border incidents as part of a grand design, and while it is difficult to substantiate or refute the specific allegation, it is certain that Delcassé had already become convinced of the necessity of achieving economic preponderance for France in Morocco.

DELCASSÉ'S "APPROACHES"

Since France had no special *entrée* to Morocco, the foreign minister suggested that territorial contiguity might serve as well as any, and from this premise postulated a great deal. Asserting that eastern Morocco was "an enclave of our African possessions," [7] he told the Senate in a speech on July 7, 1901 that it was intolerable for the Moroccan government to prevent France's economic expansion, and since everyone was aware of the decrepit state of the Moroccan economy and of the corruption of her government, both had to be modernized, a task which no one could deny was the responsibility of France. But despite certain territorial-minded militants, among whom could be counted ambitious army officers and the French minister in Tangier,

Saint-René Taillandier, who had advocated the occupation of Oujda as early as 1901, Delcassé sought to achieve his objective by peaceful economic penetration, a course which many still believed possible at that time.

To this end, he launched his "eastern approach." A Foreign Office protocol of July 1901 announced that France intended to suppress the tribal unrest around the strategic Figuig oasis and to construct a railroad to Beni Ounif, thereby placing France in control of the termini of the trans-Saharan trade routes and providing a rapid freight outlet to the coast. But tribal disorder continued, and French military activity on the border increased perforce, as did the concern of the Makhzen, which again in 1901 appealed for the intervention of France's neighbors by dispatching to the courts of Britain and Germany a mission headed by Morocco's capable and progressive minister of war, Mehdi al-Menebhi. Delcassé again assured the powers that no military occupation was contemplated, and al-Menebhi returned home empty-handed.

The mission had, however, convinced Europe that something was afoot in Morocco, and it quickly became apparent to Delcassé that a successful forward policy would entail considerable diplomatic preparation. The idea of reaching diplomatic agreements on a division of North Africa among the European powers had in fact occurred to him as early as 1898, even before he became foreign minister. Given Italian and British interests in the east and Spanish in the west, it seemed reasonable for these powers to reach an amicable balance on the whole Mediterranean coast. Thus, when the Franco-British agreement of March 1899, tentatively allotting respective spheres of influence in Central Africa,[8] aroused Italian concern over the security of Tripoli, Delcassé used the occasion to open negotiations on that quarter which culminated in a secret Franco-Italian understanding in January 1901, giving each power a free hand in its respective zone, Morocco and Tripolitania.[9]

Delcassé was contemplating similar negotiations with Spain as early as July 27, 1901, on which date he wrote to Saint-René Taillandier in Fez that Spain obviously had to be consulted. Accordingly, conversations were initiated with the Sagasta government in 1902, culminating in a draft treaty providing for the partition of Morocco; the northern half, centering on Fez, was to go to Spain, the southern half, around Marrakesh, to France.

But the Spanish refused to ratify without consulting Great Britain, to meet which condition Paul Cambon approached Lord Lansdowne on August 6, 1902 to inquire what might happen "in the event of Morocco passing into liquidation." [10] Lansdowne and Balfour failed to respond encouragingly at the time, and the vigorous protest of the sultan, conveyed to Lansdowne by Caid Maclean, may have clinched the British rejection. Meanwhile, the replacement of the Sagasta government by the Liberal Conservatives under Silvela caused the collapse of an accord on that front.

Nor were events auspicious within Morocco, for there an "English ring" was solidifying around the sultan — private adventurers who attached themselves to the service of the easily misguided monarch in pursuit of their own interests and with the connivance of Maclean. This development was taking place in 1901 and was fully operative by January 1902, and while such persons had no official connection whatever with the British government, the French were understandably suspicious and jealous. As of early 1903, Delcassé's "eastern approach" did not appear to be a rousing success.

But the persistent reluctance of the Makhzen to undertake serious reforms was working for the ambitious foreign minister of France. Al-Menebhi had been dismissed in disgrace after his fruitless overtures to Britain and Germany, and while the intervention of Sir Arthur Nicolson saved his skin, his reformist views were no longer entertained by the Makhzen. Moreover, the continued turbulence of the tribes on the Algerian border had grown completely out of hand, and the Makhzen was obliged to accept an agreement in 1902 which created a "mixed zone" on the frontier, wherein French and Moroccan authorities were to cooperate in the maintenance of order. This arrangement was almost inevitably explosive, and French military action around the Figuig oasis precipitated in 1903 what amounted to a guerilla war in that area over which the sultan had no control. To make matters worse for the Makhzen, the uprisings of the pretender Bou Hamara and the bandit Raisuli at the end of 1902 and early in 1903, and the kidnapping of American and European nationals like Ian Perdicaris and London *Times* correspondent Walter Harris set the Makhzen by the ears and caused rising anxiety in Western capitals about the prospects for reform in Morocco. By the end of 1903, it was reasonably clear to the powers that more direct action was called for, and Delcassé was not slow to respond.

The foreign minister now launched his "western approach" which focused on Morocco's financial anemia and the trouble in the Atlantic ports. The extravagances of Abd al-Aziz had finally to be reckoned with in 1903, when Morocco was obliged to borrow £800,000 from banking syndicates in Britain, France and Spain. Unable to service this debt, the sultan was persuaded in June 1904 to fund it by a French loan of 62,500,000 francs at 5 per cent, to be guaranteed by 60 per cent of Morocco's customs revenues,[11] and in 1905 and 1906 he contracted several smaller loans to buy munitions which were to be furnished by Creuzot. Despite modern nationalist revisions of Moroccan history, there is no indication that either the sultan or the Makhzen was in any way reluctant to follow Delcassé's lead in this regard.

However, the appropriation of the customs duties, Morocco's most reliable source of revenue, immeasurably weakened the Makhzen by depriving it of its sole means to finance the reforms so urgently demanded by the powers. A means of resolving this dilemma had already been suggested by Saint-René Taillandier in 1903 when he began to promote the creation of a Moroccan State Bank, to be controlled by France, simultaneously with a European police force effective enough to suppress the ubiquitous banditry which rendered unsafe even the European warehouses in the eight open ports. These two projects, the State Bank and the harbor police, were to become the main instrumentalities of French penetration in Morocco from 1904 until 1907.

By now, however, Delcassé's intricate maneuverings were being jeopardized by the emergence of powerful business interests which were raising a hue and cry for government protection from the increasing turbulence in the ports. These interests had coalesced in 1900 to form an economic colonial lobby known loosely as the Comité du Maroc and consisting of three major combines: the Société Marocaine des Travaux Publiques, interested in developing the port of Tangier and the Tangier–Larrache and Casablanca–Settat railroads, the Société Internationale des Tabacs, which came to hold the tobacco and *kif* (hemp) monopolies, and the omnipotent Union des Mines. The membership of these formidable groups was made up of the sixty or seventy large companies which were already, or would shortly become, engaged in banking, mining, transport, construction, electric power and other enterprises in Morocco. Figuring prominently among them were the Compagnie des Forges de Chatillon-Commentary, the Compagnie des Forges et Aciéries de la Marine, Schneider et Cie., Creuzot, Krupp, the Gewerkschaft Deutscher Kaiser, the Gelsenkirchener Bergwerke, the Banque de Paris et des Pays-Bas, Mendelsohn und Ko., the Nederlandsche Handel-Maatschappij, the Banque de Portugal and the Banque d'Espagne, as well as a number of British, Austrian and Italian firms, and private individuals such as Sir Ernest Cassel, who had helped Cromer to finance the Aswan Dam a number of years before. The power generated by even the loosest association of such titans was reinforced by the extensive interlocking of their directorates and by the guiding influence exercised by the Banque de Paris whose representatives sat on nearly all their boards.[12] The enormous capital, preponderantly French, which these cartels came to invest in Moroccan enterprises was customarily guaranteed by the French government in the concessions agreements, as was a stipulated annual return on investment, and any unexpected deficits were often absorbed by the government as well. The Comité du Maroc was foremost among those who were now demanding a more forward policy and who eventually were responsible for the occupation of Morocco by the French army.

But while the economic colonial lobby was pressing for outright acquisition, Delcassé stood firm on his policy of peaceful economic penetration. Speaking in the Chamber of Deputies on November 10, 1904, he reaffirmed his hope of achieving voluntary reforms along lines suggested by France in order to make possible the profitable exploitation of Morocco's natural resources. He pointed out that French control of the customs was already in hand, and, given the turbulent state of the country, he foresaw a police force and a State Bank also under French direction. Finally, there must be a railroad to Algeria and the development of port facilities. "Railways and ports and financial stability" — these were to be the instruments of French control of Morocco's economy. Although it was not explicitly stated, the implication was that no occupation was contemplated.[13]

INTERNATIONALIZATION OF THE MOROCCAN PROBLEM

Even this, however, implied a French preponderance in Morocco, which flew in the face of the provisions of the Madrid Convention and of the interests of Great Britain whose trade with Morocco in 1904 still surpassed that of France. The British were not displaying any hostility at this time, but there were a number of outstanding disputes between the two powers which French pressure in Morocco and the rising specter of a German high seas fleet served to bring to a head. Accordingly, the abortive conversations of 1902 were reopened, culminating on April 8, 1904 in the Cambon-Lansdowne Declaration, otherwise known as the *entente cordiale*. The effect of the provisions respecting Egypt and Morocco are well known. Britain was to have a free hand in the former, France in the latter, for ". . . it appertains to France . . . to preserve order in that country, and to provide assistance for the purpose of all administrative, economic, financial and military reforms which it may require." [14] Here, to all intents and purposes, was the basis for a French protectorate, although the signatories unctiously declared that "they have no intention of altering the political status of Morocco." The secret articles, which were not publicly known until November 1911, added very little to the far-reaching implications of the public declaration, providing only for the allotment of the northern coast to Spain.[15] A supplementary accord was reached on October 3, 1904 between Delcassé and de Leon y Castillo, the Spanish ambassador in Paris. The public treaty made no provision for Spanish intervention in Morocco, but the secret clauses arranged for a partition into Spanish and French spheres of influence.[16]

At this point the only power which conceivably might cause trouble was Germany, but in 1904 there was no reason for Delcassé to think that she was any more concerned for Morocco than was the United States, or Belgium, or Portugal, or any of the other signatories of the Madrid Convention, for she had provided many assurances that French hegemony in Morocco would in no way threaten her economic interests there and that her interests in Morocco were exclusively economic. The German ambassador, Prince Radolin, had assured Delcassé in March that his government had no objections to the French efforts to assure peace and security in Morocco and had shown no concern over the projected accord with Great Britain of which Delcassé apprised him at the time; [17] and when the French ambassador in Berlin, M. Bihourd, carried out his instructions to report this conversation to the German foreign minister, not a ripple was caused at the Wilhelmstrasse.[18] The public announcement of the accord produced a surprised response on the part of the German press, but there was no expression of apprehension.[19] German acquiescence seemed to be officially confirmed when von Bülow on April 12th announced in the Reichstag that Germany had no objection whatever to the Anglo-French *entente*, nor was it to be feared that her economic interests in Morocco would be jeopardized.[20]

Assuming that he had forestalled any diplomatic unpleasantness, Delcassé proceeded in March 1905 to direct Saint-René Taillandier to demand of the Makhzen the right of France to put the projected reforms into motion. But the ordinarily astute foreign minister had not reckoned with the rapidly changing outlook of German governmental officials. The Russo-German negotiations for a defense alliance had broken down in November 1904, and the German government had become greatly exercised over the erroneous but quite plausible notion that the secret clauses of the *entente cordiale* contained a provision for altering the Rhine frontier. Moreover, forces within the German government were beginning to think it necessary to reassert German prestige, and what better way could be found than to test the Anglo-French accord? The instrument chosen to make the test was none other than the Kaiser himself, who was persuaded much against his will to interrupt his Mediterranean cruise for a visit to Tangier where he announced with undiplomatic clarity Germany's determination to preserve the independence of Morocco and to safeguard German interests there on a basis of equality with the other powers. The sultan, who had already shown himself extremely unreceptive to the French proposals for reform, was now encouraged to reject them out of hand.

The violence of the French reaction to the Kaiser's pronouncement simply deepened the misgivings of Germany and the sultan as to Delcassé's designs and the secret provisions of the Cambon-Lansdowne agreement, and it was under this cloud of suspicion that the German government suggested the airing of Morocco's future status at an international conference. Delcassé thought he saw through von Bülow's game and was determined to confront him with a show of Anglo-French solidarity, but the rest of the Cabinet allowed itself to be intimidated by the chancellor's bellicosity and voted unanimously against Delcassé, who resigned. Premier Rouvier now assumed responsibility for the Quai d'Orsay and demonstrated his willingness to follow von Bülow's leading strings. Additional pressure brought to bear by President Roosevelt caused the final collapse of French resistance, and Rouvier's agreement to the conference was obtained on July 8, 1905.

As it ultimately became clear, German strategy was designed to lead, not to war, but to the public humiliation of France demanded by the arrogance of von Bülow and the Kaiser, and the Algeciras conference was intended to be its instrumentality. At the outset of the conference, world public opinion was running against a France which seemed determined to upset the status quo in Morocco. But the duplicity of von Radowitz and the bullying tactics of Tattenbach, the two German delegates, dissipated most pro-German sympathy, and while the final provisions of the General Act of Algeciras, signed on April 7, 1906, limited France's freedom of action, they were not so restrictive as Rouvier had feared at the outset.

The Act provided: first, for a police force in the eight ports open to European commerce, to number not less than 2,000 nor more than 5,000, to be supplied with French and Spanish officers, sixteen to twenty in number, and thirty or forty noncommissioned officers, the whole to be subject to a Swiss inspector-general who would report to the Diplomatic Body in Tangier and to the Makhzen; secondly, for a State Bank of Morocco to be organized under French law to act as the Moroccan Treasury and Royal Mint, with a capital of no less than 15 million francs and no more than 20 million to be furnished equally by the signatory powers, with two extra shares reserved for the French consortium which floated the loan of June 1904, and with the management of the Bank residing in a Board of Directors constituted by representatives of the signatory powers; thirdly, for public works in Morocco not to be "alienated to private interests"; and fourthly, for all concession agreements to be submitted for the approval of the Diplomatic Body and in no way to impinge on the control of the Makhzen over its public services.[21] In short, the Act gave the European powers extensive economic privileges, considerable authority over the establishment of public order, and virtually complete control over Morocco's financial administration. At the same time, however, it threw a wrench into the machinery of French intervention by pledging France to respect "the sovereignty and independence of . . . the Sultan, the integrity of his Dominions, and economic liberty without any inequality."

After Algeciras, Delcassé's policy of economic penetration was derelict, and the more aggressive program of the Comité du Maroc appeared equally so. For the time being the French government, now headed by Clemenceau, appeared willing to give the international regime an opportunity to work. The State Bank was established in 1907, and a French engineer was hired to oversee public works, but beyond that the regime proved to be a miserable failure. Throughout 1906 and 1907 banditry was on the rise, Raisuli was terrorizing Tangier, Bou Hamara was in control of the Riff, the Algerian border was in chaos, and Casablanca was under siege by the surrounding tribes. All trade across the Algerian frontier had come to a halt in 1906, and Morocco's legitimate foreign trade was 30 per cent below the level of 1903, although a contraband trade in arms was flourishing. Moreover, by mid-1907, more than a year after Algeciras, the State Bank had failed to restore the sultan's solvency, none of the projected public works had been carried out, the international harbor police existed only on paper, and Abd al-Aziz was stubbornly resisting every reform envisaged by the Act. The murders of Dr. Mauchamp in Marrakesh in March and of nine European railroad workers outside the walls of Casablanca in July were dramatic proof that the Makhzen's authority had collapsed, and provided France with an excuse to enforce the Algeciras reforms unilaterally, a prospect which seemed to vindicate the stand taken by the Comité du Maroc against Delcassé's exclusively economic policy.

UNILATERALIZATION OF THE MOROCCAN PROBLEM

The Clemenceau government responded to the chaotic conditions by occupying eastern Morocco from Oujda southward, as well as the city of Casablanca and its hinterland (the Shawiya). Since 1905 France's trade with Morocco had surpassed Britain's, and the worsening political situation could not be permitted to jeopardize this. In December 1907, Regnault, French minister in Tangier, could report: ". . . the preponderant importance, today beyond question, of our commercial interests, is such that we could not contemplate with indifference the blow which a troubled situation would mean to the economic progress of Morocco." [22]

By early 1908 the whole of the Shawiya was occupied as well as additional territory in the east, but nevertheless there is evidence that the French government had not yet entirely abandoned its preference for economic penetration over political control. In June 1907, Eugène Étienne, first undersecretary of state for colonies and later minister of war and interior and a leading figure in the Comité du Maroc, had assured the Kaiser in a private conversation that France sought in Morocco no protectorate of the Tunisian sort but "only a *prépondérance morale*, to be able to give advice." [23] This intention seemed to be confirmed by the gradual withdrawal of French troops from the Shawiya once peace had been restored, for as of April 1908 the area was occupied largely by native Moroccan auxiliaries acting in concert with a diminishing number of Europeans. The idea was "to create native forces to hold the country and to enable France to trade in peace." [24] "We will thus form the skeleton of an organism which we can leave to itself when it offers adequate guarantees of consistence and stability." [25] As late as 1910 a flurry of dispatches between the Ministry of War, the Quai d'Orsay and the representative in Tangier showed that the French government considered it imperative to restrict military operations to the Shawiya in order to avoid getting involved in internal tribal disputes; [26] and in March of that year, the government was planning a total evacuation of the Shawiya as soon as the Makhzen could maintain 1,500 troops in the area.[27]

By this time, however, it was becoming illusory to think that the Makhzen was capable of restoring order or of servicing the debt, and French actions had in fact made matters worse. In 1907 Paris had demanded reparations of 13,069,000 francs for damage sustained by French merchants during the shelling of Casablanca as well as an indemnity of 60 million francs, for which the sultan was obliged to levy new taxes. And in 1910 French financial interests required the new sultan, Hafid, to fund his debt, then estimated at 163 million francs, by floating a new loan to be guaranteed by the unencumbered 40 per cent of the customs revenues and by the proceeds of the tobacco and *kif* monopolies. Because Hafid could not touch the new loan, its entirety being earmarked for debt payments, and because this time France imposed real supervision over the collections, Hafid's only recourse to meet his mounting expenses was to raise taxes once again. So diminished was the Makhzen's authority and so widespread the dissatisfaction over the new levies that the country was reduced to anarchy. The change of sultans having done nothing to alter the basic conditions of political and financial debility, the French troops remained.

By 1909 it had become apparent to all that the reforms contemplated by the Algeciras powers were wholly unworkable and that if Morocco was to enter the modern world, her internal political situation had to be brought under direct control, and none other than French control could now be contemplated. Even Germany seemed resigned to the inevitable, for in the Franco-German Convention of February 1909, Germany recognized for the first time the "special political interests" of France in Morocco in return for a guarantee to German commercial interests and a promise to cut Germany in on future concession contracts.[28] Even many Moroccans, notably the Makhzen families and the urban merchants who stood to benefit by the restoration of order, began to favor the establishment of French political control. Only the tribes, ever jealous of their autonomy, continued to resist any sort of checkrein imposed by central authority, French or native. By 1911, both internal conditions and international opinion clamored for a resolution of the Moroccan problem.

In April 1911 former Premier Rouvier, now a spokesman for the Comité du Maroc, announced that Fez was invested by the tribes and that Europeans were in danger. So serious was the situation, apparently, that even the francophobic Hafid felt constrained to request French intervention, and General Moinier was dispatched from Rabat with 30,000 troops to relieve the capital, under a cloud of assurances that once the Europeans were secured the troops were to withdraw.

In the light of her 1909 accord with France, Germany's reaction was unpredictable and touched off another international crisis. The dispatch of the cruisers "Panther" and "Berlin" to Agadir appeared to be a tactic analogous to the Kaiser's descent upon Tangier four years earlier, but in fact it had quite a different purpose. That France would establish her preponderance in Morocco was by now an accepted fact in the Wilhelmstrasse. Moreover, German economic interests were no longer in question, for they were amply protected by a whole series of international guarantees and French assurances from the Convention of Madrid to the latest Franco-German agreement of 1909, whose ramifications were still under discussion. The dispatch of the two cruisers, then, was a means of applying leverage on France for concessions to Germany elsewhere, and, as worked out in the Franco-German agreement of November 4, 1911,[29] Germany accepted approximately half of the French Congo as the price of her blessing on a French protectorate in Morocco. Chancellor Bethmann-Hollweg's remark to Jules Cambon at the signing: "You have become the master of Morocco," [30] was simply an admission of the *fait accompli*, for Moinier had not withdrawn from Fez during the crisis. French troops had been in occupation between the coast and Fez since June, and Morocco's independence had in fact ceased to exist several months before the actual negotiation of the protectorate treaty.

The Treaty of Fez (Appendix A),[31] signed on March 30, 1911, simply formalized the French occupation and Hafid's impotence. Its terms permitted France to direct Morocco's foreign relations and to supervise her internal administration — a real protectorate — but so extensive had been the prior diplomatic arrangements that there were definite curbs placed upon what France legally could and could not do. The agreement of October 1904 obliged France to "come to an understanding with the Spanish Government . . ." which in fact necessitated a partition, and of course the powers were prepared to resist any tampering with the special status which Tangier traditionally enjoyed. Moreover, the Act of Algeciras had precedence in international law over all such agreements, including the protectorate treaty itself, and while the Act failed to preserve Moroccan independence in fact, it did preserve the legal fiction of Moroccan sovereignty. It bound France to observe an economic open door as well as the capitulatory rights of the powers, all sticky points which France never was able wholly to burke or to circumvent. Even within these confining limits, France was constrained to "safeguard the religious status, the respect and traditional prestige of the Sultan, the exercise of the Mohammedan religion and of all religious institutions, in particular those of the *habous* [charitable foundations or trusts]." [32] And if the wave of liberal humanitarianism which washed over western Europe in the first decade of the century failed to reach all colonial officials charged with the "administrative, judicial, educational, economic, financial and military reforms which the French Government" saw fit to introduce in Morocco,[33] it reached some of them and at the very least provided another kind of limitation — a continuing critique of France's performance as a protecting power.

France entered upon her hegemony in Morocco with as clear-cut a dual mandate as any imperial power had undertaken anywhere in Africa. But the dual mandate everywhere in Africa was distinguished by internal contradiction. In Morocco, as elsewhere, there emerged a struggle between those who earnestly sought to fulfill the second mandate by means of a physical and spiritual rehabilitation of the country and those who stressed the first mandate and regarded a "protectorate" as a disguised colony — a bit of pretense necessitated by meddlesome foreigners and troublesome anti-colonialists at home. The exercise of the dual mandate, therefore, sometimes produced tensions between the "exploiters" and the "altruists" within the French administrative hierarchy and sometimes caused an adverse reaction among Moroccans whose expectations either were not fulfilled or were openly subverted.

PART TWO

THE PROTECTORATE AND ITS FRUITS:
1912–1943

II

ORDER AND TUTELAGE

INTRODUCTION

Frenchmen who contemplated the rise of nationalism in Morocco were inclined to ascribe it to anything but the underlying causes, i.e., to anything but the French presence, for good or evil, and the successful penetration of native culture by European. The tendency instead was to mistake the symptoms for the disease. The colonialists, speaking through their organ, *L'Afrique Française*, professed to believe that:

> The gravity of the North African situation comes less from local causes than from collusion among people in France. In the colonies themselves all that is needed to calm the trouble is firm and resolute authority enlightened by understanding.[1]

Even the astute and sympathetic Robert Montagne focused on the proletarian unrest in Casablanca as the prime factor in Moroccan nationalism, despite the incontrovertible fact that the movement first arose not in Casablanca but among middle-class intellectuals in Fez, Rabat-Salé and Tetuan. In justice to Montagne, he was referring chiefly to the period following World War II, but he belongs to the school of specialists whose personal relations with Moroccans (though not with the nationalists) were of the best and who believed that Moroccans welcomed the tutelage of "good" Frenchmen like Lyautey, and that if the spirit of Lyautey had persisted the problem of native nationalism would not have arisen.[2] Even the most ardent French critics of colonial policy held that Moroccan nationalism was primarily an expression of discontent, the result of frustrated ambitions which arose out of the militarization of the protectorate regime, the monopolization of government jobs by Europeans, the eviction of Moroccan farmers from their land, the destruction of Islamic institutions and the deliberate division of the country between Arab and Berber; in short, they believed that the roots of the movement were to be found in the perversion of the protectorate arrangement rather than in the arrangement itself.[3]

While collusion and grievances cannot be overlooked, it seems clear that Montagne and other French writers give their country less credit than it deserves. The Moroccans complained bitterly about the abuses of French rule, but it was in equal measure the astonishing successes achieved by France in modernizing a truly medieval state in less than half a century which made possible the rise of native nationalism in the first place. France bestowed upon Morocco her first effective systems of central administration, law courts and internal communications, and it was France who introduced modern educational, health and medical facilities and charted Morocco's future economic development. More often than not the innovations were chiefly for the benefit of Europeans, but they also served to instruct Moroccans in the ways of modern society and to raise their expectations as to what good government could do for them. As was the case nearly everywhere else in the colonial world, indigenous nationalism arose in direct proportion to imperial reform.

One must search diligently in the long bibliography of French colonial introspection to find any recognition of this fact, or any awareness that the lessons of Europe were driven home more acutely by the French presence. It made little difference how the French settlers behaved; their presence alone was a constant reminder of what Moroccans had yet to achieve. The mere fact of foreign settlement among a people who had long nourished an exaggerated xenophobia provided the best excuse for its condemnation by the more sensitive among the natives. Hence, whatever good France did was execrated as a defilement of Islamic custom (though such reforms were invariably retained after independence), and whatever abuses of colonial rule inevitably occurred were denounced as deliberate violations of the protectorate treaty or of human rights. This was the case with the pacification, with French administrative, political and economic reforms, and with the national systems of justice and education introduced by France. France was damned for what she did and twice damned for what she failed to do.

PACIFICATION

An elemental factor in the rise of Moroccan nationalism was the physical creation of a Moroccan nation by the French army. Not even in the palmiest days of the medieval Moorish empires was the subordination of the mountain tribes anything more than an enforced alliance with the Makhzen. But Lyautey had met this sort of situation before, as Galliéni's lieutenant in Tonkin and later in Madagascar, and was confident that his mentor's policies of the *tache d'huile* and the *politique des races* would apply here if they applied anywhere.

Accordingly, within two years of the signing of the Treaty of Fez, Lyautey's army had spread like a "spot of oil" over the entire lowland plain north and west of the mountains and even over the western spur of the High Atlas in the south, leaving behind a deposit of pacified marketplaces wherein the economic and social life of the countryside began to revive and prosper as never before in recent history. The outbreak of World War I led to the recall of two-thirds of Lyautey's effectives to serve on the Western Front and to the Cabinet's decision to abandon all advance posts and markets in Morocco and withdraw to the principal ports. But Lyautey, understanding that any withdrawal whatever would be interpreted by the Moroccans as a sign of weakness, carried out instructions to return his troops to France, then advanced all his remaining forces to the front lines, entirely evacuating the pacified zone. There he not only maintained the line of 1914 against the Berber mountaineers, but by a strategy of bluff, diversion and diplomacy managed the seemingly impossible task of advancing further into the Atlas. Between 1914 and 1919 the occupied area was increased from 163,000 square kilometers to 235,000.[4] By the war's end, the forces of order were more strongly entrenched than ever, but they were now face to face with Berber adversaries who had successfully resisted all foreign invasions from Roman times onward and for the next fifteen years gave considerable trouble to the best army maintained in postwar Europe.

The Berber resistance might have been even more formidable had not the Riffian group been isolated from the High Atlas group by the Taza corridor east of Fez, precariously held by the French army. As it was, Abd al-Krim drove the Spanish completely out of the Riff into their coastal presidios and might well have established a Berber republic had his overconfidence not beguiled him into attacking the French zone in April 1925. His initial momentum cut the Taza corridor briefly in May and threatened the city of Fez which was held by only fifteen battalions. The threat was sufficiently serious by August 1925 to cause the government to dispatch Marshal Pétain on an inspection mission resulting in his appointment as military commander in Morocco, an arrangement which undoubtedly precipitated Lyautey's resignation by depriving him of all military control. Only the concerted efforts of the dictator of Spain [5] and the hero of Verdun in command of 150,000 French troops served to bring the Riffian warrior to heel in May 1926.

The pacification of the Riff, however, did not end the matter, for there remained the tribes of the Tadla region of the High Atlas and the Tafilelt region of the Anti-Atlas. The former held out until 1931, the latter until 1932, with the final resistance in the Anti-Atlas ending only with the capitulation of Bou Izakarene on March 18, 1934,[6] after which the historic *bled as-siba* can be said to exist no more.

After the first serious Berber resistance was encountered in the Middle Atlas in 1914, however, it quickly became apparent to Lyautey that here was a people whose traditions and way of life were distinct from, and often hostile to, those of the lowland Arabs, and who comprised, it was later discovered, at least half the population of the country. Something had to be done to reassure the tribes that their acceptance of the sultan's authority would not oblige them to forsake their customary laws and traditions. This requirement became even more imperative in the summer of 1914 when the recall of the troops to France made their grip on the *bled* precarious indeed. Obviously, a special dispensation was called for in Berber territory, and it was here that Lyautey applied Galliéni's *politique des races,* a kind of Gallic version of indirect rule which permitted the tribes to evolve along the lines of their own natural development and which altered native institutions as little as possible. This was the origin of the much maligned "Berber policy" formalized by the *dahir* of September 11, 1914, which provided that the grand vizier, with the approval of the secretary-general of the Sharifian government, should designate which tribes were to be classified as *de coutume berbère* and permitted to live not under the Sharia (Muslim law) but under their own laws and customs.[7] The Berber policy would later be perverted by politicians who regarded the protectorate as a transitional expedient on the way to becoming a true colony, but at this early date nothing more than a tactical recognition of local autonomy was intended, and the policy served its purpose in facilitating the submission of the tribal chiefs.[8]

Neither the spirited Berber resistance in general, nor the Riffian rebellion in particular was a nationalist phenomenon in the modern sense. Although Abd al-Krim dreamed of a Riffian republic after his initial victories, he was at heart the "last great chief of the Holy War in Morocco," [9] and his struggle began and ended as a tribal movement. After his defeat, the momentary unity of the Riffian tribes quickly dissolved. The scattered resistance in the Anti-Atlas had been conducted from the start on a strictly tribal basis. But while not itself an expression of nationalism, the Riff War did serve to awaken the political consciousness of the young intellectuals who were to become Morocco's nationalists. Abd ad-Krim's defeat was the trauma which precipitated the formation of the first proto-nationalist organizations.

The pacification laid the foundations for the rise of nationalism in another way by opening Morocco to external influences on a large scale for the first time in three hundred years. Not only were these influences introduced directly by French administrators and colonists, but, as in Algeria, by the indirect effects of native service in the French army. Although Moroccan enlistees were not numerous, their social effect was disproportionately great because they were drawn mostly from the traditional, rural sectors of the population, and they carried French influence into villages and homesteads which were otherwise more or less isolated from it.[10]

The pacification also helped to "nationalize" Morocco by breaking down the particularism of the leading Berber tribes and subjecting them for the first time to close and peaceful contact with one another and with the urban communities of the coast. The peaceful communion of the tribes in the reestablished markets, in the expanding ports, and in the newly opened mines destroyed their traditionally cloistered thought-world and contributed to a "national" solidarity heretofore unknown in Morocco.[11]

This solidarity could help or hinder the work of France, depending on how it was handled, and the way things were handled during the first decade of the protectorate depended directly on the colonial philosophy of the man who had become resident-general.

LYAUTEY'S PHILOSOPHY

Lyautey came to Morocco, after years of experience in Muslim countries, convinced that a form of indirect rule, some variant of the *politique des races* on a grand scale, was best suited to most colonial situations. This was a point of view which had already won over a majority of French colonial theoreticians under the name of "association," [12] and was expressed most succinctly by Lyautey himself:

> The conception of the Protectorate is that of a country retaining its own institutions, governing itself with its own organs, but under the control of a European power which assumes control over its foreign relations, its army, its finances, and guides it in its economic development. What dominates and characterizes this conception is the notion of "control" as opposed to the notion of direct rule.[13]

Specifically, the sort of regime Lyautey envisaged for Morocco was a protectorate in the real sense, not a disguised colony, but a close association of French officials and Moroccans by which the latter would be able to improve the administration of their own government along familiar lines and in accordance with their own laws and customs. Such reform would in turn be made possible by the economic development of the country under the spur of French capital and management and by the employment of Moroccan labor to the ultimate benefit of all parties concerned.[14]

The French mandate for the administrative task was clear, but the task itself was complicated by Morocco's cultural diversity. The settled tribes of the old *bled al-makhzen* (government-controlled land, i.e., the Shawiya, the Gharb and Fez) welcomed the restoration of order and submitted easily to the reconstituted authority of the sultan in the person of the *caids* (tribal magistrates), pashas (urban magistrates) and *cadis* (judges in the courts of the Sharia). And in the south, where the tribes had habitually submitted only when the sultan was strong and rebelled when he was weak, Lyautey deemed it more feasible to rule through the *grands caïds*, who were essentially feudal princes managing their own affairs. These two areas posed no great problem. But the Berber mountaineers stubbornly refused to be assimilated, clung to their local dialects, and resisted all attempts to impose *caids* and *cadis*, preferring to be ruled according to their own laws as interpreted by their councils of elders (*djemaas*). They submitted to the French army only on the understanding that their own traditions would prevail wherever they conflicted with the secular authority of the Makhzen or the religious authority of the Sharia.[15] In practice this meant that the Makhzen's domain was limited, as before 1912, to the lowland plain.

But since the French army and not the sultan's *harka* (military expedition) had conquered the tribes, and since France intended to rule the *bled as-siba* as well as the *bled al-makhzen*, an elaborate protectorate administration came into being which administered different policies in each part of the country. And because this alien administrative system was adopted *in toto* by independent Morocco, while the anachronistic Makhzen withered away to extinction, it is primarily the new administration which shall be treated in this chapter, following a brief description of the reorganized Makhzen.

REORGANIZATION OF THE MAKHZEN

On the eve of the protectorate, the Makhzen comprised, in addition to the Court Service which had little administrative significance, the State Service which consisted of the sultan, his five viziers and their subordinates. The *wazir al-adham*, or grand vizier, performed the functions of a prime minister as well as those of a minister of interior in the broadest sense. It was he who handled the internal diplomatic relations with the quasi-autonomous tribes, and who dealt directly with the powerful religious brotherhoods. He was charged with general administration, public security, the supervision of education, and what little was done in the realms of public works, hygiene and the use of the country's natural resources.[16] Only the grand vizier could be called a *vizir de délégation*, wielding the delegated authority of the sultan; the other four were *vizirs d'exécution*. Theoretically, Morocco was an absolute monarchy of the most extreme form.

The *wazir al-bahr* (vizier of the sea) was the minister of foreign affairs, but did not, in fact, deal directly with foreign ambassadors or preside over a diplomatic corps himself, for neither Morocco nor the foreign powers with whom she had contact maintained permanent ambassadors in each others' capitals. By 1912, Moroccan foreign relations were conducted through the consuls and *chargés d'affaires* resident in Tangier, or, occasionally, where Europeans were resident in other cities, through the local pasha. The *wazir al-bahr* was also responsible for commercial relations with foreign companies and for all questions relating to the system of native protection.[17]

The *wazir al-malia*, or minister of finances, was charged with the supervision of all revenues and expenditures. Formerly he was assisted locally by the *caids*, but the corruption of those feudal officials had caused Moulay Hassan to appoint special *oumana* (tax assessors and collectors) who were made responsible for local assessments and the equitable distribution and collection of the tax levies. By 1912, however, governmental authority had broken down and with it the effectiveness of Hassan's *oumana*, while at the national level the powers of the minister of finances had been drastically curtailed by the supervision of the customs revenues by the State Bank in accordance with the Act of Algeciras.[18]

There was a minister of war (*wazir al-harb*), whose duties are self-explanatory, and finally, the *wazir al-chikayat* or minister of justice. Contrary to what many have assumed, the *wazir al-chikayat* had no direct authority over any aspect of the Sharia. That was the undisputed province of the *cadis*, quasi-independent judges who ruled in accordance with interpretations of the Sharia handed down by the immensely respected *ulama* (doctors of Muslim law). Instead, the Moroccan minister of justice was a kind of "redresser of abuses" in such matters as provincial and municipal administration, tax collection, claims against the government, administration of the *habous*, and failures to carry out the judgments of the *cadis*. His function was to correct abuses of power, not in judicial matters alone, but in all branches of government, either by direct action or by referral to other viziers or to the sultan himself.[19]

Regionally there was no permanent organization save the three military districts of Fez, Marrakesh and Tafilelt, each commanded by a *khalifa* (lieutenant).[20] Local administration was supervised by a direct relationship between the Makhzen and the tribes and principal cities which were administered, in Berber territory, by the *djemaas*, elsewhere by *caids* and pashas appointed by the grand vizier. Peace was maintained in the markets by a corps of market police (*mohtassebs*), also directly appointed by the grand vizier and not until later under the authority of the pashas.[21]

The imposition of a protectorate, of course, necessitated some drastic alterations of this traditional hierarchy. The sultan's *firman* (governmental order) of October 31, 1912 abolished the Ministry of Foreign Affairs, whose duties were assumed by the resident-general in accordance with the protectorate treaty, and reconstituted the remaining ministers as a Council of Viziers whose responsibilities were defined more or less as before, save for the all-important difference that they were now to clear all their acts with the appropriate French authorities [22] (see Figure 2). The Ministry of War was also placed in the hands of the resident-general, as might have been expected, and a *dahir* of August 5, 1914 abolished the Ministry of Finances, transferring to the grand vizier what little authority it yet retained.[23] In 1913 a new ministry (*habous*) was created to administer the properties held in trust for purposes of charity or public service and which the French thought wise to leave in native hands.[24] After 1914, then, the Makhzen was considerably truncated, comprising only the grand vizier and the two vizierates of justice and *habous*, and while minor alterations were made in the following years, this was the sum and substance of the Makhzen until 1947.[25]

CREATION OF A EUROPEAN ADMINISTRATION

Parallel to the Makhzen, Lyautey constructed a separate protectorate administration, the Residency. It comprised "technical services," which amounted to a wholly new European government for Morocco, and "services of authority," which served as the agents of advisement, *contrôle* and liaison with the Makhzen and by which Lyautey hoped to reform and modernize that obsolescent body. The evolution of this complex mechanism occurred in four or five phases which embraced the entire protectorate period, because conditions changed and the French were feeling their way at the start. From 1912 to 1920, simultaneously with the reorganization of the Makhzen, the "technical services" were created. These comprised chiefly the resident-general and his "cabinet," the secretary-general of the protectorate, and the various departments of state (*directions* or *services*). In the second phase, which largely overlapped the first in point of time, attention was paid to a working relationship between the Residency and the Makhzen, and the first representative bodies were created. This had been accomplished by 1922. A lengthy interlude of comparative inactivity intervened before the beginning of the third phase. Then, from 1936 to World War II, occurred a

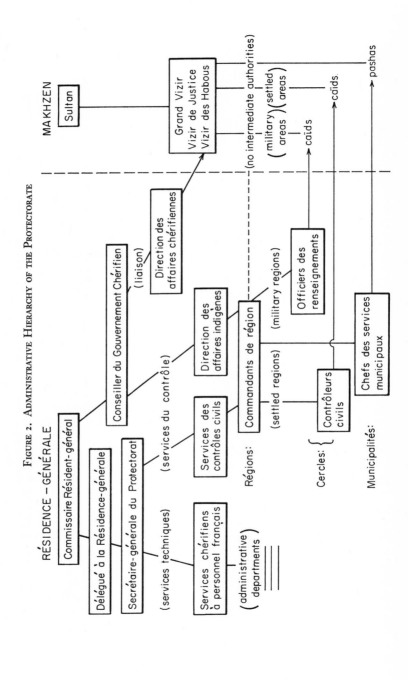

FIGURE 2. ADMINISTRATIVE HIERARCHY OF THE PROTECTORATE

MAKHZEN

Sultan

Grand Vizir
Vizir de Justice
Vizir des Habous

(no intermediate authorities)

(military)(settled)
(areas)(areas)

caïds

caïds

pashas

RÉSIDENCE – GÉNÉRALE

Commissaire Résident-général

Délégué à la Résidence-générale

Secrétaire-générale du Protectorat

(services techniques)

Services chérifiens
à personnel français

(administrative)
(departments)

Conseiller du Gouvernement Chérifien

(liaison)

Direction des
affaires chérifiennes

(services du contrôle)

Direction des
affaires indigènes

Services des
contrôles civils

Régions:

Commandants de région

(military regions)

(settled regions)

Officiers des
renseignements

Cercles: { Contrôleurs
civils

Municipalités:

Chefs des services
municipaux

reorganization of the Residency, resulting in greater centralization and assimilation as well as some change in the representative bodies. The final phase, which lies outside the scope of this study, occurred between the end of the war and 1955 when the incompatibility of centralized authority and native representation was resolved by the grant of independence.

Phase I (1912–20): Creation of the European or "Technical" Services

The administrative hierarchy of the protectorate can best be understood by reference to Figure 2. Repeated changes were made in the lines of authority and in nomenclature, but the tripartite division between "technical services," "services of control and liaison," and the Makhzen was preserved essentially unaltered throughout the protectorate period.

The decree of the French government of June 11, 1912 [26] made Lyautey virtual autocrat of Morocco. As *commissaire résident-général*, reporting to the Quai d'Orsay, Lyautey became sole repository of the powers of the Republic in Morocco; he had command of the armed forces, and was the sole intermediary between the sultan and foreign powers.[27] This absolutism persisted until the eve of Lyautey's departure, when the government's dissatisfaction with the conduct of the Riffian campaign led to the separation of the political and military commands, the latter being bestowed upon Marshal Pétain as *commandant supérieur des troupes du Maroc*.[28] Thereafter, with the exception of Noguès, no resident-general had direct control of the army in Morocco.[29] The resident-general was assisted by a deputy, the *délégué*, and by a cabinet consisting of military, political and diplomatic advisors.[30]

Government decrees of April 28, 1912 and January 15, 1913 [31] created a secretary-general of the protectorate to oversee the operation of the "technical services." These services eventually comprised the whole gamut of a French administrative bureaucracy: departments for finance, public works, public health, com-

---

Figure 2 demonstrates the increasing centralization of authority in the hands of the resident-general and the oblique though effective control exercised over the remnants of the Makhzen. Many alterations of detail were made from time to time as conditions required, but this represents the essential power structure which changed very little from 1912 to 1956.

munications, education, justice, economic affairs, agriculture, domains and forests, commerce, industry and mines, labor, social affairs, public security, and of course, for *antiquités, beaux-arts et monuments historiques*, although they were repeatedly reorganized, subdivided or amalgamated, and all of them never existed at any one time.[32] All this was necessary to give a "vigorous impulsion" to the Residency, to permit it to exercise its functions in the most direct and effective manner.[33] By 1920 the European administration of Morocco was in full operation.

PHASE II (1913–22): MAKHZEN-RESIDENCY LIAISON
AND THE FIRST REPRESENTATIVE BODIES

While the European bureaucracy of the Residency was being erected and the Makhzen reorganized, some means had to be devised to coordinate the two and to provide for the tutelage of the latter. Thus came into being the system of liaison and control which Lyautey called his *services d'autorité* and which functioned at all levels of the Makhzen from the sultan to the lowliest shaykh.

Control and advisement of the Council of Viziers was handled by a counsellor of the Sharifian government[34] who reported to the resident-general or his delegate and was assisted by a bureau known as the *Direction des Affaires Chérifiennes* organized in 1920. This administration was entrusted with liaison between the two governments, affairs of the Palace, and all native administration including Muslim justice and education as well as the *habous*,[35] an arrangement which persisted throughout the protectorate period.

For local administration the country was divided into *régions* which in turn were subdivided into *cercles*. Who was in authority at the local level depended on whether a district was "settled" or still under military occupation. The military regions, initially under army jurisdiction, were in 1917 turned over to the counsellor of the Sharifian government who administered them with the help of a separate department known as the *Direction des Affaires Indigènes*.[36] Reporting to this department through the *commandants de région* were the *officiers de renseignements* who were in direct contact with the tribal *caids*. Before 1934, military rule prevailed in the *régions* of Taza, Fez, Meknes and Marrakesh, the territories of Bou Denib and Tadla Zaian, and the autonomous *cercle* of Agadir, thus comprising the entire hinterland of the French zone as well as the coastal districts in the southwest.[37] Thereafter they gradually diminished in extent and importance, although they never entirely disappeared.

The administration of the settled regions was entrusted to the secretary-general of the protectorate and the *Corps du Contrôle Civil*[38] which was set up in 1913 and changed permanently to the *Direction des Affaires Civiles* in 1917. Each *cercle* in the settled regions was the responsibility of a *contrôleur civil* and his subordinates, the *officiers des affaires indigènes* (O.A.I.), the equivalent of the district officer in British colonial administration. Their rapport with the native *caids* and shaykhs was, on the whole, not surpassed by any other type of official. Many of the O.A.I.'s of later years, even in the 1950's, had worked with Lyautey and were still inspired by the Marshal's spirit of respect for, and genuine collaboration with, the natives.[39] In the person of the O.A.I., French colonial administration appeared in its most attractive garb. Until 1934 the civil regions were limited to the coastal districts from the Spanish zone down to Mogador and to the large province of Oujda on the Algerian border.[40]

Owing to the peculiarly urban nature of the traditional Sharifian government, the larger cities were endowed with a certain autonomy under the supervision of *chefs des services municipaux* who reported to the *commandant de région* and supervised the activities of the local pasha.[41] Very early, *municipalités* were established in Fez, Rabat, Mazagan and Casablanca, later to be extended to Fedala, Doukkala, Port Lyautey (Kénitra), Ouezzane, Meknes, Sefrou, Taza, Oujda, Settat, Azemmour, Safi, Mogador, Agadir and Marrakesh.[42] By 1922, French Morocco was being administered by a European bureaucracy exercising control at all levels over what remained of the Makhzen.

Only one development of this second phase remains to be mentioned: the emergence of the first representative bodies. Lyautey had no intention of giving political representation to the *colons*, for he scrupulously adhered to the protectorate ideal, but he did need advice, and he wished to accommodate the professional interests of both French and Moroccans under his charge. Accordingly, he created consultative Chambers of Agriculture and of Commerce and Industry for the French in 1913[43] and for the Moroccans in 1919.[44] At first both were appointive, but the French chambers became elective in 1919, while the Moroccans were obliged to wait until 1947 for this privilege. In order to augment the activities of the narrowly conceived Moroccan chambers, Lyautey inaugurated in March 1919 Committees of Economic Studies composed of all the notables in each region. The results were highly successful, for the committees compensated for the unrepresentative nature of the appointive chambers and won for the Residency the cooperation of the native leaders at all levels, enabling the work of economic development and administrative reorganization to proceed.[45]

The summit of this advisory complex was formed by the *Conseil de Gouvernement*, created in 1919 in order to ensure collaboration between the *colons* and the Residency and augmented in 1923 by a Moroccan section.[46] The first colleges of both sections comprised the presidents and vice-presidents of the Chambers of Agriculture; the second colleges, of the equivalent officers of the Chambers of Commerce and Industry. The principal function of the *Conseil* was to provide the administration with a sampling of public opinion. Budgetary and other economic matters, for the most part, were reported on by the various departments of the Residency for the *Conseil's* consideration, but the deliberations and opinions of the *Conseil* were not binding on the administration. Indeed, no votes were taken to determine the degree of consensus, but each debate was terminated by the acknowledgement of the *chef de service* of the interested department and by the expressed gratitude of either the resident-general, his delegate, or the secretary-general, accompanied by the assurance that the views expressed would be taken into account.[47]

For the sake of completeness, the municipal commissions in each of the dozen and a half municipalities created by the *dahir* of April 8, 1917 must be mentioned. These were appointive bodies of French and Moroccan membership, each section sitting separately, which assisted the pasha but had no administrative authority. Only the commission of Casablanca was empowered to supervise the receipt and expenditure of municipal funds.[48] For Fez, special deliberative assemblies (the *majlis*) representing the Jewish and Muslim populations and elected by the notables of the city, were created in 1912, but this arrangement was unique to Fez and even there it was replaced in 1934 by a municipal commission of the usual sort.[49] By 1923, then, the second phase was complete. A working relationship of liaison and control between the Makhzen and Residency had been created, and Lyautey had evolved a means of informing himself of the needs and desires of important political and economic groups at all levels of government.

Very little was done between 1923 and 1936 to alter the structure fashioned by Lyautey. Minor adjustments were necessary, of course, but the tripartite relationship of Residency, Makhzen and *contrôle*, buttressed by the representative councils, continued to function essentially as the first resident-general had devised them. Moreover, once the pacification and administrative reorganization, at which Lyautey excelled, were well in hand, the need predominated for economic consolidation and development. This required a different type of administrative talent, managerial and financial, which was personified by Lyautey's successor, Théodore Steeg. This was particularly true after the 1929 Depression set in, and thereafter residents-general were largely preoccupied with economic problems and with the demand of the French settlers for an increasing voice in government in order to secure corrective action on their economic distress. Steeg had already demonstrated his sympathy for white settler representation in 1926 when he created a third college in the French section of the *Conseil de Gouvernement*. Its purpose was to represent the professions, and it was elected directly by all French residents over twenty-one years of age who were not inscribed on the lists for the other two colleges.[50] No equivalent Moroccan college was created until 1947.

PHASE III (1936–43): CENTRALIZATION AND REPRESENTATION

The residents-general who succeeded Lyautey (see Appendix B) tended either, like Steeg, to have been reared in the authoritarian school of Algeria or, like Peyrouton and Noguès, to be temperamentally inclined towards arbitrary and centralized administration. Lyautey had lamented this penchant among French colonial officials at all levels as early as 1920. Its results became apparent even in Lyautey's last years and gathered momentum when Steeg began to import his former colleagues from Algeria.[51] The drift towards centralization also resulted from the more legitimate need to economize by pruning away some of the bureaucratic shrubbery which harbored many a nest-feathering functionary from the mid-1920's onward. The compression of services was inaugurated by Resident-General Ponsot in 1935–36 and continued by Peyrouton during his brief tenure in the latter year. A succession of decrees and *dahirs*

united the offices of the *délégué* and the secretary-general of the
protectorate and created directly under the *délégué* a *Direction
des Affaires Politiques* with combined authority over all administrative departments and the services of control, civil and military
alike. It also had supervisory authority over the counsellor of the
Sharifian government who was responsible for liaison with the
Makhzen. Only economic affairs, deemed sufficiently critical to
warrant a separate department, was excluded from the purview
of the *Direction des Affaires Politiques*, but it, too, reported
directly to the *délégué*. The net result was to bring under the
immediate control of the resident-general and his deputy virtually
every facet of native life, a regime which persisted under Resident-General Noguès until after World War II.[52]

Yet even while the assimilation of all Moroccan government by
the Residency was taking place, certain officials were beginning
to recognize a need for greater consultation and representation of
the population, a manifestation of the democratic authoritarianism
to which the French are inclined. By a Residential order of June
2, 1936, Peyrouton created a *Comité Permanent de Défense
Économique*, as well as *comités économiques régionaux*, incor-
porating representatives from all branches of economic life, native
and European alike.[53] The next month this policy was applied to
administrative matters by the creation of *conseils administratifs
régionaux* designed to provide the resident-general with fuller
reports and better analyses of regional problems.[54] The policy
was continued by Noguès who maintained throughout his long
Residency (1936-43) close ties with the *associations des anciens
élèves* of the *collèges* of Fez and Rabat. He asked their advice,
particularly on the budget, and reserved seats for them in the
Moroccan section of the *Conseil de Gouvernement*.[55] These acts,
in effect, revived Lyautey's policy of collaboration with the native
elite which had fallen into abeyance after 1925. It was given
official sanction in November 1937 by the *Conférence de Coordination de l'Afrique du Nord* which, under the presidency of
Albert Sarraut, recommended, among other things, the admittance
of more of the native elite into the North African administration
and its participation in consultative and representative bodies.[56]

Before the end of the protectorate, well before the Second
World War, Moroccans were enjoying the salutary benefits of

national unity, peace, and a modern administrative system, as well as the instructive effects of participation, however limited, in representative bodies, all of which they owed to France. Nevertheless, during the later years of the protectorate, the administrative complex created by France was patently unstable. The simultaneous pursuit of centralization and representation, however well it might work in France, was doomed to failure in a plural society, for it attempted to harmonize the essentially discordant self-interests of Moroccans and French settlers. Thus it failed, while the French presence persisted. But even the most rabid nationalist could not deny that it was such a governmental structure, and not a reorganized Makhzen, which had inspired their demands and which Morocco needed for its debut into the society of nations. This was the type of governmental structure incorporated in the nationalists' *Plan de Réformes* of 1934 and the type opted for in 1956 by the nationalists who first ruled independent Morocco, while the vestigial Makhzen was relegated to oblivion.

III

DISILLUSION

If France enlightened Morocco by reform and example, she also estranged it by abuses and discrimination. Apologists for the protectorate shrugged off Moroccan grievances as the growing pains of a new country, or as the effects of the world economic crisis, Muslim xenophobia, or foreign subversion, or any number of other things over which France had little control. None of these can be wholly discounted, of course, nor can any objective observer deny that some grievances were manufactured out of whole cloth or were grossly exaggerated, but this seems to have been a commonplace of colonial nationalism. Whatever apologists profess to believe, however, there was a variety of specific grievances that can be termed legitimate, which caused profound and sometimes unvoiced resentment among Moroccans, and which were susceptible to corrective action had the rulers of the country been sensitive to their importance. These grievances were commonly of two types: those which arose from the French practice of assimilation, on the one hand, and from its perversion, on the other.

In theory, assimilation was a process whereby the institutions of a dependent people would become one with those of the metropole, to the mutual benefit of both, and natives (the elite, at least) would learn to become loyal Frenchmen. But the presupposition that natives wanted to, or could, become Frenchmen appeared to be ill founded, and, in practice, assimilation amounted in Morocco, as it did elsewhere in the empire, to direct and often military rule, economic exploitation and acculturation of a very imperfect nature. Four aspects of assimilation — administrative, judicial, economic and cultural — and its perversion will be examined here and in the three succeeding chapters.

ADMINISTRATIVE ASSIMILATION, OR DIRECT RULE

Apart from the inescapable psychological and social dislocations which it produced in native life, assimilation, one can argue, was necessary to launch North Africa on the road to modernity. That many Moroccans did not share this view, or professed not to, was demonstrated by their armed resistance from 1907 until 1934 (and again after 1952) and by other forms of resistance which commenced shortly after World War I. What French rule became in the face of this opposition reveals the basis on which assimilation rested, unvarnished by parliamentary euphemism.

Recurrent crises in the military phases of the French occupation, for example, sometimes led to ministerial histrionics which disclosed the real concerns of Frenchmen in North Africa. On the occasion of Abd al-Krim's cutting the Fez–Taza line to Algeria in the summer of 1925, Premier Paul Painlevé declared,

We must either defend Morocco . . . or else abandon North Africa, and abandon it under what disastrous conditions, at the risk of what massacres! It would be the end of our colonial empire, the end of our economic independence, which is impossible without the colonies, the end of the prestige and influence of France in the world.[1]

The government's reaction to political resistance, though less hysterical, was equally doctrinaire and is typified by a statement made in 1934 to Allal al-Fassi by M. Girardin, then advisor to His Majesty the Sultan:

Your demands [the *Plan de Réformes*] consist of three parts: the first part can be implemented now; the second part may be implemented but only after a while; as to the third, it can never be implemented because we have no intention of voluntarily pulling out of Morocco.[2]

Had even this qualified liberalism prevailed, the nationalist movement might have been forestalled for many years, but those who ruled the country compounded their vision of assimilation with a hostility to even minimal concessions which would have impinged little on France's hegemony. Official obduracy was reinforced by settler assurances, in *L'Afrique Française*, that the definitive solution to political unrest in Morocco was the application of "firm and resolute authority." [3]

Contrary to the Treaty of Fez, the Residency almost inevitably pursued a policy of direct rule, tactfully veiled in Lyautey's time, less tactfully so by his successors. The reason for this was clear. Theoretically the system of control erected by Lyautey was perfectly compatible with indirect rule. Reform projects submitted to the sultan by the Residency could be approved and promulgated if they in no way qualified the sultan's sovereignty

or violated religious tradition, but this was an insuperable qualification, for the immovable, medieval Makhzen looked upon every
act of the Residency as an infringement of sovereignty or a
violation of tradition. Under these circumstances, the practical
result of indirect rule would have been the stultification of all
government business in a web of hostility and cross-purposes.

Under Lyautey the inevitable frictions produced by such an
arrangement were minimized by a careful observation of the
amenities, because Lyautey insisted that his system be thought of
as one of control rather than domination,[4] but subsequent
residents-general opened the old wounds by treating the officials
of the Makhzen as what in fact they were — subordinate functionaries of the Ministry of Foreign Affairs. The nationalists
complained that the Makhzen neither was kept fully informed
nor did it retain any real legislative power. Increasingly, *dahirs*
were prepared by the Residency, in what amounted to final copy,
and submitted for the sultan's approval without his prior consultation or an opportunity to assess their ramifications, an abuse of
power known in nationalist circles as the *machine à dahirs.*[5]
Lyautey had foreseen this trend as early as 1920. In a circular of
that year distributed to his subordinates, he opined that "we
[Frenchmen] have direct administration in our blood . . . coming from France as well as . . . from Algeria." [6]

Regional administration moved in the same direction. The
contrôleurs civils, instead of limiting their activities to advising
the local *caids* and monitoring the application of reforms, took
upon themselves the direct administration of their regions. What
was especially irksome to the nationalists was the rendering of
discretionary justice by the *contrôleur* in the *caid's* name and, on
occasion, without the *caid's* knowledge. In this there was a double
injustice, it was claimed, for the *caid* was ultimately held responsible for errors of judgment made by a *contrôleur civil* who was
not only an infidel but was often ignorant of, and unsympathetic
to, the local traditions which guided the administration of Moroccan justice.[7] The *commandants de région,* civilian and military
alike, were in fact little more than prefects tightly controlled by
the government in Rabat, and like Charlemagne's *missi dominici,*
had extensive authority to overrule the feudal *caids* on whom they
were assigned to report.[8] In the municipalities as well, where the
pasha wielded ostensible authority, all his acts and orders had to
be countersigned by the *chef des services municipaux.*[9]

Even religious affairs, expressly safeguarded by the Treaty of Fez, did not escape direct rule. Within the Residency was established a *Direction des Habous* to supervise the management of these religious foundations by a Makhzen official, the vizier of *habous*. The nationalists asserted that the French *directeurs*, especially after the death of Sultan Moulay Youssef in 1927, had thrust the viziers aside, usurped direct authority over the foundations, and, contrary to the instructions of the donors, had amalgamated all *habous* revenues and parceled them out arbitrarily for illegal purposes. The result was the deterioration of certain *habous* functions which the *directeur* regarded as non-critical and, owing to the European demand for land, the illegal appropriation of religious property to that end.[10]

A disproportionate number of European functionaries in a colonial government is perhaps the most telling indicator of direct rule. Lyautey had sought to limit the European bureaucracy in size, scope and privilege and to train native officials for all but the most elevated positions, but with his departure the policy was reversed. As of 1925 French functionaries numbered about 6,500. By 1932 they had increased to 19,371 [11] quite apart from the troops, and were consuming 57 per cent of the budget.[12] Herein was reflected the growing alliance between the officials, the settlers, and the colonial lobby in Paris, as well as the shift to a truly colonial policy personified by Théodore Steeg and most of his successors.

That the French imperialists regarded the Moroccan protectorate as a colony was tacitly acknowledged in February 1934, when responsibility for its administration was transferred from the Quai d'Orsay to the newly formed Ministry of France Overseas. The resulting furor on the part of both Moroccan nationalists and French settlers, for different reasons to be sure, was sufficient to cause the transfer to be reversed and the new ministry dissolved.[13] One needs but scan the pages of *L'Afrique Française* during the interwar years, where Morocco and Tunisia are customarily referred to as "colonies," to understand what the colonial lobby intended to do with Morocco.

After 1934, when the economic situation had become critical, the high percentage of funds allocated to European functionaries became intolerable and was somewhat reduced by Resident-General Ponsot.[14] But essentially the situation was irreversible, and try as they might, neither Ponsot nor Noguès was able to

pay more than lip service to Lyautey's ideal of indirect rule in the
face of the phalanx of French Algerians who had become so
strongly entrenched in the administration, in the business community, and on the land,[15] and whose parliamentary lobby in
Paris was a constant threat to the unstable coalition cabinets of
that time.

Administrative assimilation, therefore, meant in practice not the
modernization of the Makhzen and the acquisition of European
administrative skills by a native bureaucracy, but the displacement
of both by a European structure imported from France and
staffed as far as possible by Europeans imported from France and
Algeria.

TWO WEIGHTS AND TWO MEASURES

Moroccans might well have endured assimilation and the economic exploitation which accompanied it had their French masters dealt justly with them. What made the regime intolerable
was the double standard of rights, the system of the *indigénat* by
which Moroccans were subjected to discriminatory restrictions
on their rights — political, civil, vocational and personal.

POLITICAL DISCRIMINATION

Political discrimination customarily took the form of a curb
on native representation. The French Chambers of Commerce
and Agriculture as well as the French section of the *Conseil de
Gouvernement* had become elective in 1919, and by 1947 the
European population of 250,000 was enjoying universal suffrage
quite contrary to the Treaty of Fez. Moreover, through the
Comité du Maroc and powerful friends in France, the colonists
could bring exceeding pressure to bear on the Residency. By the
early 1930's, they had acquired an effective, though entirely
extralegal, voice in administration, and on occasions were able to
exert sufficient influence to have recalcitrant residents-general
removed.[16] The Residency, therefore, was usually responsive to
the wishes of the settlers and their representatives.

Unofficial power, effective as it was, did not satisfy the colonists,
however, and they began in 1935 to demand that the French
section of the *Conseil* be transformed into a fully competent
legislative body in budgetary and other matters. This, of course,

raised the question of the political rights of the Moroccans themselves, and the resulting stir led to the removal of not one, but two residents-general in 1936.[17] As it worked out, the Moroccan chambers and the Moroccan section of the *Conseil de Gouvernement* did not become elective until 1947,[18] after which date the Chambers of Agriculture could boast 3,000 electors and the Chambers of Commerce and Industry about 8,000, out of a native population of about 8,000,000, although these figures were raised to 11,000 and 220,000, respectively, in 1951.[19] Before the war, the Moroccan section of the *Conseil de Gouvernement* discussed nothing until the French section had completed its business. Unlike the French section, where criticism of the Residency was often unrestrained, the Moroccan section was expected to exercise the greatest circumspection in debate and to maintain a respectful attitude towards the government.[20] The nationalists asserted that the *Conseil*, as then constituted, did nothing to alleviate the problems which beset the country, because its membership, rules and discussions were so thoroughly inhibited that there was no opportunity for native claims and grievances to be aired.[21] Omar Abdeljalil thought it inappropriate in 1934 that a minority of 130,000 French settlers should pass on a budget for the entire Moroccan population as well as its own. To see how effectively native interests were represented, he continued, one simply need examine the budget for 1933–34, in which there was no provision for easing the deplorable plight of the fellah, the artisan or the small merchant. Nor were funds allocated to counteract the general unemployment, or to reform Moroccan justice, or to expand public education for Moroccans, all of which subjects received only the most cursory attention in the debates of the *Conseil*.[22]

If political discrimination frustrated the Moroccans, civil discrimination of various sorts made them bitterly resentful.

CIVIL DISCRIMINATION

The concept of the "rights of man" was alien to pre-protectorate Morocco. Slavery was still widely accepted in principle, if not widely practiced. Law was not the distilled wisdom of the people but the will of Allah. In this milieu, the "Declaration of the Rights of Man and of the Citizen" was regarded by Lyautey as a disturbing influence and its promulgation forbidden in the protectorate.[23] Tradition was to be a massive obstacle to the quest for civil liberties in Morocco.

But an even greater obstacle was the state of siege proclaimed by the Marshal on August 2, 1914, which technically remained in force throughout the protectorate. After 1934 there were periods of toleration, to be sure, when political parties could act as if they were legally authorized (e.g., 1934–37 and 1946–52), but this was a matter of Residential indulgence rather than legal or prescriptive right.[24] Moroccans had for centuries responded to royal despotism, which they regarded as changeless and ordained by Allah, with a mixture of resignation and sporadic rebellion. But the military state imposed by France, and hence clearly not ordained by Allah, seemed doubly oppressive because it was alien and because it was more effective. In this connection there were three uses of power which especially aggrieved the nationalists: arbitrary arrest and punishment, press censorship, and restraints on the right to associate and organize.

Administrative Justice

From 1912 until 1954 when the *code pénal marocain* was at last promulgated,[25] the individual liberties of Moroccans were unprotected by law, and those who acted contrary to administrative fiat had no recourse in the courts. The usual penalty for open participation in political activities hostile to, or even critical of, the regime was a few weeks or months in prison for disturbance of the peace. More flagrant offenses were punished by exile abroad or to another part of Morocco.[26]

Of the men who later became the leaders of the nationalist movement, Mohammed Ghazi was probably the first to attract the attention of the French authorities. Owing to articles critical of the Residency which appeared in the Algerian reformist journal *ech-Chihab*, the free school which Ghazi had founded and directed in Fez was closed in 1927 and its director exiled to Casablanca. There were few such cases before 1930, but in the next decade there were three waves of suppression: in the summer of 1930, following the demonstrations against the Berber *dahir*; in November and December 1936, after the interdiction of the Casablanca *congrès* and the resultant riots; and a period of several years beginning in September and October 1937, following the Meknes and Khemisset riots.[27]

The 1930 trouble began in Fez, where Mohammed Hassan al-

Ouezzani organized a demonstration in July to protest the Berber *dahir*.[28] Appearing before the pasha's palace, he was requested to disperse his followers and to wait upon the pasha next day with a delegation to state his grievances. On the following day the delegation was overpowered by the pasha's *makhzanis* (native gendarmes), and al-Ouezzani was held face down on the floor, severely beaten, and jailed for two weeks thereafter without medication. The incident was briefly publicized in the liberal French press at the time and was resurrected for additional propaganda mileage two years later after the nationalist press had come into being. Such treatment accorded a graduate of the Lycée Charlemagne and holder of diplomas in law, diplomacy and journalism from the École des Sciences Politiques, the École des Langues Vivantes and the École des Hautes Études Sociales caused quite a stir in Morocco and among the liberal element in Paris.

Another protest against the famous *dahir* was arranged in mid-August 1930 by the notables of Fez who sent a delegation to Rabat to express their concern directly to the sultan. When it returned empty-handed, they decided to organize a series of *latifs* (communal prayers) in the mosques throughout the country. Disturbances resulted, and among those arrested were al-Ouezzani, who spent September and October in prison, and Allal al-Fassi, who was exiled to Taza for two months. Mohammed Lyazidi, who played a leading role in the *latif* campaign, was exiled to the south from September 1930 until July 1932.[29] Several others were either imprisoned or exiled. This type of suppression only aggravated the situation. The sentences were severe enough to win public sympathy for the nationalists but not enough to deactivate them. The French might have done better either to leave them alone or to stiffen their punishments. As it was, the Residency furnished the optimum mixture of freedom and oppression before 1937 to permit the nationalists to organize and to drive converts into their ranks. Suppression was justified, of course, to the extent that the Residency was responsible for maintaining order, and the nationalists knew before they started what they might expect. What to them seemed the greater injustice was that none of these cases was ever brought to trial. Sentences were determined arbitrarily by the Residency, the *contrôleur civil*, or even the local *caid* or pasha, if the French could trust him, and there was no opportunity to defend one's basic liberties in court or, even more important, to get any favorable propaganda out of the publicity which would have attended such a trial.

A practice even less defensible than administrative justice was the threat of jeopardy to one's family. The Residency found it convenient to use the two *collèges musulmans* in Rabat and Fez as a means of controlling parents, for, with their sons under official surveillance in these two cities, otherwise intractable fathers became considerably more cooperative. Parents recognized this and sometimes resisted. Messaoud Chiguer's father was jailed briefly in 1918 for temporarily refusing to send his son to the *collège* in Rabat.[30] And though Chiguer *père* was soon persuaded, the authorities purchased trouble with his acquiescence, for Chiguer *fils* became one of the leading nationalists of the interwar years.

A final example of arbitrary interference with normal rights was the treatment accorded Allal al-Fassi, Ibrahim al-Kittani and Abdelaziz Bendriss, all of whom had passed the examinations to become *ulama* in the course of the year 1930. For their participation in the demonstrations against the Berber *dahir*, however, their degree applications were pigeonholed until December 1932 when they were invited to sign a humiliating disavowal of their 1930 activities and to bind themselves never again to engage in political activities hostile to France. Their refusal to do so led to the permanent rejection of their applications,[31] but all three went into teaching, nevertheless — Allal al-Fassi as a volunteer professor at Qarawiyin, Ibrahim al-Kittani as a teacher in one of the free schools and Abdelaziz Bendriss as the director of another.[32]

Press Censorship

From the outset of the protectorate, the press in Morocco was declared free but was in fact subjected to severe regulation.[33] French-language publications were authorized by depositing a simple declaration of intent with the public prosecutor, but Arabic journals were constrained to seek prior authorization, difficult to obtain and always revocable by vizierial decree.[34] The resident-general was given authority to ban by decree any journal published in Morocco in Arabic or Hebrew or to prohibit the entry of any journal published outside Morocco in any language.[35] Theoretically, French-language journals published in Morocco were exempt from these regulations, but in point of fact the Residential order of August 1914, which placed Morocco under martial law, permitted the commandant of troops to suspend any publication judged harmful to the public order or the security of the army.[36] This legislation, initially intended to protect France and Morocco from German and Arabic propaganda, was soon applied to Communist publications and, after 1933, to the Moroccan nationalist press.

Owing in part to this control by the Residency, but as much to the generalized illiteracy of the Arabic-speaking population, the Arabic-language press played a relatively minor role in the early years of the nationalist movement. Probably less than half a dozen Arabic-language journals were published in Morocco between 1912 and 1934, and half of these can hardly be dignified by the name "journal." Only two of them appeared for more than four years, but those which could be regarded as staunchly nationalist in character appeared for less than one, and there were long periods when no journal which could be called nationalist appeared at all, viz., 1912–26, 1930–33, 1934–35. The two which lasted more than four years were both information sheets of little political import. *Es-Saada*, founded in Rabat about 1911 and appearing two or three times per week until it ceased publication in 1956, was the only Arabic periodical legally authorized before 1937. It served, in fact, as an official outlet for the Residency, but it occasionally tolerated articles such as those by Allal al-Fassi advocating reforms at Qarawiyin University.[37] *Izhar el-Haqiqa* was another small information sheet published privately in Tangier. It was banned in the French zone in August 1915 but admitted again in the 1920's.[38] A mimeographed sheet entitled *Oum el-Bennin*,[39] published by Allal al-Fassi from 1926 to 1930, was a monthly reformist journal with a maximum distribution of perhaps two hundred copies, chiefly in Fez, Rabat, Meknes and Tetuan. It carried articles, largely by its publisher and Hachemi al-Filali, on colonization, the religious brotherhoods and Qarawiyin reforms. It was so clandestine that there is doubt that the authorities were aware of its existence, which may account for its never having been suppressed.[40] However, it had no appreciable influence on the nationalist movement, according to the men interviewed by the author (see Key to Interviews, p. 288), and is of interest only as a pioneer effort by the future leader of that movement.

Not until 1933 was a bona fide nationalist journal in Arabic published in Morocco, and it should be noted that they (for there were two) appeared in the Spanish, not the French, zone. *Es-Salam* was a monthly founded in Tetuan in October 1933 by Mohammed Daoud, and was the journal of Abdelkhalek Torrès' Reformist Party; the weekly *el-Hayat*, was founded in the same city the following year. Both were barred from the French zone after May 1934 for carrying accounts of the sultan's reception in Fez which the Residency regarded as provocative. South of the Spanish border, the first legally authorized Arabic-language papers which appeared in 1937 did not survive the suppressions of October and November of that year. All told, the life tenure of the Moroccan nationalist press published in Arabic in the French zone before 1934 had been approximately seven months.

Nationalist publications in French fared somewhat better owing to the "declaration of intent" provision, although it should be noted that the monthly *Maghreb*, the first and most important to appear before World War II, whose articles formed the mainstream of Moroccan nationalist thought, was founded not in Morocco but in Paris (July 1932) where it was wholly unaccountable to the Residency. The only other such journal to appear before 1934 was the weekly *L'Action du Peuple*, founded in Fez in August 1933, which reprinted many articles from *Maghreb* and carried original articles by the same contributors and others. *L'Action du Peuple* was suspended on May 16, 1934 for "provocation," and *Maghreb*, banned from Morocco on the same date apparently on general principles, ceased publication thereafter, having been deprived of its chief outlet. Thus the French-language nationalist press before 1934 existed about three times as long as the Arabic press, that is to say, for the still short span of two years. It was a different matter with foreign publications which the Residency found far more difficult to control.

Between 1914 and 1932, 302 foreign periodicals and over 300 other publications were officially barred from French Morocco. Of the periodicals alone, few were banned in the early years, but their numbers increased in the mid-1920's. As given by *L'Afrique Française*, whose editors had no reason to minimize a tendency which they applauded, the number of proscriptions rose as follows: [41]

1914 – 3 (none in Arabic)	1918 – 1 (none in Arabic)
1915 – 7 (one in Arabic)	1919 – 0
1916 – 9 (none in Arabic)	1920 – 0
1917 – 5 " " "	1921 – 0

1922 – 3 (2 in Arabic)	1928 – 36	Number
1923 – 14 (3 in Arabic)	1929 – 36	in
1924 – 3 (2 in Arabic)	1930 – 62	Arabic
1925 – 14 (9 in Arabic)	1931 – 46	not
1926 – 4 (none in Arabic)	1932 – 36 (Jan.–July)	given
1927 – 33 (11 in Arabic)		

Prior to 1922, then, only one Arabic-language journal had been banned, but thereafter they comprised the largest number of prohibitions in any one language. Of the twenty-eight Arabic journals banned before 1932, ten originated in Tunisia, where a militant nationalism had emerged after the war, four in Algeria, three in Egypt, four in France, and three in Brazil, where a Muslim colony of 25,000 was harboring a number of Syrian refugees eager to make trouble for the French.

After 1922, the steadily mounting proscriptions of Arabic-language journals was partly a measure of the efflorescence of Middle Eastern nationalism after World War I and partly a function of the Residency's determination to seal off Morocco from its effects and to have tranquillity and order in that corner of the empire if nowhere else. The effort was not wholly successful, as will be demonstrated later in the discussion of the influence of these journals on the nationalist movement. Many of the banned publications, especially those from Egypt, continued to enter Morocco under the aegis of the British Post Offices in Fez, Rabat, Casablanca and Marrakesh until 1937 when Britain's capitulatory rights were finally relinquished, and some continued to enter clandestinely thereafter.[42]

In the early years of their movement, it was not their inability to communicate with the masses which concerned the nationalists but the difficulty of communicating among themselves, within their own social class (which, with few exceptions, was the educated bourgeoisie), and with friends they hoped to enlist in France. One result of this, not so curious as it might otherwise seem, was that their first two propaganda vehicles were printed in French. The articles which appeared therein would not have been considered dangerous or subversive in a genuinely free society. Their language, if one has the patience to read them, must be regarded as moderate and restrained in contrast to the hyperbole and hysteria which characterize nationalist literature in other parts of the Middle East and Asia. In fact, the colonialist press of Morocco, headed by *L'Afrique Française*, could on occasion be far more provocative, and the nationalists had a legitimate grievance when their relatively mild remonstrances became the object of rigorous censorship and suppression while colonialist editors vilified and libeled them with impunity.[43]

Restraints upon Association

The right to organize labor unions in Morocco was granted to French workers, but not to Moroccans, in 1936. But even had Moroccans been authorized to join, the unions which arose were run by French Socialists and Communists with whom Moroccan workers at that time had little in common, for before World War II the latter were not sufficiently evolved to be greatly interested in trade unionism or even aware of its benefits.[44] Moreover, the nationalists, themselves, consistent with their bourgeois origins, had not yet become convinced of the need to command a proletarian audience.[45] It is true that five pages are devoted to the rights of labor in the *Plan de Réformes*, but this was intended to lure sympathizers on the French left rather than to beguile the workers of Morocco. Unlike Algeria, where Messali Hadj's organization was essentially proletarian, labor played an insignificant role in the first two decades of Moroccan nationalism.

If what the nationalists denounced had little to do with the working class, it had much to do with the restrictions placed on their own attempts to organize and to demonstrate publicly. Ostensibly the right of association had been guaranteed by the *dahir* of May 24, 1914, modeled after Article 291 of the French penal code and the Associations Law of July 1, 1901. In actual fact, public meetings other than religious were prohibited by the state of siege order of 1914, reinforced by a *dahir* of June 29, 1935. The latter was designed specifically to neutralize the National Action Bloc [46] and was used to dissolve it in March 1937.[47] Accordingly, until 1934 all native political organizations operated clandestinely, and even during the period of official indulgence from 1934 to 1937 the greatest circumspection had to be observed, each organization maintaining a secret counterpart as a hedge against the inevitable day of dissolution.

Local political organizations were not alone in their misery. The Association of North African Muslim Students (A.E.M.N.A.), founded in Paris in 1927, was never permitted to hold its annual congress in Morocco, although it held them irregularly in Algeria and Tunisia. When its third congress, scheduled for Fez in September 1933, was banned at the last minute by the Residency, Mohammed Hassan al-Ouezzani pointed out with some justice that the Institut des Hautes Études Marocaines (largely French in staff and student body) had held a recent congress in Rabat at public expense, at which the most flagrant violations of the protectorate agreement had been recommended without so much as a demur from the authorities.[48] Student organizations throughout the Middle East are notorious for their political activism, and the A.E.M.N.A. was no exception, but it concerned itself primarily with educational reform and would hardly have been regarded as subversive in a healthier political climate. Quite different was official policy towards the political activities of the European colonists. Lyautey had refused to tolerate the extension of French political parties to Morocco, but after 1925 they were able to carry on there as if Europeans possessed full political rights.[49] Thus were the native and European populations of the protectorate subjected to a system of "two weights and two measures" in civil rights.

Vocational Discrimination

The inequitable treatment accorded Moroccans in the exercise of their civil rights was equally noticeable when it came to employment. The educated young Moroccan in the job market could, of course, enter any of a number of private occupations for which he happened to be qualified, but if he sought a government job — the natural inclination of the Moroccan elite — his choices were two. He might aspire to a relatively good post in the Makhzen, on the one hand, or a more modest one in the Residency, but in either case there was limited opportunity for advancement. In the Residency the reason for this was obvious, for there the system of "two weights and two measures" prevailed, especially during the Depression when the French were hard put to find employment even for themselves. Slow advancement in the Makhzen was traceable to the practice of direct rule. Sheared of many of its functions, the Makhzen was shrinking in size and importance, and advancement depended on long established seniority. Moreover, the situation was complicated by the administrative reforms initiated within the Makhzen by the Residency. Modern organizational and administrative techniques required French-trained functionaries, which disrupted the traditional avenues of recruitment by automatically disqualifying the graduates of Qarawiyin who customarily filled these positions.[50]

But towards the increasing numbers of young Moroccans who had received a fairly good French education and were demanding recognition, the French authorities adopted a patronizing attitude which ill-suited both the protectorate ideal and the pragmatic needs of the times. This attitude has been stated most succinctly by the Moroccan specialist, Jacques Ladreit de Lacharrière, historian and semi-official apologist for the protectorate regime, who wrote in 1930 that France must not move too fast towards political emancipation in Morocco, that Morocco needed doctors and engineers above all, and that it was rather pitiful to see these young, undisciplined, half-educated Moroccans display such arrogant pretensions. France's educational duty in Morocco must be directed to the real needs of the people and avoid awakening unnecessary political aspirations.[51]

Nonetheless, one cannot help but observe that the difficulties experienced by Moroccans in finding congenial employment were partly of their own making. The French-educated had an inflated opinion of their qualifications for high office and disdained the modest administrative posts open to them.[52] There were good psychological reasons for this, and the same attitude has been observed in other suppressed groups and in most backward countries of the world, but the fact remains that such a frame of mind made job-seeking under the circumstances a doubly frustrating experience.

Of the forty-one leading nationalists on whom this study focuses, probably only eight ever held what might be called a government job during the protectorate. Three of these, Abdesselam Bennouna, Abdelkhalek Torrès and Mohammed Daoud, were residents of the Spanish zone and resigned their positions after a short and unsatisfactory tenure, with the exception of Daoud who remained director of education from 1942 to 1948. In the French zone, Mohammed al-Fassi served from 1934 to 1951 in various teaching positions and as vice-rector and then rector of Qarawiyin University. Only four were actually functionaries of the Residency: Mohammed Lyazidi, interpreter from 1926 to 1930 when he resigned to demonstrate against the Berber *dahir*; Messaoud Chiguer and Abdelkebir al-Fassi, who occupied minor clerical positions while working clandestinely with the nationalists; and Mohammed al-Kholti, who defected from the nationalist movement in the mid-1930's and collaborated thereafter with the French.

For most of the nationalists, Residency service was neither an attractive nor a hospitable alternative. Of the young Moroccans, both traditionally- and French-educated, who were not among the leadership of the nationalist movement, the proportion which entered government employ may have been higher. At no time, however, can it be said that Moroccans flocked into such jobs. They regarded themselves at a disadvantage in Residency service, a fact which even *L'Afrique Française* admitted when it reported that: "At the present time [1933], apart from rare exceptions, the young Moroccans leaving our schools, *collèges* and *lycées* find scarcely any job openings other than that of interpreter." [53] Virtually every chapter of the *Plan de Réformes* betrays an underlying concern for, and frustration over, the inequality of opportunity between French and Moroccan employees.

PERSONAL DISCRIMINATION, OR THE "SALE ARABE"

While Lyautey was resident-general, he insisted that his subordinates adhere to his *politique d'égards* — an attitude of respect towards the Moroccans with whom they had to deal. The most striking example of this which he set was his refusal to allow capitulating tribal chieftains to humble themselves before him, the sort of homage relished by most other French military commanders. Lyautey, instead, would dismount and embrace the surprised and impressed chieftain as a newly won collaborator. Ordinary Moroccans merited no such consideration, but the policy was effective in Lyautey's day when only the traditional elite counted for much in Moroccan political life.

The men who succeeded Lyautey were cut from different cloth and lived in a rapidly changing country, and their thinly disguised contempt for Moroccans of all classes and degrees of education was typical of the Algerian officialdom from which many of them were drawn. Ignace Lepp recognized this as a source of boundless resentment when he pointed out that it took a long time to undo the damage, if indeed it could be undone, when a native doctor or lawyer who had studied and lived in Paris for many years was "tutoyéed" by a minor French functionary, one of the despised *classe subalterne*, or by an uncouth Corsican *colon*. The practice of referring to Moroccans as *indigènes* in their presence, while perfectly accurate, pulsed with undertones of derision as employed by the French in Morocco.[54]

Other examples are plentiful. The French language edition of the *Bulletin Officiel du Maroc* was the only "official" edition, while the Arabic edition was not only unofficial but appeared weeks after the French one, giving the impression that it was not considered important for the native population to be informed of governmental matters.[55] Road signs were seldom rendered in Arabic until the very end of the protectorate. And the petty, unintentional humiliations suffered by young Moroccans in schools whose curricula were determined by nationalistic French pedagogues were foolish and gratuitous. "Our ancestors the Gauls" certainly had disappeared from the texts by this time, but in many of the textbooks the thinly disguised contempt for much of traditional Morocco could not help but nettle its young elite. More deliberate was the scornful treatment accorded young Moroccan *lycéens* by their French schoolmates, all the more insufferable because the privileged French youth of Morocco tended to exhibit in its most blatant form the reactionary anti-intellectualism of the typical French *colon*. Little wonder that the French lost all communication with the Moroccan elite by the time the latter reached manhood.[56]

After the Berber *dahir* fracas of 1930, the editorial temper of *L'Afrique Française* became not only patronizing but studiously contemptuous of the nationalist movement and hardly designed to foster cordial relations with the young intellectuals who were to be their country's leaders in the next generation. In August of that year a commentary on the disturbances caused by the *dahir* was published, the first indication, incidentally, that the editors were aware that organized political dissent existed in the protectorate. The riots in Salé and Fez were briefly reported as trifling annoyances attributable to foreign (i.e., Egyptian) propaganda and to young intellectuals trained (unfortunately) in the French schools. The journal asserted that

. . . a clique of a few street boys provided with a vague certificate of studies wishes to play Ghandi or Zaghloul in Morocco, without realizing that the latter are a menace for England because they represent a conscience, while these Moroccans who have escaped from primary school are nothing more than digestive tracts.[57]

Clever, to be sure, but neither accurate nor diplomatic.

In 1935 the reaction of *L'Afrique Française* to the *Plan de Réformes* was in the same vein:

> These pages, the product of the Moroccan "carp" and the Socialist "rabbit," are for the most part, despite their apparent seriousness, so tendentious, empty and incoherent that one must ask if its patrons read it before participating . . . It is only fair to add that a small number of pages express, unhappily in a maladroit and comic manner, some sincere emotions . . . As a whole, it is a firebrand thrown against the Moroccan Protectorate . . . . The authors will agitate briefly . . . but after all the art of using the Greek Fire went out with the Middle Ages.[58]

Now, while the Plan was not a document of surpassing literary merit or a draft constitution sufficiently neat and consistent to appeal to the rational French mind, it was neither empty, nor incoherent nor excessively tendentious. It was what it purported to be and no more — a practical draft for a program of long-overdue reforms.[59] The unqualified and largely unjustified derision heaped upon its authors in the article quoted above must have been deliberately contrived to humiliate them, for it could hardly have been expected to imbue in them an affection for the colonialist lobby. This nonchalant and irresponsible contempt, while not universal, was widely displayed by many French officials and colonists who were blithely unaware that it was largely their attitude which was alienating the native Moroccan and jeopardizing France's future in North Africa.[60]

Significantly, none of the nationalists interviewed by the author mentioned this grievance voluntarily. Their initial reticence may have been attributable in part to the innate dignity of the Moroccan, with which all who know him are familiar, and in part to a reserve ingrained by years of subordination. After some probing, however, it appeared that the superior attitude of their European rulers had, indeed, been a source of deep personal resentment. This is a fact recognized by the more sympathetic of the French commentators such as Ignace Lepp and Louis Jalabert, the latter being one of the first to warn his countrymen, in a perceptive essay published in 1934, that they were needlessly creating a heritage of ill will among their Moroccan subjects.[61]

Thus did discrimination and the perversion of assimilation justify nationalist complaints against the protectorate administration. Equally grievous to the Moroccans was the Residency's effort to assimilate the law of the Prophet to the *Code Napoléon*.

IV

MACHIAVELLIAN JUSTICE

While many inequities in French Morocco stemmed from willful discrimination, many, especially in judicial matters, arose from two misconceptions entertained by French officials and their advisors: the assumption that Moroccans differentiated between religious and secular law, and the belief that there was, within the Makhzen, a hierarchy of courts whose judges were vested with the delegated authority of the sultan.[1] Neither of these was the case. On the one hand, all law was considered to emanate from Allah or from the Prophet, was interpreted by the *ulama*, and was administered by the *cadis* whom the sultan appointed. Little distinction was consciously made between kinds of law, religious and secular, except that the pashas and *caids* administered the fiats of the Makhzen somewhat aside from, but within the limitations imposed by, the Sharia. On the other hand, the sultan and his entourage did not, like the medieval European *curia regis*, constitute a court of appeals, nor could the sultan retract "delegated" judicial authority for he had none to delegate, although he could intervene to have other judges reexamine a case.[2] Proceeding from these misconceptions, the Residency made secularization and centralization the bases of its judicial reform in Morocco, in conflict with religious traditions where the Muslim was most sensitive and reluctant to permit European innovations.

The Residency was also guided by practical considerations, of course. There was great need for land reform, for modernization of the judicial system, especially of the commercial code, and for the correction of gross abuses of penal jurisdiction — areas in which Muslim law was weakest and least definite.[3] Finally, the unique status of the Berber, as well as political factors to be discussed later, seemed to call for a special dispensation in his regard. These considerations led to the establishment in Morocco of a judicial structure and of civil, penal and commercial codes based on European models and served to justify the effort to merge Berber justice with French. The net result was the assimilation of much of Moroccan justice into a new European judicial system, and assimilation was to become a third basis for judicial reform in Morocco.

REORGANIZATION OF THE COURTS

Owing to the ethnic and religious diversity of Morocco, an extremely complicated system of five parallel jurisdictions was created (see Figure 3) to administer religious, secular, Berber, French and Jewish law, of which the latter two need not concern us here. The administration of the Sharia, its traditional scope much reduced, was to be centralized in the office of the vizier of justice created by a *firman* of October 31, 1912. The vizier exercised no regulatory powers, but he prepared regulations which were submitted to the grand vizier or the sultan for approval, and he supervised the *cadis*, investigated complaints about them, and settled disputes between them.[4] Prior to 1912, *cadis* were appointed by the sultan upon the nomination of the pasha, *caid* or *khalifa*, but after this time their nomination became the prerogative of the vizier.[5] The opportunity for corruption was reduced in 1937 and 1938 by legislation which provided for competitive examinations.[6] By 1954 there were about a hundred *cadis* in Morocco and as many as three in large cities like Fez and Marrakesh.[7] The *cadi* exercised his authority in a district known as a *mahakma*, created in 1914 by a reform which also weeded out some of the extraneous or incompetent judges and provided for greater care in their recruitment and training.[8]

Even before the protectorate, the administrative, or Makhzen, courts of the pashas and *caids* had usurped much of the *cadis'* traditional jurisdiction, so that as of 1912 the latter customarily judged only cases concerning the personal status and inheritance of Muslims and all cases involving real estate.[9] Hence the fundamental judicial *dahir* of July 7, 1914 did little to alter the existing situation, for it removed from the *cadis'* jurisdiction nothing but those lands which came to be registered (*immatriculées*) under French land law.[10] The *cadi* was the sole judge in his court, although he might refer to a legal expert (*mufti*) for advice which was rendered as a written opinion (*fetwa*) based on legal precedents. The role of the *mufti* declined somewhat after the regularization of the office of *oukil* (court attorney), and in the secular courts he all but disappeared.[11] The *cadi* was also assisted by one or more *adoul* (notaries or clerks) of which several were attached to each *mahakma*.[12]

FIGURE 3. MOROCCAN LAW AND JUSTICE: REORGANIZATION UNDER THE PROTECTORATE

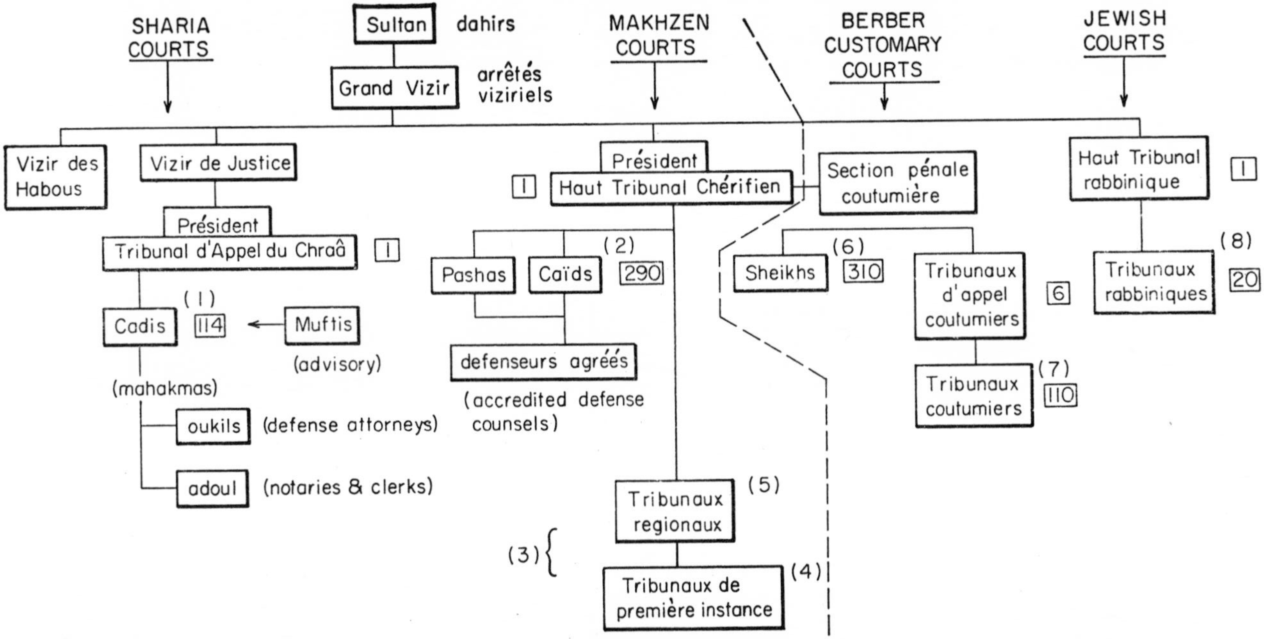

Sultan

Grand Vizir

dahirs

arrêtés viziriels

SHARIA COURTS

Vizir des Habous

Vizir de Justice

Tribunal d'Appel du Chraâ — Président [1]

Cadis (1) [114]
(mahakmas)

Muftis (advisory)

oukils (defense attorneys)

adoul (notaries & clerks)

MAKHZEN COURTS

Haut Tribunal Chérifien — Président [1]

Pashas

Caïds (2) [290]

défenseurs agréés (accredited defense counsels)

Tribunaux regionaux (5)

Tribunaux de première instance (4)

(3)

BERBER CUSTOMARY COURTS

Section pénale coutumière

Sheikhs (6) [310]

Tribunaux d'appel coutumiers [6]

Tribunaux coutumiers (7) [110]

JEWISH COURTS

Haut Tribunal rabbinique [1]

Tribunaux rabbiniques (8) [20]

For the first decade of the protectorate, appeals were handled by the vizier of justice with the advice of a *Conseil Supérieur d'Oulémas*.[13] After 1921 appellate jurisdiction was vested in the *Tribunal d'Appel du Chraa*,[14] merely the earlier council transformed into a more formal court comprising a president, vice-president, four appeals judges, four ordinary judges, and four deputy judges, appointed by vizierial decree from among *cadis*, former *cadis* and *ulama*. The *Tribunal d'Appel* was a court of second instance from which there was no further appeal.[15]

Until 1918 the Makhzen courts had functioned under the authority of the vizier of justice, but the extensive reorganization of that year (*dahir* of August 4th) placed them directly under the grand vizier, erected a *Haut Tribunal Chérifien* as the supreme court of appeals, and defined their jurisdiction to cover all criminal, civil and commercial cases, certain aspects of civil and commercial law having been withdrawn from the *cadis*.[16] Criminal cases involving more than two years' imprisonment had to be referred directly from the pasha's or *caid's* court to the *Haut Tribunal*, and civil cases involving special religious questions could be referred to the *cadi's* court.[17] The entire system was extensively reorganized in 1953 to bring it more in line with European procedures, but from 1918 until 1953 the structure and operation remained essentially as described.

Figures in squares refer to the number of courts in operation as of 1945.

(1) Jurisdiction over personal status of Muslims, their inheritance and unregistered real estate, including Jewish.

(2) After 1953 *dahirs*: where no regional courts, retained jurisdiction as before, i.e., over commercial cases, civil cases not justiciable by *cadis* (e.g., registered real estate), and criminal cases involving less than two years' imprisonment; where regional courts set up, *caids* retained only criminal jurisdiction.

(3) Wherever established (after 1953), assumed the civil and commercial jurisdiction of pashas and *caids*.

(4) No criminal jurisdiction. Lesser civil and commercial cases, only.

(5) Greater civil and commercial cases. Jurisdiction over minor crimes involving more than two years' imprisonment.

(6) Criminal jurisdiction only, with the same limitations after 1953 as applied to pashas and *caids*.

(7) Jurisdiction over all civil and commercial cases, including real estate, in Berber territory.

(8) Jurisdiction over personal status and inheritance, only.

CONTRÔLE

As was the case with the other administrative departments, the entire judicial hierarchy was subjected to the system of *contrôle* (see Figure 2). The judicial actions of the grand vizier with regard to the *Haut Tribunal Chérifien* and of the vizier of justice with regard to the *Tribunal d'Appel du Chraa* were closely monitored by agents of the *Direction des Affaires Chérifiennes* and by the *Conseiller du Gouvernement Chérifien* who were responsible as well for all other liaison between the Residency and Makhzen.[18] In the lower courts of the Sharia, the *cadis* were allowed considerable autonomy if they made an effort to curb the worst abuses, to which end in 1914 in each *mahakma* was posted a list of accredited law consultants who undertook to refrain from basing advisory opinions on doubtful legal precedents.[19] Should that be insufficient, the *cadis* could be called to account by the local French *contrôle* officials acting as representatives of the vizier of justice.[20] In each of the lower Makhzen courts, because the pasha or *caid* usually lacked legal knowledge and sometimes rendered incongruous judgments, a French *commissaire du gouvernement* was attached for legal advice to act as government prosecutor in criminal cases, to report maladministration to the grand vizier, and to appeal inequitable judgments to the higher court.[21] For periodic inspection of the court system, a body of "inspectors of the Sharifian judicial services" was created by a *dahir* of October 28, 1919.[22]

Accordingly, despite the ostensible separation of justice from administration, the system of pashas, *caids, cadis, Tribunal d'Appel* and *Haut Tribunal Chérifien* was little more than a facade behind which French officials manipulated the strings of power. There was in fact no separation of powers, for administrative and judicial authority alike were subject to the same agencies of *contrôle*, and in times of crisis all the customary rights and safeguards, i.e., defense lawyers, warrants, right of habeas corpus, appeal, and the rest, could be, and often were, subordinated to "raison d'état." [23]

THE BERBER POLICY

It remains to discuss the third system of courts which owed its existence to the traditional autonomy of the Berbers. As far back as we know anything about them, the Berbers of North Africa have energetically resisted foreign domination — Punic, Roman, Arabic or Christian. The Arabic influence was undoubtedly the most pervasive, for it converted the Berbers permanently to Islam and assimilated a portion of them to the Arabic language and way of life. But after many centuries of contact with a dominant Arab culture, at least 40 per cent of the Moroccan population, chiefly in the Riff and Atlas Mountains, still spoke a Berber dialect as their mother tongue and about three-fourths of this group spoke no other language.[24]

Their religious conversion was similarly qualified. Islam had theoretically imposed upon the Berber all the obligations of the Sharia, but in actual fact, many of his affairs continued to be regulated by his own customs. This was especially the case in disputes over personal status, property and inheritance, where his customs were at some variance with the Sharia and which, in any orthodox Islamic society, were preeminently matters for the *cadi*. But the *cadi* was seldom recognized in Berber country unless he appeared in the wake of a particularly successful *harka*. His functions were ordinarily supplanted by those of the tribal *djemaa* which composed differences by arbitration or determined which party in a dispute had violated tribal custom, leaving punishment to be imposed by unilateral action, again according to tribal custom. Hence, when the French came to Morocco, they found vigorous survivals of Berber culture which, along with the extraordinary military resistance of these mountaineers, persuaded them that a special judicial regime was needed in Berber territory.

The early motives for recognizing Berber customs were mixed, perhaps, but not unworthy of the protectorate ideal. Characteristically, Lyautey sought to honor the local traditions which he found on arrival, although he also regarded this as good tactics which could soften the impact of foreign domination during the early stages of the pacification.[25] His Berber policy did not spring from the ulterior motive of assimilation and hence did not produce the reverberations caused by the later policy.

Formal recognition of Berber customary law was granted by the *dahir* of September 11, 1914. Because the *dahir* did not stipulate what customary law was, nor designate which tribes were regarded as "Berber," these matters were left to administrative judgment, with the result that the larger proportion of tribes which ultimately submitted to the French army were declared "Berber" by vizierial decree and came under the *dahir*.[26] In 1915 the *djemaas*, contrary to custom, were given judicial powers, as part of the wider administrative effort to constitute within the tribes agencies which would represent their economic and judicial needs.[27] This early policy was not greatly resented in Morocco for it simply perpetuated, if in a more formal way, the existing situation. It was, in fact, a bit of inspired administration, for the quasi-autonomy which it guaranteed the tribes made submission more palatable to the Berber chief and helped to preserve the peace thereafter.

Towards the end of Lyautey's proconsulship, assimilationists, as distinct from the protectionists of Lyautey's stamp, were heavily infiltrating the Residency, and a shift in the motivations behind the Berber policy becomes discernible. The new men reasoned that the toleration of Berber customs, as practiced by the Marshal, was a device marvelously suited to divide the Berber from the Arab and to perpetuate French rule indefinitely. They found it difficult to believe that the Berber, beneath his superstitious, animistic heterodoxy and his rejection of much of the Sharia, still regarded himself as a devout Muslim, equated Islam with his motherland and sensed that the defense of one was inextricably bound up with the defense of the other.[28] But the assimilationists had convinced themselves that if the Berber could be isolated from all Arab influence, then gradually brought under the jurisdiction of French law, the influence of French schools, and the discipline of the Christian religion, all traces of Islamic culture could be eradicated and the Berber would become a European. Once this had been achieved among the Berber majority, the rest of the population, it was thought, would submit quietly to reality, and Morocco would become, like Algeria, a permanent overseas haven for French colonists.[29]

Commandant Paul Marty, counsellor to the vizier of justice and one of the most outspoken and influential of the assimilationist school, had asserted in 1925 in his widely read *Maroc de demain* that the Berbers were not dedicated Muslims and that the possibilities of transforming them into Frenchmen were considerable.[30] This school of thought foresaw a threat to the future of assimilation in allowing the formation of a united Morocco, and Marty's rationale for advocating the violation of the Treaty of Fez, which committed France to safeguard the religious integrity of Morocco, was in part a reaction to the charge made by nervous critics of the Residency that by unifying the country France would create a Frankenstein which one day might turn on its maker.[31] Hence, everything was to be done to avoid unification. In the minutes of a meeting (October 8, 1924) of a committee appointed by Lyautey to study Berber policy, one reads that:

There is no harm . . . in destroying the unity of the judicial system in the French Zone, since the aim is to strengthen the Berber element as a counterpoise that future exigencies may require. There is even a certain advantage, from the political point of view. . . .[32]

This faction could quote even Lyautey to the same effect, for in one of the circulars to his officers the Marshal states that ". . . our interests oblige us to help the Berber evolve *outside* the framework of Islam." [33]

From the administrative standpoint, then, the same Berber policy might be pursued for either altruistic or Machiavellian ends. Let us now see how such a policy might operate, from the nationalist standpoint, in the three areas of law, education and religion, for in a Muslim society the three can hardly be divorced.

Had it been fully implemented, the new policy would have subordinated to the French courts in Morocco roughly half the population classified officially as "de coutume berbère." The instrumentality by which this was to be accomplished was the so-called "Berber *dahir*" of May 16, 1930, the source of so many repercussions and such an important example of the attempt to divide and rule by assimilation that it merits special attention. The *dahir* itself was innocuous enough on the surface and seemed to many to incorporate the sort of reforms required to modernize judicial administration among the tribes. Its provisions were essentially four (complete text in Appendix C): [34]

1) It withdrew from the *djemaas* (without specific mention of them) the judicial powers conferred on them in 1915 and created "customary tribunals" and "customary tribunals of appeal" competent to hear all civil and commercial actions and all those involving real and personal property, personal status and inheritance. (Articles II and III)
2) It conferred on the "customary tribunals of appeal," equally with the tribal chiefs, authority to judge in the first instance all criminal cases involving less than two years' imprisonment. (Articles I and IV)
3) It gave to the French courts appellate jurisdiction over all criminal cases in Berber territory and primary jurisdiction over all such cases involving more than two years' imprisonment. (Article VI)
4) It provided for French supervision by assigning to each tribunal a

commissaire du gouvernement representing the regional control authority. (Article V)

The first two provisions, although innovations, were the natural consequence of the policy followed since 1914, and as judicial reforms one could have little objection to them. Article VI, however, created a storm of protest, not only in Morocco but throughout the Muslim world.[35] For propaganda purposes, the nationalists condemned it as a violation of the Islamic religion, expressly protected by the Treaty of Fez, but their real objection was to its political consequences, for by granting to the French courts jurisdiction over all crimes committed in Berber territory, the Makhzen would be deprived of one of its essential prerogatives. Critics of the *dahir* were rightly justified in their fear that it would weaken the always tenuous grasp maintained by the Makhzen over the rebellious Berber tribes and enable France to install herself permanently in Morocco.[36]

To the nationalists this was simply another proof of French perfidy. *Dahirs* of August 12, 1913 and September 1, 1920 had placed under French jurisdiction all cases, one of whose litigants was French, dealing with property, real estate and crimes. As it was, this had detracted much from the Makhzen; hence, the difference between all previous laws and the *dahir* of 1930 was a difference not in kind but in degree. While the former deprived the Moroccan courts of jurisdiction over scattered individuals, the latter threatened to withdraw several million people at one stroke, hardly a happy prospect for the nationalists. The Berber *dahir* was not only a grievous judicial abuse of France's second mandate; it was even more a grave political blunder.[37]

The Berber element was also to be "strengthened" by means of education. Roger Gaudefroy-Demombynes, onetime Residency official, in his doctoral thesis on French education in Morocco published in 1928, warned that it was:

. . . dangerous to allow the formation of a united phalanx of Moroccans having one language. We must utilize to our advantage the old dictum "divide and rule." The presence of a Berber race is a useful instrument for counteracting the Arab race; we may even use it against the Makhzen itself.[38]

Moroccans had no need to read Gaudefroy-Demombynes' dissertation, however, for before their eyes were the first five Berber schools established in 1923 and another thirteen erected before

1931, as well as the Berber normal school begun in Azrou in 1927.[39] The curricula of these schools were wholly French, for they were designed primarily as instruments of assimilation.[40] Commandant Marty wrote of the accomplished fact in 1925. The *école franco-berbère* is:

. . . French in its instruction and life, Berber in its pupils and environment . . . Therefore there is no foreign [*sic*] intermediary. All Arabic instruction, all intrusions by the *fqih* [Koranic school teacher], every Islamic manifestation will be resolutely avoided . . . these Berber schools should be organisms of French policy and instruments of propaganda as much as pedagogical centers properly so-called . . . that is why . . . the teachers have been flatly called upon to consider themselves agents and collaborators of the commandments . . . .[41]

Thus did the French hope to indoctrinate the Berbers in the courts and schools.

The nationalists convinced themselves that the French sought religious conversions as well. Nationalist publications of 1931 [42] pictured the mountains of Morocco swarming with Christian missionaries, a story which was echoed in the Middle Eastern press of the time.[43] The echoes were still to be heard in 1933 when an entire issue of *Maghreb* memorialized the third anniversary of the infamous *dahir*. Again the French were accused of trying to convert the Berbers and were quoted to prove the point.[44] The same fears were reflected in the *Plan de Réformes* of 1934, wherein Chapter 13 is devoted to a condemnation of the *dahir* and Christian evangelism.

It cannot be denied that there was some basis for these fears. In 1928 the conversion to Christianity of a young Moroccan — brother of a prominent nationalist, Omar Abdeljalil — had stirred up a hornet's nest among the "Young Turks" who proceeded to get the secretary of the Bishop of Rabat intoxicated and triumphantly announce his conversion to Islam.[45] While dramatic conversions of this sort were rare, it is undeniable that certain Frenchmen entertained ambitions to proselytize the Berbers, if not other Muslims. Maurice Le Glay, a Residency official, had written in 1921 that "we must abolish instruction in the Islamic religion . . . in all Berber schools. We must teach the Berbers everything but Islam." [46] And Monsignor Viel, the aforementioned Bishop of Rabat, apparently had published articles about this time in his weekly bulletin, *Le Maroc Catholique*, and in *Le Revue d'Histoire des Missions*, which could easily be construed as heralding the *désislamisation* of Morocco and a more aggressive missionary effort among the imperfectly Islamized Berbers.[47] At about the same time, Commandant Marty took it upon himself to distribute biographies of Jesus, in Arabic, to the native population and to appoint as notaries to the Berber tribunals converted Kabyle tribesmen from Algeria, while other French authorities were hindering the customary visits of the itinerant *fqihs* to the Berber schools for purposes of teaching the children Arabic.[48]

Now while there is very little evidence that a swarm of Christian missionaries had descended upon Morocco, the totality of these instances caused Moroccans even less imaginative than the nationalists to suspect that a concerted effort was afoot to eradicate Islam among the Berbers. If not entirely fallacious, the charge of evangelism was certainly grossly exaggerated, but we cannot ignore the fact that it formed part of the nationalist myth.

So intense and widespread was the reaction to the Berber *dahir* that the Residency refrained from implementing portions of it, although the Berber policy as a whole was never disavowed and continued to be reflected in such divisive tactics as al-Glaoui's descent on Rabat in 1951 and again in 1953. In the judicial sphere, however, the Residency was ultimately persuaded of its error and rectified it by issuing the vizierial decree of April 8, 1934. While it reaffirmed the authority of the "customary tribunals," the decree restored them to the jurisdiction of the *Haut Tribunal Chérifien*, within which a *Section Pénale Coutumière* was especially created for the purpose of hearing appeals (see Figure 3). Totally abandoned was the rash attempt to assimilate Berber justice to the French courts.[49]

What had the French accomplished judicially of benefit to Moroccans? They had regularized court procedures and the recruitment and selection of officials. They had standardized regional jurisdictions and introduced a rational system of appeals. Perhaps more important, they had raised the professional level of judges and established the authority of judgments at law, and they had converted the privilege of seeking royal justice into a civil right. Implicitly and explicitly the Moroccans acknowledged their debt in the nationalist literature on judicial reform.

Unfortunately, the attempt to segregate religious and secular law caused confusion, while the system of *contrôle* made a farce of judicial impartiality. Judges were supervised and often constrained, not by the accredited legal hierarchy, but by French *commissaires* of the political departments, a system which had already proved noxious in Tunisia.[50] Moreover, the French failed to provide modern legal training for sufficient numbers of Moroccan judges and attorneys, so that, as late as 1957, out of 377 licensed attorneys in Morocco, only 27 were Muslim.[51] Finally, the abortive effort to wean the Berbers away from their countrymen had convinced the proto-nationalists that the protectorate was destined for colonial status and had furnished them with a *cause célèbre* which could not have been more electrifying had it been deliberately contrived as such.

V

THE PARTIAL CORNUCOPIA

At a banquet given in 1903 by the Union Coloniale in the Grand Hotel in Paris, attended by prominent French administrators and financiers, the "Algerians" and "Tunisians" began to quarrel among themselves over the preferential treatment accorded the other by the government. So undignified did the discussion become, that Eugène Étienne, erstwhile minister of colonies and at this time vice-president of the Chamber of Deputies, felt called upon to remind them that broader vistas awaited them if they would but raise their sights.

Why! right next door to you in Morocco is a fruitful land which is doubly blessed by the rains of the Mediterranean and the Atlantic. Ah! my friends, what a fine field of action for you! There you will find phosphate beds and iron mines, wheatlands and olive plantations. There will be cotton goods to sell for the spinners of Roubaix and Tourcoing! And railroads and ports to be built for our steel makers and contractors! And loans to be floated by our bankers! Are you now going to continue to squabble among yourselves? How important are these disputes about minor tariff differentials between colonies and protectorates when such a perspective opens before you! [1]

Étienne might as well have addressed the winds. The merchants of France had long operated in the Moroccan trade, but her financiers had shown little interest in that country beyond the floatation of loans to the sultan for prepaid commissions. Why should capital be risked in such an inhospitable political climate? If North Africa invited capital, let Algeria and Tunisia suffice. Delcassé was visionary, indeed, to expect the financial houses of France to jeopardize everything as the spearhead of French influence in Morocco!

Within ten years, however, much had changed. By virtue of the Treaty of Fez, if properly interpreted, France had acquired sufficient political control to shield invested capital from the vagaries of Sharifian officials, and the financiers were ready to play ball — on certain conditions. The open-door agreements of 1880 and 1906 obviously posed a problem, but this might be re-

solved by a little discreet chicanery in the form of subsidies or
other preferments for French producers.

The conditions of the protectorate agreement which guarded
the sultan's sovereignty presented another kind of problem. In
political and judicial matters, where France found native authorities and institutions viable, the semblance of indirect rule
could be preserved, but in the economy, where no such authorities or institutions existed, or were rudimentary in the extreme, where a massive injection of capital was necessary, and
where everything had to be done simultaneously, indirect rule
was out of the question.

So intimate was the link between the reforms envisaged by
the Treaty of Fez and Morocco's economic viability that
nothing pertaining to the latter should be left to chance, or even
worse, to the incompetence of native officials. This was the
opinion of the French financial world, and if the development
program announced by Lyautey in 1912, for land reform and
public works, was to be financed by French capital, private as
well as public funds were needed and had to be catered to. Thus,
Morocco's economic transformation was to be effected from the
top down. Whatever economic powers still rested with native
officials were drastically curtailed or simply overridden, and all
authority was vested in a specially created department of economic affairs within the Residency.[2] France's long-standing
tradition of state intervention and regulation on behalf of the
powerful business community was imposed on all aspects of
Morocco's economy.

The *Service de l'Agriculture, du Commerce et de la Colonisation* was created in 1913 and until 1930 was under the direction
of François Malet, "père de la colonisation."[3] Elevated to the
status of a *direction* in 1915,[4] and of a *direction-générale* in 1921,[5]
this department was responsible for the study and administration
of all the agricultural, commercial and industrial affairs of the
protectorate, as well as of all matters relating to European colonization. After 1921 it was assisted by advisory councils for
agriculture and for commerce and industry,[6] and after 1926
by a council for livestock management.[7]

FINANCIAL BASE

To carry out his economic program, Lyautey insisted upon
an ample supply of capital, and Morocco benefited from the

start from a faster rate of investment than either Algeria or Tunisia had enjoyed. Owing to the inertia of the Chamber of Deputies, Lyautey had to rely from 1912 to 1914 entirely on private funds, but much was accomplished nonetheless. By the end of 1913 the French population had quintupled to 26,000, and Casablanca was rapidly becoming a modern commercial city with impressive port facilities. Public funds were soon forthcoming, however, for loans totaling 242.2 million francs were authorized by the Chamber of Deputies in 1914 and 1916 [8] and an additional 744 million in 1920, of which 528 million was ultimately drawn.[9] During the first decade of the protectorate, Morocco's backward economy was adequately provided with all the capital funds it could absorb.

The costs of the military occupation were also a considerable investment factor in Morocco and one which was not charged to the Moroccan budget but borne directly by France. In the period 1914–27 military expenditures were estimated at 5.8 billion francs, about six times the total of the loans granted in the same period and probably equal to the total of all French capital, private and public, invested in Morocco as of 1927.[10]

Owing to the regularization of taxes after 1912, Morocco itself was soon able to pay the ordinary expenses of government. The two most productive taxes, the *tertib* (5 per cent on estimated gross farm income) and the customs duties of 12½ per cent ad valorem on imports and ½ per cent on exports, had existed before the protectorate, as had the city taxes (created by the Act of Algeciras) and the traditional domainal revenues. Other levies inaugurated by Lyautey — *patentes* (trading and monopoly licenses), *prestations* (for road maintenance), *taxes d'habitation*, consumers' taxes on sugar, tea, matches, etc., and various registration and stamp-taxes — became increasingly remunerative until by the mid-1930's they overshadowed the old *tertib* and altogether more than equalled the rapidly growing customs receipts.[11] The four major revenue sources — the consumers' taxes, the *tertib*, the customs duties and the income from phosphates — alone furnished over 80 per cent of Morocco's budget receipts in 1932.[12] To supervise the receipts and expenditures, a vizier of finances was created in the Makhzen in 1912 [13] and a *directeur-général des finances* in the Residency in the following year,[14] the customary *contrôle* being exercised over the former by the latter.

By the time of Lyautey's departure, Morocco's solvency had been restored, although on a rather unsound basis. Taxation was not exorbitant (the average per capita tax was 75 francs, as against 80 in France) and the debt stood at 705½ million francs, most of which was guaranteed by the French government. While the debt service absorbed one-sixth of the revenues, they were at a high level owing partly to the military expenditures, and annual budgetary surpluses were accumulating because the military expenditures were not being charged to the Moroccan budget.[15]

Thereafter the situation deteriorated rapidly. Subsequent residents-general adopted spending policies which made Lyautey's seem parsimonious by comparison. As early as 1926, rapid capital investment, including the costs of the Riff War, had driven prices high enough to justify price ceilings, a condition aggravated in the 1930's by the arrival of much of the flight capital then leaving France.[16] Yet the investment policy was continued. By the end of 1927, the debt had risen to 900 million francs. A new loan of 820 million was authorized in 1928,[17] and the practice of state guarantees for the financing of municipalities, port facilities, railroads and electrification added another billion francs to the debt by the end of 1931. After 1930 the budget surpluses evaporated. The budget of 1931 ran a deficit of 7½ millions; that of 1932, 50 millions; that of 1933, 65 millions. Throughout the crisis, Resident-General Lucien Saint doggedly persisted in the stop-gap policy of balancing budgets with credits and negotiated additional loans in 1932 totaling 2,755 million francs, increasing the debt by half in one fell swoop.[18] At the going rates of interest set by the Banque de Paris, which controlled directly or indirectly much of the economic life of the protectorate, this raised the interest charge on the Moroccan budget to about 25 per cent. This was partly financial misjudgment, based on an erroneously optimistic assessment of the alacrity with which a backward economy could react to forced feeding, and partly political necessity, caused by the reluctance of unstable governments to revoke the subsidies committed to powerful business interests and European settlers.

For a country like Morocco with a perpetually unfavorable trade balance and with annual budgets of less than a billion francs for the years 1931–1933, these loans were regarded by the nationalists as dangerously large, to say the least, if not deliberately

intended to bail France out of the Depression at the expense of
Morocco.[19] Such an attitude was not altogether justified, however, even though great profit accrued to French financial interests, for if the Moroccan peasant bore a heavy tax load it was
shared by the French taxpayer, owing to the military expenditures and to the state guarantees behind the loans. And whatever
faults and discrepancies can be found with the size or timing
of the loans, one must remember that Morocco could never
have been shaken out of its lethargy by an investment of lesser
proportions, and that French capital would never have undertaken the risk under open-door conditions without substantial
governmental assurances of protection. Owing to Morocco's
utter backwardness and the speed with which modernization
was undertaken, the convulsions caused by massive doses of
capital were probably unavoidable.

INFRASTRUCTURE

Whatever its political repercussions, large-scale capital investment endowed Morocco with what economists call an infrastructure, the kinds of public works essential for the development
of agriculture, trade and industry, i.e., irrigation, ports, power,
transport and communications.

The development of the port of Casablanca was a favorite
project of Lyautey. Utilizing private resources at first, work
began immediately in 1912, and by the end of that year there were
already 12,000 European residents in the city.[20] In July 1914
Lyautey was fortunate enough to have in hand 70¼ million
francs of his first loan, and the work proceeded rapidly. By 1918
the native population had risen from 10,000 to 82,500, the
European to 37,500, the port could claim a trade equal to that
of Oran, and Lyautey had already held the first of a long series
of trade fairs which have since won global recognition. In 1925
the population totaled 116,000 and Casablanca handled 70 per
cent of Morocco's foreign trade.[21] By 1936, imports totaled
706,000 tons, exports 1,847,000, including phosphates, and total
ship tonnage had risen from 484,710 tons in 1912 to 8,908,000.
The total cost had been high — approximately 1⅓ billion
francs — but in 1936 Casablanca could boast port facilities as
modern as any in the world and the distinction of ranking
seventh among all French ports. Some modernization had oc-

curred in the seven or eight secondary ports of Morocco,[22] but as of 1936 their combined tonnage amounted to about one-tenth of that of Casablanca.[23]

In the era between the Roman and French empires in Morocco, it is doubtful that the native population built or maintained a kilometer of hard-surfaced road. None existed when the French arrived; Morocco traveled by foot or horseback, and internal trade and communications moved at a pace comparable to that of medieval Europe. Eighteen kilometers of road had been constructed by 1913, 3,000 by 1926, and in 1937 there were 7,055 kilometers of first class roads as well as 20,000 kilometers of *pistes automobiles*,[24] a development which shares credit with the pacification for the revival of Morocco's *souks* and internal trade. The total cost had been 450 million francs.

Early railroad construction was limited to the narrow-gauge (60 cm.) track to which the French army seemed peculiarly addicted overseas. In June 1921, the Casablanca–Oujda line was completed, linking Marrakesh and Casablanca with Tunis. By 1925, 1,660 kilometers were in operation, mostly narrow gauge except the Casablanca–Rabat–Fez section. By 1938, at a cost of some 3 billion francs, the mines and major cities of Morocco were served by a modern railway network of 1,753 kilometers, mostly electrified and mostly standard gauge, all but 137 kilometers of the original 60-centimeter track having been replaced.[25]

Although the water resources of Morocco officially became public property by a *dahir* of July 1, 1914, the *Caisse de l'Hydraulique Agricole et de la Colonisation*, to coordinate all dam construction and irrigation, was not formed until 1927, the first hydraulic engineering projects were not begun until 1929, and progress thereafter was slow. The dam at al-Kansera was completed in 1935 and perhaps one-sixth of its irrigation potential (an estimated 75,000 acres) was actually realized before the Second World War. A second large dam was completed near Kasba Tadla in 1939, but its potential was hardly touched until after the war.[26]

If irrigation was not strikingly achieved, the electrification program, at least, benefited from these hydraulic projects. Whereas not a kilowatt of hydroelectric power was produced in 1929, 108 million kilowatts were produced in 1938, and a high tension network of 1,427 kilometers at 60,000 volts was in service, furnishing power to most Moroccan cities and the railroad system.

The total cost of irrigation and hydroelectric development had been 1.1 billion francs up to 1937, but there were indications that some of the increments had been exorbitant; the al-Kansera project, for example, had cost five times the original estimates, owing to hasty surveys and politically influenced administrative decisions. Al-Kansera was promoted because it would serve the water needs of the Sidi Slimane area, one of the chief centers of European colonization.[27]

The creation of an infrastructure and the pacification of the countryside, along with incidental innovations such as the generalization of the metric system, were eventually to metamorphose Moroccan economic life, and they edified and impressed Moroccans with what could be achieved by a well-organized modern state. Sophisticated European critics observed that Lyautey's preoccupation with commerce and mining caused his public works program to neglect improvements in farming and herding which might have been of more immediate benefit to the Moroccan fellah.[28] But when it came to the "plight of the fellah," the more naive Moroccan nationalists, themselves, failed to make this criticism, attributing the fellah's troubles to such observable abuses as land expropriation, inequitable tax assessments, and the mismanagement of credit and marketing facilities, all of which could be related more directly to agricultural development or its failure.

AGRICULTURAL DEVELOPMENT

The landholding system in traditional Morocco was complex and chaotic in the extreme. Land use varied according to whether its owner was nomad, transhumant, pastoralist or sedentary farmer. Landownership was equally varied along lines which cut across all forms of land use, the chief categories being private land, domainal land, *habous* land and communal land, each subject to different laws. Moreover, Arab lands were generally regulated by the Sharia, Berber lands by tribal custom, while the townsman and rustic generally observed different methods of landownership and exchange. To complicate matters, under the last two independent sultans much of the best domainal land had been improperly alienated to wealthy subjects (reducing the sultan's patrimony by two-thirds), the income from *habous* property had been grossly misappropriated, and collective tribal lands had become the object of illicit speculation. Furthermore, the practice of sharecropping, sanctioned by the Madrid Convention of 1880, whereby the European entrepreneur advanced capital and furnished protection to his native associate (*mokhalat*) in return for half the crop, was being systematically abused. Land systems in all Muslim countries are complicated, but nowhere had the French encountered conditions as disordered as they were in Morocco, and land reform became one of the most pressing tasks of the early protectorate. The Makhzen had to establish control over a more orderly land regime, the natives had to be protected from improper alienations, and, of course, land had to be made available for European colonization.[29]

Before anything else could be done, the various categories of land had to be defined, and this was accomplished by the grand vizier's circular of November 1, 1912, which formed the basis for all subsequent land legislation.[30] Next, many of the domainal lands were restored by forcing illegal owners to disgorge some 230 million francs' worth, and some of the *guich* lands were taken from the military tribes on the grounds that their title terminated when their military functions were taken over by the French army. *Habous* lands were then surveyed, placed officially in the hands of a vizier created for that purpose, and rigidly earmarked to prevent their use for any other than the donors' purposes. And by a *dahir* of July 7, 1914 an attempt was made to protect small native landowners by forbidding private or unofficial alienations of the communal lands.[31]

Provision for the European settler was inaugurated by the *dahir* of August 12, 1913, which applied to Morocco the modified Torrens System of land registration previously used in Tunisia. Under this arrangement collective lands could be individualized so as to make them available for alienation, and the *dahir* of July 1914 stipulated which lands were available for such purposes.[32] Under this arrangement, the voluntary immatriculation of land commenced in 1915, only to have the Algerian experience repeated all over again. So seldom did the natives take advantage of it, that an alternative approach was taken in 1919 when the pressure for colonization land was increased by promises held out to war veterans. *Dahirs* of that year provided that collective lands not actually "in use" by the tribes could be made available to European settlers on perpetual leases,[33] and a *dahir* of 1922 established special rules, outside Muslim law, for the alienation of property to settlers in Berber territory.[34]

None of these schemes, however, was able to overcome native resistance. So unfavorable, indeed, were the conditions for land acquisition in Morocco, that even official encouragement of land settlement, begun in 1916, produced astonishingly meager results throughout the protectorate period. By 1925 there were approximately 100,000 European residents in Morocco, but fewer than 500 of these were actually *colons* living on the land. What European landownership there was, a scant 390,000 hectares (hectare = 2.47 acres), had resulted from the tedious accumulation of scattered parcels into farms typically 200 to 400 hectares in extent.[35] There was very little "small farming" and only a few of the enormous estates which characterized Algerian landholding, and the prospects for any change in the situation looked poor indeed. Whatever could be appropriated from the domanial lands was exhausted by 1925. *Habous* lands were protected by official policy. The few private parcels made available by voluntary immatriculation sold at a premium price few settlers could afford. And the communal lands, the thorniest problem because they promised the greatest potential, were held in the grip of tradition, ignorance, religious taboos and native apathy.[36]

After Lyautey's departure, his concern for securing settlers of a high type and his scrupulous observance of legality were abandoned for a policy of *petite colonisation* based on a thinly disguised system of arbitrary land expropriation. Under the new regime, the number of actual *colons* rose to nearly 4,000 by 1934 (6,000 by 1950) and European landownership to about 840,000 hectares, while the average size of their holdings declined to about 200 hectares.[37]

Despite the hurdles over which land reform in Morocco stumbled, something had been achieved by France before World War II. The total land area under cultivation had risen from less than 2,000,000 hectares in 1919 to over 4,000,000 in 1938,[38] and Morocco's total exports had jumped from 40 million francs in 1913 to 807 million in 1936, agricultural products accounting for roughly three-fourths of the gain. Qualitatively, the most striking progress had been made in the production of the soft wheat most desired for flour milling. Soft wheat was unknown in Morocco in 1912, yet in 1931 she produced 2,150,000 quintals (i.e., hundredweights) and in the period 1936–40 a yearly average of 4,376,000 quintals, emanating about equally from European and Moroccan farms. The relative importance of soft wheat can be measured by the simultaneous drop in hard-wheat production (4,806,000 quintals in 1920, 2,928,000 per year in 1936–40) and the rather substantial rise in barley production (7,293,000 quintals in 1920, 14,649,000 per year in 1936–40). By 1936, soft wheat had become Morocco's second most valuable agricultural export.[39] The only difficulty with this development was that, in the years when the world cereal market was good (before 1929), France encouraged the cultivation of very little else in Morocco. Accordingly, until after World War II, over 90 per cent of Morocco's cultivated land was in cereals, and 95 per cent of that was concentrated in barley, hard and soft wheat, and maize.[40] This created a serious problem for Morocco after 1929 when the world's wheat markets became glutted.

To encourage the native as well as the European farmer, agricultural credit and marketing facilities were established early in the protectorate period. The needs of the *colons* were served from 1912 to 1919 by extending to Morocco the activities of the *Crédit Foncier d'Algérie et de Tunisie*.[41] In the latter year, agricultural credit was reorganized under a *Crédit Agricole Mutuel* which operated *caisses de crédit agricole* for short-term loans and a *Caisse de Prêts Immobiliers* for long-term loans.[42] The fellah could obtain credits from the *sociétés indigènes de prévoyance*, experimentally created in 1917 and formally reorganized in 1922.[43] By 1937 there were fifty-four such societies, whose membership embraced about one million of Morocco's five million fellahin. The *sociétés de prévoyance* were supposed to provide credit, improved seed, agricultural information, and collective insurance against fire, pest and epidemic, to furnish machinery for collective use, to create marketing cooperatives and experimental farms, and to wipe out the usury which so often dispossessed the small Muslim farmer.[44] So much for the positive side.

The nationalists saw quite another side, of course. Prior to 1926, land reform had affected chiefly those property rights which were being grossly abused: domainal, *habous* and *guich* lands, much of which were of marginal value and of little concern to the ordinary Moroccan. It was not these, but the attempted alienation of the collective lands which became an extremely sore point with the nationalists.[45] In Lyautey's time that attempt had failed because the Marshal had refused to endorse *petite colonisation* or a coercive registration policy. But Lyautey's successor, Steeg, reared as he was in the Algerian administration, believed

not unnaturally that the best way to exert French influence in the
countryside was to plant the greatest possible number of *colons*
on the land,[46] and the same opinion was held by Augustin Bernard,
professor of geography and North African colonization at the
Sorbonne and mentor of many a North African official:

We did not come to Morocco only for the happiness of the natives or to
restore a few ruined mosques. North Africa will finally be welded to
France only if we succeed in establishing there a solid core of colonists
. . . . [who must be provided] the most favorable conditions for success
by installing them on choice land, close to railroads, and by endowing
them with all the necessary economic facilities.[47]

Bernard originally wrote these words in 1912. When the eighth
edition of his book appeared in 1932, what he foresaw had become
the established practice in the Moroccan protectorate. *Dahirs* of
1927 and 1928 had set a new precedent in the colonization effort
by equating land alienation with "public utility." This put on
the pressure for obligatory registrations and forced sales either
by impoverished farmers or by the native *mokhalat* who could be
obliged, under French law, to sell out to his European associate,
often at a depressed price.[48] Permitting individuals to acquire
land for private purposes by exerting the power of public
authority was regarded by the nationalists as little short of
legalized theft.[49]

Most of the settlers who benefited from the policy of official
colonization after 1925 were *petits colons*, several cuts below the
type admitted by Lyautey. Lacking capital and other resources,
many of them collapsed under the impact of the Depression and
made strident demands upon the government to bail them out.
Since they constituted the "imperial apparatus of France" and
could not be allowed to perish, a charge of 90 million francs was
laid upon the Moroccan budget of 1931, as well as additional
sums later, to pay their debts,[50] a privilege denied the Moroccan
fellah who found himself in far worse straits. The inopportune
demands of this vociferous minority of settlers was seen by one
French observer, by no means unsympathetic to colonization, as
serving no purpose but to set a bad example of insubordination
for the Moroccan nationalists.[51]

The total area of European land acquisition accounted for only
5–7 per cent of the arable portion, but much of this was found to
be the richest in Morocco — in the Meknes–Sidi Slimane Plain —
and much of it had been taken by forced sale. The consequences

for the evicted landowners had been disproportionately great, owing partly to the superior quality of the land expropriated and partly to the fact that most of their farms had been only one to five hectares in extent. Thus, the installation of a single *colon* could dispossess as many as forty or fifty fellahin, swelling the growing mass of jobless proletariat in the cities by whoever of these could not be absorbed as agricultural laborers.[52]

The discriminatory administration of credit and marketing facilities was another major source of grievance, and here the problem centered on the rising importance of soft wheat in the export market. The *sociétés de prévoyance*, supposedly created for the fellah's benefit, limited themselves to providing as little seed and credit as they could get away with. Moreover, the nationalists claimed, allotments of soft-wheat seed were difficult to obtain, being reserved for the *colons* in case of short supply. It was immaterial that the *colon* paid dearer for his seed, or that his selling costs were higher, because up to 50 per cent of his seed cost was refunded by the government, and he received a higher price for his product in the French market, which, for reasons about to be explained, were closed to the Moroccan producer.[53] These arguments carried considerable weight even before the Depression but became even more cogent after 1929.

The widespread overproduction of wheat of that year caused France to establish quotas in an effort to support her domestic price. Owing to the political power of the Moroccan *colons*, however, drastic quotas could not be imposed in that quarter, and Morocco emerged from the controversy with an export quota to France for 1929 of 1,700,000 quintals, which was raised to 1,800,000 in 1932. Most of the quota (1,650,000 quintals) was in soft wheat.[54] The significance of this lay in the inequity of marketing facilities, with regard to which the nationalists justifiably charged the French with bad faith. The European wheat grower in Morocco had at his disposal government-sponsored storage facilities — the two largest being the *Union Dock Silos* and the *Commerce d'Exportation Marocaine* — which, unless he happened to be a wealthy native proprietor, were not available to the Moroccan. Accordingly the French producer could store his wheat and ship it to France under favorable market conditions, while the Moroccan was generally forced to sell his entire harvest locally on a glutted market. During 1934–35, European soft-wheat growers were realizing 94 francs per quintal on the French

market while the same wheat brought 51 francs in Morocco. The
hard-wheat differential was about the same: 75 and 47 francs,
respectively.[55]

Insofar as farm credits were concerned, the grievance arose
from a double standard of allotment. The nationalists asserted
that up to 1932, the 3,000 *colons* had received credits, long- and
short-term loans, advances, indemnities and discounts to the extent
of 765 million francs, not including favorable land settlements and
special school privileges, while in the same period some 850,000
Moroccan farmers received 35 million francs.[56] If the fellah had
at the same time been given proper guidance in the use of these
funds, the sum would have been woefully inadequate, but in the
absence of such guidance, the money was really a disservice to
him, for he usually spent it unwisely and had little to show for it
when the time came for repayment. At that point, moreover,
his plight differed from that of the *colon*, for the debts of the
colon were on occasion assumed by the state, while the fellah was
usually forced to sell out.[57]

The third major economic grievance was the inequitable
assessment of taxes, especially of the *tertib*. As early as 1922,
François Piétri, director of finances in the Residency, was becoming concerned over the uneven distribution of the tax burden.
Averaging 75 francs per capita throughout the country, it was
much heavier (about 200 francs) on the farmer owing to the
relative importance of the *tertib* in the early years.[58] European as
well as native farmers were liable for the *tertib*, but in order to
encourage modernization, a schedule of rebates up to 50 per cent
of the tax was adopted in 1923 wherever "European" or "improved" methods of cultivation were used. In effect, this shifted
the net tax burden from the European farmer, who qualified, to
the native farmer, who usually did not, a situation not rectified
until 1957.[59]

The Moroccans also thought it unfair that the *tertib* should be
levied at all in years when the crop yield was too meager to
produce a surplus, or that a sheep should be assessed as heavily as
a horse, when most native pastoralists earned their entire livelihood
with their flocks while relatively few Moroccans could boast the
ownership of a horse worthy of the name. Worse, the assessments
were made by the notoriously venal shaykhs and *caids* on the
assessment commissions, who received, respectively, 4 and 6 per
cent of the tax proceeds.[60] Worst of all, the rate of the *tertib*

had risen each year from 1928 to 1931 at a time when expropriations were reducing the area and quality of the fellah's land, and the rigorous collection of his debts, in marked contrast with the treatment accorded the *petits colons*, was often forcing him to sell out.[61] Thus, while France introduced improved methods in agriculture, the fellah bore much of their cost and enjoyed few of their advantages.

INDUSTRIAL DEVELOPMENT

French Morocco was ill-suited to heavy industry owing to the poverty of her fuel resources. Bituminous coal was never found, her anthracite deposits were thin and hard to mine, her petroleum resources, even in the 1950's, provided only one-sixth of the country's needs, and hydroelectric development was in its infancy.[62]

Another hindrance to economic development was France's effort to assimilate Moroccan industry, just as she tried to assimilate the country in other ways. Both René Hoffherr, Steeg's administrative assistant, and Resident-General Lucien Saint were pressing as early as 1930 for what they called a "complementary economy" in Morocco,[63] and when the effects of the Depression began to be felt in 1931 in the form of dumping through Morocco's open door, additional pressure to this end was applied by the powerful Casablanca Chamber of Commerce and Industry. Chamber President Chapon, speaking for the French business community, pointed out that:

. . . Morocco has no means of defending itself but the protection of France, a protection which has now become hesitant, temporary and fragmentary, lacking all proportion to France's obligation in the matter. It is therefore necessary that France frankly welcome Morocco into her own economy; or that she give the country the possibility of negotiating its purchasing power to its own best interests.[64]

The latter alternative was obviously no alternative at all, for it would have subjected heavily subsidized French enterprises in Morocco to the hurricane of foreign competition.

Fuel shortages and the assimilative drive of the business community limited Morocco's industrial development either to industries which were not highly mechanized and could take advantage of the cheap labor supply or to those which were complementary to, rather than competitive with, the economy of France. This meant little more than mining, fishing and selected converting industries. To be sure, within these limits ample official encouragement was offered in the form of low-cost loans and credits, direct subsidies and preferential shipping and customs arrangements. Even so, a brake on rapid industrial development was constantly applied in the early years by Lyautey, whose notions of industrialization were limited, and in later years by the politically powerful *colons*, who feared the loss of their cheap labor supply to the mines and factories and the inevitable rise in wage scales which attends industrialization.[65] Thus, Moroccan industry developed slowly and late. Phosphates, which became Morocco's major export, were known to exist long before 1912, but the first extensive study of the deposits was not completed until 1919.

Nonetheless, whatever industrial development occurred was, naturally, the work of France, and the exploitation of Morocco's mineral resources was a good example of the *économie mixte* so characteristic of domestic French industry. It was a joint effort undertaken by the Moroccan "State," as the French euphemistically dubbed their protectorate, and a small number of large companies nearly all of whom were associated with the Comité du Maroc and the Banque de Paris. Phosphate mining was an out-and-out state monopoly. In order to circumvent the economic equality which the open-door agreements bestowed on all comers, the Office Chérifien des Phosphates was founded in 1920, ostensibly as a competitive private company which paid "taxes" to the government but was in fact wholly owned by the Moroccan "State." [66] Coal and oil production were controlled by the Bureau de Recherches et de Participations Minières (B.R.P.M.), a public corporation founded in 1928 whose initial capital was furnished by the Phosphate Office but in which private interests were allowed to participate to the extent of 50 per cent ownership. The B.R.P.M. held the controlling interest in the anthracite monopoly, the Société Chérifienne des Charbonnages,[67] later extended its control to oil prospecting, acquired large interests in manganese and lead mining, and in 1938 was given authority to license all mineral exploitation in Morocco with the exception of phosphates. The private interests involved were represented chiefly by the Banque de Paris and its subsidiaries which exploited manganese, cobalt and some of the lead mines in concert with the B.R.P.M. The richest lead and zinc deposits, at Bou Beker, were mined by the Walter Group, the only large private combine in Morocco not associated with the Banque de Paris.[68] In this fashion French interests exercised a virtual monopoly over not only Morocco's mineral resources but over her fisheries and other industrial potential as well.

So impressive were the phosphate ores discovered in 1919 (the lodes on the Khouribga Plain averaged 70–75 per cent) that operations were undertaken immediately, and the first shipments arrived at the docks of Casablanca in 1922. By 1927 production had surpassed one million tons, and the interwar peak of 1,828,000 tons was reached in 1930. After 1931, production dropped off to about half, but the worst years of the Depression were over in Morocco by 1935, and with the added productivity of the high-grade lode discovered at Louis-Gentil in 1934, production in 1939 had very nearly recovered to the level of 1930. On the eve of World War II, Morocco ranked second in the world's production of phosphates, unquestionably France's most successful business venture in that country.[69]

The only other mineral exploitations which reached significant levels before World War II were manganese, lead, anthracite and cobalt, all of which were discovered in the decade from 1919 to 1930. Production of all of them sank nearly to zero during the depth of the Depression (1933 to 1935), but by 1939 they, too, had rebounded and were exceeding their 1930 levels by several times. By 1939 Morocco was supplying one-sixth of the world's cobalt ore (6,000 tons) and ranked third in world production.[70] The extraction of zinc, tin, molybdenum and petroleum, which became very profitable after World War II, had barely begun by 1939.

The expansion of Morocco's fishing industry, while not so striking as phosphates in international trade, was nonetheless significant. Before 1912 there were no distribution or preservation facilities, and native fishing boats of the flimsiest sort furnished irregularly a meager supply of fresh fish to local markets on the coast. The protectorate brought power-driven boats and distribution and canning facilities. In 1927 there were eleven trawlers averaging 55 tons burden in the fresh fish business; by 1939, twenty-five trawlers averaging 33 tons. The annual catch of fresh fish in the same period rose from 2,000 to 7,000 tons, exceeding local needs by an exportable 1,500 tons in 1938, most of which went to France.[71] With the improvement of their harbors, Casablanca, Fedala, Safi and Agadir became great fishing ports, the last three devoting almost their entire catch to canning.

Canning in Morocco means sardines, although a small quantity of tuna is also processed, and the first cannery was established in Fedala in 1925. By 1927, thirty-five powered sardine boats averaging 3 tons burden were delivering 3,000 tons of fish annually to the canneries. So rapidly did the industry expand that by 1933, forty-four canneries were handling 15,000 tons of fish per year, and by 1939, 123 sardine boats averaging 10 tons burden were delivering 24,000 tons to be processed, most of which was exported to France. By 1936 nearly half the annual catch was being taken by Casablanca, making it the fourth largest fishing port in the French empire.[72]

The development of other industries was rather modest before World War II. The sole "modern" industrial plant which Morocco could boast in 1912 was the Grand Socco Flour Mill in Casablanca.[73] Natural shortages of flour caused by World War I permitted high-cost Moroccan mills to flourish, and after the war they were protected by quotas from 1923 to 1928 and by a ban on wheat and flour imports permanently imposed after 1929. Similar conditions prevailed in most other Moroccan industries. Sugar refining, begun in 1932, was operated by Cosuma, in which the Banque de Paris held a large interest. Here, too, means had to be found to protect high-priced Moroccan sugar from cheaper foreign competition, and devious forms of subsidy were employed to circumvent the open door. Cement manufacturing by the Société des Chaux et Ciments, also controlled by the Banque de Paris, thrived in Morocco during the building boom of the 1920's; but again, costs were high, and when the Depression resulted in the dumping of cheaper foreign cement, Moroccan producers were protected by outright subventions and by circuitous subsidies such as shipping rate reductions on Moroccan railroads.[74] Flour, sugar, cement and canned fish were the only finished products other than beer and wine which Moroccan industry manufactured in significant amounts before World War II. Even these did not satisfy local needs (except beer and wine) and had to be supplemented from abroad.[75] The great variety of manufactured products on Morocco's export list today — textiles, chemicals, soap, paste, canned fruits and vegetables, and a host of food products such as biscuits, chocolate, cheese and vinegar — are the result of postwar developments.

Morocco before World War II was still overwhelmingly agricultural. Even in 1950–52, for which the first reliable statistics are available, industry employed only 100,000 Moroccans out of a labor force of about 3,000,000,[76] so the proportion before World War II must have been smaller yet. The fact was that Moroccan industry held a relatively minor place in the total employment picture during the interwar era, and was not expanding rapidly enough to absorb the unemployment caused by the agricultural crises of the 1930's. The plight of this small but unfortunate proletariat was of such little import to the nationalists of the time that it affected their political doctrines hardly at all. Being largely bourgeois in origin, they were neither sympathetic, nor fully conversant, with the problems of the industrial worker, and most of their pronouncements on the subject have the ring of being borrowed from their socialist friends in France.

POSITIVE RESULTS

Despite the spottiness of economic development in Morocco, France could lay claim to real achievements. When one examines the nationalist proposals which appear in the *Plan de Réformes*, it becomes apparent that France had taught the Moroccans to think in terms which were totally foreign to them in 1912 — "farmers' cooperatives," "agricultural credits," "standard of living," "organization of production," and the like. And while most Moroccans did not benefit from the improved agricultural methods employed or profit directly from the nascent industrial development, witnessing what the Europeans could accomplish along these lines raised their own expectations and stimulated their demands.

During the first decade of the protectorate, Morocco was transformed from an economic backwater into the third most productive of France's dependencies. From 1913 to 1924 Morocco's foreign trade nearly trebled, from 221 million francs to 1,548 million, although a 250 per cent inflation must be taken into account. Much of the rise was based firmly on the more effective exploitation of agricultural resources.[77] The peak was reached in 1929 — an impressive 3,780 million francs which thereafter fell off to 2,015 million in 1936.[78] Perhaps the most interesting aspect of Morocco's trade expansion was that, while the percentage of exports to France was about the same at the beginning and end of the period under study (having fluctuated widely during the interim), imports from France rose to a peak in 1923 and then fell steadily (see Table 1).

The significance of the statistics in Table 1 is that France's proportionate share in the trade of her protectorate increased during the first decade but suffered a substantial decline thereafter, so that in 1936 for the first time Morocco was able to sell more to France that she bought. This resulted from Morocco's peculiar status in international law which preserved equal economic privileges for all the powers within that country, so that English, German and other goods could in fact compete with French

TABLE 1.   MOROCCO'S FOREIGN TRADE AND TRADE BALANCE WITH FRANCE
(in millions of francs)

YEAR	TOTAL	% WITH FRANCE	EXPORTS	% TO FRANCE	IMPORTS	% FROM FRANCE	BALANCE WITH FRANCE
1913	221	60%	40	53%	181	61%	− 89.2
1923	1,052	76	272	53	780	78	−464.3
1929	3,780	52	1,233	44	2,547	56	−883.8
1932	2,470	56	685	71	1,785	51	−424.0
1936	2,015	45	807	57	1,206	38	+ 5.7
1938	3,629	44	1,502	57	2,127	35	+111.0

Sources: Melvin M. Knight, *Morocco as a French Economic Venture: A Study of Open Door Imperialism* (New York, 1937), p. 40; Charles F. Stewart, *The Economy of Morocco 1912–1962* (Cambridge, Mass., 1964), p. 38; Résidence-Générale . . . au Maroc, "Situation politique et économique: mois de mai 1939" (Rabat), p. 4.

imports to good effect whenever France did not resort to subsidies or other preferential devices. France tried to make trade with the metropole more attractive to Moroccans by authorizing free entry of a number of important Moroccan products,[79] but the chief result was to create for France the unfavorable balance we have noted. This, of course, was of no particular benefit to France, but it was tremendously beneficial to Morocco, for it meant that France was helping to subsidize Morocco's overall trade deficit while Morocco simultaneously diversified her overseas suppliers. Morocco's economic development was in some respects "a product of high taxes in France," [80] rather than the other way around.

Another criterion of Morocco's growing economic vigor was the remarkable rise in tax revenues during the first three decades of French rule. Revenues from the *tertib* rose from 21 million francs in 1915 to 71 million in 1935, a 240 per cent increase which was largely offset by inflation. But customs receipts jumped 450 per cent, from 21 million francs in 1911 to 115 million in 1935. Revenue from the Phosphate Office and the licensed companies skyrocketed from 3.5 million francs in 1920 (the year of the first phosphate concession) to 33 million in 1935, and consumers' taxes, inaugurated in 1915, had by 1937 become Morocco's largest revenue source at about 200 million francs.[81] The phosphates industry alone, in 1930, contributed directly or indirectly over 200 million francs to the Moroccan budget which stood at only 802 million francs in that year.[82] Thus, France not only endowed Morocco with a more modern economic structure, it was a structure which worked in spite of (or perhaps, because of) its artificial props and supports.

NEGATIVE RESULTS

On the negative side, the assimilation of Morocco's economy to that of France was sufficiently complete to cause excessive suffering in Morocco during the Depression. Assimilation was partly responsible for the failure of Morocco's high-grade phosphates to compete as well as might have been expected. In 1933 the companies exploiting the lower-grade Algerian and Tunisian deposits formed a sales cartel which the Moroccan Phosphate Office was obliged to join and whose quotas discriminated in favor of the long-established Algerian and Tunisian interests. But these interests did not profit proportionately, for Europe's demand for high-grade phosphate rock was met by Soviet Russia in the 1930's. Political influence thus curtailed the income from Morocco's most valuable mineral product at the moment of her direst need.[83]

Assimilation also aggravated Morocco's agricultural crisis, and it was unfortunate that her increased agricultural production came to depend so heavily on her export trade to Europe at the precise moment that the world's trade shrank so rapidly. Moreover, the official encouragement of cereal culture and viniculture put Morocco in the unfavorable position of competing with the overproduction of those commodities in Europe after 1928. (It was only after World War II, as a result of this experience, that crop diversification was seriously undertaken.) The resulting agricultural crisis accelerated the migration into the towns, which had been started by the land expropriations of the 1920's and was fostered even more by a succession of bad harvests caused by locusts in 1930 and a tragic succession of droughts in 1935, 1936 and 1937. By 1936 the stream of unemployed farmers and artisans to the cities had swelled to unassimilable proportions.[84] Even before their arrival, the towns of Morocco had been trying vainly to absorb the growing number of unemployed immigrants. Moroccans were beginning to show a preference for European manufactured goods against which the country's traditional artisans could not compete. Thus, in the 1920's, and especially during the Depression, traditional Moroccan industry suffered chronic unemployment. Most of those who joined the procession to the *bidonvilles* found their skills unadaptable to modern industry and unwelcome to their urban counterparts whose business had also suffered from European competition.[85]

Social conditions in the towns and cities of Morocco were serious indeed after 1930, for the decline of handicrafts caused the traditional urban corporations to deteriorate, and this in turn led to a deterioration of the whole urban social structure analogous to the detribalization occurring in the countryside. Fez was most seriously affected. Before the protectorate, its corporations had been one of the few stabilizing factors in Moroccan government, while in the 1920's their stability had so far decayed that Fez became the chief center of nationalist agitation.[86] The swelling population of the unfortunates who congregated in the *bidonvilles* of Casablanca and Rabat also presented a threat to the security of the regime. The only effective method devised to handle the problem before World War II was known as "purifying" the towns, whereby mass roundups were carried out and those who did not happen to be carrying satisfactory credentials were shipped back to their places of origin,[87] a practice reminiscent of Tudor poor-law administration.

Another aspect of Morocco's economic assimilation was the policy of protecting high-cost production, already mentioned. Protection, in fact, was the key to whatever success Moroccan industry, including food processing, enjoyed during the protectorate. Not only did this place native industries on an uncertain footing in the event of independence, it meant that Moroccan production flourished at the expense of the consumer and the taxpayer, Moroccan as well as French. The high costs of Moroccan beer, wine and cement were borne largely by the European settlers, who were their largest market. But the artificially high cost of flour and sugar, staples in the native diet, was an unjustified burden on the Moroccan and an unjustifiable subsidy to the producer made possible only by violating the open-door agreements. As Stewart points out, the economy of Morocco under French protection operated on the premise that the high-cost producer should be subsidized by the low-income consumer.[88]

The Moroccan nationalists had no fundamental objection to the economic tutelage of France. Indeed, they greatly admired what had been achieved, especially in terms of infrastructure and industrial development, and were inspired to believe that even more was possible, and for this France must be given credit. They even had no real objection to being assimilated into the European economy, for they readily saw its advantages and in these early years were not as clearly aware of its drawbacks, save in the matter of national debt, as were some of its European critics.

What chiefly bothered the nationalists economically was the application of "two weights and two measures" to loan and credit policies, taxation, and the land regime, whereby it was primarily the French who prospered while the Moroccans benefited incidentally when at all. That the nationalists may have exaggerated the woes of the fellah, or ascribed to France more than her share of the blame, is quite irrelevant, for it bears repeating that nationalisms are often based on myths. This chapter has attempted to show to what extent French policy did bear the blame and to what extent Morocco's afflictions were a function of her backwardness and of world conditions beyond anyone's control. The fact remains, so deeply did Moroccans feel those economic afflictions, and so convinced were they that France was somehow to blame, that more ink and paper were expended on them than on any other grievance except the Berber *dahir*.

VI

RISING EXPECTATIONS, OR EDUCATING NATIVES TO BE FRENCHMEN

Traditional Muslim education, at the primary level, focused on the memorization and recitation of the verses of the Koran. Formerly, drill in reading and writing had preceded and facilitated the Koranic studies and rendered them meaningful to the young student, but at the beginning of the twentieth century, language study had long been abandoned in Morocco, and students simply memorized the Holy Book without much explication and with little understanding, in order to qualify for the paradise guaranteed those who could accomplish the feat.[1] Each town of Morocco and each *douar* (tent, or hut, city) had its *msids* (elementary Koranic schools), the total number of which is difficult to estimate, but at the turn of the century there were 120 in Fez alone.[2] The total number of students enrolled is equally indeterminable, but it is safe to say that a large proportion of Moroccan youth attended these schools at one point or another in their lives. Education for girls, in the formal sense, scarcely existed, however. Aubin remarked in 1906 that there were fifteen girls' schools in Fez, without exception small private classes conducted by educated women as charitable undertakings, and there were also "technical" schools where girls learned the arts of sewing and embroidery. Most women were educated at home if at all, but this did not prevent a few of them from receiving an excellent education.[3]

In the heyday of the Merinid sultans (1213–1465 A.D.), advanced instruction had been given in a number of mosques and *medersas* (boarding schools) throughout Morocco but preeminently at the great Qarawiyin mosque in Fez.[4] There, in surroundings reminiscent of the colleges of medieval France, aspiring young men from all parts of the Maghreb and Muslim Spain, and even a trickle from Christian Europe, had received an education which rivalled that of Cairo's al-Azhar. There were found the most learned scholars in Koranic exegesis, metaphysics, Sufism, divination and the Sharia. There, too, one could sit at the feet of masters of theology, philosophy, history, geography, grammar, rhetoric, philology, lexicography, mathematics, astronomy, medicine and alchemy, the peers of any at Paris or Bologna. But most of this had disappeared by the end of the nineteenth century. Qarawiyin was the sole remaining center for higher studies, and what survived of the old curriculum were the Traditions of the Prophet, the principles and practice of Koranic law, and dilute vestiges of theology, grammar, rhetoric, logic, prosody and Arabic literature.[5]

At the turn of the century, the *ulama* at Qarawiyin must have numbered about fifty, with an attendance of between 800 and 1,000 students. Well-to-do young Fassis lived at home, but the poorer students and out-of-town boys stayed in the nine *medersas* still maintained as dormitories by the *habous* and by the benefactions of wealthy Fassis and the sultan. Each student bought a key to his cell, received a daily loaf of bread from the *medersa* and either purchased or depended on charity for the remainder of his diet. Virtually all the bourgeoisie of Morocco were literate, and certain rural areas like the Djebala and the Sous sent numerous students to Qarawiyin. Some of the university's graduates became *ulama* in turn, but more took positions in the secretariats and law courts of the Makhzen, which befitted their literacy and legal training. By virtue of this, the *ulama* of Qarawiyin exerted an indirect but profound influence in public affairs quite apart from their religious and pedagogical authority.[6]

The French authorities were reluctant to intervene in the affairs of Qarawiyin, entwined as it was by the coils of Islamic religion, and no reform or modernization was attempted there until 1933. In that year two *dahirs* reorganized the program of studies, but the resulting curriculum, based on Koranic law and the Arabic language, was less a modernization than a resurrection of courses long ago discontinued.[7] Apparently the reform was fruitless, for Qarawiyin dwindled in significance as modern educational institutions arose in Morocco. In 1952 there were only seventy-eight students enrolled in its program of higher studies beyond the secondary level.[8]

A number of schools were opened before 1912 by Catholic and Protestant missionaries and by the Alliance Française. None of them, however, was well attended and they all gradually disappeared after 1912. The schools of the Alliance Israélite Universelle were far more numerous and important. They were taken over by the Residency in the years following 1915 when an at-

tempt was being made to standardize their programs in official
écoles franco-israélites, but the arrangement proved unsatisfactory,
and the Alliance Israélite schools gradually regained their autonomy during the 1920's. They served a community whose members
seldom entered public life in Morocco and who were more inclined to collaborate with the French than with the nationalists.
A "Moroccan Jewish nationalist" was almost a contradiction in
terms, and there were exceedingly few of them. As we might
expect, Jewish schools had little effect one way or another on the
nationalist movement.

EDUCATION UNDER THE PROTECTORATE

The goals of Muslim education had been to cultivate mental
agility and to perpetuate tradition, especially religious tradition,
and the finished product of the Islamic school could recite Scrip-
ture and perform arithmetical calculations in his head which
astonished the Western visitor. What he received in the way of
humanistic studies however, was impregnated with mysticism and
tended to range indiscriminantly over the broad spectrum of
Islamic culture rather than to focus on a narrower, national culture. Accordingly, Muslim education neither prepared one for
citizenship as we know it in the West, that is, for popular participation in public life, nor for a professional career, except insofar as literacy was always a highly marketable commodity, but
rather for a kind of philosophical acceptance of whatever fate
had in store for every man.

The goals of French education, on the other hand, have been to
inculcate students with the scientific method and a deep affection
for the national language and culture. The dedicated French
educator seeks to form patriotic and cultured, as well as professional men and women. Hence, the French *licencié* is not only a
professional person; he is to one degree or another an ordained
nationalist and a priest of his national culture. Translated to the
colonies, this commitment came out as the *mission civilisatrice*
and *assimilation*, a peculiarly French compulsion to "educate
natives to be Frenchmen" and then absorb them into a "Greater
France." The French overseers have insisted, more than any other
imperialists, on the use of their mother tongue as the language of
instruction, whatever the racial origin of the students, and this
was proclaimed official policy in Morocco in 1914 by Gaston

Loth, then director of education.[9] Loth's successor, Georges
Hardy, who was already a convinced assimilationist when he
arrived in Morocco in 1920, wrote that ". . . every native who
speaks French is half won over to our cause by that fact alone. . . .
The educational significance of our work pales before its importance in the penetration of native culture." [10] Those Frenchmen who came to Morocco for something more than economic
gain sought nothing less than a "conquête morale" of the country.[11] This was the theory.

In practice, the civilizing mission and assimilation fell far short
of the ideal. The French found in Morocco an aristocratic,
hierarchic society to which their own aristocratic, hierarchic
notions of education were easily applied. They also found political
turmoil which they did not wish to aggravate by disseminating
revolutionary ideas from Europe. Lyautey cautioned, in a speech
to his Government Council in 1924, that:

> We should be attached to the principle of education, professional [i.e.,
> vocational] for the masses, general for the elite. But we must have a
> care that these young men do not become the propagators of revolutionary
> ferment and disorder. They must be convinced that their first duty is
> to help us preserve their heritage.[12]

Louis Brunot, then chief of the Office of Native Education, was
even more explicit:

> The school should in no case be the propagator of political ideas which,
> from the sole fact of their novelty, will never be anything but pernicious
> elements of trouble . . . . The school limits itself to increasing the pro-
> fessional capacity of the native . . . . Politics, in the European sense, is
> not suited to the progress being accomplished here. Consequently, let us
> not think of emancipating the Moroccan citizen, nor of freeing the slave,
> nor of the liberty of women; when you get to know the situation in
> Morocco, you will understand that those dogmas, when transplanted
> here, are dangerous.[13]

For the Moroccan masses, the school was not to be an instrument
of enlightenment but an agent of social equilibrium.

The limitations which the French felt obliged to place on
Moroccan education meant, of course, that native children could
not be permitted in the schools established for the children of the
French settlers, and segregation became established policy in the
interwar years. In 1939 the director of primary education could
report that:

> For many political and technical reasons . . . access to the European

schools is forbidden, with some exceptions, to the Muslim . . . . Thus, the
admission of a native into a European school is to be regarded as a great
favor.[14]

However, the ambivalence of the native policy, in which the
mission civilisatrice struggled with the fear of propagating
revolutionary doctrines, did permit a small elite to partake fully
of the fruits of French culture, while limiting the education of the
remainder to what amounted to vocational training. The resulting school system was as complex a contraption as one could
imagine and a fine example of the *contrôle* the French intended to
exert over the minds of their Moroccan subjects (see Figure 4).
There were primary, secondary and higher institutions for the
French, primary and secondary schools for the Moroccan elite,
and for other Moroccans, a variety of urban and rural, professional and technical, schools, night classes for adults, and special
schools for girls. The system was further confused by the possibility, which tempered the policy of segregation, of a small
number of Moroccans finding their way into the French schools.
A rather detailed survey of the whole system, more explicit than
might otherwise seem appropriate, will be necessary if we are to
understand the substance of the education received by some of
the later nationalist leaders and to what extent this affected the
nationalist movement.

FRENCH SCHOOLS

Primary education for the children of the French settlers was
essentially a transplant from the metropole. By the end of 1912
there were already over a thousand European children in these
schools. By 1930–31 the population of the European schools had
risen to 22,770, of whom 144 were Muslims, and by 1938–39 to
30,648, of whom 450 were Muslims.[15]

The first *lycée* had been opened in Tangier in 1909, three years
before the Treaty of Fez, and the first in the French zone in Casablanca in 1913. By 1931 there were nine *lycées* in the French zone
and Tangier. No others were established before 1941. In addition
to the *lycées*, there were six *collèges* and a few *écoles primaires
supérieures* and *écoles techniques* in existence before the Second
World War. The total attendance at these secondary schools rose
from 754 in 1914–15 to 5,644 in 1931–32. The number of Moroccan Muslims attending them rose from 9 to 122 in the same period,

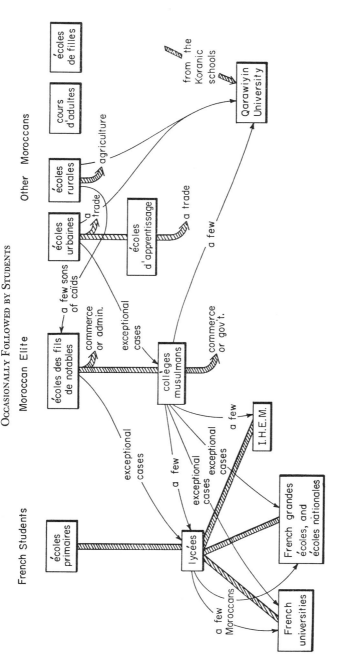

FIGURE 4. A SIMPLIFIED FLOW CHART OF THE TRIPARTITE EDUCATIONAL SYSTEM ESTABLISHED IN MOROCCO BY THE FRENCH BEFORE WORLD WAR II, SHOWING THE ROUTES CUSTOMARILY AND OCCASIONALLY FOLLOWED BY STUDENTS

and of Moroccan Jews from 67 to 633.[16] Of approximately 1,400 baccalaureates granted in Morocco in the two decades after 1920, only forty-three were earned by Moroccan Muslims, and all but a dozen or so of these had been granted after 1934 when the formation of the nationalist leadership had already taken place.[17] The curriculum of the *lycées* was nearly identical with that offered in France, and the baccalaureate obtained was the sole *entrée* to the French universities, for it was not awarded by the secondary schools created for the benefit of Moroccans.

Most of the young Europeans and Moroccans who wanted a genuine higher education went, or tried to go, to France. There was in Rabat, however, an institution which can be regarded as "higher" in the same sense as the École des Langues Vivantes in Paris or as the collegiate technical and professional institutes of this country. This was the Institut des Hautes Études Marocaines, founded in 1912 to brief newly arrived functionaries in the language, customs and civilization of the country in which they were living and to train teachers, administrators and interpreters, French and Moroccan alike, for their particular functions in the protectorate administration. The Institute also sponsored research in many aspects of Moroccan culture and published several scholarly journals of which *Hespéris* is the most highly regarded.[18] It was essentially a research institute and language school for interpreters, French officials and visiting scholars from France, rather than the "university" it became in the panegyrics of Residential propaganda. Language study (chiefly Moroccan Arabic and the Berber dialects) dominated the curriculum, and passing attention was paid to Muslim law and civilization and to Moroccan history, geography, archeology and ethnography. But since no courses in Western civilization were taught prior to World War II, and since its faculty was far less interested in teaching than in the marvelous research opportunities it offered, the Institute lacked the prestige of the French universities for the bright Moroccan boy who sought a European education. Even the two sections for law and science, founded in 1920 and 1921, respectively, which were affiliated with the University of Bordeaux and offered a genuine *licence*, convenient as they may have been for the French settlers, did not attract significant numbers of young Moroccans. After an initial flare of interest in 1920–22, Moroccan enrollment dropped off,[19] and we shall see later that so-called "higher" education in Morocco had far less impact on the nationalist movement than did university education in France, where greater numbers went and a higher proportion finished.

"Franco-Moroccan" Schools

Schools for Moroccans were created in accordance with existing class lines and public policy. It was natural for a man of Lyautey's aristocratic predilections to lay down an educational policy which would set apart the Moroccan elite and train it for the non-manual professions. Thus, the sons of the Makhzen families, of the upper middle class, and of the rural *caids* received in the *écoles des fils de notables* an education similar to that given in the primary schools of France, with the intent of equipping them for positions in the Makhzen, the liberal professions and the business world. A few exceptional students were admitted to these schools from the *écoles urbaines* and *écoles rurales*, but this was not normal procedure. The *écoles des fils de notables* were the only public schools in Morocco for which an annual tuition was charged.[20]

There were never more than six of these schools in French Morocco. The first opened its doors in Fez in 1912, and others were established in Casablanca in 1914, Marrakesh in 1919, Rabat and Salé in 1921, and Meknes in 1929.[21] In towns where there were *collèges musulmans*, the *écoles des fils de notables* were regarded as the preparatory classes for secondary education; where no *collège* existed, they served as the terminal course for the primary schools. Each of these schools had five grades: a preparatory level, two elementary and two upper grades. The curriculum was similar to that of the *école primaire ordinaire* of France except, of course, that instruction was not given in the students' mother tongue. French language and literature filled twelve and a half hours per week in the *cinquième*, and diminished to eight and a half in the *première*. Arabic was taught two to four hours per week and the Islamic religion half an hour to an hour. Modern "sciences," which included ethics, history, geography, arithmetic, writing, singing and design, increased from six and a half to twelve and a half hours per week in the course of the five years.[22] Accordingly, over three-fourths of the instruction was given in French, and we cannot help but recall Georges Hardy's assurance that ". . . every native who speaks French is half won over to our cause. . . ." Provision for studying the Koran had to be made outside of regular class hours.

The recipient of the certificate of primary Muslim studies (C.E.P.M.) from the *écoles des fils de notables* was qualified to enter the *collège musulman*, or, in exceptional cases, the *lycée*. Graduates with limited academic aptitude were encouraged to get a job. The *collège musulman* was designed as a terminal institution for the young Moroccan who was not sufficiently talented to pass on to the university. It was supposed to inject discipline into the easygoing Moroccan temperament, to increase proficiency in the arts of commerce and government, and in general to help the upper-class Moroccan in his future contacts with the French.[23]

Prior to 1936 there were two *collèges* in Morocco: the Collège Moulay Youssef, founded in Rabat in 1916, and the Collège Moulay Idriss, founded the same year in Fez, both of which catered to the sons of Makhzen officials, landed proprietors and the larger merchants. A few scholarships were available for qualified students from poorer families.[24] At Azrou in the Atlas foothills, the normal school for Berber teachers which was opened in 1927 became known as the *collège berbère* after 1931. Its course was less advanced than that of the other *collèges*, for it was an outgrowth of the Berber policy and served even more than the others as a propaganda and indoctrination center. A third *collège musulman* was founded in Marrakesh in 1936. There were no others before 1945.

From 1921 onward, the *collèges* had six grades in two cycles of four and two years. At first a good deal of the curriculum was devoted to Arabic language and literature, the Muslim religion, and Moroccan history and geography,[25] but this was altered by the *dahirs* of May 17 and 21, 1919, which laid out a more deliberate program of studies and greatly increased the emphasis on French. In the first cycle, nine hours per week were given over to Arabic (grammar, reading and writing) and eighteen hours to French (language, history, geography, mathematics, science, commerce and design). The general section of the second cycle prepared students for government and professional careers and offered ten hours of instruction per week in Arabic, twenty in French; the commercial section, four hours in Arabic, twenty-six in French.[26]

From 1921 to 1931 the *collèges* granted a diploma of secondary Muslim studies (D.E.S.M.), but after 1931 the first part of the baccalaureate could be earned. Only after 1948, when the *baccalauréat classique marocain* was invented, could graduates of the *collèges* go directly to the French universities. Before that a small but increasing number of Moroccans prepared for higher education in France by attending a *lycée* for a year or two after graduation from the *collège*.

In 1930–31 there were about 1,600 Moroccan Muslims enrolled in the *écoles des fils de notables* and the *collèges musulmans* altogether.[27] For the *collèges* alone, only scattered statistics are published. In 1917, for example, there were 96 students in the Rabat *collège* and 150 in Fez.[28] In his *doctorat-ès-lettres* thesis, Lucien Paye states that by 1929 only about 500 Muslims had progressed as far as secondary education but that very few of these, indeed, had completed it.[29] It was mentioned earlier that about a dozen Moroccan Muslims earned baccalaureates from the *lycées* in Morocco between 1920 and 1934. The number who received the D.E.S.M. from the *collèges* in the same period was not far in excess of that (about 35).[30]

For ordinary Moroccans there were only elementary and technical schools. The former were of two types, urban and rural. The *écoles urbaines* were designed to foster a basic literacy for the greatest possible number and, by combining vocational training with the usual elementary subjects, to improve productivity and the standard of living without disturbing class distinctions.[31] In Lyautey's mind, the *école urbaine* was to shore up the proletarian and clerical foundation on which a modern Morocco could be built. It was attended free of charge by all boys who presented themselves, although it catered chiefly to the sons of workers, small shopkeepers, and lesser employees of the government and commercial enterprises. In 1925 there were twenty-five *écoles urbaines*, and by 1937, thirty-nine.[32] The course of studies was ordinarily six years in length and was not unlike that of the *école des fils de notables*, with the exception that less attention was paid to Arabic (two hours per week) and four or five hours of manual training was added. Like the elite school, it granted the C.E.P.M., but of an inferior grade — *mention professionelle* rather than *mention générale*. Upon graduation the best students could take further professional or technical training which qualified them for a trade or a berth in the lower echelons of business or government.[33] A few exceptional graduates went on to the *collèges musulmans*.

The *école rurale* was not, properly speaking, an *école de diplômes* but only a two-year survey of elementary French, arithmetic and agronomy, designed to help the Moroccan fellah improve his productivity and to understand the advice proffered him by agricultural inspectors and other government agents. From a social and political standpoint, the *école rurale* was intended to keep the fellah down on the farm, to preclude his swelling the masses of landless urban handworkers, and to enable him to be employed advantageously by the *colons*.[34] In 1931 there were thirty-six of these schools, eighteen of them for Berbers alone,[35] and by 1937, forty-four.[36] Two-thirds of the curriculum was devoted to academic studies, one-third to practical work. French was taught three hours per week, arithmetic one hour, agricultural practice two hours, and ethics was interlarded with the rest. As in all other public schools of the protectorate, instruction in the Koran had to be given outside regular class hours by the local *fqihs*. The best students emerging from the *écoles rurales* could receive additional technical training in the *écoles régionales* and then in an *école agricole*, but these were not designed as way stations to a *collège*. The fellah was to remain a fellah and go back to the soil, although a few sons of rural *caids* could climb out of this groove and pass on to the *écoles des fils de notables*.[37]

The *écoles d'apprentissage* have already been mentioned in connection with the *écoles urbaines*, of which they were an extension. Their stated purpose was to prepare young men for jobs in industry by training them in woodworking, cabinet-making, ironmongery, bookbinding and printing, but since most of these were skills at which Moroccans were already adept, the *école d'apprentissage* did little more than formalize and lengthen (to three years) the customary apprenticeship and throw in a smattering of French. There were only eighteen of these schools by 1931,[38] and a few others were opened in the next ten years, but none of them was very successful, and in all probability fewer than a thousand Moroccans, all told, attended them in the years prior to World War II. The technical schools unquestionably were a stimulant to postwar proletarian nationalism in Morocco, but there was little commerce between their graduates and the bourgeois nationalists in the interwar years.

The first *cours d'adultes* were started in 1913 as language centers and became quite popular, particularly among the more urbanized Moroccans of the northern part of the French zone. By 1922 there were twenty-two such courses attended by about 1,500 people from all classes of urban society, and the course offerings had broadened to meet the special regional and professional demands of the students. By 1928, *cours d'adultes* were to be found in all the major cities of Morocco.[39] These schools may in part account for the fact that a large proportion of the native population today speaks French of a sort, but to assess their effect on the rise of Moroccan nationalism would be a task beyond the scope of this book and the competence of the author.

The French also found it necessary to establish special schools for Moroccan girls until the taboos on coeducation began to break down. The first *écoles de filles* opened in Salé in 1913; there were fifteen by 1931 and eighteen by 1937.[40] They were designed to inculcate clean, orderly, economical household habits and to provide, for those obliged to support themselves, a more honorable means of livelihood than is customary among too many unmarried Moroccan women.[41] By 1931 about 2,000 girls were in attendance.

The repercussions of the new educational system were diverse and profound. While no more than half the interwar nationalist leaders were European-educated, those who were, received an excellent education, and their expectations for a better Morocco rose in proportion to their schooling. It was they, rather than the traditionally-educated, who were most vociferous in their criticism of French educational policy. They wanted more — much more — and could point with authority to a variety of incongruities and inequities which the French permitted to creep into the educational system or simply could not avoid, owing to racial prejudice and assumptions about the universal applicability of French culture (see Appendix D).

INCONGRUITIES, DIFFERENTIALS AND ABUSES

For one thing, the nationalists objected — or said they did — to educational assimilation. The substitution of the French language for Arabic in the Berber schools and the disproportion of French in the Arab schools were seen as part of a master plan to obliterate Arabic culture in the Maghreb. And when, in 1934, a plan was announced to fuse the two Muslim *collèges* with the French *lycées*, Omar Abdeljalil condemned it as an effort to downgrade the study of Arabic and to foster the assimilationist tendency even more.[42] He and others felt that two out of nine daily class hours were insufficient for instruction in their native tongue and its relegation to the end of the day, when students were tired, as further proof of the bad faith of the French.[43] The prospects for expanding instruction in Arabic appeared to be slim, however, for qualified teachers were scarce in Morocco, and the Residency, fearing the introduction of subversive doctrines from the Middle East, refused to import more than a handful of well-screened teachers from Algeria. Moreover, Arabic was ill-suited to the teaching of modern sciences, and much as the nationalists lamented the preponderance of French in the humane studies as well, they recognized as readily as anyone else its utility in modernizing their educational system. With this qualification, the Moroccan nationalists, imbued as they were with Islamic reformist doctrines, not unnaturally believed in the feasibility of a modern Arabic education borrowing from, but not assimilated to, the French system.[44]

Their strictures on educational assimilation notwithstanding, the Moroccans objected far less to the accent on French studies than to the system of "two weights and two measures" which affected the schools as much as other institutions where the two peoples were thrown together. Despite the theory of the *mission civilisatrice*, Residency educational policy tended to deny Moroccans all instruction of a nature which might arouse political aspirations, and this, of course, covered a good deal. The nationalists asserted with justification that most Moroccans were not being fitted for self-government but were being fobbed off with manual training and a smattering of French to qualify them as useful servants of their new masters.[45] The fact that 10,289 out of 11,907 Muslims in school in 1930 were being given this kind of training would seem to bear out the contention. Moreover, the nationalists complained, Moroccans were denied the right to establish private schools which might rectify this situation, because the *dahirs* of February 18, 1916 and October 14, 1919 authorized private schools for Europeans alone.[46] In fact, private schools operated by Muslims were not legalized until 1935,[47] although some were condoned before then.

The other side of the argument, maintained by many French educators who perhaps had a better perspective of Morocco's real needs, was that the intellectual type of education demanded by the nationalists did not suit the conditions. The metamorphosis of Morocco had to be based solidly on the modernization of its economy, which presupposed a supply of skilled workers and progressive farmers trained in vocational schools, and there was precious little money even for this during the Depression. This argument made a good deal of sense to its proponents, but unfortunately their rationality was not shared by most of their subjects. Moroccan peasants derided the whole concept of schools for farmers, for it was apparent to anyone that a son went to school not to instruct his more experienced father in farm management but to rise above his father's estate. Education was not a means to prepare for manual labor but to avoid it.[48] Accordingly, there was a certain amount of built-in traditionalist resistance to the kind of practical education which the French thought this backward country required, and the complaints of the nationalists on this score must be discounted proportionately. Nevertheless, obstacles far greater than native conservatism stood in the way of educating Moroccans, and foremost among these were discriminatory budgetary allocations.

In the protectorate budget for 1921, 9,255,400 francs were allotted for the education of Europeans and 2,970,390 for the education of Moroccan Muslims.[49] Ten years later the respective allocations were 41,712,348 and 14,863,385 [50] and in fiscal 1938, 58,114,130 for French and Jewish education combined, 21,185,670 for Muslim.[51] Accordingly, before the Second World War, approximately twice the educational funds provided for a Muslim population of nearly six million were made available to a European population of 200,000, resulting in a considerable inequity in school facilities. During the year 1930–31, some 27,000 European school children (all there were) were accommodated in nine *lycées*, a number of *collèges* and technical schools, and 117 primary and professional schools. In the same year 12,000 Muslim children, out of a school-age population of about half a million, were privileged to attend two *collèges* and 100 primary schools (including eighteen purely vocational institutions and fifteen schools for girls). In Marrakesh, for example, in 1933, there were only five primary schools for Moroccans, or one school for every 38,000 inhabitants.[52] All indications are, that despite native conservatism, Moroccan school attendance would have been far greater had facilities been available.

In the realm of secondary education, the chief complaint other than the scarcity of facilities, was that most Moroccans were denied entrance into the French universities because the degrees awarded by their *collèges* were not equivalent to the *baccalauréat*.

It is true that occasional graduates of the *collèges musulmans* found their way directly into French institutions of higher learning, as did Omar Abdeljalil from the Collège Moulay Idriss into the École Nationale d'Agriculture in Montpellier. But Abdeljalil's was an exceptional mind and an exceptional case, and the facilities of the French universities ordinarily were not available to Moroccans who held only the D.E.S.M.

As early as 1918 the grand vizier, al-Mokri,[53] had expressed the wish that the programs of the *collèges musulmans* should be made equivalent to those of the *lycées*, and Lyautey had transmitted the request to the Ministry of Public Instruction in Paris, but no action was taken at the time,[54] and even the inferior *baccalauréat marocain* was not created until 1948.[55] Denied admittance to the French universities from their *collèges*, a number of young Moroccans (122 in 1930) successfully sought entry into the *lycées*. This privilege, however, was accorded less frequently for merit than for political acceptability.[56]

Higher education in Morocco was for years a stepchild of the French university system, relegated to the academic scullery, for the nearest thing to the French *licence* offered by the Institut des Hautes Études Marocaines was its second-rate *licence-en-droit*. As already pointed out, the Institute was primarily a language and research center which could boast neither a complete curriculum nor a full-time faculty.[57] If an aspiring Moroccan candidate in law sought to circumvent this by studying in Paris, he found that scholarships were available for French students from Morocco but not for the likes of him.[58] The maladroit Louis Brunot had a hand here in the making of a Moroccan nationalist when he refused such a scholarship to Omar Abdeljalil, explaining pontifically that the course of studies the boy had in mind was too long and that his family should not be asked to bear the expense. Brunot added that a scholarship to study agriculture might be arranged, so Abdeljalil made the best of his opportunity and went to tranquil Montpellier rather than to infectious Paris.[59]

The authorities sometimes withheld passports from individuals regarded as potential troublemakers. Before 1930, when the applications had been few in number, the government had caused little difficulty on this score, but after the Berber *dahir* disturbances, the list of undesirables lengthened and passport rejections increased. In 1932, when thirteen fathers from Rabat alone applied for passports for their sons to study abroad, all thirteen were

denied, and the next year over fifty applications were rejected.[60]
It is probably true that many of these applicants intended to study
in the Middle East and one can hardly censor the French for trying
to isolate Morocco from the subversive doctrines then emanating
from Cairo, Jerusalem and Damascus. But despite the obstacles,
a small number of Moroccans managed to reach both France and
the Middle East for their higher education.

One must keep in mind that French educators in Morocco had
to storm the walls of a nearly impregnable obscurantism far more
case-hardened than elsewhere in the Middle East, and that the
interwar years witnessed pressing economic needs which pre-
empted many of the limited funds otherwise available for educational reform. Nevertheless, French educational achievements in
Morocco were less than astonishing prior to the Second World
War, and the increase in Muslim school attendance from 600 in
1912 to about 25,000 in 1939 compares unfavorably with at least
twice that number of European children in school or with the
estimated 1,300,000 Moroccan school-age children not provided
for.[61] And if the number of Muslims beginning school was small,
the exceptionally high attrition rate as they moved towards a
certificate reduced the number of actual graduates to infinitesimal
proportions. This, of course, may indicate a number of things
other than unsatisfactory performance — a lack of motivation,
contentment with a little education, family hardships, or what
have you — but the important thing to note is that many of the
withdrawals were voluntary. As we read the complaints of the
nationalists, we should remember that the failure to educate
Moroccans did not lie entirely with the French, and where the
system did fall down, it was owing as much to the recusancy of
the Moroccans in the early years as to the shortcomings of French
authorities and the shortage of funds.

French policy, however, was ambivalent. It sought to galvanize
the Moroccan into activity without awakening his political
consciousness, to infuse him with rationalism but deny him its
revolutionary implications — in short, assimilation of a very imperfect nature. For those Moroccans who did succeed in attending French schools and universities, appetites were whetted and
expectations rose for an even more sumptuous banquet to come.
The Moroccan nationalists complained loudly of cultural as-

simlation, and where assimilation was perverted by French administrators, or where discrimination was shown, the complaints were genuine. But on closer inspection it will become clear that what the nationalists really wanted was *more* assimilation for themselves, in the form of an open door to the universities, and *less* for the lower classes, by the elimination of the French language from their schools. What concerned them most was the education of a Moroccan elite (themselves) in sufficient numbers to restore control of their country to native leadership (their own).

SUMMARY OF PART TWO

Modern nationalism would unquestionably have arisen in Morocco had she remained independent after 1912, but the character of her nationalism would have been quite different without both the beneficial and detrimental effects of the French imperium. The stimulative effect of France's material contributions to Morocco can hardly be overestimated, for the ports, roads, cities, mines, dams and modern farms have transformed the face of the country. Psychologically, too, France gave much to Morocco, for she demonstrated that rebellion need not be endemic and taught the Moroccan to appreciate effective government, sober justice, secular education and an expanding economy. The miracles that France wrought in this medieval land opened the Moroccan's eyes, broadened his horizons, raised his standards, girded up his confidence, and propelled his expectations upward to uncontrollable heights from whence they would crash down like Zeus's thunderbolts upon the heads of the imperialists. France created a nation in Morocco; is it any wonder she created nationalists?

And yet it is safe to say that France's imperial rule caused more frustration, created more misgivings, and built up more tension in the breasts of her dependent subjects than did Britain's nation-building policy. British dependencies could anticipate an evolution towards self-government; but *assimilation*, as practiced by France, whatever the mummery about *association*, endowed French dependencies with all the weaponry of the West but denied them the joy of anticipating a political, economic or cultural future of their own. Where France chiefly blundered, however, was in her native policy — in her failure to treat the Moroccan with respect, sensitivity and equity. The discriminatory practices, of which the French were guilty, provided the *raison d'être* of the nationalist movement, and are accurately reflected in the *Plan de Réformes*. As was the case in most colonial situations, the imponderables aroused the deepest bitterness.

Thus, the material and moral rehabilitation of Morocco, owing in part to its success, in part to its faulty execution, and in part to France's compulsion to damp down its natural effects, got out of hand (at least from the French viewpoint). By raising Moroccan expectations, France had seemingly created more problems than she had solved. Far from being grateful, the Moroccans became greedy. They wanted more of what France had shown and taught them. Even had France been able (as she was not) to restrict French education to ". . . une toute petite élite, diligement sélectionnée, attentivement surveillée, progressivement initiée à une culture qui est loin d'être sans périls pour des cervaux neufs . . . ," [62] it was too much to expect these "inexperienced minds," once pried open, not to essay a practical application of the revolutionary ideas which flowed in from East and West.

PART THREE

EXTERNAL FACTORS

VII

THE IMPACT OF THE ARAB AWAKENING

Mohammed al-Fassi, former minister of public instruction and presently (since 1958) rector of the University of Morocco, asserts that the Middle East provided the inspiration and the philosophic basis for the nationalist movement in his country, and most nationalists of the early days concur. For Mohammed Lyazidi it was the flow of news and ideas from the East which gave them the will to assert themselves against the French. And authoritative French observers have concluded that the basic political concepts of Moroccan nationalism were derived from the Middle East. This is all quite general, however, and not very instructive, for any intelligent student of these matters would be surprised had Cairo and Damascus failed to exert a wide influence in the Muslim world. What, then, is the meat of the matter? What can be said more tangibly about the repercussions in Morocco of the religious and secular reform movements which comprised the Arab Awakening?

SALAFIYYA

As a fundamentalist movement, Salafiyya, like Wahhabiyya, sought a return to the pristine faith as conceived by the "pure ancestors," the *salaf al-salih*. But Salafiyya arose during the years when the Ottoman Empire was dissolving under a renewed tide of European imperialism, and the advanced political, social and technological concepts borne upon that tide inescapably penetrated the doctrines of the movement as developed by that great hortatory triad, Djamal al-Din al-Afghani (1839–97),[1] Mohammed Abduh (1849?–1905),[2] and Rashid Rida (1865–1935).[3] Whereas Wahhabiyya had been puritanical and conservative, had largely ignored changing conditions and regarded religious purification as an end in itself, Salafiyya looked upon religious reform as the initial act in a sequence of social regeneration. Once Islam was restored to its original purity by the elimination of corrupt medieval accretions, it could then assimilate selected elements of

European culture without danger of the secularization which customarily attends Westernization. In this way Islamic society would simultaneously recover its religious vigor and revitalize its material and intellectual life, great aspirations in themselves, but having the further advantage of rearming Islam to withstand Western imperialism.

When Djamal al-Din, Abduh and Rida ventured beyond religious matters, they differed widely in detail as to which Western ideas and techniques were to be adopted and how they should be applied. They agreed, however, on certain general principles of reform which are especially relevant to the study of colonial nationalism. They thought that religious reform was the proper locus for political progress, and that nothing fundamental to Islam would be found to be incompatible with Western constitutional and democratic institutions. They advocated the unification of Islam under a caliphate based on consultative, representative government and popular sovereignty, and in this sense Salafiyya was a pan-Islamic movement. Finally, they agreed that successful religious reform and all its social derivatives depended in the long run on mass education, for only thus could modern ideas penetrate the fossilized Arab mentality to strip away the falsifications of Islam and the foolish superstitions which had accumulated over the centuries. Abduh was particularly concerned about education, arguing that the deterioration of scientific studies was a disgrace in the Arab world which had so long led the West in this regard, and as a member of the administrative committee for al-Azhar from 1895 on, his reforms of the administration and curriculum of the university, while not permanent at the time, served as precedents for reforms which only since 1964 have been undertaken in an effective way.

Reform of the canon law was another matter which greatly attracted Abduh and Rida. They both thought that the Sharia needed revision, especially as regards slavery and the treatment of women, to accord with the conditions of modern society. As grand mufti of Egypt after 1899, Abduh found himself in a unique position to breathe a fresh spirit of justice and modernism into the courts of the Sharia in order to reconcile them with the administrative reforms being introduced by Cromer and his successors.[4] Rida further pursued his master's lead by urging that those portions of the Sharia which treated civil and commercial transactions and social relations should no longer be held sacrosanct and immutable, but should be reinterpreted and amended by the *ulama* to accord with the greatly altered conditions of the family, the community and business in the modern world. Rida's originality lay in understanding that the problems of twentieth-century Islam were moral problems, not to be overcome by institutional reform alone. He completed the work of Djamal al-Din and Abduh by emphasizing the ethical aspect, the notions of public and private responsibility, which his predecessors had failed to develop.[5] It was this aspect of fully developed Salafiyya which especially appealed to the Young Moroccan reformers of the 1920's who were morally incensed to see their country held in servitude by a coalition of corrupt pashas and *caids*, unregenerate religious brotherhoods, and power-seeking French functionaries.

Salafiyya made an especially deep impact on Morocco because its doctrines were maturing at just the right moment to fit the rapidly changing conditions which followed the turn of the century. Morocco had always leaned towards fundamentalism in religion — the Malekite ritual prevailed there — and hence was potentially receptive to a movement such as Salafiyya, but during the time of Djamal al-Din and Abduh it had made little headway because the other conditions were wanting. Before 1900, Moroccan intellectuals had not been fully awakened to either the degenerate state of their religion or the imminence of European intervention in their affairs. Therefore, when al-Sanussi returned from Cairo in the late 1870's imbued with a missionary zeal for introducing Djamal al-Din's reforms, he so outraged the Royal Council that even the sultan's patronage failed to shield him from heresy proceedings, and he deemed it wise to emigrate for a number of years until the trouble blew over.[6]

After the advent of the new century, however, the situation altered markedly. A land which had not experienced foreign rule since the eighth century found itself facing an imperialism which had already engulfed all surrounding territories, and its occupation by one European power or another seemed imminent. Furthermore, the degeneracy of Islam in Morocco was becoming painfully apparent in contrast to the modern world of which Morocco was now forcibly becoming a part. Just as some of the sixteenth-century Protestant sects had given rise to aberrations in Christian practice, so did the Malekite school, the "low church" of Islam, condone mysticism and saint worship, both of which had proliferated in North Africa. The powerful religious brother-hoods which perpetuated these practices were, in Morocco, among the most conservative and at the same time among the most politically active in the Muslim world.[7] Unlike the brotherhoods of Algeria, the Moroccan orders tended to mirror the distinctions, ethnic, political and social,[8] between Arab and Berber, and during the first half of the twentieth century the brotherhoods which remained most active in Morocco, with one or two im-portant exceptions, were those which reflected Berber particular-ism.[9] This inevitably conflicted with the broader aspirations of the nationalists. Thus, while staunchly Berberist orders like the Derqawa and its derivative, the Kittaniyya, originally opposed the French occupation, when they were later confronted by a reforming sultan who openly sympathized with the aims of the Salafiyyist nationalists, they often leagued themselves with the French authorities who promised, however ambiguously, to re-spect their prized autonomy, religiously as well as politically.[10] The basic incompatibility of the brotherhoods with the religious and political aims of the nationalists did not prevent the two from cooperating temporarily during the furor over the Berber *dahir*,[11] but with the major exception of the Tijaniyya of Tetuan, the Moroccan brotherhoods were anti-nationalist, and even the Tijaniyya looked askance at the Salafiyyist strain in the nationalist movement. Thus, to progressive-minded Muslim intellectuals, Salafiyya stood opposed to everything they hated and seemed especially suited to deal with the dual problem of the French occupation and religious petrifaction. This was the case in Algeria where it motivated the nationalist association of *ulama*,[12] and it was the case in Morocco where it permeated the thinking of the early nationalists and played a more prominent role than in any other Middle Eastern nationalist movement. After the turn of the century, then, Moroccan intellectuals became far more receptive to teachers and publications which carried the Salafiyyist message.

When the Shaykh Abu Shuaib al-Dukkali (1878–1937) returned home from his studies at al-Azhar, having imbibed the atmosphere of reform surrounding Rashid Rida and the *Manar* group and become as thorough-going a Salafiyyist as his predecessor, al-

Sanussi, the French army was standing at Morocco's door. When the shaykh was admitted to the faculty at Qarawiyin in 1908, the French were occupying Oujda and Casablanca, and when he became vizier of justice in 1912, the country for whose laws he was responsible had become a French protectorate. As exegete of the Koran at Qarawiyin, the position to which he owed most of his later influence, al-Dukkali's eloquence, his interest in youth, and his vast Islamic learning converted to Salafiyya two young men who were to become great teachers in their turn, Mohammed bel-Arabi al-Alaoui and Abdesselam Serghini, as well as some still younger men of the next generation who were to become the militant nationalists of the interwar years. The shaykh became a hero to these young men for his attack on the religious brotherhoods which were now beginning to collaborate with the French. And in keeping with the Salafiyyist stress on education, he promoted the free-school movement which arose in Morocco after World War I.[13]

Bel-Arabi ranked foremost among al-Dukkali's disciples. After graduation from Qarawiyin he taught there and at the Collège Moulay Idriss as well. In the 1920's he served as a *cadi* in Fez, later became president of the Court of Appeal of the Sharia in Rabat and, finally, vizier of justice in the Makhzen. His nationalist sympathies caused him to retire from public office after the riots of January 1944, but after independence his status as elder statesman led to his appointment as one of the three minister counsellors to the Throne, a position which, quite aside from his scholarly reputation, marked him as one of the leading notables of Morocco. Like his master, Bel-Arabi was more of a Salafiyyist than a nationalist, which is to say that he insisted on religious reform as the basis for all other, and it was the profound impression which this made on the young men in his circle that gave Moroccan nationalism its uniquely religious bent. Most of the leading nationalists of this era regard Bel-Arabi as the spiritual fountainhead of their movement.[14] Al-Dukkali's other disciple, Serghini, also taught at the university and the *collège* after graduation, and at least two of the nationalists noted his effect on their thinking.[15] Nevertheless, he is chiefly remembered as a colleague of Bel-Arabi.

If apostles like al-Dukkali and Bel-Arabi were the primary agents, publications from the Middle East were also instrumental in spreading Salafiyyist doctrine. The leading periodicals were

al-Manar, al-Fath and *al-Zahra* from Cairo, and *ech-Chihab* from
Constantine (Algeria), and by all odds the most widely read of
these in Morocco was Rida's *al-Manar*, a monthly review of
philosophy, religion and social affairs reflecting about the same
proportion of political overtones as the reform movement it
represented. During World War I, copies of *al-Manar* and
reprints of an earlier journalistic enterprise of Djamal al-Din and
Abduh [16] were beginning to circulate in Morocco, and *al-Manar*
was one of the sources to which al-Dukkali directed the attention
of the young Bel-Arabi.[17] When the editors of *L'Afrique Française* asserted that Muslim public opinion began with the pan-
Islamic press founded by Djamal al-Din, Abduh and Rida, it was
chiefly *al-Manar* to which they referred.[18] Rida's serialized
"Commentary on the Koran," which appeared in the journal
almost from the beginning, was probably inferior only to the
lectures of al-Dukkali and Bel-Arabi in spreading the good word
of Salafiyya to Morocco, and the older nationalists agree that, for
those who had no direct contact with the two teachers, *al-Manar*
may have been the primary agent of their conversion.[19]

Al-Fath was a reformist weekly with a decidedly Salafiyyist
tinge whose popularity in Morocco was all the greater because it
was one of the few eastern journals to take Moroccan nationalism
seriously in the late 1920's. In 1930 it figured prominently in the
international campaign against the Berber *dahir* for which it was
banned in Morocco, although it continued to come in via the
British Post Offices. Moroccans not only read it, they wrote for
it, notably Hassan Bouayad, then in Egyptian exile, and Omar
Abdeljalil. Mohammed Hassan al-Ouezzani rates *al-Fath* second
only to *al-Manar* for its influence on Moroccan intellectuals.[20]
Al-Zahra, like the other Salafiyyist journals, mixed political with
religious concerns, but its moderation kept it from being banned
in Morocco despite occasional contributions by that *bête noire*
of French imperialism, Shakib Arslan, and it was widely read
there in the 1920's and 1930's.[21]

Ben Badis' journal, *ech-Chihab*, reflected the outlook of the
Algerian *ulama* who had taken up with Salafiyya, and its mention
by the nationalists interviewed raises the question of the extent
of Algerian influence on Moroccan nationalism. Louis Jalabert
asserts that the Algerian *ulama* carried little weight beyond their
own border and that both Morocco and Tunisia received their
Salafiyya directly from Egypt,[22] while Julien implies that the

point of contact was Paris where Moroccan and Tunisian students met their Egyptian, Syrian and, presumably, their Algerian co-religionists.[23] On the other hand there seems to have been some top level contact within North Africa, for Allal al-Fassi, the acknowledged leader of the Moroccan reformers, appears to have been in correspondence with Ben Badis before 1930, although al-Fassi's papers are not yet available to prove it. At the very least, it can be said that Moroccan intellectuals read and contributed to *ech-Chihab*, and therefore must have corresponded with its editor. It was the articles submitted by Mohammed Ghazi which caused the journal to be banned in Morocco in 1927 (it continued to infiltrate) and led to Ghazi's exile the next year.[24]

To a lesser extent than periodicals, books on Muslim fundamentalism were responsible for propagating Salafiyya in Morocco. Ibn Taimiya's fourteenth-century classic on religious reform, *The Separation between the Disciples of God and the Disciples of Satan*,[25] was a factor in converting Bel-Arabi to Salafiyya [26] and exercised a considerable influence on intellectuals of the next generation as well, including Allal al-Fassi.[27] The writings of the Grenadine Moor, al-Shattibi, were used by Serghini as the basis for his lectures on Salafiyya at Qarawiyin University [28] and served as the basis for Mekki Naciri's polemic of 1925 attacking certain of the religious brotherhoods.[29] Mekki Naciri was one of the most active and prolific of publicists among the early Moroccan nationalists. In 1928, *L'Afrique Française* complained that the works of medieval masters such as Ibn Taimiya were selling in Fez faster than ever before,[30] and their influence on Moroccan reformist thinking seems beyond doubt.[31] Among contemporary works the ten-volume *Arab Encyclopedia* lent scholarly authority to the attack on unreformed religion,[32] but far more influential were the works of Rashid Rida, primarily his great *Caliphate*,[33] but also his three-volume biography of Mohammed Abduh.[34] All the Moroccans interviewed for the present study acknowledged his influence.

Among the other sources of North African reformist thought, Julien cites the schools and universities of the Middle East.[35] They unquestionably influenced Moroccans of the Istiqlal era. Of the forty-one leading nationalists of the interwar years, however, in all likelihood no more than six went to school in Egypt or Palestine and only one in Syria, and perhaps only four of these had even begun this schooling before 1930.[36] Moreover, French schools were earlier and better attended by the nationalists (18 of the 41), and traditional Moroccan institutions even better attended (24).[37] Accordingly, the influence of Eastern education was slight before World War II, even slighter in the formative years before 1934, and trifling in the period before 1930 when Salafiyya was making its greatest contribution to Moroccan nationalist thought and when the impact of local teachers and publications was much greater.

The pilgrimage has also been cited as a vehicle which spread Arab reformist doctrines, but again, as far as the Moroccans are concerned, the evidence is to the contrary. Allal al-Fassi has never taken the pilgrimage and Omar Abdeljalil was five years old when taken by his father. Mohammed Lyazidi and others claim that pilgrims were customarily too busy with a multitude of religious preoccupations to concern themselves with much else. Certainly there were opportunities during the trip to exchange views, but the Moroccans involved deny that the pilgrimage played any significant part in the rise of their nationalist movement.

The permanent results of Salafiyyist indoctrination varied of course with each person. As they listened to al-Dukkali and Bel-Arabi, the future nationalists undoubtedly reacted as did an earlier generation which attended Abduh's commentaries in Cairo: "We felt in our souls that any of us was capable of reforming a province or a kingdom." [38] Later on, time, maturity and political immediacy qualified the early enthusiasm, but nonetheless, in talking with many of the older nationalists, one becomes aware of a fundamental religiousness on their part even after three decades of distraction by an essentially secular struggle with the French in which the question of religious reform was largely submerged. Omar Abdeljalil and Mohammed Lyazidi are among the best examples of this type of person; deeply affected by Salafiyya, they still retain today their attachment to its religious ethic quite apart from the many political implications the movement later had for them.

SECULAR MOVEMENTS

If religious reform was for some Middle Easterners the imperative for an Islamic revival, for others — the "secular" reformers — it was of decidedly secondary importance. One must distinguish, however, between the two types of secular reformism, pan-Arab and parochial, which arose in the Middle East. Within the first category are found the comprehensive Arabist philosophies of writers like al-Kawakibi (1849–1903) and al-Manfaluti (1876–1924), as well as the pan-Arabism of Shakib Arslan (1869–1946). They differed from pan-Islamism chiefly in their insistence that the Arabs should play the leading role in the Islamic revival and that the Islamic renaissance they anticipated would find its political expression in an Arab caliphate restored to Mecca.[39]

The Moroccans were familiar with much of the literature of this school. Al-Kawakibi's *Attributes of Tyranny*,[40] a scathing attack on despotic government, and his *Mother of Villages*,[41] a fictitious account of a society to regenerate Islam, were widely read in the Middle East at the end of the nineteenth century. A generation later in Morocco they impressed young reformers like M. H. al-Ouezzani as "war machines" for democracy against tyranny.[42] The histories and novels of the prolific Jurgi Zaydan (1861–1914) were well known, as were the works of the Egyptian sociologist, al-Manfaluti, whose collected articles on social reform, education and politics became an Arabic best-seller just before World War I. Of the lesser lights of the Arab renaissance, the historian Amin Said, the novelist Niqula al-Haddad (1870–1954) and the poet Khalil Jibran (1883–1931) were also read in Morocco, but al-Kawakibi, al-Manfaluti and Zaydan were clearly the best known. The Amir Shakib Arslan's philosophical contribution to this broadly conceived Arab renaissance took shape in his extensive annotation of Lothrop Stoddard's *The New World of Islam*[43] and in the columns of his propaganda sheet, *La Nation Arabe*, which appeared irregularly from 1930 to 1938 and furnished native elites from the Java Sea to the Atlantic with helpful hints for their budding nationalist movements.[44]

Nevertheless, the prospect of a resurgent Arab hegemony had a limited appeal in Morocco, which had permanently thrown off Arab imperialism in the eighth century, and the pan-Arab myths of ethnic unity and a common language had little more appeal in a country where Syrian and Egyptian vernaculars were nearly incomprehensible and where even the most ardent Arabist was obliged to cater to Berber particularism. *La Nation Arabe* continued to be smuggled into Morocco and read by, or to, a large audience even though banned (August 1930) by the authorities,[45] but its pan-Arab complexion was not especially appreciated there. Both Julien and Rézette have remarked on the importance of Arslan's pan-Arabism for Moroccan nationalist philosophy,[46] but the Moroccans interviewed thought that French observers ordinarily tended to overrate his ideological impact.[47] The pages of *La Nation Arabe* and the amir's other writings unquestionably inspired a vague sense of dignity and personal worth in the Moroccan reader, but visions of a united *nation arabe* or even a more limited pan-Maghrebian union were of little practical value to Moroccans who sought specific correctives to specific problems raised by the French presence. Accordingly, a pan-Islamic philosophy like Salafiyya could strike a responsive chord in Morocco because its stress on religious reform and the vagueness of its precepts of Islamic unity did not jeopardize Moorish independence, while the broad, philosophic Arabism of an al-Kawakibi, romantic as its appeal undoubtedly was, never seemed particularly useful to Moroccan reformers; and the allure of pan-Arabism and Arab unity tended to vary inversely with its attainability, as is true elsewhere in the Middle East.

Far more appealing in Morocco it seems, by virtue of their concrete achievements, were the activists, the practitioners of parochial nationalisms such as Mustafa Kamil of Egypt, Shaykh Thaalibi of Tunisia, and even non-Arabs like the Turk, Mustafa Kemal. In this group can also be included Shakib Arslan whenever he abandoned his pan-Arab role to deal with the regional problems of the Maghreb or the immediate, local concerns of the Moroccans. As permanent representative in Geneva of the Syro-Palestinian committee, Arslan kept in touch with most of the interwar leaders of the Muslim world and taught political action to many, especially those of Syria, Lebanon, Palestine and North Africa. Possessed of a wider perspective than most Arab leaders on the realities of Middle Eastern politics, Arslan quickly understood that the rigid formulae of the "Arab Pact" of 1931 were virtually inapplicable in a place like Morocco whose historic and cultural ties with the Arab world had been loose and intermittent. He therefore remodeled the Pact to accommodate North Africa. In recognition of its linguistic, cultural and religious personality, he devised the concept of pan-Maghrebism, while simultaneously urging each country to pursue its independence apart. It was hardly by coincidence that Tunisian, Algerian and Moroccan nationalists before World War II proposed very similar programs: each was to proceed towards independence with the blessing of France, who, faithful to her democratic genius, would cooperate in the creation of a firm union of North African states bound to her by gratitude and common interests.[48] As one might expect of even a "secular" Arab nationalist, Arslan cautioned against the neglect of religion under the pressure of events. The Arab recovery was the prime goal, but religious and political revival must proceed side by side.[49] The qualification appeared sounder than the basic premise to the Moroccan nationalists whose political orientation was already profoundly tinged with Salafiyya.

Arslan's influence in Morocco was more tactical than ideological, and as such, resulted less from his publications and propaganda than from personal associations. Of the three Moroccans who knew him best, Ahmed Balafrej, Mohammed al-Fassi and M. H. al-Ouezzani, the former two visited him on several occasions during their university days in Paris (1926–32) and were treated like sons by the amir. It is said that Balafrej, thoroughly Gallicized as he is, was more profoundly affected politically by Arslan than by his formal education.[50] Al-Ouezzani served as the amir's secretary from September 1932 until the following summer, and in the late 1930's, when the nationalists were threatening France with non-cooperation, he clung to Arslan's counsels of moderation.[51] On the masthead of his journal, *L'Action du Peuple*, appeared Arslan's epigram: "To be the enemy of a policy or a method is not to say that one is the enemy of a nation." [52] Arslan apparently resisted the temptation to use his Axis connections as leverage against France in the matter of North African nationalism, and there is no doubt that his moderating influence helped to maintain nationalist loyalty to France on the eve of the war. His associations with North Africans, however, reached beyond his personal acquaintanceship. He carried on an extensive correspondence with Mohammed Lyazidi from 1935 on, most of which was burned by Lyazidi's family to keep it out of the hands of the French authorities. Abdesselam Bennouna and Allal al-Fassi corresponded with him for years before meeting him in 1933, and Mohammed Daoud claims to have in his possession nearly a hundred of his letters. It was frequently through such correspondence that Arslan introduced Moroccans to other Arab nationalists and to Frenchmen sympathetic to their cause.[53]

It was also Arslan who directed the foreign campaign against
the Berber *dahir*, and his journal, *La Nation Arabe*, was most
significant for Moroccan nationalism in its role as a propaganda
weapon during that campaign. The founding of the Moroccan
nationalist journal, *Maghreb*, under the direction of Balafrej, was
undertaken in 1932 after a conference in Geneva between Arslan
and Ahmed Mekouar, who financed it. And it was Arslan who
counseled the Moroccans to aim for reform rather than independence in the late 1930's. In some respects, Arslan was the
prime mover of active nationalism in Morocco, and if Bel-Arabi
can be characterized as the spiritual guide of that movement,
Shakib Arslan unquestionably qualifies as its tactician.[54]

Among the parochial nationalists, Mustafa Kamil clearly made
the greatest impression on the Moroccans. His newspaper, *al-Liwa*,
flourished before their time, but they read his books, especially
Égyptiens et Anglais,[55] and his posthumously published correspondence with Mme. Juliette Adam,[56] as well as the biography
by his brother which contained many of his speeches and
articles.[57] The young and impressionistic Moroccans were stirred
by the portrayals of Egyptian nationalism and of Kamil's leadership in the poetry of Ahmed Shawqi and Mohammed Hafiz Bey
Ibrahim,[58] and they toured their country in the late 1920's with
Kamil's drama, *The Conquest of Spain*, which dealt with a heroic
era dear to Moorish hearts.[59] Because Kamil was first and foremost an Egyptian nationalist and not especially interested in
Abduh's religious reformism or in a revived caliphate, he advocated
the separation of religion and the state and the responsibility of
a secular executive to an elected legislature. As might be expected, it was this part of his program which least appealed to the
Salafiyyist Moroccans; nor did they feel that the subordination
of the executive to a fully sovereign legislature was particularly
suitable to the Sharifian state, whose monarchy was not only
greatly revered but was cooperating increasingly with the nationalists. They were more impressed by two of his other ideas:
free and compulsory primary education and the gradual downward extension of popular sovereignty by means of general,
provincial and local councils. These of course are of central
concern, if only propagandistically, to any aspiring colonial
nationalist movement. In the eyes of Allal al-Fassi, Kamil's impact
on Moroccan nationalism ranks second only to Salafiyya.[60]

After Kamil's mantle fell upon Zaghlul, the Moroccans could

defer to a man the end of whose career was contemporaneous with their own fledging movement, which meant that the news of his activities had more immediacy for them and came to them more directly by way of current periodicals and through their friends, for a few Moroccan students were now beginning to find their way into Middle Eastern schools and universities.[61] The most influential of the journals which served this function, owing perhaps to its Salafiyyist tendencies and despite its editorial differences with Zaghlul, was the weekly supplement of the Liberal Constitutionist organ, *al-Siyasa*, which carried articles bearing on the Egyptian national revival by many Egyptian men of letters.[62] *Al-Ahram*, though less frequently read by the Moroccans, was important enough to be frowned upon by the Residency, and both journals customarily circulated by way of the network of British Post Offices. Two other Cairo journals, more literary than political in content but nonetheless influential owing to the eminence of their contributors, were Zaydan's old monthly, *al-Hilal*, and the newer (founded in 1933) *al-Risala*, of which Mohammed Lyazidi still owns a complete collection.[63] In the early days students played a somewhat limited part in this liaison. M'Hammed Bennouna returned from his studies in Cairo in the summer of 1926 to rehearse Zaghlul's reforms for his friends in Rabat,[64] and Hassan Bouayad, who studied in Cairo from 1929 to 1933, brought home and put to use his knowledge of the Egyptian Constitution of 1923 and of Zaghlul's judicial and educational reforms. Quite possibly Ahmed Balafrej and Mekki Naciri did the same, but, as pointed out earlier, few of Morocco's future leaders went to the East for study before 1930.[65]

Among the lesser lights of Egyptian reformism, Kasim Bey Amin (1865–1908) is mentioned by Ignace Lepp as having made a lasting impression on the Moroccans by virtue of his novel concern for the plight of women in the Muslim world. Abduh had advanced some feelers in this regard without much effect, but Amin's *The Emancipation of Women* and *The New Woman* [66] stirred up a controversy in which the Moroccans ultimately opted for the author. Lepp points out that all the Moroccan nationalist leaders of his acquaintance, whether French-educated or not, were monogamous, and the nationalists themselves attest to the influence of the movement started by Amin.[67]

Syrian nationalism, closely linked to Egyptian nationalism as it was by ties of tradition, sympathy and personal involvement

(Rida, Arslan and Zaydan, for example, were either Syrian or Lebanese), can be regarded as a kind of appendage of the Egyptian movement insofar as its effect on Morocco is concerned. Apparently Allal al-Fassi corresponded before 1930 with Hashim Bey al-Atasi, head of the Syrian nationalist bloc, and the monthly review, *al-Irfan*, came directly from Saida into the hands of Moroccans carrying accounts of such things as the Druze rebellion of 1925–27. News from Syria, however, ordinarily reached Morocco via Cairo by means of the Egyptian journals already mentioned, and dramatic events such as the French bombardment of Damascus were recounted in the works of the Egyptian poets Shawqi and Ibrahim.[68]

Odd as it may seem, the Moroccans appear to have known or cared very little about the program of the Tunisian Destour. In a general way, it is true, they adhered throughout the interwar years to its principal aim as stated in Thaalibi's *La Tunisie martyre* in 1920, namely, reform within the framework of the protectorate towards the eventual goal of self-government; but this may as well reflect Arslan's influence, and it was not so much the doctrines as the organization and methods of the Tunisian nationalists which made an impression in Morocco.[69] Chiefly by means of student contacts in Paris and reading Tunisian periodicals, the Moroccans acquainted themselves with the more advanced techniques and rather impressive activities of their colleagues: press campaigns, delegations to Paris, attempts at economic boycott, parades in uniform, paramilitary use of Boy Scouts, carefully planned "spontaneous" street demonstrations, and the structure of local cells under orders from a central committee. Student contacts were maintained through the Association of North African Muslim Students in Paris, whose ostensible purpose was to assist struggling North African students in the capital with their rooming and boarding problems but whose meetings inevitably gravitated to French policy in the Maghreb. The Association served to keep the North Africans in touch with one another and was an education to the less experienced Moroccans.[70]

Of the journals which brought news of Tunisia to Morocco, *es-Sawab*, *ez-Zohra*, and *en-Nahda* were the most important of those not affiliated with the Destour, but their moderate, or even neutral, line did not immunize them from trouble with the authorities. The latter two were banned from Morocco in 1925 at the height of the Riff War, although all three continued to circulate clandestinely.[71] The Destourian journals, of course, were rigorously proscribed in the French zone of Morocco, but this problem was resolved, somewhat unexpectedly, by the ultra-colonial mouthpiece, *L'Afrique Française*, which began to print excerpts and summaries of the Tunisian press in order to fill its European readers with pious horror of the pernicious character of Thaalibi, Bourguiba and company. In October 1928, for example, *L'Afrique Française* paraphrased an article from *Lisan ech-Chaab*, banned by the Moroccan Residency in 1923, which informed Moroccans that the Tunisians were thinking of publishing a propaganda journal in Paris to get some mileage out of the recent Socialist pledge to protect France's dependent peoples from their imperialist exploiters.[72] This information undoubtedly contributed to the foundation of just such a journal by the Moroccans a few years later, and by repeated examples of this sort (they are found in nearly every issue), *L'Afrique Française* became unwittingly a prime vehicle for the exchange of nationalist views across North Africa. Finally might be mentioned the journalistic efforts of the Tunisian, Ahmed Tawfiq al-Madani, who was exiled to Algeria in the early 1930's and established there a liaison with the association of Algerian *ulama* whose reformist views were reflected in his periodical, *el-Basair*, and his annual almanac, *Taqwim el-Mansur*. He was better known in Morocco for his *Book of Algeria*, ostensibly a geographical and historical guide, but interlarded with so much polemic on the iniquities of French rule that it stood higher than most guidebooks on the reading lists of North Africans.[73]

While not an Arab movement, Turkish nationalism had repercussions in Morocco quite as significant as some of the Arab movements themselves. The war of 1914–18 marked off the Young Turks and the Committee of Union and Progress as part of a bygone era, but the activities of Mustafa Kemal at the time of the Turko-Greek War were very much alive for the Moroccans, although the Tetuanis, who were not especially drawn to Salafiyya, were more affected than their colleagues in the French zone.[74] But even there, Kemal's struggle to establish a Turkish state, his educational reforms, the Fundamental Law, and the emancipation of Turkish women were observed with interest if not always with complete approval. As was the case with Syrian nationalism, news from Turkey customarily arrived by way of

Egyptian periodicals or Arabic translations of Turkish books printed in Cairo. Allal al-Fassi remembers discussing the Turkish revolution at home in the years before he went to Qarawiyin University, and M. H. al-Ouezzani claims to have studied ten or fifteen books on Turkish nationalism. Even after the secularization of Turkish institutions (1924) somewhat clouded Kemal's reputation in the Muslim world, he was still a subject of discussion in the secret societies, active in Fez and Rabat during 1925–30, which formed the nucleii of the Moroccan nationalist movement.[75]

In summary, the inspirational or psychological impact of Salafiyya was felt in various ways. For some it was the spirit underlying all reform; for others it opened the mind to the possibilities of reform; for still others it awakened their political consciousness. It also prevented in Morocco the secularization experienced in Turkish, and to a lesser extent in Egyptian, society. Ideologically, Salafiyya furnished the nationalists with such general concepts as consultative government, popular sovereignty, educational reform, and the congeniality of constitutional government and democracy with Islam, and in one case with a specific remedy, the separation of certain rules of law, especially civil and commercial law, from the Sharia. Tactically, Salafiyya served as a refuge, a sheltered staging ground for attacks on the French regime. Religious reform as the basis for a national revival would remain an important though declining factor in Moroccan nationalism until at least World War II, or even longer in the minds of the older men.

The secular reformers breathed life into the Arab renaissance by creating a new psychological atmosphere in which nationalism was fashionable. Ideologically, they propagated such general principles as women's rights, the independence of Arab peoples, and the novel idea that political corruption and oppression are not ordained but are remediable by education and free expression, as well as specific programs such as the gradual extension of popular sovereignty by means of general, provincial and local councils, and the judicial reforms which reflected the influence of Zaghlul. Finally, their tactical influence is manifest in the techniques borrowed from the Tunisians and in the advice accepted from Shakib Arslan about founding a propaganda journal in Paris and cooperating with the French authorities.

VIII

THE IMPACT OF THE EUROPEAN
REVOLUTION

It might be well to note at the outset that the terms "French" and "Western" are often used synonymously in this chapter, because, in the treatment of generalized phenomena, such as the ideas of the Enlightenment, specifically French contributions are frequently indistinguishable from the broader pattern. Moreover, in the years before World War II, when their experience with non-French Westerners was limited and officially discouraged, Moroccans themselves customarily used the terms *occidental* and *français* interchangeably. Emphasis more than anything else will determine the usage here.

Europe has so profoundly altered the non-Western world that the latter's development in modern times is a kind of compressed rehearsal, or reflection, of the growing pains of Europe since the Renaissance. Europe's political and economic philosophies, her science and technology, humanitarianism and Protestant ethic, organizationism and militarism, racism and materialism, and the psychology of optimism, to name but a few of the facets of the European revolution which have impinged on non-Western societies, have so reoriented the way Asians and Africans think and act that to attempt to evaluate or even describe the net result would be a task far beyond both this author's capacity and the scope of this monograph. Fortunately an assessment of that aspect of the non-Western reaction with which this study is primarily concerned — colonial nationalism — can be made reasonably understandable even if its European input is treated rather selectively. The choice of liberalism, socialism and totalitarianism, as agents of colonial ferment in this study, has not been made arbitrarily, but arose quite naturally out of what appeared to be the case after a number of possibilities was explored.

Before examining the qualitative effect of these agents, it is necessary to have some idea of the number of Moroccans who were more or less directly affected by the European revolution. To a large extent this limits our inquiry to the French-educated, especially in this formative period between the great wars, for it was the French schools and universities which served to open other avenues of contact later on. How many Moroccans, then, received a French education, and what proportion of them became nationalists? The qualitative effects of French education shall then be examined, with the conclusion that French education was not only a vehicle of transmission but can be regarded as a fourth agent of the European revolution which had a significant impact on Moroccan nationalism.

FRENCH EDUCATION

Of all the Western-educated Moroccans who were old enough to finish secondary school before 1930 or their higher education before 1934 (the year of the *Plan de Réformes*) and thus be in a position to influence the rising nationalism, none received a Western education that was not French. In later years, a few from the Spanish zone attended the American University in Cairo, Robert College in Constantinople or the University of Madrid, but they were not among the forty-one early leaders. Undoubtedly a number of Moroccans were in Spanish primary and secondary schools in the northern zone, but the development of educational facilities there was even more retarded than in the south, and the number could not have been large. It should be kept in mind that the nationalists of Tetuan never rose above the second or third rank in the movement. The important nationalists were from the French zone, and when they received a Western education it was French, a generalization which holds true after, as well as before, World War II.

Of the hundreds of Moroccans who received some degree of French education only nineteen became top-ranking nationalist leaders before World War II.[1] One is tempted to conclude either that the French-educated as a whole were lukewarm nationalists or that French education made no more than a minor contribution to the psychology of nationalism, and in some respects both are true. Most of the French-educated either defected from the movement when things grew difficult or never closely associated themselves in the first place. Some of them surrendered to the attractions of Gallic culture from the very beginning and went quietly along the road towards assimilation. Others saw no point in being sent to jail for breast-beating and regarded cooperation with the Residency in the interests of piecemeal reform as the better part of valor.[2] But one must remember that most of those who were *not* French-educated reacted in the same fashion.

Our assessment of the French-educated changes somewhat if we limit our consideration to those who went on to the university or who at least finished their secondary schooling. It is difficult to determine how many progressed this far, owing to the unreliability of official statistics. But after consultation with both French and Moroccan school officials in Rabat and with a number of private individuals, the author feels justified in asserting that in the decade before 1930 not more than ten Moroccans were awarded the *baccalauréat* from Moroccan *lycées*, a few from Parisian *lycées*, and about thirty-five that consolation baccalaureate, the *diplôme d'études secondaires musulmanes* (D.E.S.M.), from the Moroccan *collèges*. We are confronted by the same difficulty as regards higher education. The published figures for the Institut des Hautes Études Marocaines in Rabat do not distinguish between French and Moroccan students, and an official record (if it exists) of Moroccans who went to France was not available to the author. Nevertheless, by interpreting information provided by the Bureau Universitaire de Statistique in Paris, it can be estimated that, in the period when the early nationalist leaders were getting their higher education (i.e., 1923–32), about thirty Moroccans must have attended universities in France.[3] In the Depression years which followed, neither were the funds available nor was the need for a university education greatly felt as yet by Moroccans, and the number who progressed to the university level increased very slowly, so that in the year 1939 there were only thirty-nine enrolled.[4]

Of the ten baccalaureates earned by Muslims at the *lycées* in Morocco before 1930, at least two were granted to future nationalists, and four other budding nationalists received baccalaureates in Paris during the same period, all the more interesting if it is remembered that these early scholars and their families were customarily screened for their political reliability. Of the thirty-five who earned the D.E.S.M., about fifteen were to become nationalist leaders, and of the thirty in French universities between 1923 and 1932, nine became nationalists. Accordingly, about one-third of this group found its way into the upper ranks of the nationalist movement, a far higher percentage than among the non-French-educated.

Nevertheless, in this day when unreconstructed imperialists deplore the baneful effects of Western schooling on peoples unprepared for it, the question remains as to why a majority of the French-educated failed to become leaders of the national movement in Morocco. The answer is not to be found by asserting that there was limited room at the top, for the fact is that more than half of those who rose to the top were not French-educated. Individual temperament probably accounts for a good deal of it. French education, in and of itself, could neither prepare the retiring person to lead nor the phlegmatic to expose himself or his family to the inconveniences which attended nationalist activities.

The level of education attained, however, seems to have had some relevance, because the proportion of committed nationalists rises sharply among the better educated as well as among those schooled in France as opposed to those schooled in Morocco. But even here one must distinguish among those trained in medicine, who tended as a rule to be politically passive, those trained in law, who unfortunately for a nice sociological distinction, chose to split about evenly, and those who studied literature or journalism, who were inclined to be the more active nationalists. It is not hard to account for this, because the legal and medical professions offered sufficient vocational outlets at home quite apart from any political involvement, whereas it was too much to expect a journalist or teacher to skirt for long the broad areas of political discussion forbidden by the Residency without impinging on them sooner or later. Notwithstanding, the chief factor which differentiated the nationalist was probably temperament, and a striking example is provided by the two brothers Abdeljalil, each of whom received his higher education in France. Hadj Omar, *diplômé* of the École Nationale d'Agriculture at Montpellier, became a very active nationalist, while his brother, the Reverend Father Jean Abdeljalil, a graduate of the Sorbonne, was converted to Catholicism in 1930 and became a Franciscan monk in Paris until just prior to his death in 1962 when he recanted and returned home. The case is atypical, but it illustrates the preponderance of the factors of personality and individuality over mere education in the determination of careers.

Bare statistics, then, do not seem to clinch the case for French education, and one might conclude at this point that it did not play as crucial a role in the rise of nationalism as is commonly thought. While numerous French commentators have observed that nationalist agitation did not occur until the first classes had graduated from the Moroccan *collèges* about 1925, the possibility of coincidence should not be ruled out. It may be that the *Zeitgeist* of our century would have generated such a movement had not a single Moroccan been admitted to a European school.

But if the case for Western education is not quantitatively proved, we shall find its qualitative ramifications far more convincing. Besides acting as the primary agent for acquainting young Moroccans with novel ideas and techniques, French schooling left each of them with a disciplined mind and many of them with serious psychological problems, both of which fed the nationalist movement.

Whereas traditional Muslim education sought to indoctrinate by developing the memory, the mental exercise encountered in French schools was rather in the nature of understanding and organizing material. One cannot generalize from this that all the French educated acquired methodical intellectual habits and that all others retained encyclopedic but disorderly minds, but it is still true that the French-educated usually were better able to organize their ideas and their work, and the foremost nationalist who did not receive a Western education (Allal al-Fassi) attests to this fact.[5] Mohammed Hassan al-Ouezzani, Ahmed Balafrej, Mohammed Lyazidi and Omar Abdeljalil, all French-educated, comprised with al-Fassi the leading echelon of the national movement. It is precisely they who were also the most Westernized from the standpoint of regular, organized habits of work and thought.[6] And al-Fassi, while he received no formal Western schooling, claims to have studied in Arabic translation both Descartes' *Discourse on Method* and all the works of Descartes' disciple, Malebranche, and to have been deeply affected by both. Whether his organizational talents were thus acquired or simply reinforced, he possesses them to a degree not customary for Moroccans, and he regards the scientific approach as one of France's great gifts to Morocco.[7] It was in French schools that Moroccans learned the Cartesian methods of ordered thought and exposition, and acquired a taste for rational criticism as well as a Gallic clarity of expression. By focusing these newfound skills on heretofore confused ideas and feelings, they were able to create a national program of

reform out of the embryonic nationalistic sentiments of the mid-
1920's. In this way French education reinforced Moroccan
nationalism by furnishing it with more effective techniques of
organization and propaganda. It will be seen that the orderly
thought processes of the French-educated qualified them to be
the theoreticians of the nationalist movement and to sit as its
"board of directors," and some of the Moroccans interviewed
(though by no means all) took the position that to have deprived
their movement of the French-educated would have deprived it
of its best organized and most effective leadership.[8]

Another direct effect of French education was the psychological
dislocation it caused for many young Moroccans, but especially
for those who chose professions other than medicine or law. The
attitudes of superiority and racism, mild as they were, displayed
by the French in Morocco were less evident in the metropole,
where whatever social contact existed was more easy-going and
where the young Moroccan tasted real equality with the European, often for the first time. He also tasted alcohol, prohibited
by his religion, but after all he was a long way from home. He
found attractive not only European dress but European ways of
life, especially the freedom of the individual, and he ended by
forsaking some of his own ways for those of the West. In the
process, he also came to consider himself superior to his rustic
coreligionists at home and to entertain job expectations far beyond
his real abilities.[9]

On his return to Morocco, he found he had become a stranger
in his parents' eyes. Nor was he accepted on an equal footing by
the French *colon*, who complained that a European education
had made of him a functionary instead of an industrious citizen,[10]
that is to say, a competitor for government jobs (especially during
the Depression was this resented) rather than a docile native who
worked hard and kept meticulously out of politics. He was
labeled a *jeune tarbouche* to contrast him with his father, an "old
turban." Rather than take him into the administration at a level
justified by the training he had received, the French authorities
often sought to discredit him among his own people, already
suspicious of him, by branding him a dangerous innovator, and
no treatment could have been better calculated to transform him
into that very thing. Finding that French democracy, which he
had learned to prize in Paris, was not for export, that his job
expectations were not to be fulfilled, and that he was treated as

a cultural anomaly, neither Muslim nor French, he not uncommonly turned to nationalism as a welcome nostrum.

One must beware of overstating this point, however. For one thing, direct testimony about their psychological problems from Moroccans themselves is scanty, probably because it is a matter of some delicacy. What evidence there is derives largely from French sources which must always be scrutinized for the predisposition to regard as mentally disturbed anyone betraying anti-French, nationalistic inclinations. Secondly, psychological maladjustments did not occur, or were not apparent, in all or even a majority of the French-educated. The more phlegmatic personalities found that their education did, indeed, improve their job opportunities. Striking examples of this were Brigadier-General Mohammed Kittani, the only Moroccan general officer in the French army; Mohammed Zeghari, vice-premier and minister of defense in the first two independent governments and a member of the Istiqlal *Conseil Supérieur* after 1945, but prior to World War II a director of the Compagnie Algérienne in Fez and advocate of moderate reforms in collaboration with the French; and M'Barek Bekkai, first premier of independent Morocco, also an officer in the French army and a member of its General Staff after 1943. Even some of the more ardent nationalists held jobs which seemed to satisfy them for a while. Omar Abdeljalil was a successful plantation manager. Messaoud Chiguer served as a secretary to the Makhzen from 1927 until his clandestine nationalist activities came to light in 1944. Mohammed al-Fassi taught at the Lycée Lyautey and the Institut des Hautes Études Marocaines, and was for a time tutor to the present king. Abdelkader Benjelloun was, and is, a successful Casablanca lawyer. Economic well-being did not, however, compensate the Moroccan for all other grievances, and despite the qualifications noted, we may conclude that his psychological reaction at finding himself in, but not of, Moroccan society as well as excluded from the ruling elite was an important component in the makeup of the French-educated Moroccan nationalist.

LIBERALISM

For the sake of convenience we shall distinguish between the doctrinal and institutional aspects of liberalism as they affected Moroccan nationalism. The former would embrace the ideas of the Enlightenment and the French Revolution as they were absorbed into French liberalism during the ninetenth century; the latter the embodiment of those ideas in French administrative, representative and judicial institutions.

Ignace Lepp asserts that the appearance of the Moroccan movement can be explained in large part by the dissemination of the French Revolutionary myths in the primary and secondary schools of the protectorate.[11] Indeed, teachers of history could hardly be expected to avoid these ideas if the history of modern France was to make sense, even though Lyautey had ordained that the "Declaration of the Rights of Man and the Citizen" be expunged from such courses. Moroccans derived from this source less in the way of specific remedies than general concepts such as equality and justice, freedom of association and expression, and others relating to national consciousness such as the *patrie*, self-determination and national education.[12] These had great appeal to young men who sought to jar their fatherland out of five centuries of stagnation and transform it into a modern state, and their effect was to broaden the intellectual horizon of the reformers, to convince them that Salafiyya alone was no longer adequate to their purposes and to encourage them to look further into the secular philosophies and institutions of the West.[13] The reader will protest that the fundamentals of Western liberalism had already penetrated the Arab world long before the first Moroccan attended a French school. True, indeed, and because the Moroccans first encountered them in Arabic literature, the ideas were at first naively regarded as indigenous to the Arab Awakening. But when the young Moroccans began to attend French secondary schools and universities in the 1920's they were soon disabused of this illusion, and it was at that point, when the ideas encountered were no longer visionary goals but could be seen to have molded every institution of French life, that liberalism began to exert a more direct, more personal, and therefore more effective impact on their thinking.[14]

It would appear that their professors did not in any appreciable way mold the political conformation of the Moroccan nationalists. This is curious when one reflects on the procession of famous political disciples which has marched out of the classrooms of French academicians, and the question bears further investigation.

Within Morocco, of course, the academic community was far more subject to official control than it was in France, and the teacher who valued his job seldom ventured into the political arena. Whatever the explanation, professors appear to have been no more than a minor political influence. Only one or two of the nationalists interviewed could name teachers whom they remembered as outstanding in this respect.[15]

Far more important for the transmission of liberal doctrines were the course readings and other works which the student encountered in the academic community. The eighteenth-century philosophers were as widely read in the French schools in Morocco as they were in France. Nor were the literati of the nineteenth and twentieth centuries ignored, for Victor Hugo and Jean Jaurès are quoted side by side with Voltaire and Mirabeau on the pages of the nationalist journal, *L'Action du Peuple*. And those who did not read French discovered through their friends that many of the European philosophers existed in translation. Descartes, Malebranche, Voltaire, Rousseau and Diderot were all available in Arabic and were being read in Morocco in the 1920's, as were Seignobos' *History of Modern Civilization* and Guizot's *History of Civilization in Europe*.[16] From the testimony of the Moroccans, there can be no doubt that they were profoundly affected by the liberal ideas which they discovered on the bookshelves of the French schools and universities.[17]

Liberalism also filtered into Moroccan thinking by way of the periodical press, as one would expect, but what one would not expect is the preponderance of journals from the center or right wing of the republican tradition. *Le Temps* seems to have been favored by the French-educated as well as by some of those who were not, for Allal al-Fassi, who did not learn to read French until his Gabonese exile (1937–46), made a pest of himself by his constant requests to have *Le Temps* read to him or translated for him by his friends. *Le Figaro*, the *Revue de Deux Mondes* and the *Revue de Paris* are also mentioned by Moroccans as influential in their political formation during the 1930's.[18] More curious is the influence of *Le Petit Parisien* and *L'Echo de Paris* which emerged from World War I as mouthpieces for the *bloc national*, but it should be noted that, conservative as they may have been, neither was captive to the colonial lobby. *Le Petit Parisien*, indeed, embarked on a kind of anti-colonialist crusade in the 1930's, and its correspondent, Louis Roubaud, who had published

Vietnam in 1929 condemning French atrocities and military
oppression, took a second opportunity in 1933 to denounce
colonial policy in a series of articles which were reprinted by the
Moroccans in *L'Action du Peuple*. And *Echo*, before it was taken
over by rightists in 1936, pursued a similarly independent line.
Several articles highly critical of the Moroccan administration
were contributed by René Vanlande in 1934 and were also
reprinted in *L'Action du Peuple*. In fact, Roubaud and Vanlande
were probably quoted more frequently in that nationalist journal
than any other French political commentator.

In Part Four of this study it will be seen that liberalism had a
greater impact on the doctrines than on the methods of the
nationalists, but it did affect somewhat the terminology of the
movement, for the Moroccans early discovered that the language
of liberalism was a useful propaganda instrument, and by couching
their grievances and demands in phraseology familiar to the Gallic
ear, they expected to evoke the sympathies of open-minded
Frenchmen.[19] The most comprehensive exposition of the nationalist program, the *Plan de Réformes* of 1934, bears the stamp of
French liberal (and socialist) terminology throughout.

That the institutional expression of liberal doctrines impressed
Moroccans was eloquently attested to by Ahmed Rida Guedira
in 1956. Acting as spokesman for the Moroccan delegation which
negotiated the Franco-Moroccan treaty of independence, Defense
Minister Guedira voiced the sentiments of the older men around
him when he said:

For us who have drawn upon the spiritual resources of France, who have,
for the most part, had our higher education in France, I must say that
the French Government corresponds exactly to the image which we have
always had of France: a country generous, free and democratic, the
land where the principles of 1789 were born.[20]

While some of this language can be attributed to the euphoria
of independence day, many of those who listened to Guedira had
come to this conclusion years before by observing and studying
the operation of governmental institutions in France and in
Morocco. As students in Paris they had sat fascinated at the
sessions of the Chamber of Deputies and the court days at the
Palace of Justice. In the daily press they had followed with keen
interest the activities of the ministers, and had seen how democratic

elections were conducted and how they could be manipulated. Those who stayed in Morocco acquired notions about democracy and the forms of constitutional government not only from their textbooks, but from the periodical press, and by observing the growth of the representative bodies of the colonists, the Chambers of Agriculture and of Commerce and Industry. When the time came to draw up the *Plan de Réformes*, they augmented their observations by studying the legislative codes applying to Morocco which appeared in the *Bulletin Officiel*. There were few educated Moroccans on whose thinking the governmental institutions of France did not have a profound impact.[21]

SOCIALISM

In 1925 when the editors of *L'Afrique Française* were seeking scapegoats for the Riffian rebellion, they hit upon three likely prospects: the world economic crisis, agitation from the Middle East, and the activities of French Socialists, whose patriotism was clouded by their ideology.[22] We shall see, however, that the Socialists were disposed to reject rather than endorse Moroccan nationalism until as late as 1936, and even in 1937, when they had begun to patronize it, Léon Blum, with an assist from Resident-General Noguès, found it quite possible to suppress the Moroccan National Party for disturbing the peace. Nevertheless, some Moroccans, especially those closely associated with the labor movement, regard the doctrines and methods of French Socialism as the most significant of all Western influences on Moroccan nationalism, and militant French Socialists are quite willing to take credit for having provided the Moroccans with a ready-made ideology.[23] Given these diverse and often contradictory observations, let us now try to determine the extent to which Socialism did or did not exert a measurable influence.

Colonialism, with its host of attendant problems, was one of those embarrassing skeletons in the closets of the Élysée Palace, and the Socialists took it as part of the political game to rattle it now and then. Even though the Popular Front revealed that a responsible Socialist government could not afford to be militantly anti-colonialist in practice, it was so in theory, and the encouragement this gave to Moroccans served to stimulate their innate antipathy to alien rule. But the Moroccans interviewed could be far more specific than this, and their concerted opinion was that

Socialist doctrine was most deeply felt, understandably, in the area of social reform. In the *Plan de Réformes*, the rubric *réformes sociales* covers education, *habous*, public health, welfare and labor. Labor reforms, in particular, were derived from French models virtually unchanged,[24] which should not be surprising if one recalls that most of the early Moroccan nationalists were bourgeois who had little personal experience with or sympathy for the laboring classes but thought it good strategy to impress their French readers with their advanced notions about the rights of labor.

The Moroccans were also affected psychologically by French Socialism. Sought out and feted by leftist politicians, often for their own ends, and by left-leaning scholars who began in the 1930's to write seriously about Muslim reform movements, the young Moroccans acquired an inflated sense of self-importance and gradually became convinced that circumstances had bestowed upon them a mandate to liberate their country.[25]

Finally, Socialism had an important methodological impact on Moroccan nationalism. Socialist techniques and organization were put into practice by the Moroccans in such matters as the conduct of meetings, the planning of demonstrations and other types of agitation, the organization of press and propaganda campaigns, the presentation of reports, and the issuance of policy statements.[26] This type of influence is clearly reflected in the journalistic effort of 1932–34 conducted by *Maghreb* and *L'Action du Peuple* and elsewhere, in which the Moroccans expressed themselves in terminology drawn partly, as we have seen, from the liberal tradition, but partly, too, from the Socialist dialectic. In all likelihood, *Maghreb's* "editorial board" — actually a committee of patronage whose membership was entirely French and whose political flavor was predominantly Socialist — directed the campaign to some extent.[27]

The diverse impact of Socialism resulted most directly from personal contact with French politicians and intellectuals who were willing to take the Moroccans under their wing. Prominent among the older men were Edouard Depreux, Jean Longuet, and the old Socialist war-horse and colleague of Jean Jaurès, Pierre Renaudel, who broke away from the S.F.I.O. in 1933 to form the Neo-Socialist Party. Both Longuet and Renaudel were friends of Shakib Arslan, and it was owing to Arslan's instigation that they were instrumental in helping Ahmed Balafrej found *Maghreb* in

1932. It was they, too, whom Ahmed Mekouar consulted before he agreed to become *Maghreb's* principal financial backer.[28]   All three wrote for *Maghreb* and *L'Action du Peuple*, although Omar Abdeljalil claims that Depreux alone prepared his own articles, the others having relied on data or even suggested drafts provided by the Moroccans. These men helped to apply Socialist doctrines to problems specifically Moroccan, and it was in consultation with them in both France and Morocco that the social reforms suggested first in *Maghreb*, then in *L'Action du Peuple*, and finally in the *Plan de Réformes* were worked out.[29]

Among the younger men who might be classed as colleagues or collaborators, rather than mentors of the Moroccans, was Robert-Jean Longuet, lawyer, militant Socialist, son of Jean Longuet, and a personal friend of Allal al-Fassi, Omar Abdeljalil, Ibrahim al-Kittani, Ahmed Mekouar and possibly others. The younger Longuet served as nominal editor-in-chief of *Maghreb*, and Georges Monnet, Radical-turned-Socialist, a deputy from Aisne, was on *Maghreb's* editorial board. Among the writers in this group, who inadvertently fed the Muslim ego, were three well-known Arabists, Émile Dermenghem, Henri Laoust and Louis Massignon. Dermenghem, already the author of a life of the Prophet, was so impressed by the Salafiyya movement during a visit to Morocco in 1925 that he wrote a treatise on its doctrines and objectives. Laoust published a serialized article on Salafiyya which appeared in the *Revue d'Études Islamiques* in 1932 and was reprinted in *L'Action du Peuple* in 1933–34. Massignon contributed a number of books and articles on various aspects of Islamic society, including an article in the *Revue du Monde Musulman* in June 1920, entitled "Introduction à l'étude des revendications islamiques" which was reprinted in full in *L'Action du Peuple* in 1933.[30] Many of the Moroccans, French-educated or not, knew these men personally, and many were the conversations held in the cafés of the Latin Quarter and the Avenue Maréchal Lyautey and at Socialist congresses in both France and Morocco.[31]

The Socialist press was probably not so influential in Morocco as were the more widely read moderate and conservative journals, but its influence was, nonetheless, measurable. The Moroccans were, of course, familiar with *Le Populaire*, the official organ of the S.F.I.O., but the party journals published in Morocco, *Le Cri Marocain* and *Le Populaire Marocain*, both of Casablanca, had a

more direct impact on the nationalists. They first attracted
nationalist attention in 1930 when they alone, among all the
French newspapers in Morocco, took to task the Residency's
Berber policy. And if, in the ensuing years, the Socialists could
never quite make up their minds about espousing the bourgeois
nationalists, there nevertheless was a certain collaboration between
the two, and the Moroccans not only read but contributed to both
journals. Mohammed Lyazidi, for example, published occasional
articles on political problems in *Le Cri Marocain* and was a friend
of its editor, M. Carette-Bouvet.[32]

The acquisition of leftist doctrines from the study of books,
such as the works of Gustave Le Bon, was apparently not very
common. Ibrahim al-Kittani, one of the more scholarly of the
nationalists, whose opinion is probably as valid as any on this
point, asserts that while most of Le Bon's works [33] had been
translated into Arabic before 1920 and were available to the young
Moroccan reformers during the following decade, their influence
does not seem to have been profound.[34] The relative weight of
the other factors mentioned was apparently far greater.

While acknowledging the debt of the Moroccan nationalists to
the French Socialists, it should be recognized that active collaboration between the two was always somewhat restrained. A resolution adopted at the congress of the Fédération Socialiste du
Maroc, held in Casablanca, May 16–17, 1936, made it clear that
the party would not be taken into camp by bourgeois Moroccans
seeking to replace colonial exploitation by their own. Deploring
the resurgence of religion in the form of Salafiyya, and recalling
the historic treatment of Christian captives by the Moors, the
congress somewhat fatuously denounced the nationalists as clerical
and racist and warned against the extension, then under consideration, of the third college of the *Conseil de Gouvernement* to
immature and unreliable Moroccan politicians. Only a minority
of militant individuals on the extreme right and left of the party
were inclined to sympathize with the budding nationalist movement. The Federation's posture softened to a degree the following year when the more liberal Fez and Casablanca delegations
came out in support of the nationalists at the Marseille congress,
but the S.F.I.O. as a whole remained uneasy about the liaison.[35]

The Radical Socialists were equally uneasy. Their relations
with the Moroccans became very strained after 1932 when
Maghreb charged that the purpose of Premier Herriot's trip to

Spain in November, billed as a literary and artistic vacation, was in fact to negotiate with President Zamora for the extradition of 10,000 Moroccan rebels who had taken refuge in Rio de Oro. It was also reported that the *London Daily Herald* correspondent, Tom Beckett, was in possession of documentary evidence to the effect that Herriot had offered to exchange French possessions in the Orient for a large portion of Spanish Morocco,[36] an eventuality which would have given France a virtual monopoly in Morocco and have limited even more the opportunity of Moroccans to play off Paris against Madrid. Whatever the authenticity of the charges, the underlying suspicion which they reflected precluded total confidence between the Moroccans and the Radicals.

For their part, the Moroccans were far from eager to affiliate formally with these parties, although an invitation to join the S.F.I.O. was extended by Georges Monnet in 1933. Suspicious of the party leaders, the Moroccans reproached them for trying to lay hands on the nationalist movement for their own ends. The Moroccans declared that they did not wish to be assimilated by anybody, even by friends. Moreover, they had observed that the French Socialists residing in Morocco could be quite as determined as other *colons* when it came to defending their special privileges. And finally, one must recognize that some aspects of Socialist doctrine were not especially appealing to the Muslim mind, for neither the concept of the class struggle nor the underlying secularism of French Socialism proved very attractive to a people whose class consciousness was but a minor thread in the complex fabric of Islam and whose reformers started from a philosophical position closer to Luther than to Marx or even to the *philosophes*.[37] In the final analysis, the union of French Socialism with Moroccan nationalism seemed more like a marriage of convenience than of love, but though the two were often separated by differences of philosophy and temperament, they were never completely divorced.

Here it might be appropriate to comment briefly on the position of the Spanish Socialists vis-à-vis Morocco. The Spanish monarchy had been frankly reactionary to the end and had conceded nothing to the timorous Moroccan demands in spite of the republican threat. Accordingly, with the departure of Alfonso XIII in April 1931 and the adoption of the republican constitution in December, the Spanish zone nationalists had reason to hope for better things. At its thirteenth congress held in Madrid in October 1932, the Spanish Socialist Workers Party called for reforms in the Spanish protectorate, and the newly formed Radical Socialist Party, at its first congress, heard its delegate from Morocco, José Alberolda, urge the government to prepare the protectorate for full sovereignty. The Moroccan nationalists were surprised and embittered, however, when it became apparent that these proposals either referred exclusively to the sovereign rights of Spanish settlers in Morocco or were couched in terms which little accorded with the nationalists' demands. The proposals of the Spanish left during this period had an orientation towards reform quite different from that to be found two years later in the *Plan de Réformes* and reveal how little the former affected the latter.[38] A single preposterous incident clearly demonstrates the lack of mutual sympathy or even respect which prevailed between the Spanish republicans and the Moroccans. President Zamora, in his capacity as president of the Spanish Rotary Club, invited Abdesselam Bennouna, secretary of the Tetuan Lodge, to speak before a Madrid audience of republican deputies, journalists and others. Bennouna, a dignified, scholarly and aristocratic Tetuani, not given to hyperbole or histrionics, was pelted with eggs and tomatoes by the intellectuals of Spain. Zamora neither apologized nor reprimanded his impetuous colleagues, and suppressions followed Bennouna's return home.[39]

TOTALITARIANISM

Throughout most of the interwar period, the more ardent French nationalists found repeated occasions to exercise their literary talents on the machinations of "the enemies of France" in North Africa.[40] The editors of *L'Afrique Française* discerned a secret agent in every critic and were highly incensed at what they considered the lenient treatment accorded the "subversive press" by the colonial authorities. Of all these *bêtes noires*, the Communists were the special targets of outraged colonialists.[41]

According to *L'Afrique Française*, the Communist propaganda machine was focused on North Africa shortly after World War I to encourage it to rise against the French imperialists with the assurance that the French Communist Party would lend a helping hand. The journal's editorial staff informed its readers that the Étoile Nord-Africaine was a Communist organization in spite of protests to the contrary, that Communists had helped Messali Hadj found it in Paris, and that its upper echelon met there and distributed subversive tracts among the Muslim workers of the city, all of which was quite true.

It was further charged that the encouragement which Abd al-Krim received from Communists such as deputy Jacques Doriot (Seine) accounted for the stubborn opposition of the Moroccan leader, and the charge was given considerable scholarly support by Louis Jalabert, who in 1938 confirmed the suspicion that French Communists had, indeed, helped Messali, while pointing out that it was hardly unusual for French Socialists and Communists to take Algerian and Tunisian nationalists under their wing and to furnish them with the tools of propaganda and agitation.[42]

To what extent did these charges apply to Morocco? Jalabert's article is significant in that it deals exclusively with Algeria and Tunisia, and a close scrutiny of *L'Afrique Française* reveals that the bulk of the subversive activities enumerated took place in those two dependencies alone, to the virtual exclusion of Morocco. Moreover, in reading over the relatively objective official reports as well as other authoritative assessments of the Moroccan situation for the interwar period, one is struck by the almost total absence of allusions to Communist subversion.[43] One might conclude from this that colonial Cassandras had been exaggerating Communist influence in Morocco, but since the Moroccans themselves acknowledge it, we must make an effort to measure its character and extent.

Mohammed Lyazidi asserts that when the suppressions of 1930 obliged the nationalists to improve upon their necessarily clandestine organization, they fashioned it after the Communist model. To this end, Lyazidi, Allal al-Fassi and Mohammed Hassan al-Ouezzani studied the history and organization of the Communist movement and, more particularly, the statutes of the Parti Communiste Français in Arabic translation. Al-Ouezzani also attended P.C.F. meetings in Paris to learn its methods, and al-Fassi was in correspondence, around 1930, with Gim Argila and other Spanish, French and Algerian Communists as well as with Messali Hadj. This seems to have been about the extent of the liaison. No evidence has yet been brought to light that any of the prominent nationalists were in touch with Communist cells which were established in Casablanca in the late 1920's.

The question of the influence of Communist doctrine remains. *L'Humanité* was obtainable in Morocco during the interwar years despite the ban of May 1925 imposed for its advocacy of fraternization between French and Riffian soldiers. But neither was

there much fraternization nor were the early Salafiyyist reformers much taken in by the Communist line.[44] The Communist
gospel related only casually to the national aspirations and the
technological problems of the Arab peoples in the modern world
and was wholly incongruent with their culture and theology. In
North Africa neither Communism in general nor the concept of
the class war in particular struck congenial soil unless modified
almost beyond recognition. If Communism is a doctrine, Moroccan nationalism was its antithesis. Rarely could one meet two
Moroccans who agreed about the future shape of their country
or the route to independence. It is astonishing how few Communists or fellow travelers there were among the prewar nationalist leaders. Many of them had been attracted by Marxism as
students in Paris, but on their return to Morocco, nearly all
severed whatever affiliations they had contracted. What little
Communist influence there was on nationalist ideology appears
to have had its effect for but a short while after the crystallization
of the Popular Front in 1936.[45]

Moroccans were fully aware of all that Soviet Communism
implied and were willing to accept what it had to offer without
becoming bound by it. Many of them unquestionably shared
Shakib Arslan's sentiments:

> We have never defended the Bolshevists because they do not believe
> in liberty. But we have never felt obliged to fight them for crimes com-
> mitted by others.
> To profess the right of oppressed peoples to complete independence is
> most unpardonable to the pitiless imperialists. That the Communists
> profess this political doctrine out of systematic hatred for the capitalist
> regime in order to make that regime less powerful and less harmful, and
> not out of simple justice, is quite possible, is perhaps most likely, but in
> any case, on this ground, and on this ground only, we can only applaud
> the Bolshevists by reciting the verse of Abmotanabbi: "Sometimes you
> are obliged not to praise an actor, but to praise his act." [46]

We can safely conclude that the organizational techniques of
Communism attracted Moroccans who were obliged to operate
sub rosa, whereas the appeal of Communist ideology was rather
dilute.

Germany and Italy had fascinated Arab nationalists long before
the days of Hitler and Mussolini, for their unifications showed
what could be done to fabricate nationalities out of disparate

provincial loyalties. But the attraction of the strident dogmas of Nazism and Fascism, however powerful in the Middle East, was more limited in Morocco than is commonly assumed.

Moroccans had long nursed a fondness for Germany in her role as protector of Islam. They had retained a warm memory of the Kaiser's visit to Tangier in 1905, paid in an effort to outflank Delcassé's maneuvers, and had looked with approval on Langenheim's efforts to aid Abd al-Krim in the mid 1920's.[47] German intervention had a certain nuisance value in obstructing French and Spanish designs in Morocco, and as yet the Moroccans did not consider German imperialism a serious threat to Moroccan sovereignty. Accordingly, when Langenheim, resident in Tangier since 1905, brought the agitator, Karl Schlichting, to Tangier in 1932 for purposes quite obvious to the Comité du Maroc, most Moroccans failed to realize that they might be in danger of exchanging French whips for German scorpions in the very near future.

After the Nazi triumph of 1933, and especially after the rise of Franco, the German propaganda effort in Morocco moved into high gear, stressing the anti-Semitic theme to which Goebbels apparently thought Moroccans would be most responsive. An increasing volume of hate literature was deposited by German vessels on the quays of Ceuta and Las Palmas for Moroccan consumption, and Arab-speaking German agents such as Dr. Fritz Kern of Bonn University and his Algerian colleague, Takki eddin al-Hilali, a disciple of Shakib Arslan, infiltrated the French zone and established contact with Moroccan nationalists.[48] L'Afrique Française, of course, had much to say about Nazi provocation in North Africa. In December 1932, it reported the creation in Vienna of the "Islamischer Kulturbund"[49] by Shakib Arslan, and noted that among those attending the founding dinner were Mekki Naciri, Mohammed Hassan al-Ouezzani and Abdesselam Bennouna. The editors also alleged that trips made to Germany and Austria by Moroccans were financed by Herr Goebbels,[50] and while the charge was unsubstantiated there is little reason to doubt it.

After the Fez riots of October 1937, Ibrahim al-Ouezzani, brother of Mohammed Hassan, fled to Tetuan and founded there a pro-Nazi organization called the Bureau de Défense Nationaliste, and in the late 1930's and during the Second World War, he served rather indiscriminately as an agent for the Nazis, the

Italians and the Spanish.[51] As the ninth anniversary of the Berber *dahir* approached, *L'Azione Coloniale* published an utterly un-founded panegyric of al-Ouezzani as the leading nationalist leader at liberty,[52] part of a coordinated Axis propaganda effort which embraced Radio Bari, Radio Berlin, where Takki eddin al-Hilali launched a vicious attack on France, and the Spanish station at Alcazarquivir, where the Spanish high commissioner did what he could to assist Mekki Naciri, even to providing him with an official car.[53] Finally, it can be noted that Ahmed Balafrej spent much of his voluntary exile (1937-43) shuttling between Tangier and Germany, and that he, as well as Omar Abdeljalil and a num-ber of other nationalists from the French zone, happened to be in Tangier to welcome Franco in June 1940 when the city was occupied by Spanish forces.[54]

How shall this accumulation of uneven and conflicting evi-dence be appraised? As far as concerns the Islamischer Kultur-bund, the three Moroccans most prominently linked with it were never, after 1934, in the mainstream of the nationalist movement. M. H. al-Ouezzani's influence began to wane after the suppression of his journal, *L'Action du Peuple*, in May 1934 and the sub-sequent airing of his personal differences with Allal al-Fassi; Mekki Naciri fled the French zone for Tetuan in December 1934 and ceased thereafter to exert much influence except in the northern zones; and Abdesselam Bennouna, patriarch of nationalism in Tetuan, had always been somewhat outside the flow of activity in the French zone. Clearly, then, the Islamischer Kulturbund cannot be regarded as a primary factor. Secondly, if the tenets of National Socialism percolated into Morocco through men such as Ibrahim al-Ouezzani, they arrived too late to alter significantly the doctrinal foundations of nationalism, because what little there was of real collaboration with the Nazis occurred just before the outbreak of the war, long after the pattern of Moroccan nationalist ideology had become fairly well formulated. And Balafrej, how-ever useful he may have regarded collaboration, showed that he was fully aware of the risks involved and made known his hos-tility to Nazi ideology as early as 1934 in an article which ap-peared in *el-Hayat*.[55] Nor were the incitements of Radio Berlin and the others very effective, for they failed utterly to disturb the tranquillity of Morocco during the 1939 anniversary of the Ber-ber *dahir*, after the followers of Allal al-Fassi had counseled against demonstrations.[56]

As for the Nazi influence in general, which might have come — quite apart from any direct connection — from the simple existence of such a creed in the world or from the affinity felt for the "enemy of our enemy," it is quite true that from 1933 until well along in the war Moroccans regarded Hitler as a potential ally of Islam and were not much repelled by his anti-Semitism.[57] L'Afrique Française cites three clashes between Moroccan Muslims and Jews in 1933 (an anti-Jewish riot in Rabat on May 10, quelled after 150 arrests, and two disturbances in Alcazarquivir and Tangier on July 1) and interprets these as the reawakening of traditional Moorish Jew-baiting under the fine hand of foreign agents and young Moroccan nationalists. But the correspondent simultaneously acknowledged that the two disturbances in the north were provoked, respectively, by a Muslim and a Jew, each under the influence of alcohol, and that none but the Rabat riot amounted to anything; [58] — altogether a rather incongruous article. Nevertheless, the editor of the Survey of International Affairs, an otherwise reliable source for this period, concluded from these isolated cases that in the early 1930's a militant anti-Semitism had begun to emerge in Morocco. The Survey, indeed, concedes that the predisposition was less pronounced in Morocco and Tunisia than in Algeria where the old prejudice had been aggravated by the Jewish citizenship law of 1870.[59] But in searching L'Afrique Française from 1925 to 1939, the author discovered no other documented report of anti-Semitic activity. The least one can conclude from this is that the Nazis failed to provoke a full-blooded anti-Semitism in Morocco. In modern Morocco, anti-Semitism lay dormant until the French themselves once again revived it as official policy during the fortunately brief Vichy interlude.

A phenomenon related to, but distinct from, anti-Semitism — and one which had a greater impact on Morocco — was anti-Zionism. Rising spontaneously throughout the Arab world in the years following the establishment of the British mandate in Palestine, its repercussions began to be felt in Morocco about 1926. From 1929 on, Mohammed Lyazidi, Ahmed Balafrej and Ahmed Cherkaoui, among others, raised funds on occasion for the Palestinian Arabs, and photographs of the Islamic Conference of December 1931 were put on sale in Morocco for the same purpose. But while anti-Zionism aroused the sympathies of Morocco as anti-Semitism did not, it had very little if any direct bearing on the nationalist movement.[60] Provisions in the *Plan de Réformes* specifically accorded Jews full equality with Muslims in the new Morocco, a commitment made good when Dr. Léon Benzaquen, a French-educated Moroccan Jew, accepted the invitation to serve as minister of posts, telephone and telegraph in the first two independent Moroccan governments of 1956–58.

As could be expected, *L'Afrique Française* also warned of the baneful effects of Fascist propaganda among the colonists of Italian extraction in North Africa — propaganda which encouraged them to organize into *fascios* and to incite the native population against the French.[61] Radio Rome preached emancipation for France's North African dependencies, while Tripolitanian publications in Arabic, which penetrated the Maghreb by way of the Italian consulates, extolled the idyllic life of the Muslim population of Libya. Members of one Moroccan family prominent in nationalist circles, the Diouris, enjoyed Italian protection and made little effort to hide their Fascist sympathies. Indeed, the major nationalist organ during 1937, *L'Action Populaire*, was directed by Mohammed Diouri's wife and printed in Rabat at the Foch Press, which was run, it is said, by an Italian who was an influential member of the Fascist Party.[62]

But what evidence there is for Fascist influence on North African nationalism seems to be largely circumstantial and not very impressive. The fact was that the North Africans knew the score quite early. The Tunisians, observing the spectacle of Italian rule in neighboring Libya, knew what they would be up against if the Fascists came to power in French North Africa, and during the Fascist noise-making of 1938–39, most Tunisian nationalists rallied behind France.[63] The Moroccans were no less wary of the Fascist embrace. Ahmed Balafrej wrote as early as 1933:

. . . we know the real goals of Italy. She fights French imperialism simply to replace it with a Fascist imperialism a hundred times more dangerous. We can judge the Italians by their work in Tripolitania.[64]

One might well expect Fascist Spain to have influenced Moroccan nationalism, for Franco's initial blandishments were attractive indeed. It is well known that Moroccan warriors from the Spanish protectorate who joined Franco's rebellion were allowed to entertain hopes of self-government as their *quid pro quo*. Their hopes were short-lived, however, for in North Africa the chief result of Franco's victory was a torrent of press and radio propaganda emanating from Seville, Tetuan and Alcazarquivir, inviting Moroccans of the French zone to demand the liberties already enjoyed by their brothers north of the demarcation line. But the Moroccans in both zones soon awoke to the illusory nature of Franco's liberalism, and the star in the Iberian heaven dimmed as the Second World War approached. Even had Franco been able to exert a continuing influence, it would have been too late to have had much effect on Moroccan nationalist doctrines which, at the time of Franco's emergence, had already been well formulated for nearly two years.[65]

Axis activities aggravated the growing restiveness of the Moroccan nationalists by beguiling them with the illusion of great-power support and by the tempting, though entirely misleading, contrasts which were drawn between conditions in the French and Axis dependencies in North Africa. But any direct relationship between the two parties was opportunistic on both sides. Neither was in the least interested in the objectives of the other, and the Moroccans actively feared the consequences of a triumphant Axis, although both were desirous of exerting leverage on France. But from the moment their European confederates threatened to extend their regime to North Africa, the Moroccan nationalists backed away from the liaison. This occurred early in the case of Fascist Italy, a bit later with Falangist Spain, while the Germans managed to preserve good relations with the Moroccans until after 1940.

What, then, can be said in summary of the impact of the West? Ahmed Mekouar, with little French education and with adequate personal reasons for cordially detesting all things French, can claim that he was little affected by Western culture, while Mohammed Hassan al-Ouezzani, whose six years in Paris thoroughly Gallicized him, can assert that Western philosophies and techniques were the primary molders of Moroccan nationalism. Both judgments are extreme, but the latter seems to be more clearly demonstrated. Unquestionably the French-educated were powerfully attracted by Western ways, and by indirection, despite Mekouar's claim, most of the Muslim-educated were affected to one degree or another, Mekouar, himself having established direct contact with some of the friendly Socialists in Paris.

More specifically, we have noted the psychological impact of French education and Socialism. The former, whether received in Morocco or in France, had the effect of aggravating existing grievances by raising expectations which inevitably were thwarted when the student left school and by causing cultural and psychological disorientations which divided families and often plagued the victim for the rest of his life. It would be curious if a university education, especially in France, did not endow its recipient with a measure of self-confidence and momentum as well, but this is extremely hard to assess, and the Moroccans interviewed were more inclined to credit that sense of mission and of personal importance, so vital to every reformer, to their Socialist associations than to their education.

In the most general ideological sense, French education opened to Moroccans a new world of ideas as well as exposing them to a variety of other influences. From Socialism they received a rationalized anti-colonialism which before had been little more than inarticulate emotion, and from the broad spectrum of the liberal and republican traditions they derived notions of equality and justice, freedom of expression and association, and an understanding of the concept of the *patrie* and of the vital importance of a system of national education. More specific doctrines are traceable to the same sources: labor and public welfare reforms, especially the former, from French Socialism, and their conceptions of administration, parliamentary procedure, elections and judicial methods from their observation of the liberal institutions of France, however imperfectly these may have operated in the interests of Moroccans.

Finally, all sources of Western influence had a noticeable effect on the nationalists' tactics. It was in French schools and universities that they learned the arts of mental discipline, organization and verbal expression. From the Socialists they learned how to conduct meetings, plan demonstrations, organize propaganda campaigns and present their demands, and their terminology was an amalgam of Montesquieu, Voltaire, Rousseau, Saint-Simon and Jaurès, none of whom, it should be noted, was representative of the extreme wings of French political philosophy. Not its dogma, but only the organizational structure of the Communist Party did they find useful.

PART FOUR

THE RISE OF MODERN NATIONALISM: 1921–1944

IX

THE DECADE OF GESTATION: 1921–1930

The Moroccan Salafiyyists became convinced, during and after World War I, that a system of modern Islamic education was essential for the rejuvenation of the Moorish people. In this way, Salafiyya became the source of the free-school movement and, thereby, by derivation, the wellspring of Moroccan nationalism.

THE FREE SCHOOLS

The free schools were so called not because there was no charge — there was, in fact, a modest tuition (7 to 15 francs per month, depending on family resources) — but because they were the only elementary schools in Morocco to furnish a modern education free from state control. The first school was opened in Fez, the Athens of Morocco, and there, also, the movement reached its fullest development. The Sidi Bennani school was founded in 1921 [1] by Ahmed Mekouar and was directed by him until taken over by Abdelaziz Bendriss from 1934 to 1944. It was later renamed Benkirane, after a benefactor, and now comprises seven branches, of which one operates as a *collège*. The an-Najah school was founded later in 1921 by Mohammed Lahlou, but its direction was relinquished the next year to Ahmed Mekouar and in 1934 to Hachemi al-Filali. The Naciriya school, so called because it met in a *zawiya* (religious sanctuary or headquarters) once belonging to the religious brotherhood of that name, became the most famous of the schools owing to the difficulties its director, Mohammed Ghazi, encountered with the French authorities. Founded in 1921 or 1922, it was closed down in 1927 when Ghazi was exiled to Casablanca for articles contributed to the Algerian reformist journal, *ech-Chihab*. During its last two or three years of operation, Mokhtar Soussi, Allal al-Fassi, Ibrahim al-Kittani and Mohammed al-Korri taught there — a veritable nest of proto-nationalists. Shortly after this the al-Mounia and Zawiya Charradiyya schools were founded, and four more were opened in the next decade, so that by 1935 there were nine such schools in Fez.[2]

In Rabat both the Arrakiya school, founded by Seddik Cheddadi, and the Wazahra school, founded by a group of wealthy citizens who put Fatmi Bargach in charge, opened their doors in 1921 or 1922. A third, financed by another group of Rabati notables and directed by Ahmed al-Moudden, opened in 1924 or before, and the al-Hayat school was founded about the same time.[3]

Elsewhere the movement was slow in starting. For a number of years Casablanca had only a single school, the Lalla Taja, founded in the early 1920's apparently at the instigation of the Shaykh al-Dukkali himself.[4] In Tetuan, the Ahliyah school was founded at the end of 1924, and in all likelihood there were two or three in Marrakesh at this time, as well as one in Salé, in Kénitra and in Sidi Kacem.[5]

Prior to 1935 the free schools were tolerated but not legally authorized. The basic law pertaining to private schools was the *dahir* of October 14, 1919, which provided for foreign schools like that opened by the Italians in Casablanca in 1920. The law established a scale of penalties for failure to obtain a permit or refusal to allow periodic inspections, and also made the teaching of French obligatory.[6] The free schools, unable to qualify on two counts — they were not "foreign" and their directors were hostile to instruction in French — were able to evade the regulations only by setting up as "Koranic" schools.[7] But the *dahir* of April 1, 1935 [8] changed all this, and a great expansion of the free-school movement ensued under the new dispensation. Within two years there were twenty institutions in Fez alone, enrolling 1,500 students,[9] and country-wide enrollment totaled 5,000 as compared to about 20,000 in the government schools.[10] The free schools unquestionably did much good by making it possible for Moroccan children to receive a relatively modern education in keeping with Muslim traditions. Perhaps they did much harm by misleading young Moroccans into overestimating the adaptability of their native culture to the modern world without drastic alterations.

Programs and Purpose

The free schools were customarily referred to in French as *msids renovées*, the first word being the Moroccan term for a Koranic school, the second implying the revival of traditional Muslim education as it was at its best. Actually, the word *renovée* is somewhat misleading, for the free schools inclined toward the Salafiyyist ideal and were traditional only to the extent that Salafiyya embraced selected elements of Islamic tradition. Their curricula could more accurately be styled "modern Islamic" and comprised Koranic studies (the catechism and memorization of the Koran) taught, of course, from the Salafiyyist standpoint, as well as Arabic grammar, writing and logic, ethics and the life of the Prophet, Islamic history and geography, and arithmetic, of which only the last was offered by the protectorate schools. The sciences were not taught in the lower grades and were often missing in the upper grades as well, owing to the expense of facilities and the shortage of trained teachers. Because it was difficult for an Arabic press to operate freely for any length of time, most of the textbooks came from Egypt or Lebanon.[11]

One of the major aims of the free-school movement was to counteract the denigration of Moroccan history as taught in the government schools. No one could deny that the *élan* of Islamic society as a whole had faltered in recent centuries, but what humiliated the Moroccans was the contention that their own corner of Islam, whose independence was for so long and so vigorously maintained at a level of culture at times superior to that of Europe, had deteriorated so conspicuously by the twentieth century that a foreign protectorate was the only realistic solution to its problems. That this was essentially the case was most inconvenient for the free-school enthusiasts, and the curriculum which they established sought to offset the demoralization this had caused by directing attention to the earlier glories of the Moorish civilization of Andalusia, which was thoroughly justified, and by depicting Morocco in 1912 as a modern state, which was pure fabrication. Pursuant to this fiction, it was held that the early twentieth-century sultanate had become a representative, constitutional monarchy served by a cabinet of ministers and a fully articulated local administration in the European style, that an atmosphere of progressive reformism prevailed, and that there was no justification for the protectorate which had been imposed by force of arms.[12] The minute element of truth in this rendered it all the more plausible to the Moorish patriot, for the French occupation was attended by a good deal of fighting. But in order to accept the whole myth, one had to suppress the fact that the Arab fraction of the population, especially those who were then trying to promote this rewriting of history, was the very fraction, one generation removed, which had welcomed the peace and security provided by the French army after 1907, the Berber mountaineers almost alone having resisted the French occupation until their final defeat in 1934. Subversive information such as this was carefully overlooked in the history classes of the free schools.

POLITICAL ORIENTATION

Despite this growing bias in free-school instruction, the men at first responsible for the schools were neither resolutely anti-French nor consciously nationalistic. Their intellectual focus was Salafiyya, their objective a cultural revival, and at this early date no other influences are discernible except an understandably latent hostility to foreign rule.

What these men sought was to offer their countrymen an alternative to assimilation: the vision of a modernized Islamic society which, they were supremely confident, could compete with and ultimately drive out the undesirable elements of European culture introduced by France. What eventually hardened them against the French were the Residency's Berber policy, its opportunistic support of the reactionary elements in Moroccan society, and the secular curriculum in the government schools which gave short shrift to Arabic language, literature and history — all of these policies being equally repugnant to the Salafiyyists.[13]

From this position to a conscious nationalism was no great distance. When the first secret societies which can be called "nationalist" were founded in Fez, Rabat and Tetuan in 1925 and 1926, they absorbed the free-school movement, and the attempt to counteract the teaching of history in the French schools, originally intended to restore cultural identity, was transformed into a propaganda effort with a frankly political end in view. Many of the founders and directors as well as some of the teachers of the first free schools became prominent nationalists in these years. The first secret society to be founded was composed entirely of teachers at the Naciriya school in Fez: Mohammed Ghazi, the director, Mokhtar Soussi, Allal al-Fassi and Ibrahim al-Kittani. Abdelaziz Bendriss and Hachemi al-Filali, who in 1934 took over from Mekouar the Sidi Bennani and an-Najah schools, respectively, had become members of the Fez society shortly after its inception, and Mekouar himself, long sympathetic with its aims, officially joined the national movement in 1930 and rose rapidly to top leadership.[14] In Rabat, Ahmed al-Moudden was one of the early members of the secret society founded by Ahmed

Balafrej. Ahmed Cherkaoui founded a free school in 1927 and joined the nationalist movement about 1933, becoming number-three man in Rabat. Balafrej, outranked in the nationalist hierarchy only by Allal al-Fassi, founded his own school in 1934, naming it the Institution Mohammed Guessous after his wealthy uncle and benefactor. In Tetuan, the three most prominent of the eight teachers at the Ahliyah school, Abdesselam and M'Hammed Bennouna and Mohammed Daoud, who also served as directors of the school, comprised the core of the secret society established there in 1926, and one of the early graduates, Abdelkhalek Torrès, later founded the Islah (Reform) Party.[15]

The second generation of nationalists, who rose to positions of leadership after World War II, learned their political catechism in the free schools, and for this reason the schools are often regarded as the cradle of Moroccan nationalism. But of the first generation of nationalists, only Hassan Bouayad, Hachemi al-Filali and Mekki Naciri knew these schools as students rather than teachers. For most of that older generation, the free school was an instrument — the first effective instrument which Moroccans had devised to resist the onslaught of European civilization.

THE SECRET SOCIETIES

The autumn of 1925 was a turning point in the Moroccan reform movement. It was a lively season for the Middle East. The Druze rebellion in Lebanon had begun that summer. September witnessed the suppression of the religious orders by Kemal's government in Turkey, the demand by the Indian nationalists for a series of round-table conferences looking towards responsible government, and in Morocco, the climax of the Riffian rebellion and the resignation of Lyautey. October saw the great proconsul's replacement by the civilian, Théodore Steeg, and the forty-eight hour bombardment of Damascus. But the event which more than any other jolted the Salafiyyist reformers out of their narrow cultural preoccupations and initiated their conversion to conscious nationalism was the entry of France into the Riff War. Pétain's offensive against Abd al-Krim opened in September. By October the last bright hope of Moroccan freedom was in full retreat. In November the first secret society was founded in Fez.[16]

Lyautey's replacement by a functionary of the Third Republic was, as it turned out, prophetic of the shift from "protectionism" to an all but overt colonialism. And while the young proto-nationalists were innocent of this perspective in 1925, the evolution of their secret societies from a cultural to a political orientation during the half-dozen years which followed showed that they were intuitively aware of this tendency at work within the Residency and among the French colonists.

FOUNDATION

The founders of the Fez society were Allal al-Fassi, president, Ibrahim al-Kittani, vice-president, Mokhtar Soussi and Mohammed Ghazi. They were soon joined by Abdelaziz Bendriss, Hachemi al-Filali and Bouchta Jamai, all of whom became prominent in the nationalist movement, and by Mohammed al-Fersiwi and Ahmed Medkouri, who did not. Hassan Bouayad, who became one of the foremost leaders, joined the group sometime before 1930. All were then students at Qarawiyin, except Ghazi and Soussi who had graduated a few years before. Almost simultaneously another group was forming in Fez comprising Mohammed Diouri, Mohammed al-Fassi, Abdelkader Benjelloun, Mohammed al-Kholti and Thami al-Ouezzani, all in process of receiving a French secondary education at the Collège Moulay Idriss. The two groups were linked almost immediately by Mohammed bel-Arabi al-Alaoui whose Salafiyyist preaching and activities had attracted members of both.[17]

The Fez society sported neither name nor organization, partly because security lay in anonymity and partly because neither the purposes nor the techniques of organization, in the occidental sense, were clearly understood by its members. The oath of secrecy, which was sworn on the Koran, reflected a clandestinity more oriental than European in character. The society continued to function until 1931, though depleted somewhat by the departure in 1926 of all the *collège* contingent except Diouri for one or another *lycée* in Paris, by Ghazi's exile to Casablanca in 1927, and by Soussi's voluntary exile to Marrakesh about the same time.[18]

In August 1926 the nucleus of a second society began to meet in Rabat, partly on the instigation of M'Hammed Bennouna of Tetuan who had recently returned from Egypt full of the activities of Zaghlul.[19] Its leading members, Ahmed Balafrej,

Mohammed Hassan al-Ouezzani, Omar Abdeljalil, Mohammed Lyazidi, Abdelkebir al-Fassi and Abdelkader Tazi, had all received, or were in process of receiving, a Western education. Also prominent were Mekki Naciri, then attending a free school, and his brother Mohammed Naciri and Mohammed ben Abbès Kabbaj, both receiving a traditional Muslim education. Four other founders who took no active part in the later movement and who were traditionally educated were Omar Kabbaj, Mohammed ben Mohammed Kabbaj, Abou Bakr Bennani and Ahmed al-Moudden, the free-school director.[20] Like that of Fez, the Rabat society had neither an organization nor a formal name, although its members sometimes referred to themselves collectively as *muslihin* (reformers).[21] It customarily met twice a week on Wednesday and Friday evenings, often in the homes of Ahmed Balafrej or Mohammed ben Mohammed Kabbaj. It seems to have been the most active of the early societies and in time came to be regarded as the "mother club"[22] in the tradition of the "mother *zawiyas*" of the religious brotherhoods.

While the Rabat and Fez societies were founded independently, they established contact within the year, a fact documented in the introduction to a book published by Mohammed Naciri in December 1926,[23] wherein members from both the societies are listed together as a reform group (*hizb al-islah*).[24] The significance of this liaison should not be exaggerated, for contact was not continuous throughout the period 1925–30, but, nevertheless, a link had been forged which grew in strength and efficacy.[25]

A third society was founded in Tetuan in 1926 by Abdesselam Bennouna and Mohammed Daoud and included M'Hammed Bennouna, Ahmed Ghilane and Mohammed Tnana, as well as four others who soon became inactive: Mohammed Moudden, Mohammed Nabkout, Mohammed ben Mohammed Ouezzani and Mohammed Zowak. All had received a traditional education except the youngest, M'Hammed Bennouna, who was then attending the Egyptian University in Cairo. The group met on Wednesday nights; its program, typically Moroccan, consisted of mint tea before dinner, a session of music after dinner and finally, a discussion. Fifteen or twenty usually attended, mostly Tetuanis, but occasionally a visitor from the French zone was included.[26]

Moroccans differ over the relationship of the Tetuan society to the others in these early years, some regarding it as a branch of the Rabat group, others as a branch of Fez. Abdesselam Bennouna and Daoud had both attended Qarawiyin and undoubtedly had connections there, but Daoud had graduated in 1924 and Bennouna even earlier, and neither was particularly impressed by the Salafiyyist doctrines of Bel-Arabi.[27] On the other hand, M'Hammed Bennouna had attended and made the major address at the founding meeting of the Rabat group in August 1926. But what the formal relationship was probably makes very little difference, for contact between Tetuan and the French zone was intermittent at best.[28]

The branch established in Tangier in January 1927 by Abdullah Guennoun, with the advice and counsel of M'Hammed Bennouna and Mohammed Daoud, was never more than an agency of the other societies. At first it was under the influence of Tetuan but later maintained a closer contact with the French zone and served as a relay station to Spain when it became politic for leading nationalists to absent themselves for the time being from Morocco. Besides Guennoun, it comprised three other members who were not especially prominent in the nationalist movement as it developed: Mokhtar Ahardan, Mohammed Boudakka and Mohammed Haddad.[29]

ACTIVITIES

In spite of their independent inception, all the societies were agreed on a common purpose: to create a current of reformist thought by propagating the modern Islamic ideologies of the Middle East among the intellectuals of the principal cities of Morocco.[30] In the French zone, though not in Tetuan,[31] the dominating spirit of Salafiyya led the reformers to focus their attention on the destruction of the worst of the religious brotherhoods by dispelling the ignorance and superstition on which they bred.[32] For this reason, the vitality and continuation of the free schools was regarded as of paramount importance, and many of the nationalists were involved in that effort.

Another public service to which these young men devoted themselves was the foundation and operation of *maisons de bienfaisance*, privately supported institutions whose purpose was no less ambitious than the abolition of the eternal beggar from the streets of Morocco by putting him to some useful task in what amounted to workshops. By 1927 there were three hundred inmates in the Rabat *maison* and over five hundred in each of the two *maisons* in Fez.[33]

That this period was one of transition from religious reform and cultural nationalism to political nationalism is demonstrated by an examination of the other major activities of the secret societies: group readings and discussion, "churning" the countryside, press propaganda, and cooperation with the Association of North African Muslim Students.

The societies began as discussion groups, essentially. They customarily met in private homes (often at Bel-Arabi's in Fez) where the members read aloud passages from books and newspapers emanating chiefly from Algeria, Tunisia, Egypt and Syria. Topics were then assigned for reports to be given at the next meeting, to be followed by discussion. Copies of the reports were sometimes forwarded to Tetuan which kept in sporadic touch with the French zone. It is difficult, and probably not very important, to determine whether religious, cultural or political topics first dominated the discussions, for there is evidence of all three, and the most that can be said with certainty is that the range of subjects was wide. Owing to the members' philosophical background, the doctrines of Djamal al-Din, Abduh and Rida loomed large in their talks, and Salafiyyist publications, along with others, were purchased and passed around among themselves and their student colleagues.[34] Even before the collapse of the Riff rebellion, however, their attention began to shift to more secular and political matters. Foreign newspapers entering Morocco, legally and otherwise, carried the news of Pétain's offensive mounted in the autumn of 1925 and of the impending Riffian disaster early in 1926, as well as accounts of the Tunisian Destour and of Saad Zaghlul's activities in Egypt. The grievances created by the French regime in Morocco and the administrative organization of that regime also became matters for discussion, as did the history and literature of the Arab world, the interest value of which was enhanced by virtue of their proscription in the public schools operated by the Residency.[35] Starting as simplistic Salafiyyists, the Moroccans were beginning to understand the complexity of their world and to be caught up in the diversity of forces which were to shape their national movement.

"Churning" the countryside, to use Ibrahim al-Kittani's phrase, was an activity of the societies which resulted from more or less fortuitous circumstances. Within two years of the formation of the Fez group, Mohammed Ghazi was exiled briefly to Meknes for articles which appeared in *ech-Chihab*, and then to Casablanca where he carried on among the young intellectuals the proselytizing begun in Fez. Shortly thereafter, Mokhtar Soussi thought it prudent to leave Fez for similar reasons and moved to Marrakesh where he undertook the same missionary role as Ghazi; Bouchta Jamai's exile to Oujda in 1930 similarly helped to spread the word. Soon the intelligentsia of the foremost cities of the country was being agitated by reformist ideas, so that by 1930 it was prepared to respond as it did to the Berber *dahir*.[36]

Another propaganda medium could not fail to suggest itself, for Moroccans are inveterate thespians, and it was only natural that they should hit upon theatrical performances as an effective means of arousing the country. Troupes were formed in Fez, Rabat and Salé, the latter two being managed by Mohammed Lyazidi and Abdellatif Sbihi, respectively. The score or so members of the Rabat troupe presented on Saturday evenings plays such as *Saladin*, portraying the struggle against the Crusaders, and Mustafa Kamil's *The Conquest of Spain*, both of which typified the anti-Western character of the repertoire. The players frequently took advantage of their captive audiences to speak out for reform, especially educational reform, and during their years of greatest activity from 1927 to 1929, they customarily dedicated their proceeds to the free schools or to the support of students in Paris.[37]

The use of the press for propaganda purposes at this time had not progressed beyond its initial stages. In Fez, Allal al-Fassi is supposed to have published *Oum el-Bennin* (see page 55 above), but apparently not a single copy has survived. Unquestionably of more consequence were the articles contributed to the organ of the reformed Algerian *ulama*, *ech-Chihab*, by Allal al-Fassi, Mohammed Ghazi, Mokhtar Soussi and Mohammed and Mekki Naciri, all members of the Rabat or Fez societies. These articles dealt with the same topics which arose in the discussion groups — religious reform, the protectorate administration, Arabic history and literature — and were read throughout Morocco. Finally, it may be recalled that Mohammed Lyazidi, at least, was contributing pieces critical of the Residency to the Casablanca Socialist daily, *Le Cri Marocain*, as early as 1925 or 1926.[38] These were small but significant preambles to the ambitious press campaigns of the next decade.

With the exception of the free schools, possibly the most productive effort to which the early North African nationalists lent themselves was the formation of the A.E.M.N.A. in Paris, sometime between January and June of 1927. Its prime movers among the Moroccans were Ahmed Balafrej, also its first secretary, and Mohammed al-Fassi; both were attending Parisian *lycées* at the time. Other Moroccan founders were Mohammed Hassan al-Ouezzani, Abdelmalek Faraj, Mohammed al-Kholti, Thami al-Ouezzani, Madani Mekouar (Ahmed's brother), also in Parisian schools, and Omar Abdeljalil who visited France several times during the priod 1927–29. Its first president was the Tunisian, Salem Chadli.[39] Tunisian students had been in Paris for many years before the first Moroccan appeared, but since there had been very few Algerians, there was little reason for the existence of a pan-Maghrebian students' association. But even after the arrival of the Moroccans justified one, it appears that they, rather than the more numerous and experienced Tunisians, took the initiative in founding it. While no direct control was exercised over the Association by the North African nationalist groups, there was overlapping membership and close collaboration between the two, as well as with the alumni associations of the two Moroccan *collèges*, Moulay Idriss in Fez and Moulay Youssef in Rabat.[40]

The original purpose of the A.E.M.N.A. was to help North African students in Paris to obtain adequate rooming and boarding facilities and financial aid, but it soon concerned itself with the educational facilities available to Muslims in North Africa. Since educational and political policies were closely linked in the French colonial world, however, the Association inevitably found itself embroiled with the two protectorate regimes in North Africa and branded as a nationalist organization, which, of course, it was.[41] It was not long, in fact, before the political activities of the Association began to outstrip all others. Its headquarters on the Left Bank, free of the restrictions imposed in Tunis or Rabat or Fez, was an ideal rendezvous, and its greatest contribution undoubtedly was the opportunity it provided North African nationalists to exchange ideas and to encourage one another. It served as a mutual admiration society at a time when colonial nationalism was admired by very few. Its members studied and discussed nationalism, reform and independence, recruited new members, maintained contacts with interested parties in France and at home, including French journalists as well as other students from the Levant, and published an annual bulletin for several years after 1931 containing chiefly the *procès verbaux* of its yearly congresses.[42] Apparently it was a time-consuming activity.

Beginning in 1931, the Association held, or tried to hold, annual congresses in Tunis, Algiers, Fez and elsewhere. Educational items dominated the published agenda, but of course politics was in the air, and the congresses deepened the sense of pan-Maghrebian identity which had emerged since 1927 and furnished a clearinghouse for consideration of problems and grievances common to both protectorates.[43] And once the Association reached outside Paris to North Africa, its sense of solidarity was heightened and its political tendencies intensified by the inclusion of members who had not the least personal connection with the educational system of France. Such were Abdelhadi Chraibi and Ibrahim al-Kittani, Moroccan delegates to the congresses of 1932 and 1935, respectively.[44]

NATURE OF THE NATIONALIST MOVEMENT: 1925–1930

Having reviewed its various activities, how might one characterize the incipient, proto-nationalist movement of this era? That Salafiyya remained its firm foundation is convincingly demonstrated. Correspondence still available for 1927 finds the Rabatis urging upon Mohammed Daoud in Tetuan the importance of adhering to the spirit of Salafiyya.[45] And in 1925 Mekki Naciri published a polemic in the Salafiyyist vein, based on the writings of Abou Ishaq al-Shattibi, which attacked certain of the religious brotherhoods.[46] The shaykh of the Cherkawiya brotherhood replied to the attack with an insulting book entitled *Inkisar*, which in turn elicited the response, mentioned earlier, from Mekki Naciri's brother, Mohammed, defending the rites of the Naciriya brotherhood as being in accord with Salafiyyist doctrines but assailing the heterodoxy and deviations of the Cherkawiyyin. Neither of the two Naciri books would be regarded as "nationalistic" today; neither would be considered an attack on the policies of the Residency except by the broadest implication. Their significance lies in the fact that they document the primarily cultural, even religious, orientation of early Moroccan nationalism,[47] an orientation paralleled by early manifestations of European nationalism such as the sixteenth-century German Reformation or nineteenth-century German and Italian Romanticism.

We can also trace the influence of Salafiyya in the free-school movement, taken over by the nationalists after 1925, and in the likelihood that religious and cultural reform was initially the chief topic of the group discussions of the secret societies. Mohammed Ghazi and Mokhtar Soussi, who espoused Salafiyya more ardently if anything than the other founders of the Fez society, helped to establish the character and direction of the national reform movement in the third and fourth cities of Morocco, Marrakesh and Casablanca.[48] The educational interests of the theatrical troupes which toured the country also reflected a central point of Salafiyyist doctrine. And finally, Allal al-Fassi's clandestine sheet, *Oum el-Bennin*, was largely concerned with religious and educational reform, while the articles on religious reform published in *ech-Chihab* received wide circulation among Moroccan intellectuals who were interested in what the Salafiyyist *ulama* of Algeria had to say.

Nuseibeh's charge that the Arab world is guilty of "cultural inanity" in failing to decide where religion fits, or does not fit, in political life may apply to the rest of the Middle East but probably does not to Morocco, where a conscious effort was made to synthesize religious and political reform as inseparable aspects of the same goal — the modernization of Islam.[49] The Moroccans held that some of the most serious social problems of modern Europe could be traced to the separation of church and state, which should be avoided in Morocco, but this does not mean that they argued for the domination of the latter by the former. The prospects for a theocracy are, in fact, far less likely in Islam today than they were in medieval Islam or even in ante-Enlightenment Christendom, because the evolution of an organized Islamic "church" has not kept pace with the perfection of political parties and governmental administrations. All the Moroccans meant to say was that reformed religion and reformed politics were to be equally important parts of a revived Moroccan culture and society. And this position was not so unrealistic as it might appear at first glance, for the possibility of achieving such a symbiosis was far greater in Morocco, where the sultan traditionally exercised the duties of the caliph and continued in the twentieth century to act with universal approval as both spiritual and temporal head of his people, than it was further east where the dynasts had nearly everywhere lost their spiritual inheritance and prestige by the end of World War I, if not long before. Accordingly, in a society where secularism had failed to make the

inroads it had made further east, Salafiyya remained the under-
pinning of nationalism, indeed its dominant attribute until at least
1930, and never ceased to be a potent if secondary factor thereafter.

The decline of the religious brotherhoods was both a result and
a cause of this. Whereas in 1920 the adult male population of the
country was almost universally enrolled in the brotherhoods, their
identification with Residency intrigues soon called contumely
down on them, and in each succeeding political crisis, whenever
they aligned themselves with Residency policy, they lost a portion
of their remaining credit. As their appeal declined, that of
Salafiyya rose proportionately, making the heterodoxy and
reaction of the brotherhoods even less attractive, so that they lost
heavily in membership in the decade prior to World War II.
The Vichy regime tried vainly to revive them during the war as
a counterweight to pro-Allied sympathies, and their involvement
in the popular sultan's exile in 1953 destroyed the vestiges of their
political power.[50]

Thus the significance of Salafiyya in Morocco was twofold:
its fundamental dissonance with the official policy of assimilation
in general, and with the Berber policy and official collaboration
with the brotherhoods in particular, made its active opposition to
French rule inevitable, while at the same time it caused the
nationalist movement, thus derived, to be linked tightly to the
Islamic religion quite unlike most other Middle Eastern nationalisms.

But the gradual consolidation of their position, in their own
minds, at least, awakened the young reformers to new considerations: the host of grievances against French rule, which they
now began more deliberately to add up, as well as the more
secular ideas of the East and West, which in the latter part of the
decade began to flow more freely into Morocco. Moreover,
France's intervention in the Riff War and Pétain's first offensive
in September 1925 came as a profound shock to the young
Moroccan idealists. And when the second offensive of May 1926
resulted in the total collapse of the Riffian "Republic," the patent
folly of armed resistance persuaded the secret societies to accept
for the time being the *fait accompli* of the protectorate and to
seek reform by more pacific, political means, there being no
alternative at their disposal. Thus the immediate effect of the
Riffian surrender was not to eliminate resistance but to transfer it

from the military to the political front [51] and hence, into the hands of the reformers who would soon begin to talk in terms of "nationalistic union," of the need to unify "confused Arabs and Berbers who have nothing in common but their religion," and even of eventual independence, although they had in mind no program at all save the education given in the free schools. [52]

This did not mean that Salafiyya was overthrown. On the contrary, it came to be recognized as an instrument admirably suited to the new character of the resistance movement, for it now acquired a tactical value over and above its substantive appeal by enabling the nationalists to attack Residency policies from a religious position immune from reprisal, owing to the customary abstention of the French authorities from intervention in native religious affairs. Henceforth, the religious and political aspects of Moroccan nationalism were even more closely intertwined. [53]

But apart from its tremendous inspirational power and a few specific notions about judicial and educational reform which could be derived from it, the philosophy of Salafiyya had proved too abstract to furnish practical solutions in the new circumstances, and during 1925–30 the reformers began slowly to turn to other sources of inspiration. The internal grievances caused by French rule were now becoming significant enough to be a subject of concern for the secret societies and the A.E.M.N.A., an object of propaganda for the theatrical troupes, and the substance of articles in *ech-Chihab* and *Le Cri Marocain*. Specifically, we can identify a reaction against economic assimilation in the articles on colonization which appeared in *Oum el-Bennin*. And civil discrimination against Moroccans, in the form of press censorship and the prohibition of public meetings, was beginning to react on nationalist tactics in three ways: it called for clandestine operations, it made Salafiyya even more valuable as a base of operations, and it led to the establishment of the first propaganda organization in France rather than at home (see Chapter XII).

Western influences are hardly visible at this early date. One could be persuaded of the appeal of Socialism as early as 1925 in the airing of nationalist grievances in *Le Cri Marocain*, but more likely this was sheer opportunism on the part of both parties. The prestige of the S.F.I.O. was still very tenuous in Morocco, for the Casablanca section was not even founded until shortly before 1930, and none but exploratory contacts had yet been made between Moroccans and Socialists in France. Furthermore, the Moroccan Communist Party, which was to originate within the fold of the Casablanca section of the S.F.I.O., would not materialize until the eve of World War II. As to French education, by 1925 only three members of the secret societies had reached the university level and only seven more the secondary. During the years 1925–30 most of these young men were primarily occupied with their studies, and the ideas of the Enlightenment and the French Revolution were not yet reflected in their activities or their publications. Much the same can be said of French governmental institutions. The administrative machinery of the protectorate had indeed come to the attention of the nationalists and was discussed with interest in the meetings of the secret societies but without concrete result. Those who were visiting parliamentary and court sessions in Paris, of course, would bring their observations home with them, but only after the termination of their studies.

To identify other influences before 1930 would be premature. It is true that the ideas of the Arab renaissance, in general, and the activities and writings of the Turkish, Egyptian, Syrian and Tunisian nationalists, in particular, were read and discussed from the middle of the decade onward, but they were not echoed in the publications or activities of the Moroccan nationalists before 1930. The Moroccans were mulling them over but had not yet reached any conclusions.

How "national" was the reform movement before 1930? The author of a monographic work is always in jeopardy of over-pleading his case; hence, the safest position to take at this juncture, and probably the most accurate, is to acknowledge that the Moroccan nationalist movement amounted to very little before 1930. The nuclei of cells had been implanted in most of the major cities, but with the notable exception of the A.E.M.N.A., which as yet had few tangible victories to its credit on the political side, Moroccan nationalism in 1930 was characterized by little formal organization, no program of political or administrative reform, the inconclusive discussion of ideas, and some tentative propaganda efforts.[54] Furthermore, there was very little unity or even unanimity of purpose among the three societies of Fez, Rabat and Tetuan, which were never closely or continually in touch before 1930. This was especially true as regards Tetuan, which formed a sort of eddy in the nationalist current, and where the reform spirit had been relatively secular from the start.

Neither Abdesselam Bennouna nor Mohammed Daoud had been particularly attracted by Salafiyya, which they felt would sow dissention within the ranks of the reformers, many of whom in the Spanish zone still clung to membership in the religious brotherhoods.[55] Daoud himself belonged (and still belongs) to the Tijaniyya order and repeatedly sought to moderate the appeal to Salafiyya being made by his colleagues in the French zone.[56] And it was typical of Bennouna that the secularization of the Turkish state never soured his admiration for Kemal as it did that of the nationalists of Fez and Rabat.[57] Hence, because Salafiyya played so strong a role in the French zone, this difference in attitude constituted a serious qualification to the truly "national" character of the movement and an impediment to real unity of action and organization. Very early, certainly as early as 1927, the Tetuani nationalists began to drift apart from the mainstream of the movement. Nevertheless, contact between all the societies had been established very early, and spasmodic as they may have been, the attempts made to coordinate their efforts from 1926 onward led to a noticeable similarity in activities and objectives which at the very least can be termed "proto-national."

X

THE CAMPAIGN AGAINST THE BERBER POLICY: 1930–1931

By 1930 the reduction of Morocco to Sharifian authority was complete, save for a few tribes entrenched in their eyries at the western extremities of the Atlas. But Morocco did not lack disruptive forces, for drought and locusts plagued North Africa in 1930, and the onset of the Great Depression roiled the political climate of the Maghreb for the next several years. The forces of nature and the declining demand for phosphates caused farmers and miners to seek refuge desperately — where there was none to be found — with friends and relatives who had migrated to Casablanca or Algiers or Tunis. Thus was compounded the economic misery which in these years provoked outbreaks of anti-Semitism in Algeria, exacerbated the cemetery issue in Tunisia, and kindled in Morocco a discontent which boded ill for the hot summer months to come.

THE BERBER DAHIR

Under these storm clouds the youthful sultan of Morocco, on May 16, 1930, signed into law the *dahir* (see Chapter IV) whose import apparently escaped him but which was intended to curtail sharply his authority over the Berber tribes. The act occasioned him no obloquy among the people at large or even among the nationalists, for it was widely believed that he had acted innocently and on orders from Resident-General Saint and the Grand Vizier al-Mokri.[1]

When considered together with the zealotry of the Franciscan mission under Monsignor Viel, Bishop of Rabat, with the subsidies received by the Catholic Church out of the Moroccan budget, with the provocative articles appearing in *Le Maroc Catholique* and *La Revue d'Histoire des Missions*, with Commandant Marty's distribution of copies of a *Life of Jesus* in Arabic translation, with the foundation of the normal school for Berbers at Azrou, with the proviso that even merchants and tourists must obtain passports in order to visit Berber areas — documents unavailable to the Arab *fqihs* who had traditionally visited the Berber tribes in the summertime — the *dahir* clearly appeared to even the most phlegmatic of Moroccans as the culmination of a plot to eradicate Islam among the Berber population. Thus was created a long-standing grievance against French rule which became part of the nationalist dogma and which provoked repeated, if increasingly ritualistic, protests during the next several years. The initial reaction, however, was anything but ritualistic, and the spate of nationalist activity which erupted in 1930–31 marks these years as a railhead in the history of Moroccan nationalism in the sense that they witnessed the culmination of old lines of development and the inception of new ones.

REPERCUSSIONS OF THE DAHIR

It becomes evident in this period that the transition from cultural to political nationalism was being completed. The *dahir* of 1930, by seeking to undermine Berberized Islam, struck at the heart of that very religious movement which the reformers were using to counteract the effects of French cultural assimilation, and since religion had been the only remaining bastion of Moroccan sovereignty as yet unassailed by the French, the *dahir* completed the identification of Salafiyya with political resistance to the French and invested the entire reform movement with a decidedly political flavor. In this sense it was a period of culmination.

It was a period of inception because the *dahir* consolidated opposition to French rule for the first time on a truly national scale. The *Survey of International Affairs* of 1937 observed that the Moroccan nationalist movement embraced, in "unresolved contradiction," "zealots" of the type of the Algerian *ulama* and the Tunisian Destourians as well as "Herodians" of the type of the Neo-Destourians.[2] But however this distinction might apply to Algeria and Tunisia, there was no "unresolved contradiction" in Morocco after 1930, because Moroccan "Herodians" were not deeply involved in the nationalist movement. The typical Moroccan nationalist of 1930, although he often donned the trappings of Western culture, was not the secularized reformer of the Neo-Destour variety but was fully committed to the Muslim orthodoxy which characterized both the traditionalist and reformist *ulama* in Algeria and Morocco. While it is true that their European education rendered the proto-nationalists somewhat suspect to the *ulama* on grounds of secularism, even before 1930 it was clear to the *ulama* that these young men were sincerely hostile to the unholy alliance of the Residency and the heretical religious brotherhoods. And when the Berber *dahir* convinced the *ulama* that the French intended to destroy Islam in Morocco, they began to regard the Salafiyyist-nationalists, who alone organized an effective resistance, as defenders of the Faith, and thereafter any contradictory tendencies inherent in the two groups were subordinated to mutual concerns.

Because the Berbers constituted a far larger proportion of the Moroccan than of the Algerian or Tunisian populations, and because the issue of 1930 happened to be a law profoundly affecting the Berbers, it was crucial for the cohesion of the nationalist movement to rally the Berbers firmly to its cause or, at the very least, to forestall their assimilation into the French judicial and educational systems which the *dahir* threatened to do. The heterodoxy of the brotherhoods had traditionally received a ready acceptance among the Berber tribes, but heterodoxy and impiety are hardly synonymous, and the French failed to understand that Islam as a whole meant far more to the Berber than did these unorthodox sects which he customarily embraced. Accordingly, when the Berber discovered his European conqueror, against whom he nurtured an abiding resentment, supporting the brotherhoods and *marabouts* (holy men), these time-honored institutions of Moroccan life became discredited in his eyes and caused him to drift towards an orthodoxy more acceptable to the Salafiyyist reformers and *ulama*. Under any circumstances, the Berbers would have resisted the *dahir* as an attempt to replace their ancient overlord by a new one even more hateful because more effective, but under the circumstances of 1930, with an infidel army swarming over their mountain retreats, the Berbers were even more repelled by the *dahir* as a joint attack on their religion and their traditional autonomy. Thus were the tribes united with the *ulama* and the Salafiyyist reformers. Nothing better than the Berber *dahir* could have been designed to consolidate Moroccan resistance to French rule. It provided a nucleus around which confused and disparate aspirations were crystallized. It created a movement out of what had been no more than a tendency.[3]

THE NATIONALIST RESPONSE

The measures taken by the Moroccans to consolidate national support were chiefly three in number: the *latifs*, the Fez delegation and the campaign abroad.

THE LATIFS

Initially the Moroccan public had reacted to the *dahir* with opaque indifference, much to the chagrin of the reformers, but they might have expected as much in a land where illiteracy was nearly universal and where the nationalist impulse was no more than embryonic. A propaganda effort was obviously called for if the people were to be made to understand what the *dahir* portended, and so, partly because religious assemblies were the only privileged form of public communication, and partly because Muslims have always done so in times of crisis, the reformers repaired to the mosques and began to recite the *latif*. Customarily reserved for occasions of public calamity such as earthquakes, droughts, visitations of locusts and the like, this communal prayer was now adapted to political purposes by Mohammed Lyazidi and Abdellatif Sbihi and terminated with the supplication: "O Savior (*Ya Latif*), protect us from ill treatment by fate and allow nothing to divide us from our brothers, the Berbers." [4] Henceforth, the *latif* was widely employed in Morocco to express popular grief on days which the nationalists designated as the anniversaries of national calamities: e.g., March 30th (Treaty of Fez, 1912), or May 16th (Berber *dahir*, 1930), or October 26th (arrest of Allal al-Fassi, 1937).

Mohammed Lyazidi had been employed as an interpreter in the office of the Land Registry since 1926. After the promulgation of the Berber *dahir*, he asked for a leave of absence (which was to become permanent) and returned on June 1st to Rabat where, in the great mosque, and across the river in Salé as well, the first prayers were recited on June 20th. They proved so successful, from the standpoint of popular appeal, that they were recited all over Rabat-Salé one week later and on subsequent Fridays in Marrakesh (arranged by Sbihi and possibly Mokhtar Soussi), in Safi and Casablanca (by Lyazidi and Mohammed Ghazi), and in Meknes, Tangier and Fez. The resulting disturbances led to Sbihi's arrest and forced residence for two years, first in Marrakesh, then in Tiznit, after which he withdrew from active participation in the national movement.[5]

It was in Fez, in July and August, that the *latifs* probably reached their greatest intensity. The first was held on July 4th in the Qarawiyin mosque without public disturbance, but on July 18th the speeches made by Abdesselam ben Brahim Ouezzani and Ben Hadj Fateh Sefrioui were followed by street demonstrations which led to the arrest of twenty-four of the agitators. On the following Friday, the Residency was sufficiently uneasy to place units of the Foreign Legion around the *medina* (Arab quarter), and a few police actually entered the mosque, making additional arrests. On July 29th a group of Fassi notables including Ahmed Mekouar, met with the colonel in charge and agreed to form a committee to discuss the problem on condition that those arrested be released, which condition was met on the next day. The first meeting of the committee with Commandant Miller took place on August 2nd, and other meetings with Miller and the grand vizier followed during the next few days. On August 11th a letter from the sultan, asking an end to the agitation, was read in the Qarawiyin, and, during the following two days, the committee agreed to call off the *latifs* and decided to send a delegation to discuss the whole matter with the sultan.[6]

For one of the young nationalists of that city, however, the protest was not sufficiently vigorous. Accordingly, Mohammed Hassan al-Ouezzani organized on July 16th a street demonstration before the pasha's residence, much against the advice of his colleagues. The pasha asked him to return next day with a committee to discuss grievances, but when it arrived, two of its number, al-Ouezzani and Hachemi al-Filali received the punishment mentioned earlier (p. 53) which did very little for the popularity of the pasha and his French military collaborators. Allal al-Fassi and Abdelaziz Bendriss were arrested on the same day and briefly imprisoned. Meanwhile, Lyazidi and Ahmed Cherkaoui continued to conduct the *latifs* in Rabat and Salé until about September 1st, when, after the return home of the Fez delegation, they, too, were arrested.[7]

THE FEZ DELEGATION

Meanwhile, the Fassi aristocracy had remained unconvinced by Residency assurances that the motives behind the *dahir* were entirely innocent, and something more than a hundred of them convened on the night of August 22, 1930 to proceed with the election of a delegation to make known their views to the sultan. Twenty-one in all were nominated, but owing to business responsibilities and other reasons only seven or eight ultimately went to Rabat.[8] A brief memorandum (the "Thirteen Demands") was drawn up and signed by those present, protesting the Berber policy in general and the *dahir* in particular and demanding its revocation.[9] On the following evening, ten of the younger men met at Mekouar's house in the Batha to form an organization which they called the "National Group" (*Djemaa al-Wataniya*) [10] which would defend their "religion, their country and the throne," and to this group fell the arrangements for sending the delegation to Rabat, although only one (Mohammed Diouri) actually accompanied it. The other leading members of the Group were Allal al-Fassi, Mohammed Hassan al-Ouezzani, Ahmed Mekouar, Hassan Bouayad and Abdelkader Tazi, most of whom had been members of the secret societies of the mid-1920's, all of whom were nationalists by 1930, and all of whom, except al-Ouezzani and Tazi, were to remain at the center of the movement until independence.[11]

The delegation left for Rabat on August 26th, was received by the sultan the next day, and returned to Fez on Friday evening, August 29th, having been warned that they were about to be arrested. On the following morning, the delegation reported to their Fassi colleagues that the sultan had replied, "We are going to consider your demands and answer you." This, apparently, was regarded as a negative response, for the decision was taken to revive the *latifs*, and emissaries were sent out to alert Rabat, Salé, Casablanca and Marrakesh of this decision.[12] This time, however, the Residency was prepared. Hadj Mohammed Lahlou, who had received the largest vote on August 22nd, was arrested with a few others on Sunday, and on Tuesday, September 2nd, other arrests were made. In Fez, Allal al-Fassi, Mohammed Hassan al-Ouezzani, Abdelaziz Bendriss, Ibrahim al-Kittani, Hachemi al-Filali and Ibrahim al-Ouezzani were taken into custody and jailed until October 27th in Taza where they were joined by Ahmed Cherkaoui from Rabat.[13] Of the other Rabatis, Mohammed Lyazidi was packed off to Marrakesh for a forced residence of two years' duration (until July 1932), and Mekki Naciri was expelled from the country, whereupon he betook himself to

France and played an active role in the foreign campaign against the *dahir*.[14]

Such a campaign seemed to be the only feasible course at the time, the protest movement having been severely limited within Morocco. On Arslan's advice, the group rejected any course of action which might savor of a *jihad* (holy war), deeming it more politic to pose as victims of an abridgement of civil rights — an abridgement in direct violation of the solemn international commitments to respect and protect the Moroccan religion undertaken by France in the Treaty of Fez. The campaign was launched in the fall of 1930 as a joint effort on the part of Balafrej, Mekki Naciri and Mohammed al-Fassi in Paris, Shakib Arslan in Geneva, and the editor of *al-Fath* in Cairo. It was decided that the most effective propaganda would result from dramatizing the *dahir* as an attempt to Christianize the Berber majority of Morocco's population, and the results more than fulfilled expectations, for the Muslim world from Dakar to Djakarta took up the cudgels on behalf of Morocco.

Led by *al-Fath* and *al-Manar* in Cairo, the Arabic press in Jerusalem, Beirut, Tunis, Tripoli and elsewhere fanned the Muslim world into a minor frenzy. In Constantinople the Shaykh of Islam, Mustafa Saleri Effendi, vilified France in an article in *Biâm Islam*. The French Embassy in Cairo received petitions inscribed with several thousand signatures protesting the Berber *dahir*, and the *ulama* of al-Azhar petitioned King Fuad to intervene personally with the French government. A "committee for the defense of Moroccan Muslims" was formed in Cairo under the presidency of Prince Omar Tossoun, and similar committees sprang up elsewhere, as far east as Java and as far north as the Muslim community in Berlin. The Quai d'Orsay was flooded with protests from all corners of Islam.[15]

Two publications of particular interest for this study issued from the international propaganda effort. One was the 76-page polemic, *Le Tempête sur le Maroc, ou les erreurs d'une "politique berbère,"* published in Paris early in 1931 by a group which adopted the rather droll pseudonym of "Mouslim Barbari." *Le Tempête* traced the evolution of the iniquitous Berber policy from its inception in 1914 to its odious climax in 1930, analyzed the import of the provisions of the latest *dahir* for Moroccan society, recorded the indignation which it evoked throughout the Muslim world, and concluded with several suggestions to the French authorities for resolving the crisis. The Residency should permit the teaching of Arabic and the Muslim religion in the *écoles franco-berbères*, restore the judicial authority of the pashas, *caids* and *cadis* in Berber territory, put a stop to missionary efforts of all types and cut off their official subsidization, suppress the requirement of passports for travel in the interior, and dismiss French officials who promoted these practices, all of which were in violation of the letter or the spirit of the Treaty of Fez.[16]

Le Tempête was, in reality, the work of Ahmed Balafrej, Mohammed al-Fassi, Abdelkader Benjelloun, Mohammed al-Kholti and Abdelmalek Faraj, all about to complete their studies at either the University of Paris or the "Sciences Po," and of Mekki Naciri who was whiling away the first year of his exile at the Sorbonne and the Institut des Études Islamiques. Omar Abdeljalil may also have participated in the writing; in fact, he may have been its chief author.[17] It should be noted that Balafrej, Naciri and Abdeljalil had been members of the secret society of Rabat back in 1926, while Mohammed al-Fassi, al-Kholti and Benjelloun had belonged to the Fez society, an indication of the continued, indeed, increasing collaboration of the two main groups which opposed the Residency.

Le Tempête clearly demonstrates that Moroccan nationalism had completed the transition from a predominantly religious to an overtly political movement and was no longer concerned exclusively with the free-school effort to resist assimilation by educational means. The reforms suggested in the book touch nearly all areas of official administration, judicial and political as well as religious and educational, although there is little more than an intimation of what might be done in each case — nothing in the way of a broadly conceived program of reform. Translated into Arabic and published in Cairo later that same year, it was available to the delegates attending the first Islamic Conference in Jerusalem, December 7–16, 1931.

The second of the two publications referred to above was the work of Mekki Naciri. By mid-1931, Naciri had gravitated to Geneva where he collaborated with Arslan and his lieutenant, Ihsan Djabri, in the preparation of a report on the Berber *dahir* which he read before the Islamic Conference and which was another factor in persuading the conference to forward its protest to the secretary-general of the League of Nations.[18] This report was later elaborated upon and published in Cairo in December 1931 or early 1932 as a 92-page booklet (in Arabic) entitled *France and Its Berber Policy in Morocco*.[19] It is noteworthy because the demands cited on Page One, although no more than a bare listing, are couched in terms which demonstrate the broadening perspectives of the Moroccan nationalists and a growing perception of their place in the world of European imperialism and colonial nationalism. Not only should justice reign in Morocco, not only should the unity of Morocco be preserved as an Arabic nation submitting to Islam alone, all of which had been said before, but now for the first time is clearly proclaimed the idea that the protectorate regime should help Morocco regain its freedom as a Muslim nation.[20]

The managers of the propaganda campaign also tried to bring economic pressure to bear by promoting an international boycott of France. On November 21, 1930, an article by Shakib Arslan in *al-Fath* assured the Arab countries that this was "the one weapon that the Europeans, who worship money in place of God, fear most," [21] but interestingly enough, while India decided to apply the sanctions, Egyptian merchants were not sufficiently aggrieved over their coreligionists' plight to consider the game worth the candle.[22] Some effort was made inside Morocco to boycott locally the sale of sugar, cotton cloth and tobacco, all French monopolies, and to discourage the patronage of French cafés and public transportation, but the populace as a whole was not yet sufficiently exercised to deprive itself for long of these conveniences. Economically, the campaign against the *dahir* was a fizzle; propaganda-wise, it was an immense success.

RESULTS OF THE CONTROVERSY

The fact that the diligent authors of the Berber *dahir* had achieved a partial victory should not be overlooked, however. The "customary tribunals" were maintained, even extended, and the use of Arabic was still forbidden at the normal school in Azrou. The authorities continued to hinder the visits of the *fqihs* to the Berber schools, and the old Koranic schools tended to retreat before the advancing line of the *écoles franco-berbères*.[23]

But the French derived little concrete satisfaction out of these developments, because the customary tribunals, if anything, strengthened the *djemaas* and did nothing to foster assimilation, and the artificial separation of Arab *fqih* and Berber schoolchild simply created resentment among the Berbers who had valued Arabic culture as much as they resisted Arab domination.[24] In one case the policy backfired ironically, for the school at Azrou, so carefully screened from Arabic influence, became a veritable seedbed of militant nationalists later in the protectorate period. Finally, the outcry against Article VI of the *dahir* had been so vehement and detrimental to French popularity throughout the Muslim world that it was abrogated on April 8, 1934 by a new *dahir* which restored the jurisdiction of the pasha, *caids* and the High Sharifian Tribunal over criminal cases in Berber territory.[25]

The real significance of the *dahir*, however, lay not in its success or failure as an administrative decree, but in its effect on Morocco's sense of nationhood. Most French observers, including many who should have known better, dismissed the agitation as an expression of youthful turbulence confined to several hundred activists and their sympathizers, while *L'Afrique Française*, understandably, poured undiluted contempt upon them.[26] But Daniel Guérin, writing in the November 1, 1930 issue of *Monde*, admonished his readers that the repercussions caused by the effort to assimilate the Berbers were far more profound than most Frenchmen realized, and that the Berber policy had stirred up "une véritable tempête au Maroc." [27] The *dahir* was, in fact, the first serious blow to French prestige and authority in Morocco. The legitimate Berber policy, administered since 1914 on the premise that certain aspects of the unique Berber culture should be tolerated though not encouraged, was weakened and discredited by this attempt to enlist it in the cause of colonialism. It was this display of official ineptitude which made it possible for a comparative handful of determined young men to discommode the Residency and to frustrate in part the execution of the policy of "divide and rule" by demonstrating how effectively they could master the indignation of the Moroccan people to combat foreign interference with their religion. The agitation against the *dahir* marked the first occasion in modern times when the Moroccan people responded on a national basis to an external challenge, however transient that response was to prove in the end.

In doctrinal terms, however, the national reaction of 1930–31 was patently deficient. Whatever there was of rational expression in the "Thirteen Demands" of Fez was meager in content and limited in scope, addressed as it was to a specific grievance. Even in *Le Tempête* of the following year there was hardly more than the intimation of a broader program of reform and not much more than that in *France and Its Berber Policy in Morocco* which appeared a few months later. Moreover, while the *latifs* and the campaign abroad reflected an improved sense of organization, the nationalists had, by the end of 1931, no national political structure comparable to the *Destour* to show for their year's efforts.

What influences can be discerned at this point? Of the Middle Eastern factors, Salafiyya was no longer the guiding force as before, for the matter of religious reform was largely over-shadowed by the controversy of 1930–31. Instead, the charac-teristics of the campaign against the Berber policy marked the rising influence of Middle Eastern secular nationalisms and the emergence in Morocco of a predominantly secular political movement. The greater confidence and assertiveness of the nationalists in this period reflect their own maturation as well as the continued impact of the Arab renaissance on their sense of personal dignity and worth. The influence of Arslan is noticeable both in his advocacy of a propaganda campaign abroad rather than a kind of *jihad* at home and in the Moroccan realization that pan-Arabism had its uses, if for nothing more concrete than the establishment of sympathetic public relations with the Levant. The influence of Tunisian nationalism may well have been reflected in the use of the press campaign and the economic boycott, for both of these devices had been employed by the old *Destour* in the previous decade, and there was every opportunity for the Moroccans to become aware of them through their con-tacts with the Tunisians in the A.E.M.N.A. after 1927. Moham-med Hassan al-Ouezzani, however, contends that the boycott, at least, was borrowed directly from Indian nationalists whom the Moroccans met while at school in Paris.[28] It is quite possible that both Tunisian and Indian nationalism influenced the Moroccans. What is important to note is that these Middle Eastern secular influences were almost entirely of a tactical nature up to this point. As was the case in the period 1925–30, the doctrines of Arab nationalism were being discussed in Morocco but were reflected in only a most superficial way in specific recommenda-tions for reform.

The struggle against the Berber policy was also in part a response to the internal grievances against educational, religious and judicial assimilation. In its literary form, that response was often well argued, but it was almost totally negative in character, for none of the nationalists had as yet any well considered alternatives to offer. Another internal grievance, viz., civil discrimination in the form of press censorship and the prohibition of public gatherings, forced the nationalists to conduct their propaganda campaign in the mosques and in the foreign press of Paris, Geneva and Cairo, and to take advantage of other promising forums such as the Islamic Conference of 1931. As with Middle Eastern influences, before 1931 internal grievances evoked a tactical rather than a doctrinal response in Morocco.

Western influences, barely noticeable before 1930, were about to become a major factor in the rise of nationalism. The French-educated were still in a minority among the top leaders, although they were becoming more important than their numbers indicate. Mohammed Lyazidi and Abdellatif Sbihi, it was noted, played a leading role in the *latif* campaign, and three of the six leading members of the group which arranged for the Fez delegation (Mohammed Hassan al-Ouezzani, Mohammed Diouri and Abdelkader Tazi) were French-educated, as were all those who collaborated on the two books published in Paris and Cairo in 1931, except Mekki Naciri; even he rectified this deficiency by attending the Sorbonne, the Institut des Études Islamiques and the University of Geneva during his years of exile from 1930 to 1932. One can now begin to detect the substantive impact of French education on the Moroccans, for they displayed an increasing dexterity, accuracy and relevance in their use of criticism as well as a greater aptitude for organizing work and people. The former is quite apparent from reading the articles and booklets prepared for the international press campaign, although one must not discount in this connection the advice and counsel which the Moroccans undoubtedly received from their French friends. Their growing administrative aptitude is descernible in the role played by Lyazidi and Sbihi in directing the *latifs*. Lyazidi himself testifies that his French education had endowed him with far more regular and organized work habits.[29] Enlightenment and French Revolutionary dogmas, which the French-educated had by now fairly well assimilated, had already gone far to convince them that Salafiyya was inadequate as a program for political reform, that to it must be grafted a broad spectrum of ideas drawn from the abundant heritage of European political philosophy, of which their French education had first made them aware.

The years 1930–31, then, constituted a new departure for Moroccan nationalism, because they marked the emergence of a truly political consciousness and the impingement of a multitude of secular influences from both East and West, as well as the first demonstration of a really national opposition to foreign rule. But something further had been demonstrated — the need for a vastly improved organizational structure and a broader, more appealing program of reform, and to these two ends the novice nationalists bent themselves in the years after 1931.

XI

BUILDING AN ORGANIZATION: 1931–1934

Beginning in 1931, three concentric organizations were created by the nationalists to pursue their new goals: the Zawiya, the Taifa, both clandestine, and the Kutlat. This chapter deals with their foundation and purposes, their organization and membership, and their activities; the next, with their program of reform.

FOUNDATION AND PURPOSES

The word *zawiya* came very early in the Muslim world to be applied to that corner of a mosque occupied by teachers and their pupils. Its use was progressively extended to mean the abode of any religious teacher, the seat of a religious organization which such a teacher may have founded, the headquarters of a religious brotherhood, and finally, the brotherhood itself. It was only natural for the Salafiyyist reformers to apply quasi-religious terms to their activities; hence, "Zawiya" was the name given the first nationalist group founded in Fez in the summer of 1930 after the tremendous effort required to sustain the *latif* campaign had demonstrated the need for better organization.[1] That had been a one-cause campaign, but the Zawiya was formed to study and act upon the entire gamut of problems created by foreign domination.

Very soon new people began to filter into the movement, but as they were not yet trusted implicitly, they were first taken into a larger, but still clandestine, organization also created in 1930 and known as the Taifa.[2] (The word conveys a less precise meaning than Zawiya and can be translated as "group," or "congregation," or simply, "sect".) Under the aegis of the Taifa, additional cells were founded in the principal cities not already represented.[3]

The third concentric body, the only one publicly known, was the *Kutlat al-Amal al-Watani*, in English, the "National Action Bloc," and less accurately in French, the "Comité d'Action Marocaine." The Kutlat began life in the summer of 1933 as a committee of the Zawiya assigned to draft a plan of reform, and when the first nationalist "party" was founded in May 1934, it adopted the committee's name.[4]

ORGANIZATION AND MEMBERSHIP

Compared to the secret societies of the previous decade, the Zawiya was well organized. It was endowed with a written charter and required an oath of secrecy and sacrifice.[5] Of the initial cells, in Fez and Tetuan, Fez was the "mother cell" to which most of the important leaders belonged. Limited to those who had demonstrated their discretion and fidelity, it never much exceeded the membership of twenty-five here listed.[6]

FEZ CELL	Allal al-Fassi	(joined about 1936)
	Mohammed Hassan al-Ouezzani	Abdelaziz Bendriss
	Omar Abdeljalil	Hachemi al-Filali
	Mohammed Ghazi (Casablanca repres.)	Bouchta Jamai (Casa-
	Ahmed Mekouar	blanca repres.)
	Hassan Bouayad	
	Mohammed Diouri (Kénitra repres.)	
	Abdelkader Tazi*	
	Mohammed Sebti	
	Omar Sebti	
	Lghali Sebti	
	Ahmed Bouayad	
	Larbi Bouayad	
	Hamza Tahiri*	
TETUAN CELL	(soon drifted apart)	(joined 1932)
	Abdesselam Bennouna	Abdelkhalek Torrès
	Mohammed Daoud	
	Ahmed Ghilane	
RABAT CELL	(founded 1932)	(joined 1933–34)
	Ahmed Balafrej	Ahmed Cherkaoui
	Mohammed Lyazidi	
	Ahmed bel-Koura*	

* Abdelkader Tazi, Hamza Tahiri and Ahmed bel-Koura left the nationalist movement soon after 1931. The others remained active.

At its core were nine men who comprised the "board of directors" of the nationalist movement in the years 1932–34, who are here ranked in order of their influence (in the author's estimation) during that formative period:

FEZ   RABAT

1. Allal al-Fassi
2. Mohammed Hassan al-Ouezzani

3. Ahmed Balafrej
4. Mohammed Lyazidi
5. Omar Abdeljalil
6. Mohammed Ghazi
7. Ahmed Mekouar
8. Hassan Bouayad
9. Mohammed Diouri

Allal al-Fassi stood out above the others for his charisma, and al-Ouezzani never outranked him except in the eyes of the French, who saw and heard more of him because he was educated and active in France. Owing to their personal differences, al-Ouezzani's authority waned after 1934. Ahmed Balafrej and Mohammed Lyazidi did not join the Zawiya until June or July 1932, when the former returned from his studies in Paris and the latter from exile in the south.[7]

After 1934 the "board of directors" became even more select as the natural result of the leadership shaking down, five of the original nine rising to supreme authority: al-Fassi, Balafrej, Lyazidi, Abdeljalil and Mekouar.[8] The other members of the Zawiya followed the lead of the "board." Something to remember in examining successive nationalist organizations after 1931 is that this inner circle acted as the executive committee of the movement and ruled on major policy from 1931 until at least 1944, when Istiqlal was founded, and possibly until independence. Everything that was done was controlled by the "board," with the possible exception of the military and terrorist activities of the Army of Liberation which got somewhat out of hand on the eve of independence. The other members of the Zawiya often joined the inner circle in its consultations but were not privy to everything that transpired.[9]

The distinguishing feature of the Taifa was its more fully developed cellular structure which was extended to Rabat, Salé, Kénitra, Casablanca, Safi, Marrakesh and Tangier in the years 1930-32. The membership of each cell was known only to itself and to the "mother cell" in Fez to which they all reported, a structure undoubtedly inspired by the Communist Party of France which was closely studied at this time by Allal al-Fassi, M. H. al-Ouezzani and Mohammed Lyazidi.[10] At its inception, the Taifa numbered thirty or forty members, and it probably totaled about a hundred by the time it was disbanded in 1944, although its intervening membership may have risen somewhat higher. It included the entire Zawiya, of course, in addition to which its most prominent members were the following: [11]

FEZ	Abdelaziz Bendriss (joined Zawiya about 1936)
	Hachemi al-Filali (″ ″ ″ ″)
	Mohammed al-Fassi
	Abdelkader Berrada
RABAT	Ahmed Cherkaoui (joined Zawiya about 1934)
	Messaoud Chiguer
	Abdullah Regragui
SALÉ	Said Hajji
	Boubker Kadiri
CASABLANCA	Bouchta Jamai (joined Zawiya about 1936)

The Kutlat was a more amorphous body to which nearly anyone could belong and whose continuance or suppression had very little effect on the existence of the core groups. It was outlawed by the Residency in March 1937, reappeared as the National Party in April, and was finally disbanded in October, while the Zawiya and Taifa continued almost uninterrupted with their clandestine activities.

An "official document," cited but not identified by Rézette, whose friends in the Residency possibly gave him access to confidential files, estimates the membership of the Kutlat for all three zones of Morocco in 1934 at twelve "leaders," 150 "militants" and 200–300 "sympathizers," three categories which, in retrospect, we can identify very roughly with the Zawiya, the Taifa, and the rank and file of the Kutlat. Before its first dissolution (March 1937), membership had risen sharply to somewhat over 6,500, excluding the Spanish zone. It declined to about 4,000 before its final dissolution (October 1937) and the secret organization which persisted thereafter shrank even further, although no accurate figures are available.[12] Some of the most prominent members of the Kutlat were never admitted to the Zawiya or Taifa (e.g., Ibrahim al-Kittani from Fez, Mekki Naciri and Abdelkebir al-Fassi from Rabat, Mohammed Hassar from Salé and Abdullah Guennoun from Tangier), but these five, along with the leading members of the Taifa mentioned above, can be regarded as among the forty-one individuals who directed the nationalist movement before World War II and who form the dramatis personae of this study.

LEADERSHIP FUNCTIONS

Because so many a priori assumptions are entertained about the direct relationship between European education and colonial nationalism, this seems as appropriate a place as any to analyze more precisely the respective roles played in Moroccan nationalism by the French-educated and the Muslim-educated. Five functional types can be distinguished: a "board of directors," comprising the inner circle of nine, "theoreticians," "organizers" in the various cities, "propagandists" at home and abroad, and "financial backers." In Table 2 the leaders are ranked in order

TABLE 2. FUNCTION, RANK AND EDUCATION OF LEADING NATIONALISTS

DIRECTORS	Allal al-Fassi	Mt†
	Mohammed Hassan al-Ouezzani	Fsh
	Ahmed Balafrej	Fsh
	Mohammed Lyazidi	Fsh
	Omar Abdeljalil	Fsh
	Mohammed Ghazi	Mt
	Ahmed Mekouar	Mt
	Hassan Bouayad	Mm
	Mohammed Diouri	Fs
THEORETICIANS	Allal al-Fassi	Mt
	Mohammed Hassan al-Ouezzani	Fsh
	Ahmed Balafrej	Fsh
	Omar Abdeljalil	Fsh
	Mohammed Lyazidi	Fsh
	Mohammed Ghazi	Mt
	Hassan Bouayad	Mm
	Mekki Naciri*	MmFh
	Mohammed al-Kholti*	Fsh
ORGANIZERS:		
Fez	Allal al-Fassi	Mt
	Mohammed Hassan al-Ouezzani	Fsh
	Mohammed Ghazi	Mt
	Abdelaziz Bendriss	Mt
	Hachemi al-Filali	Mm
	Ibrahim al-Kittani*	Mt
Rabat	Mohammed Lyazidi	Fsh
	Ahmed Balafrej	Fsh
	Ahmed Cherkaoui	Mt
Salé	Said Hajji	Mm
	Boubker Kadiri	Mt
Casablanca	Mohammed Ghazi (1930–31)	Mt
	Bouchta Jamai (1933 ff.)	Mt

TABLE 2 (*Continued*)

Kénitra	Mohammed Diouri	Fs
Oujda	Bouchta Jamai (1930–33)	Mt
Tetuan	Abdesselam Bennouna	Mt
	Mohammed Daoud	Mt
	Abdelkhalek Torrès (1932 ff.)	Mm
PROPAGANDISTS:		
In France	Mohammed Hassan al-Ouezzani	Fsh
	Ahmed Balafrej	Fsh
	Mohammed al-Fassi	Fsh
	Abdelkader Benjelloun*	Fsh
	Mohammed al-Kholti*	Fsh
In Morocco		
Fez	Allal al-Fassi	Mt
	Omar Abdeljalil	Fsh
	Abdelaziz Bendriss	Mt
	Hachemi al-Filali	Mm
Rabat	Ahmed Cherkaoui	Mt
Casablanca	Bouchta Jamai (1933 ff.)	Mt
In the Middle East		
(*Cairo and Jerusalem*)	Hassan Bouayad	Mm
	Mekki Naciri*	MmFh
FINANCIAL BACKERS	Ahmed Mekouar	Mt
	Mohammed Diouri	Fs
	Mohammed Sebti	Fs
	Omar Sebti	Fs
	Lghali Sebti	Mt
	Ahmed Bouayad	Mt
	Larbi Bouayad	Mt

* Not a member of either the Zawiya or the Taifa.
† Initials signify education received by each man: F(French); M(Muslim); s(secondary); h(higher); t(tradition); m(modernized). See Appendix D for details.

of their prestige and the authority they commanded insofar as these could be determined by an analysis of nationalist publications and by extended consultations with many of the men involved.[13] The education received by each man appears after his name and is explained in the note.

It should be noted that the majority of the "directors" and "theoreticians" received a French or Westernized education, and it should hardly be surprising that all the "propagandists" in France received the same. The propaganda function in Morocco and the Middle East was assumed by the Muslim-educated for the most part because the French-educated tended to lose rapport with the people. Loss of rapport was not critical as long as the nationalists regarded their organization as an elite political club, but it began to concern them in 1936 when they made the decision to rally the masses to a truly national party. For this reason the majority of the "organizers" were Muslim-educated, while the "financial backers" were divided about evenly and are neither so easy nor so important to categorize.

ACTIVITIES

Throughout this period, the nationalists continued to sponsor the free schools, but there is little need to elaborate on the discussion of Chapter IX. By far the most important activities of the Zawiya were the publishing of *Maghreb* (1932–34) and *L'Action du Peuple* (1933–34) and the preparation of the *Plan de Réformes* (1933–34), for out of these efforts emerged the fullest exposition of the doctrines of Moroccan nationalism to be formulated prior to independence. These will be treated in detail in the chapter on doctrine (Chapter XII). Here other activities will be briefly reviewed.

Outlets were never lacking for articles on the inequities and iniquities of French colonialism in Morocco, and the Zawiya accommodated itself to the demand. Shakib Arslan's *La Nation Arabe* was always available, as was the Cairo weekly, *al-Fath*, whose editor worked closely with the amir. To a lesser extent *al-Risala* (Cairo) was employed for this purpose, as was *al-Manar* until it ceased publication shortly after Rida's death in 1934. The two Salafiyyist journals of Algeria, *ech-Chihab* (Constantine) and *Oued Mzab* (Algiers), also carried articles written by the Moroccan nationalists who, through these media, publicized their grievances in Europe, North Africa and the Middle East.[14]

Further support was enlisted by taking advantage of a variety of opportunities for personal contacts with other Muslims and sympathetic Europeans in the Middle East, in Europe and in Morocco itself. Constitutionally, France controlled all official relations between Moroccans and foreigners and tried to discourage all unofficial relations, and since the propaganda activities of the nationalists were decidedly unofficial, this might have created a serious obstacle to effective contact. It was an obstacle easily surmounted, however, for conservative as the protectorate regime may have been, it was not totalitarian, and a considerable amount of foreign "cultural" contact was tolerated.[15]

One locus of such contact was the Association Hispano-Musulmane (*al-Jamiya al-Isbaniya al-Islamiya*) founded in Madrid in October 1932 after the consolidation of the republican government promised a change in colonial policy.[16] Shakib Arslan was instrumental in its inception and became one of its two vice-presidents, and Rashid Rida apparently was also involved. Its leading Moroccan members from the French zone were Ahmed Balafrej, Mohammed al-Fassi, then president of the A.E.M.N.A., and Mohammed Hassan al-Ouezzani, then serving briefly as Arslan's secretary. The Spanish zone was represented by Abdesselam Bennouna, Mohammed Daoud and Abdelkhalek Torrès. Its ten Spanish members included deputies, journalists and lawyers, all of whom were invited to join *Maghreb's* committee of patronage and four of whom accepted: Gim Argila, the Communist writer, Edouard Ortega y Gasset and Melchior Marial, both deputies, and the Spanish minister of instruction, Fernando de los Rios. The ostensible purpose of the Association was to exploit the historic racial and cultural affinities between Spain and Morocco in order to create an atmosphere of sympathy for the latter's claims for independence, but more immediately it sought to create pressure on the French zone by causing the Spanish government to liberalize its policies in the Spanish zone, just as it was then liberalizing them in Catalonia. For several years the Association conducted a campaign of vilification against France, notably in the journal *El-Pais*, against which the French government protested in vain. It also sponsored an Arab school in Grenada. But other than this the Association was not particularly effective, and after 1935 it was allowed to wither away despite Franco's interest in exploiting such instrumentalities.[17]

A similar organization was *al-Jamiya al-Taqafa al-Islamiya* (Islamischer Kulturbund) founded in Vienna on December 6, 1932, also by Shakib Arslan,[18] and already mentioned in Chapter VIII. Mohammed Hassan al-Ouezzani was a member of its bureau, and it had branches in Tetuan and Tangier.

Within Morocco such contacts were somewhat hindered by the sporadic arrests and detainments of the time, but rarely were many of the nationalists in jail simultaneously or for very long before the wholesale suppression of 1937. The free schools and theatrical troupes mentioned earlier operated openly, and there was ample freedom during these years for any agitator to mingle freely in alumni associations, scouting troops and literary societies.

The *associations des anciens élèves* of the *collèges* in Rabat and Fez, founded in the early 1920's, had languished after their early years of activity, but from 1933 onward they were rejuvenated and transformed into political action groups on the initiative of members of the Zawiya who were alumni of the *collèges*.[19] The executive boards of the revived associations, owing to their earlier experience, proved to be better organizers, indeed, than the novice nationalists, and while one might have expected the Zawiya once founded to stage a series of public demonstrations, the period from September 1930 to September 1936 was surprisingly free of disorder, and the only two noteworthy demonstrations of the time, both remarkably peaceful affairs, were staged by the alumni associations. On November 15, 1933 was held the first *Fête du Trone* commemorating the sultan's accession six years earlier. Organization committees were formed in Fez, Rabat, Meknes, Casablanca, Marrakesh and Tangier, on which members of the alumni associations predominated. Telegrams of felicitation were dispatched to the sultan, tea (Morocco's national drink) was offered the people who turned out, and there was dancing in the streets, but that was all.[20]

A more lively demonstration occurred on May 8, 1934 on the occasion of the sultan's annual visit to Fez to proclaim the "Sultan of the Students," a demonstration which may well have been provoked by the riotous protests staged in Rabat and Casablanca four days earlier by French civil servants angered by salary reductions.[21] It was organized by the editorial board of *L'Action du Peuple* in conjunction with the alumni association of Fez as a show of loyalty to His Majesty. More than the usual number of Moroccan flags appeared, and cries of "Long Live the Sultan!" and "Down with France!" were heard. The enthusiastic crowd molested and slightly injured the unpopular pasha, voiced some uncomplimentary sentiments under the windows of the French commandant, and ripped up a *tricolore*, but there was no general rioting. The young sultan was flattered and surprised at this untoward display of fidelity, but the French authorities were greatly displeased, and the sultan was obliged to return to Rabat next day on the pretext of safety to his person. When *L'Action du Peuple* made propaganda out of the incident, a Residential order of May 16th not only closed down that journal but for good measure banned *Maghreb, es-Salam, el-Hayat* and other subversive foreign publications.[22]

The nationalists also infiltrated the Moroccan scouting movement, the *éclaireurs marocains*, the first section of which was founded in 1931 in Casablanca by a certain Jean-Pol, a dissident from the Federation of Scouts of France. By 1933 there were troops in Rabat and Tangier and two in formation in Fez and Marrakesh. In 1932 they reunited with the metropolitan organization but continued to nurse an Arab or national tendency towards autonomy. As elsewhere in the Middle East, *le scoutisme* was not so much a movement for children as for young men, and it furnished the nationalists with an excellent tool to shape and discipline the minds of Moroccan youth. Indeed, the scouts played a leading role in the street demonstrations which began in the autumn of 1936.[23]

The speaker's rostrum also served nationalist ends. Allal al-Fassi's personal magnetism drew students by the hundreds to his lectures on the life of the Prophet given at Qarawiyin during 1933. In actual fact, these lectures were somewhat more than they purported to be. They were studies of the political situation in Morocco and did much to help indoctrinate the young men who were to become active in the nationalist movement after World War II.[24] The forum offered by cultural and literary societies in France furnished another outlet for nationalist propaganda. Ahmed Balafrej, for example, availed himself of such an opportunity in May 1932 when he delivered an attack on the Berber *dahir* before the Fifth Arrondissement section of the League of the Rights of Man and the Citizen. This particular talk led the section to urge its central committee to remonstrate with the government on the subject.[25]

Telegrams were a favorite means of expressing displeasure over official acts and were used on many occasions. In February 1934, for example, Moroccan and Tunisian affairs were placed under a newly created Ministry of France-Overseas in the Daladier government, although, as protectorates, they could not technically come under the authority of a "colonial" administration. Telegram of protest "in the name of the population," but actually containing only a few dozen names, were sent from Fez, Rabat, Salé, Casablanca and Marrakesh to Premier Daladier, to the presidents of the Committees of Foreign Affairs of the Senate and Chamber, and to Jean Longuet, vice-president of the Chamber. But Daladier's government, already embarrassed by the Stavisky riots, solved its problems by resigning before it had served a month, and the controversial new department was inherited by Gaston Doumergue who disbanded it within the month. Such telegrams were not usually so effective, as for example those sent repeatedly to the S.F.I.O. at its national congresses vainly asking it to adopt a plank for Moroccan independence, or those protesting the mass arrests of October 1937 which prostrated the national movement for the next six years.[26]

SPANISH ZONE ACTIVITIES

Although the Zawiya had been founded jointly by Fassi and Tetuani nationalists, the two began almost immediately to drift apart. A completely separate organization, the *Kutlat al-Wataniya* was founded in Tetuan that same year (1930) by Abdesselam Bennouna, his brother M'Hammed, Mohammed Daoud, Ahmed Ghilane, Thami al-Ouezzani, Mohammed Tnana and Mohammed Masmoudi, who were later joined by Abdelkhalek Torrès, Taieb Bennouna, Abdesselam Benjelloun, Mohammed al-Khatib and others. It was not a secret organization, nor was it suppressed by the Spanish authorities, because, according to Daoud, its activities were more peaceable than those of the French zone.[27]

The schism began in 1931 when the installation of the new republican government in Spain persuaded Abdesselam Bennouna that something could be gained for the northern zone by a direct appeal to Madrid. On May 1, 1931, a bare fortnight after the overthrow of the Spanish monarchy, a delegation of Tetuani notables presented Alcalá Zamora, provisional president of the new regime, with a petition bearing eight hundred signatures and requesting what Bennouna considered the maximum concessions Spain would consider.[28] Although an abbreviated instrument (a single page), it has the distinction of being the first integrated program of reform advanced by Moroccans. This initiative, however, produced no tangible results. After making a few gestures towards granting some of the demands, the Spanish government drew back. The petition was presented again, unchanged, at the time of Zamora's visit to Tetuan at the end of 1933. The fact that it had remained unaltered during the intervening two years showed not only that the Spanish republicans had proved reluctant patrons but how little close contact after 1931 there was with the French zone where the nationalists of Fez and Rabat had been working out a far more elaborate plan of reform for nearly a year. The content of each set of proposals will be discussed in the following chapter.

The activities of the Spanish zone nationalists in the interwar years were limited largely to their participation in the ineffectual Association Hispano-Musulmane and to the establishment of an anti-French "nationalist" press with the connivance of the Spanish authorities. The first of these journals to appear, the monthly es-Salam, survived only ten numbers (October 1933–November 1934), having lost most of its circulation after being prohibited in the French zone in May, although it continued to enter that zone briefly by way of the British Post Offices. Owing to es-Salam, Daoud was declared persona non grata in the French zone and Tangier, and forbidden to enter them for ten years. After a sojourn in the Middle East, when he was barred from Syria and Lebanon, he returned to Tetuan and on March 15, 1936 launched a weekly newspaper, el-Akhbar, of which only five numbers appeared.[29] It, too, was prohibited in the French zone, but its cessation seems to have had less to do with official discouragement than with the prewar honeymoon between Franco and the Spanish-zone nationalists (see Chapter XIII).

The weekly el-Hayat appeared from February 1934 until August 1935. Like the others, it was banned in the French zone in May 1934, but is demise was actually caused by the heavy taxes levied by the faltering republican government. It was succeeded in the same year by er-Rif, directed by Thami al-Ouezzani and affiliated with Torrès' Islah Party which had just been founded. It, too, was banned in the French zone, disappeared, and was succeeded in turn by the daily el-Hurriya in March 1937, also affiliated with Islah. Spanish strategy permitted these journals to indulge in unrestrained condemnation of the French protectorate so long as criticism of the Spanish regime remained circumspect. As a result, they constitute a fuller commentary on events in the French zone than in the Spanish zone, and an Arabist who has the time to examine them closely might turn up a rather different slant on French-zone nationalism than appears, for example, in L'Action du Peuple.[30] A few of the French-zone nationalists contributed to these journals, including Allal al-Fassi, M. H. al-Ouezzani, Ahmed Balafrej and undoubtedly others anonymously, but this was not common practice.[31] From 1931 onward, the climate in which the Tetuani nationalists operated was quite different from that of Fez and Rabat, and caused the two movements to grow apart.

The year 1934 witnessed the sultan's first significant contacts with the leaders of the nationalist movement. As a young prince, Mohammed ben Youssef had been introduced to Salafiyyist doctrine by Ahmed Tijani and Mohammed Mammerie, both Algerian *ulama* imported by the Residency as tutors. They were not members of the Association of Algerian *ulama*, but the French authorities either failed to realize, or were not concerned, that they both shared its Salafiyyist viewpoints and imparted them to their pupil. Later, this influence was reinforced by Mohammed's association with Mohammed bel-Arabi al-Alaoui when the latter served as president of the *Tribunal d'Appel du Chraa* and then as vizier of justice.

From his accession in November 1927 until 1930, Mohammed was isolated as much as possible from his subjects as a matter of Residency policy. The stir caused by the Berber *dahir*, however, could not help but attract his attention, and he insisted on receiving the deputation from Fez which presented its memorandum of protest on August 27, 1930 and gave him his first real contact with the grievances of his people. But as the agitation died down that autumn, so, it seems, did the sultan's interest, for there is no indication of any initiative on his part or of any contact with the rising nationalist movement from 1930 until 1934.

During 1933 and 1934, however, his curiosity was aroused by some of the articles which he read in *L'Action du Peuple*, and whenever a grievance seemed to merit attention, he made it a practice to investigate and sometimes to demand redress from the French authorities. He had also been impressed by reports of Allal al-Fassi's lectures at Qarawiyin and moved by their author's subsequent flight (September 1933) to escape his projected arrest, and when al-Fassi deemed it safe to return, a meeting was arranged in February 1934, the first between the leader of Moroccan nationalism and his monarch.

The Residency had been dismayed by the popular demonstration which attended Mohammed's appearance in Fez on May 8, 1934. Hence, when the subsequent suppression of the nationalist press caused a delegation of protest to wait upon the sultan, it felt

obliged to shield His Majesty from any further contagion, and the
delegation had to content itself with an audience with the viziers.
Nevertheless, indirect communication with the sultan was so
arranged on this occasion as to exclude French interception, and
declarations of mutual fidelity and sympathy were exchanged
between the sultan and the delegation which comprised Allal
al-Fassi, Omar Abdeljalil, Abdelaziz Bendriss and Mekki Naciri.
Later that year, when the *Plan de Réformes* was presented, the
sultan wished to make a sympathetic public response, but the
Residency could not tolerate such a breach in its authority and
even sought to exile the authors to Gabon. At loggerheads, both
Mohammed V and Resident-General Ponsot managed to back
down on this occasion, and a compromise was arranged whereby
the banishments were suspended at the price of Mohammed's
silence.

The year 1934 had witnessed the nearest approach to nationalism made by the Palace before the end of World War II.
Thereafter, contact once again became sporadic. Only after the
1942 conference with President Roosevelt, which enhanced Mohammed's ego as much as the French had deflated it and which
raised immediate hopes for the restoration of Morocco's sovereignty, was regular contact reestablished, although on a clandestine
basis. Henceforth, the sultan became increasingly outspoken and
recalcitrant until his exile (1953–55) finally confirmed his image
as a national, and nationalist, hero.[32]

Before turning to doctrinal matters, let us pause to review those
influences which had some bearing on the expressions of nationalism treated in this chapter.

The spirit of Salafiyya was still discernible in the free-school
movement which maintained its momentum during the mid-1930's.
But the activities just described had become far more characteristic of Moroccan nationalism and demonstrated that the leaders
had come to recognize that the problem of reform was less a
function of righteousness than of politics. The influence of
Shakib Arslan is evidence of this, for the foundation of the
Islamischer Kulturbund and the Association Hispano-Musulmane
had no ideological basis whatever, but was essentially a maneuver
to alter the power structure by marshalling international public
opinion on the side of Morocco. No other Middle Eastern

influences can be identified at this juncture, with the exception of the obvious local precedent set by the religious brotherhoods for the oaths of absolute fidelity and sacrifice adopted by the Zawiya.

Western influence can be seen in the Communist-style infiltration of cultural and youth organizations by the nationalists. The structure of the Communist Party was reflected in the cellular structure of the Zawiya and Taifa, and the reader will recall that Lyazidi, Allal al-Fassi and M. H. al-Ouezzani had studied the history of the Communist movement and the statutes of the French Communist Party. We should recognize, however, that a predisposition for totalitarian organization was inherited from the age-old religious brotherhoods, for even the nationalists could not emancipate themselves in a moment from the traditions of an institution which was thoroughly imbedded in their culture.

Western education began to play a larger role as the movement became more specialized, for the French-educated gravitated increasingly to certain functions. It is always difficult to assess the relative "importance" of the French- and Muslim-educated in such a movement, but it can be maintained that the former constituted the dynamic element. They dominated the inner circle where doctrine was established, policy was formed and orders were issued. They also bore the chief responsibility for the propaganda effort abroad, at that time far more important than public relations at home. The Muslim-educated predominated only in functions which had to do with the execution of orders — that is, in recruitment and certain phases of public relations.

The increasing initiative being taken by the French-educated, the diligence with which they went to work, and their growing confidence, all reflect the sense of mission and personal importance imparted to them by the superiority of their education and by the flattering attentions of the French left. The influence of French politics is also noticeable in the use of propaganda techniques such as telegrams of protest and speeches before cultural and literary societies, as well as in the role played by the French left in the press campaign launched against the Berber *dahir* and continued on a reduced scale in the following years.

XII

FRAMING A PROGRAM: 1932–1934

Eighteen months of flaying the Berber *dahir* with diminishing effect had made it clear to the nationalists that limited causes produce limited results. Accordingly, in 1932 and 1933 two propaganda journals were founded in Paris and Fez which agitated the whole spectrum of grievances suffered (or imagined) under the protectorate regime and roughed out suggestions for reform. Corroborating Bacon's axiom that writing maketh the exact man, in the columns of *Maghreb* and *L'Action du Peuple* the ideas of Moroccan nationalism were tested, corrected and refined until they emerged in December 1934 as the *Plan de Réformes Marocaines.*

MAGHREB AND L'ACTION DU PEUPLE

Rézette makes the statement that *Maghreb* was founded by Robert-Jean Longuet, apparently with the backing of the militant wing of the S.F.I.O.[1] This would seem to be borne out by the names of the "editorial committee" appearing in each issue, for not a single Moroccan is included. Longuet is listed as editor-in-chief, François Albert, chairman of the Chamber of Deputies' Committee on Foreign Affairs, as president, and other left-wing deputies as members: Gaston Bergery, Jean Longuet, Pierre Renaudel, Anatole Sixte-Quenin (November 1932 ff.) and Georges Monnet (March 1933 ff.). In actual fact, this was not an editorial board at all but a committee of patronage, a device for attracting support from the French left. Léon Blum, for example, while never a member of the board, was persuaded to write articles in *Le Populaire* in support of *Maghreb* and the Moroccan nationalists.[2]

Although published in Paris, *Maghreb* was almost entirely a Moroccan undertaking. The possibility exists that it was first inspired by a Tunisian project of 1928, for in that year *L'Afrique Française* announced that the Tunisians were thinking of founding a propaganda journal in Paris, financed by wealthy compatriots, to advertise their grievances before the Chamber of Deputies and especially among the Socialists who had resolved at their 1928 Brussels congress to protect the peoples of the dependencies.[3] This project could not have escaped the attention of the Moroccans in Paris at that time, who were not only reading *L'Afrique Française* but were rubbing elbows daily with their Tunisian schoolmates.

But while the seed may have been planted in 1928, it bore fruit only after Shakib Arslan cultivated it in the mind of Ahmed Mekouar in Geneva late in 1931. Mekouar returned to Paris, where he discussed the project with Balafrej, and thence to Fez, where the Zawiya thought well enough of the plan to give it financial backing. Accordingly, Mohammed Hassan al-Ouezzani was dispatched to Paris at the end of 1931 to organize the journal with Balafrej, but the two fell out when Balafrej, for tactical reasons, refused to permit the other to list himself as director, for which al-Ouezzani considered himself qualified by virtue of his diploma in journalism from the École des Hautes Études Sociales. The group in Fez concluded that Balafrej had the better case, and henceforth sent to him directly the funds necessary to maintain the review, the first installment being 80,000 francs. It was also Arslan who asked Jean Longuet and Pierre Renaudel to help Balafrej as much as possible. They complied by recruiting the committee of patronage mentioned above, the so-called "editorial board." [4] The power behind *Maghreb*, then, was the Zawiya, and its chief editors were the French-educated members of that group: Balafrej, who handled the editorial task almost single-handedly in Paris, and al-Ouezzani, Abdeljalil and Lyazidi, who fed him material from Morocco.[5]

The first issue of the new review appeared in July 1932. It was banned in Morocco on September 9th by the Residential order of Lucien Saint (also responsible for the Berber *dahir*), although it continued to trickle surreptitiously into the country. M. Guernat, head of the League of the Rights of Man, happened to be in Morocco shortly after the ban was imposed, and on his return to France, he and Pierre Renaudel successfully exerted pressure on Premier Herriot to have it lifted on November 1st.[6] Throughout the two years of its publication, *Maghreb* was read by, or read to, enough of the wrong people in France and Morocco to stir up a minor storm. *L'Afrique Française* testified to the effectiveness

of the journal by asserting that tranquillity would have reigned
in Morocco after the Residency's skillful disposition of the Berber
dahir affair had it not been for the inauspicious birth of *Maghreb*.
According to the article, everything on its pages had been said
before, the only difference being the reaction it now evoked
among powerful elements of the French parliament.[7] The left
clamored for reform and annulment of the *dahir*, while the right,
seconded by *L'Afrique Française*, noisily demanded suppression
of these heresies as well as revision of the Treaty of Fez to abolish
the irksome restrictions of Algeciras. The beleaguered, well-
meaning Lucien Saint was only too happy to retire to the relative
calm of the French Senate in July 1933. *Maghreb* ceased publication after it was permanently banned by the Residential order
of May 16, 1934, an act which inaugurated a three-year period
in which no nationalist publications whatever were tolerated in
the French zone.

After al-Ouezzani fell out with Balafrej and found himself
overruled by the Zawiya, he returned to Morocco and insisted on
founding a French-language journal in Fez. This the Zawiya
reluctantly approved,[8] and the first issue of *L'Action du Peuple*
appeared on August 4, 1933. Rézette regarded the editorial board
of *L'Action du Peuple* as the most important nationalist organization of that time and the embryo of later organizations.[9] Of
its six leading members, however, only al-Ouezzani, Abdeljalil,
Lyazidi and Abdelkader Tazi belonged to the Zawiya, and Tazi
was never in its inner circle. The other two, Mohammed Hassar
and Mohammed al-Kholti, were not in the Zawiya at all. In actual
fact, the editorial board of *L'Action du Peuple* was no more than
a propaganda agency of the Zawiya.[10]

The editorial offices of the new journal were located at 168,
Kasbah de Boujelloud, in Fez. Owing to the press regulations of
the protectorate, a French national (in this case, Georges Hertz)
was listed as managing editor, but al-Ouezzani was its director
and editor-in-chief and did most of the work himself. It styled
itself the "weekly organ for the defense of Moroccan interests,"
and the masthead carried for the first four months a quotation
from Zaghlul Pasha on freedom of the press. Owing to a row
between al-Ouezzani and Hertz over a technicality, the Tribunal
of Fez, in a decision of November 30, 1933, suspended the journal
and confiscated the issue of December 1st. It was replaced by
La Volonté du Peuple on December 8, 1933 at the same address.

The Rabat Court of Appeal reversed the lower court's decision on February 20, 1934, and the paper reappeared as *L'Action du Peuple* on March 16th. After the sultan's visit to Fez was used as propaganda leverage in the issue of May 11th (see Chapter XI), the paper was suspended permanently.

Brief as were the careers of the two journals, they chronicle the growing sophistication of nationalist thinking, and a glance at their leading contributors ought to reveal something about the developing character of the movement. Many of the articles ostensibly written by Frenchmen, such as the two Longuets and Émile Dermenghem, were often the work of Moroccans who supplied the documentation, the arguments — indeed everything but the final literary polish. Edouard Depreux, who contributed the articles on the Syrian independence movement, apparently was the only French collaborator who did his own research.[11]

By far the most prolific contributor to both periodicals was Mohammed Hassan al-Ouezzani, who supplied a total of fifty-two articles during the two-year period, mostly under his own name. Omar Abdeljalil furnished forty-one articles, either under his own name or under the pseudonyms "Bouazza Zemmouri," "al-Fallah," or "Abou Hafs." Mohammed al-Kholti, retrieved from Paris by al-Ouezzani to work on *L'Action du Peuple*, contributed thirty signed articles to that journal alone, mostly on the subject of law and justice. Mohammed Hassar was next with twenty-three articles. Ahmed Balafrej never wrote for *L'Action du Peuple* but contributed to *Maghreb*, under various pseudonyms such as "A.B." and "Ahmed al-Mansour" (Ahmed the Great!), twenty-two identifiable articles and probably more. The wife of Abdelkader Benjelloun, as "N.B." or "Romeikya," wrote clandestinely a total of twenty-two articles, and her husband, later a successful Casablanca lawyer, sixteen articles, usually under the pseudonyms "Ezembour" and "Kadour." Georges Hertz furnished fifteen articles to *L'Action du Peuple* before he fell out with al-Ouezzani, and Mohammed Lyazidi contributed a total of fourteen pieces to both journals, mostly in his own name. No other person contributed more than three articles apiece.[12]

Without exception, the leading contributors to the two journals were French-educated, which is to say that those who were first responsible for formulating the broader doctrines of Moroccan nationalism were those through whom the philosophies of Western civilization percolated into that movement. It is true that the offices of *L'Action du Peuple* served as a rendezvous for others besides the *licenciés* just returned from France and the *diplômés* of the *collèges* and *lycées* in Morocco; they were also frequented by some of the students and younger professors at Qarawiyin whose acquaintance with French culture was slender, indeed. The latter, however, seldom wrote for the two journals, even in translation, and the problems of peculiar concern to them were infrequently discussed in the journals.[13] What those problems were is hard to determine and may even be irrelevant, for the fact remains that the French-educated did most of the writing for both *Maghreb* and *L'Action du Peuple*, and their Westernized outlook inevitably governed the content of the two journals.

However, among the leading contributors, neither Georges Hertz, nor Mohammed Hassar, nor the Benjellouns apparently carried much weight as theoreticians. Mohammed al-Kholti defected from the movement soon after 1937, collaborated with the French, and is now regarded by the nationalists as a traitor. Some referred to him as a theoretician of secondary importance, and one nationalist called him a "writing machine." Nevertheless, as the leading contributor on juridical matters, he must have had some influence before his defection. Mohammed Lyazidi contributed relatively few articles but his moral prestige gave them a disproportionate authority. We may conclude, then, that the three most frequent contributors to *L'Action du Peuple* (al-Ouezzani, Abdeljalil and al-Kholti) and the chief contributor to *Maghreb* (Balafrej), along with Lyazidi, should be regarded as the principal theoreticians of the movement at this time.[14] The preparation of the *Plan de Réformes* would call forth the same talent in others.

THE PLAN DE RÉFORMES MAROCAINES

The Plan owed its origin partly to the well-founded charge that the Moroccans complained a lot but had nothing constructive to offer, and partly to the remark of retiring (and hence no longer responsible) Resident-General Lucien Saint that the mistakes made by France in Morocco ought to be rectified in simple justice to the native population.[15] Although they recognized Saint's pronouncement as the confession of a dying warrior, the nationalists professed to take it at face value and set about to turn it against their rulers.

TABLE 3. TABLE OF CONTENTS OF THE PLAN DE RÉFORMES MAROCAINES

The project for composing a plan of reform took shape among the members of the Zawiya in the summer of 1933, and in July or August a small committee was appointed to draft it. Working in Rabat, usually at the home of Mohammed Lyazidi, the committee had completed the first draft by the time of the press suppressions of May 1934. At that juncture Allal al-Fassi felt that demonstrations were called for, but he was overruled by the majority of the Zawiya which opted to complete the Plan, to present it formally, and to await results. The final revisions were probably made in Fez during the spring and summer of 1934 at the homes of Omar Abdeljalil and Mohammed Hassan al-Ouezzani. The participants testify that, except for the political section (Chapters 1–3), the original draft was little altered. Some chapters were composed almost entirely by individuals and presented later to the group. Others were the product of group discussions, where Omar Abdeljalil, as secretary, recorded the conclusions. All notes were taken in Arabic because some members of the committee were not fluent in French. Successive drafts and even the final manuscript were also in Arabic, and a preliminary edition in Arabic was in fact published in Cairo in September 1934, although the reason for this is obscure, because insufficient copies were printed for wide distribution. The French edition, for presentation to the authorities, was published in Paris in November 1934 (see Table 3).[16]

The preparation of the Plan was a closely guarded secret until a month or two before publication,[17] when a committee of patronage was formed in Paris consisting of eight deputies, two former deputies, four writers and one professor, many of whom had already collaborated on *Maghreb*.[18] On December 1, 1934 the Plan was presented in Paris to Foreign Minister Pierre Laval by Omar Abdeljalil and M. H. al-Ouezzani and by Jean Longuet, Jean Piot, Pierre Renaudel and François de Tessan representing the committee of patronage. In Morocco it was presented to the sultan by Abdelaziz Bendriss, Ahmed Cherkaoui, Mohammed Ghazi and Boubker Kadiri, and to Resident-General Henri Ponsot by Mohammed Diouri, Allal al-Fassi and Mohammed Lyazidi.[19] It was rejected immediately by the government as a matter of principle, and, as we have seen, the sultan purchased the freedom of its authors only by abstaining from any public acknowledgment of the Plan.

Page II of the Plan lists the members of the Comité d'Action

Marocaine as the authors: Omar Abdeljalil, Abdelaziz Bendriss, Ahmed Cherkaoui, Mohammed Diouri, Allal al-Fassi, Mohammed Ghazi, Boubker Kadiri, Mohammed Lyazidi, Mekki Naciri and Mohammed Hassan al-Ouezzani. Because only four of the ten were French-educated, Rézette concluded that the Plan was largely an emanation of Islamic culture, although this contradicts his previous statement that the Plan was scarcely more than a compendium of the articles which had appeared in *Maghreb* and *L'Action du Peuple*, articles which he correctly recognized as the work of the French-educated and which largely ignored questions of exclusive interest to the traditionally-educated.[20] This puzzlement might have been avoided had the identity of the real authors been known in 1955. Of those listed on the Comité, Bendriss, Cherkaoui and Diouri, in fact, had nothing to do with its preparation.

The members of the original committee assigned in 1933 to draft the Plan were Lyazidi, Abdeljalil, Hassan Bouayad, Ghazi, and Said Hajji, the first three being the principal contributors. Lyazidi worked on all chapters of the Plan, which is not surprising since most of the early meetings were held in his home. Abdeljalil was responsible for much of the economic section. Bouayad, who preferred to remain anonymous owing to his status as a British protégé, was largely responsible for the political section and probably contributed to the chapters on justice and education as well. In all likelihood Ghazi's influence was rather general, for his intellectual conformation was essentially Salafiyyist, a philosophy characterized as much by its weakness of detail as by the vigor of its fundamental principles. Said Hajji participated only sporadically, and before the first draft was complete was replaced by Boubker Kadiri who was too young to be of much influence. Abdelkebir al-Fassi and Messaoud Chiguer, who took part clandestinely in order not to jeopardize their minor posts in the Residency, translated the Arabic draft into French and may have had something to do with the chapter on justice, both having been trained in the law.[21]

The only major revision of the Plan resulted from the press suppressions of May 1934, and probably was made in Fez by Lyazidi, Abdeljalil, Bouayad and Ghazi, representing the original committee, and by M. H. al-Ouezzani and Mekki Naciri who had no part in the Plan before that crisis but made substantial alterations in the political chapters thereafter. Possibly Allal al-Fassi and Ahmed Mekouar helped to revise the drafts, but their contribution does not appear to have been significant. Ahmed Balafrej at this time was preoccupied with the founding of his free school and took no part in the Plan's preparation. Accordingly, the five principal authors were Lyazidi, Abdeljalil, Bouayad, al-Ouezzani and Naciri, of whom only Bouayad had received an exclusively traditional education.[22] In the analysis which follows, the Plan will be seen to reflect the predominant influence of the Western-educated.

SOURCES OF THE PLAN

The French-educated stood out among the authors of the Plan because most of it was prepared by assembling ideas which had previously appeared in *Maghreb* and *L'Action du Peuple* and in exploring for ammunition the French edition (the only complete edition) of the *Bulletin Officiel du Maroc*. Rézette calls the Plan a "codification of the claims already presented" in the two periodicals, and the authors of the Plan themselves consider it a "synthesis of demands already expressed . . . on diverse occasions." [23] The best illustration of this is the article by Omar Abdeljalil in *La Volonté du Peuple* entitled "Programme," an outline of all aspects of the agricultural problem which distressed the Moroccan farmer and quite obviously an early version of the reforms suggested in Chapters 10, 11 and 12 of the *Plan de Réformes*.[24] Mohammed al-Kholti's articles on judicial abuses and the attacks by Balafrej and al-Ouezzani on the administrative organization of the protectorate are other examples of the same kind (see analysis beginning on p. 216). In dealing with colonial nationalisms, a good case can be made for asserting that if grievances had not existed they would have been fabricated, but sufficient grievances of a genuine nature existed in Morocco to endow the *Plan de Réformes* with real substance. Some parts of the Plan, however, were not derived from *Maghreb* or *L'Action du Peuple*, because they did not emanate from distress conditions but reflected institutions and reforms that France had introduced in Morocco, which were adopted as prototypes by the nationalists. Thus, the achievements as well as the failures of French rule formed the content of the Plan and since both have been extensively described in Part Two above, it will only be necessary to allude to their influence from time to time in the analysis which follows.

There were four possible influences which one might assume the Plan would reflect.[25] One might expect the Moroccans to have adopted many ideas from their more experienced coreligionists of Tunisia, but such was not the case. The nine-point program of the Destour of 1920 called for a popularly elected deliberative assembly of Tunisian and French deputies possessing equal rights, for a ministerial government responsible to the assembly, and for the participation of Tunisians in the acquisition of crown lands and other lands open for colonization. None of these provisions, however, appears in the Moroccan Plan. The Destour project also called for a clear separation of the executive, legislative and judicial functions, a matter of apparent indifference to the authors of the Plan. In such matters as equal pay for Tunisian and French functionaries, the opening of official posts to capable Tunisians, freedom of press and assembly, elective municipal councils, and compulsory primary education, the Plan does resemble the Tunisian program,[26] but these ideas could have derived as readily from internal grievances in Morocco or from elsewhere in the Middle East where they were all common coin. The number of discrepancies between the Plan and the Destour proposals makes a direct relationship questionable at the very least, and we should probably take at face value Mohammed Lyazidi's claim that the authors of the Plan were not familiar with the Destour program.[27]

The Egyptian Constitution of 1923 might also be considered a likely prototype for Moroccan reformers, but like the Turkish Constitution of 1908 and the Moroccan Constitutional Project of the same year, it was designed for an independent country rather than for the reform of a protectorate regime. It provided for a bicameral parliament rather than the single *Conseil* of the Plan, and there was nothing in it about social welfare, agriculture, colonization or education (except that it be free and compulsory), the last three of which occupy a prominent place in the Plan.[28] Clearly the influence of the Egyptian Constitution was slight.

Rézette's assertion that Abdesselam Bennouna's petition of 1931 was the first integrated doctrinal statement of Moroccan nationalism and that it was closely paralleled by the *Plan de Réformes* is plausible to the extent that a one-page document can resemble one of 134 pages. The petition was couched in terms of loyalty to the protectorate regime; it requested elected municipal councils, a higher council responsible for the interests of Moroccans and the approval of the budget, liberty of press and association, better schools and a system of credit to help the fellah improve his lot. Moreover, the nationalists of the French zone were acquainted with it, for M. H. al-Ouezzani had given it full treatment in *Maghreb* in 1932, and it was reprinted in *La Volonté du Peuple* a year or so later.[29] Be this as it may, Bennouna's petition was the most summary of plans, occupying no more than part of a single newspaper column. Its proposals for municipal and higher councils and for agricultural credit facilities were too brief to have been of much help to the authors of the Plan. Its proposals for liberty of the press and of association allude to the Arab "sense of dignity" and the need to "educate them [Moroccans] in their opinions and aspirations," whereas the provisions of the Plan are clothed in the vocabulary of French liberalism, typified by such phrases as ". . . unify the legal status of all the press in Morocco. . . ." or ". . . guarantee the rights of Moroccans. . . ." In its phraseology and its lack of detail the petition smacks strongly of Middle Eastern reformism, while its proposals on education, especially higher education, are quite unlike those of the Plan. Here, too, we should probably accept Mohammed Lyazidi's contention that it did not serve as a model for the Plan, although it may well have had a very general influence.[30]

The fourth potential influence which was not, in fact, reflected in the Plan, despite its proximity, was Spanish Socialism. The Spanish left was even less in tune with Moroccan nationalist aspirations than its French counterpart (see p. 150 for a discussion of the thirteenth congress of the Spanish Socialist Workers Party which opened in Madrid on October 6, 1932).

ANALYSIS OF THE PLAN

If the subject matter of the Plan was determined by conditions internal to the protectorate, the reforms proposed were shaped largely by external factors, Middle Eastern and Western, but predominantly the latter.

According to the Plan's *Avant-Propos*, Morocco suffered from a profound political, social and economic malaise attributable to colonization and to a foreign administration which was characterized as racist, obscurantist, anti-liberal, assimilationist and discriminatory. This comprehensive digest of malfeasance was supported by particulars and statistics and concluded with the statement that, after the crisis of May 1934, two courses were open to the Moroccans: energetic direct action which might provoke grave events, or the presentation of moderate and practical proposals for reform. The latter course was chosen, the Plan which followed was the result, and it was presented in a spirit of cooperation and of confidence in the good will of the Residency.[31]

Mohammed Hassan al-Ouezzani wrote the *Avant-Propos* in Paris, probably in the summer of 1934. The enhancement of his innate organizational ability by his French education, as well as his capacity for hard work and his voracious appetite for reading, enabled him to integrate vast quantities of factual material into meaningful and persuasive form, a talent quite as evident here as in his articles in *Maghreb* and *L'Action du Peuple*, and in the Introduction to the Plan which is largely attributable to him.[32]

The influence of Shakib Arslan is revealed in the simultaneous adoption by the Moroccans, the Algerians and the newly founded Neo-Destour of a policy of cooperation, reform and peaceful political action.[33] This decision to work within the framework of the protectorate was more than a mere tactical maneuver. As of 1934 the Moroccans believed as sincerely as Ferhat Abbas that French culture had much more to offer than their own, and to jeopardize its acquisition by demands for independence would have been considered the height of folly. Nothing could reflect more strikingly the conversion of the French-educated by Enlightenment and Revolutionary philosophies and European governmental institutions and technology.

Part I of the Introduction discussed the treaties, the principles of international law, and the official French declarations of duty and intent which should have constrained French rule in Morocco but did not. Part II reiterated the stated goal of the protectorate — the moral and material revival of Morocco with the aid of France — and asserted that this goal had been sacrificed to colonization, assimilation and discrimination. It concluded with the charge that France had violated not only the Treaty of Fez but the civilized world's sense of justice by gradually replacing Lyautey's system of indirect rule by a direct colonial regime which had reduced Moroccan sovereignty to a mere shadow.

The concept of national self-determination which dominated the Introduction was, of course, such a commonplace that it cannot be attributed to any single source. The one clear influence on the Introduction was French education, for the three principal contributors were educated in France. Al-Ouezzani was probably responsible for most of the final version, and he drew heavily not only upon his own articles in *Maghreb* and *L'Action du Peuple*, especially the series of eight entitled "Le Protectorat," but from a large number of articles written by Ahmed Balafrej and Madame Benjelloun. Balafrej was the most Westernized of the nationalist leaders in every way, and Mme. Benjelloun was a French Jewess of Austrian descent who had received her diploma from the École des Sciences Politiques at the same time as her husband in 1930.[34]

The first chapter of the Plan, which dealt with Administrative Organization, called for a restoration of the system of *contrôle* to something like the original stipulations of the Treaty of Fez. This would have reinstated a form of indirect rule wherein each department established by the Residency would become a vizierate within the Makhzen responsible not to the Residency or to a legislature but to the sultan, the *contrôleurs civils* being relegated to a staff position advisory to the local authorities of the Makhzen. Job discrimination against Moroccans and the preferential treatment of French functionaries were to be abolished, and employee benefits granted Moroccans and Frenchmen on equal terms. Representative government was to be introduced, consisting of municipal, tribal, regional and national councils, the last of which, although consultative in nature, would initiate resolutions for the sultan's consideration on all economic and financial matters as well as on "all reforms of general interest."[35] Finally, the National Council was to be elected by universal manhood suffrage employing a system of *scrutin de liste* in two stages.

The original proposals for administrative reform had appeared in articles contributed to *Maghreb* and *L'Action du Peuple* chiefly by Balafrej and al-Ouezzani (eight or nine articles apiece) and to a lesser extent by Omar Abdeljalil and Abdelkader Benjelloun. This material was of course available to Bouayad and Lyazidi when they drafted this chapter of the Plan. Al-Ouezzani and Mekki Naciri probably changed or added a great deal during later revisions, and Messaoud Chiguer may have collaborated on the original draft in Rabat. Accordingly, the primary educational influence here is French, since of those named, only Bouayad received a traditional education. Lyazidi, for example, while he regards himself as inherently systematic, acknowledges that his mental processes became far more orderly as a result of his French education.[36]

Other Western influences are to seen in the proposal for a ministerial system fashioned after that of France and altered only to fit the requirements of a still absolute monarchy. The French administration in Morocco provided sufficient precedents for the provisions on personnel policies with regard to the appointment, promotion, leaves, discipline and retirement of government employees. The proposal to transform the Chambers of Agriculture and of Commerce and Industry into regional councils grew quite naturally out of the observation that the colonists had already converted these institutions successfully into instruments of political power. The electoral system of France served as the model for Articles 37 and 47–50, providing for universal manhood suffrage, *scrutin de liste*, and the arbitration of electoral disputes.

The impress of the Salafiyya movement is still to be traced at this date in the non-revolutionary mildness, even gentleness, of the Moroccan nationalist leaders and in their optimism about the compatibility of Islam with representative government and popular sovereignty. A very specific Middle Eastern influence can be seen in the adoption of Mustafa Kamil's proposal for the gradual extension of popular sovereignty by means of local, provincial and general councils, mirrored in Articles 31–46 of this chapter, but it should be noted that Kamil in turn derived some of these notions from Lord Dufferin's proposals of 1883 which were incorporated in the Organic Law of that year. Finally, one might observe that Kasim Amin's influence on the emancipation of Moroccan women did not yet extend into politics. No mention of women can be found in the sections on the rights of civil servants, nor were they to be enfranchised.

Justice and the Berber Policy were covered in Chapters 4 and 13. Chapter 13 provided for the abrogation of all aspects of the Berber policy by proposing an end to Christian proselytizing (of which there was very little) and the subsidization of churches out of local receipts, and by providing that the entire population submit to a single code of laws and a uniform educational program.

Chapter 4 described a thoroughly Gallic judicial system modified only where demanded by the requirements of reformed Islamic law. The jurisdiction of the Sharia was to be limited to matters of personal status, inheritance and real estate, leaving civil, commercial and criminal law to be subsumed under the Western system. The *code marocain*, thus founded, would have been derived not only from Muslim law as interpreted by the Salafiyya fundamentalists, but from all the *dahirs* in force in the protectorate (which in themselves would have introduced a measure of Roman law) and from "established principles of jurisprudence," presumably occidental as well as oriental. The rights of the accused were recognized and provisions were made for his defense and arraignment without undue delay. There was to be a Ministry of Justice comprising a *procureur-général* (attorney general), district attorneys in all districts, and a corps of inspectors. A dual system of courts for religious and secular law was to be established in three degrees: courts of the first and second instance and a High Court of Appeal. A High Court of Cassation was to function as the ultimate court of appeal directly under the aegis of the sultan, the chief exception to the principle of the separation of judicial and executive power. French tribunals were to be reduced to their former and, according to the Treaty of Fez, their proper, status as consular courts. Each Moroccan court was to be staffed by a president, judges, assessors, legal advisors, clerks and interpreters. All personnel were to be salaried out of the national budget, all receipts being remitted to the State Treasury. Judges, clerks and other personnel were to be recruited by means of competitive examinations. The suggested reforms of the penal system forbade the use of forced labor and the maltreatment of prisoners, and provided for libraries, workshops, proper sanitary conditions and reformatories for young felons. Political prisoners were to be accorded full civil rights other than freedom of movement.

Mohammed al-Kholti, who held the diploma in law of the University of Paris, was by far the largest contributor of articles (over twenty) on legal matters to *L'Action du Peuple* and *La Volonté du Peuple* and to a lesser extent to *Maghreb*. M. H. al-Ouezzani was next with at least five articles, while Lyazidi and Balafrej each contributed one or two. All of this material was assembled for Chapter 4 of the Plan, primarily by Hassan Bouayad and Mohammed Lyazidi, the former of whom had just returned from Egypt much impressed by the judicial reforms of the late

Saad Zaghlul. Mohammed Ghazi appears to have helped in a general way with the preparation of this chapter, and Messaoud Chiguer and Abdelkebir al-Fassi, both lawyers, may have collaborated to some extent. Here again, the influence of French education is clearly preponderant. Only Bouayad and Ghazi were traditionally educated and the latter's contribution was relatively minor.[37]

The provisions for judicial reform have been treated in detail because they occupied more space in the Plan than any other topic, twenty out of a total of seventy-five pages. The reason for this is clear. Discrimination in any form was galling enough to the native Moroccan, but when it was legalized by the system of so-called justice which the Residency condoned in the protectorate, it became perhaps the most distressing of all grievances. The nationalists studied and wrote more about this inequity than any other, and in his far from flattering appraisal of the *Plan de Réformes*, Julien acknowledges that the recommendations for judicial reform reflected a reliable knowledge of the failings of the protectorate.[38]

The influence of one of the basic tenets of Salafiyya on the judicial provisions of the Plan is discernible both in the separation from the Sharia of all matters more properly secular in nature and in the care exercised to avoid the complete secularization of Moroccan society, as had occurred in Turkey. Another Middle Eastern influence can be seen in the impression which Zaghlul's judicial reforms had made on Hassan Bouayad. Nevertheless, other than Salafiyya, Middle Eastern influences appear to have been rather dilute.[39]

According to Abdeljalil and al-Ouezzani, it was the judicial system of France and of her Moroccan and Tunisian protectorates which served as the model for Chapter 4 of the Plan, and to anyone familiar with that legal system, its similarity to the preceding description is sufficiently apparent to dispel any doubt. As for the penal reforms, to anyone acquainted with the treatment of prisoners in traditional Arabic countries, the humanitarian influence of French liberalism is obvious enough to need no further comment.

Economic and Financial Reforms were treated in Chapters 9–12 of the Plan. The section opened with a number of generaliza-

tions about raising the standard of living by creating work and
increasing wheat consumption, about encouraging agricultural
and industrial production, about protecting Morocco against
dumping, and about the nationalization of mines, oil production,
mineral waters, transportation facilities, electric power, the
tobacco monopoly, and credit and banking facilities. Next, in considerable detail, were suggestions for the improvement of agriculture by the creation of experimental farms and the reform of
the *sociétés de prévoyance* so as to break the settler monopoly of
credit and storage facilities, disaster insurance and the like. The
fellah was to be protected against the kind of seigneurial system
prevailing in Morocco which permitted the *colon* to levy arbitrary
local fines and dues, to requisition labor, to exploit native women
for entertainment at official ceremonies, and to inflict punishment
on his Moroccan employees without being accountable to the
courts. The provisions for land reform included the cessation of
expropriations and all extra-legal practices relating thereto and the
allotment of land to the indigent fellahin. The section concluded
with financial reforms which provided that improper loans over-
loading the Moroccan budget were to be prohibited, tax differentials between Moroccans and Europeans eliminated, tariff duties
raised to the extent permissible by the Act of Algeciras, and an
income tax assessed on all salaries over 12,000 francs.

Virtually the only formulator of nationalist agricultural policy
was Omar Abdeljalil, who furnished at least thirty-eight articles
on the subject to *Maghreb* and *L'Action du Peuple* and was largely
responsible for Chapters 10 and 11 which treated agriculture and
land reform. As a graduate of the École Nationale d'Agriculture
at Montpellier, an apprentice for one year at the experimental
farm at Grignon, and an active farm manager after his return to
Morocco, he was as familiar with the grievances of the fellah as
he was with modern farming methods, and the soundness of this
portion of the Plan is testimony of his expertise.

The other economic provisions of the Plan, however, were
rather weak, for even the French-educated Moroccan usually
neglected the study of economics and was not quite at home in
the world of industry and finance. The usually articulate M. H.
al-Ouezzani had contributed a meager five articles on general
economic policy to *Maghreb* and *L'Action du Peuple* and the
Benjellouns another four, all of which were somewhat elementary
and virtually exhausted their fund of knowledge and experience

on the subject. And since the laws and regulations published in the *Bulletin Officiel* were a poor resource for the drafters of the Plan, because they dealt chiefly with the needs of the *colons* rather than the particular economic requirements of Morocco, about the only source materials available for financial and industrial matters were the above-mentioned articles. They consisted largely of ideas borrowed from French Socialism such as nationalization plans, make-work projects and government subsidies for anyone in trouble. It was from these that Chapters 9 and 12 were fashioned. The treatment was not especially profound, but it did reflect the French influence, for no one with a traditional education had anything to do with this section of the Plan.[40]

One minor Middle Eastern influence can be noted here — that of Kasim Amin on Chapter 10, Article 26, which relieved women of their customary obligation to perform at ceremonies, a traditional Arab practice considered degrading by the young reformers.

Chapter 5, on Education, provided for a government ministry, including a corps of inspectors, responsible for academic standards and sanitary conditions. The program of studies was to be standardized for all Moroccans regardless of territorial, racial or social distinctions. There were to be primary, secondary and higher, as well as agricultural, commercial and professional, schools. The state was to provide scholarships, and girls were to receive formal training. Only eleven of the fifty-four articles dealt with Islamic education, and only a single article provided for the creation of free schools and the abrogation of all impeding legislation in their regard.

Omar Abdeljalil had contributed six articles on education to *Maghreb* and *L'Action du Peuple*, Mohammed Lyazidi and the Benjellouns, four apiece, and M. H. al-Ouezzani, three. Since no one interviewed could assign specific responsibility for the drafting of this chapter, in all likelihood it was one of those produced from notes as a result of group discussion.

The Salafiyya influence is still discernible in the relative importance attached to educational reform (only two other chapters of the Plan equal or exceed Chapter 5 in length), but the relegation of the free-school movement to a single article out of fifty-four betokens its declining prestige. Another oriental influence now beginning to supercede Salafiyya was the secular notion, characteristic of the Arab renaissance in general, that education was an important means of combatting governmental corruption and tyranny, both of which were believed to be inherent in any colonial regime. The ideas of free and compulsory primary education and the promotion of higher education could have come from Kamil and Zaghlul. Articles 25 and 30 on the education of women might well reflect the work of Kasim Amin, and all of these notions must have been familiar to Hassan Bouayad and Mekki Naciri who spent several years at universities in Cairo.

But most of these provisions could just as well suggest the direct influence of France. The underlying assumptions that the proposed educational system should be "national" without consideration for "territorial or social distinction" probably discloses an influence more French than Middle Eastern, and the other provisions of the chapter outlined above are clearly patterned after the French system in Morocco and in the metropole, modified only enough to still the anguished cries of the traditionalists.[41] Moreover, the intellectual conformation of those who must have dominated the discussions, if the final result is any indication, was clearly Western. Even the reform notions which Naciri picked up in Egypt must have been greatly altered by the special study of pedagogy which he took the trouble to make at the Sorbonne and the University of Geneva. It seems reasonable to conclude that, insofar as educational reforms are concerned, oriental and occidental influences reinforced one another, heightening the impact of both, but that the French influence predominated.[42]

Public and Private Liberties were covered in Chapter 2. The first eleven of the eighteen articles of this chapter provided for the rectification of the abuses of individual liberties discussed in Part Two of this book. Article 12 sought to enforce existing laws against slavery and the slave trade. Article 13–18 dealt with freedom of expression, assembly, association and movement.

This was one of the shorter chapters of the Plan, because much of its subject matter was subsumed under judicial reform, but in *Maghreb* and *L'Action du Peuple*, civil liberties had been the subject of over seventeen articles by al-Ouezzani, Balafrej and the Benjellouns. According to the author's informants, Bouayad, al-Ouezzani and Naciri were the principal collaborators on this portion of the Plan,[43] demonstrating once again the preponderant influence of the French-educated.

Specific grievances alone account in large part for Articles 1–11 of this chapter. European liberalism, embodied in the rights enjoyed by Frenchmen in Morocco, served both to heighten the sense of injury in those denied such rights and as an inspiration for this chapter as well. Page 34 of the Introduction revealed that Moroccans considered the legislation already in force for the European colonists as perfectly satisfactory for extension to the native population. We should note at this point that the "Declaration of the Rights of Man and of the Citizen," while it must have had a general inspirational impact on Moroccans, had little direct influence on this chapter of the Plan, for nowhere do we find reiterated the ideas basic to the "Declaration," viz., that law is the expression of the general will, that the rights of man are liberty, equality, security and property (although the implication is there), or that a man is innocent until proved guilty.

It is even more difficult when considering the subject of civil liberties than it was with education to differentiate between oriental and occidental influences. Both are discernible, for example, in the article on slavery, an institution as loathsome to Kasim Amin and other enlightened Muslims as to the European. And in the provisions for freedom of the press, assembly, and association, the mark of the Arab renaissance as well as of the Enlightenment and the French Revolution can be seen. Exponents of the Arab renaissance, like Kawakibi, regarded a free press, along with education, as the guarantor of government responsibility and accountability, while the beneficiaries of the French Revolution — the settlers who brought with them their precious heritage of civil liberties — by denying the same to Moroccans, taught their charges even more to cherish those liberties for themselves.

Nothing on the subject of industrialized labor had appeared in *Maghreb* and very little in *L'Action du Peuple*. Omar Abdeljalil had contributed two articles to the latter dealing exclusively with the problems of the dispossessed farmer who moved to town and of the traditional Moroccan handicrafter faced by foreign competition, and Mohammed al-Kholti had contributed one article of like nature. This chapter of the Plan (Chapter 8) was drafted by

Mohammed Lyazidi, with Mekki Naciri collaborating on a later revision.[44] The French educational influence seems to predominate here, too, but not conclusively.

Moroccan nationalists in 1934 were not as yet much concerned with the problems of the laboring class, owing perhaps to their bourgeois origins. The fact that Lyazidi was one of the few among them who came from humble parentage (his father was a *chaouch*, or messenger boy) may account for his almost solitary responsibility for this chapter. For this reason, most of its provisions were lifted bodily out of the *Bulletin Officiel* wherein was recorded the labor legislation already in force for French workers in Morocco, which was patterned after the labor legislation of the metropole: the eight-hour day, health standards in rural workshops, workers' housing, the creation of *syndicats*, the establishment of mutual funds subsidized by the state for sickness and unemployment, and limitations on child and female labor. The notion of the right to organize came directly from France, since even French workers were not permitted to organize in Morocco until 1936.[45]

Very little on the subjects of public health and welfare had appeared in the pages of *Maghreb* and *L'Action du Peuple*; Abdeljalil, al-Kholti and Mme. Benjelloun each had contributed one article. None of the nationalists interviewed could recall who composed this chapter in the Plan (Chapter 7); in all likelihood, it was a joint production.

The provisions for the reform of public health facilities were obviously modeled after the health services established in Morocco by the French for themselves and were aimed at improving the facilities provided for the native population, which were, of course, inferior. Since any facilities whatsoever constituted a gain over conditions existing in 1912, the Moroccans had little to complain about on this score, and few of the provisions of this chapter can be traced back to legitimate grievances.

The influence of the French left is clearly discernible in the welfare provisions of the Plan: with funds to be established for orphans, the aged, paupers and the unemployed, with special privileges on the railroads to be accorded large families, and with the general provision for state subsidization of all these benefits.

Little or nothing on the subjects of Moroccan Nationality and Civil Status had appeared on the pages of the two propaganda journals, and no one could name the person who might have drafted this chapter of the Plan (Chapter 3). About all that can be said is that its content reflected a predominantly Western influence. Although the concepts of "nationhood" and "nationality" could have originated in the Middle East, their detailed treatment in this chapter was obviously derived from French law on the subject, mostly Revolutionary in origin, such as, for example, the right of option between Moroccan and foreign nationality for persons born in Morocco of foreign parentage, the artificial creation of nationality through naturalization, and the explicit inclusion of Jews as Moroccan citizens. Much of French law on these matters found its way into the French code for Morocco, and the authors of the Plan stated in the Introduction that such legislation need simply be extended to Moroccans.[46]

The remaining chapters (6, 14 and 15) concerned with the administration of the *habous*, the official use of the Arabic language and the Moroccan flag, and the recognition of legal holidays were devoid of any ideological significance not already mentioned and occupied a total of only seven pages in the Plan.

GENERAL CHARACTERISTICS OF THE PLAN

While the Plan has been criticized for the weakness of its economic theory and its questionable representativeness, its authors have been charged most severely with inconsistency and opportunism. The first charge has usually been made with regard to the provisions on the separation of powers. Separation was explicitly provided for in Article 14 of Chapter 4, which guaranteed to judges freedom from administrative interference in the exercise of their functions. Elsewhere the separation was only implicit, as in Chapter 1, Article 47 (c) where civil servants were declared ineligible for election to the National Council. The principle seemed to be openly violated, however, in Article 44 of Chapter 1 and in Article 28 of Chapter 4, which vested ultimate legislative and judicial power in the sultan. Charles-André Julien, erstwhile dean of the Faculty of Letters of the University of Morocco and as sympathetic a friend as the Moroccans ever had, has pointed out that preserving the absolute power of the sultan appeared to be incompatible with a regime based on universal manhood suffrage.[47] But Allal al-Fassi, while admitting the contradiction, rejoined that even had the nationalists been ardently democratic, which they were not, one was obliged to start with the fact that the sultan was still absolute, in theory if not in fact, and that the constitutional provisions of the Plan were intended as nothing more than "a preliminary phase towards a genuine constitutional government . . . in the belief . . . that it was necessary to follow a gradualist course in the . . . application of democracy through a trial period of participation in municipal and regional councils." [48] Seen in this light, these provisions appeared to make sense, and it ought to be noted that this was precisely the procedure adopted after independence. Both Mohammed V and his successor, Hassan, have taken the initiative in establishing representative institutions so that today the ballot, while not always honest, is taken seriously in Morocco, and in 1963 the last of the absolute Sharifian dynasts became Morocco's first constitutional monarch.

Some Frenchmen descried another inconsistency in the partly religious basis of the judicial section of the Plan which they ascribed to the Salafiyyist background of the nationalists. These, said Julien and others, conflicted with the provisions for democratic liberties, an observation which, though characteristic of the secularized French liberal, is quite beside the point, for the Moroccans were seeking consciously to integrate religion and politics and were hopeful (though it has proved a fond hope) that their country could avert the amorality or downright corruption which marked public life in France.

If such contradictions seriously compromised the merit of the Plan in the eyes of its French critics, they failed to disconcert the Moroccans who could rationalize both of them. Furthermore, the point of such charges was somewhat blunted by the Moroccans' awareness that French Socialist theory, from which milieu many of these criticisms arose, did not always jibe with the practices of Socialist deputies in France or of Socialist *colons* in the protectorate. Those who accuse African nationalists of inconsistency might well heed Emerson's reminder that "a foolish consistency is the hobgoblin of little minds, adored by little statesmen and philosophers and divines." [49]

The charge of opportunism can be better substantiated, for the Plan's economic provisions were clearly such. On the one hand, they advocated an open door policy vis-à-vis the West in order to appeal to the French left, to the signatories of the Act of Algeciras, and to the Moroccans themselves, whose industries, such as they were, were not competitive with those of the West. On the other hand, the Plan demanded protection for traditional Moroccan industries, such as the manufacture of babouches, against foreign dumping (in this case, Japanese), a demand which not only appealed to Moroccan artisans but conveniently did not conflict with the Act of Algeciras of which Japan was not a signatory.[50] Need it be said, however, that this sort of opportunism can hardly be condemned by Europeans who have taught the rest of the world what it knows about tariff protection.

Opportunism can also be seen in the proposals for the nationalization of industry, utilities and finance. These were designed to appeal to the Moroccans who lacked the private capital required by such enterprises, to the socialism of the French left, and to the protectorate authorities who would like to have closed the door held ajar to foreign competition by the Act of Algeciras.[51] Thus did Morocco's industrial and financial weakness, her strategic geographic location, and her place in international trade and international law play into the hands of the nationalists who wove these factors most astutely into proposals which could appeal to all but the most unregenerate imperialist.

Finally, it might seem too obvious to mention that the *Plan de Réformes* was "reformist," but the point merits attention, nonetheless, that the Moroccan nationalists of 1934, like Ferhat Abbas, were not seeking independence. Nowhere in the Plan is there mention of terminating the protectorate, or of independence, or even a suggestion that France relinquish her control of Morocco's foreign affairs or the responsibility for her defense. The Plan was not a separatist instrument such as the later North African manifestos. The aim of Morocco's nationalists in the interwar years was, purely and simply, reform of the protectorate regime.

With the exception of such matters as industrial labor, the French presence determined the content of *Maghreb*, *L'Action du Peuple* and the *Plan de Réformes*. Certain topics predominated, and in the articles written by the seven leading contributors to the two journals, economic and judicial grievances appeared more frequently than any other, nearly fifty times each, and this was reflected in the prominence of economic and judicial reforms in the Plan. There were over twenty-five articles on administrative assimilation and about twenty apiece on education (cultural assimilation) and public and private liberties (civil discrimination) in the two journals, and again, the same matters occupied a preponderant place in the Plan. All other topics received relatively short shrift.

The Salafiyyist foundations of the movement remained undisturbed, but the influence of that philosophy on the daily course of events had diminished in proportion as the Moroccans were faced with the realities of French rule and the allure of Western doctrines. Under these circumstances, the tenets of Middle Eastern secular nationalism had become increasingly attractive, although their appeal was rather general or inspirational. Nevertheless, two specific results can be attributed to them: the constitutional provisions of the Plan in regard to elected local, regional and national councils and the foundation of *Maghreb* wherein Shakib Arslan played a central role.

It would have been strange, indeed, if French education had not affected the articles in *Maghreb* and *L'Action du Peuple*, for had it not been for French education, there would probably have been no French-language journals in the first place. Moreover, it was precisely the French-educated, and the most Gallicized among them, who were most sensitive to the derision of the colonists and to the disappointments encountered on the French left. In the columns of the two propaganda journals and in the pages of the *Plan de Réformes*, it was the French-educated who showed themselves the most articulate and constructive critics of the protectorate regime, employing a style and a terminology learned in France, or at least, in French schools.

French leftists can be credited with assisting in the propaganda game by virtue of their advice to the young editors of *Maghreb* on the arts of presenting demands, issuing policy statements, and of journalism in general. As for Western ideas, it is now clear that, by 1933 or 1934, these had begun to dominate Moroccan nationalist doctrine. All the writing in the two journals and in the Plan savors of Europe liberalism and socialism, partly to impress French friends, to be sure, but partly because French education had impregnated the Moroccans with European liberal and socialist thought. The combined ingredients of European liberalism, French socialism and French governmental institutions in both France and Morocco furnished most of the specific remedies which the nationalists had to propose. The *Plan de Réformes* was a conclusive refutation of the charge that the Moroccans had nothing constructive to offer.

XIII

SPREADING THE WORD: 1935–1937

The rejection of the *Plan de Réformes* momentarily unhinged the nationalist movement and caused a perceptible slackening of activity during 1935 and early 1936. So completely had the Zawiya-Kutlat committed itself to the Plan that alternative courses of action had hardly been contemplated. The initiative of the central organization failed, and what activity there was, transpired at the local level.

In place of the former "cells" reporting to Fez, there arose "sections" in the principal cities, usually under the leadership of one of the former "directors" and unquestionably patterned after the sectional structure of the S.F.I.O. By the end of 1935, there were five sections in Fez, four in Casablanca, two in Rabat-Salé and one in Kénitra.[1] It was not an elaborate organization; indeed, it was hardly an organization at all. But what it had lost in centralized policy control, it gained in local vitality, and it showed that the nationalists had taken seriously the charge that their movement represented no more than a handful of malcontents and were attempting to rally popular support. Hence, the dispersion of central authority caused local groups to form around individual leaders and permitted the movement to gain power at the base. Much of this haphazard, local activity achieved results which proved helpful when the time came to attempt a new synthesis of power on a national scale.[2]

The interval of localized activity was marked by little else save a few desultory efforts to protest displeasing developments by means of telegrams or conferences with the authorities. In late 1935, for example, when the French settlers demanded a deliberative voice in the administration of the protectorate, the nationalists objected loudly to what they regarded as another conspiracy to incorporate Morocco in the French empire.[3] And when the question of settler representation arose again in the spring of 1936, Allal al-Fassi and others met with the new resident-general, Marcel Peyrouton, but Peyrouton, a later Vichyite, was not the soul of diplomacy and the discussion degenerated into an exchange of invective.[4]

At the moment when the nationalists seemed frustrated at every turn, however, a series of events occurred outside Morocco which opened new perspectives and revived hope. The worsening situation in Palestine, which erupted in civil war between Arabs and Jewish immigrants in April 1936, caused a reaction throughout the Arab world. In North Africa it broke out in Algeria and Tunisia in the form of strikes and riots in the spring, spreading to Casablanca in June.[5] But the most electrifying developments for the faltering Moroccan nationalist movement were the rise of the Popular Fronts in Spain and France and the rebellion of General Francisco Franco. These events injected the movement with new life but at the same time threatened to destroy what little unity remained between Tetuan and Fez, for the conflicting political orientations in France and Spain attracted the nationalists in each zone to opposite poles.

THE STIMULUS OF THE POPULAR FRONT: MAY–NOVEMBER 1936

No sooner was the Popular Front installed in Paris than it received from the hands of M. H. al-Ouezzani a petition entitled "Appel du Peuple Marocain au Gouvernement du Front Populaire." This document contained only limited demands for the relaxation of press and association laws,[6] but on July 7th a complete dossier of Moroccan claims and grievances, including the *Plan de Réformes* and a documented case against Resident-General Peyrouton, was presented by al-Ouezzani and Omar Abdeljalil to Pierre Viénot, undersecretary of state for foreign affairs.[7] Viénot received them cordially, though non-committally, and the delegation left with expectations that official policy was about to change course.[8] As it turned out, no concessions were made with regard to the Plan, but two months later the nationalists could congratulate themselves on a concrete success when the despised Peyrouton was replaced by General Noguès, although the change was caused more by settler hostility to Peyrouton than by the pleas of the nationalists.

The young Moroccans might have saved themselves from future disappointment had they heeded the realities of French politics as well as Shakib Arslan's warning not to rely too heavily upon the French left. For one thing, as of 1936 they lacked the official support of the Socialist Party.

The annual congress of the Fédération Socialiste du Maroc (the Moroccan branch of the S.F.I.O.), held in Casablanca on May 16–17, 1936, was so far from sympathetic to their cause that it denounced them in a public statement as a privileged minority which wanted to replace imperialist exploitation by its own. The same congress condemned as dangerous and premature the projected admission of Moroccans to the third college of the *Conseil de Gouvernement*[9] and refused to bestow its imprimatur on the delegation of Moroccan nationalists about to embark for France to appeal to the annual congress of the S.F.I.O., characterizing them as ". . . bourgeois; the bourgeois of Islam . . . clerical, racist, and even anti-socialist . . ."[10] The Casablanca congress wanted it known that any alliance with the nationalists would put the party in the position of favoring a reactionary movement under the pretext of combatting imperialism,[11] and al-Ouezzani and his friends haunted in vain the corridors of the S.F.I.O. congress at Huyghens on May 31st.[12]

Moreover, by 1936, neither the government in Paris nor the Residency, had they been so inclined, was in a position to alter official policy significantly, for they found themselves caught neatly on the horns of the dual mandate dilemma. On the one hand were the obligations contracted under the protectorate treaty, as well as the real desire of altruists to administer Morocco for the benefit of the native population. On the other were the strident demands of the French residents in Morocco and their supporters in France, few of whom were predisposed to cooperate with the Popular Front in the first place or to sacrifice the privileges of the settlers for the welfare of mere natives, especially in the midst of a Depression. By 1936 the settlers were sufficiently numerous and powerful to remove undesirable residents-general and to block any policy change which displeased them. Blum's government, faced by the Comité du Maroc, by Algerian settlers in an angry mood over the Blum-Viollette proposal, and by the constant pressure of the North African lobby, spiked its guns and scuttled away into the recesses of the Élysée Palace. Even the presence of nationalist sympathizers in high posts was of no help to the Moroccans. Pierre Viénot, undersecretary for foreign affairs in both Blum cabinets, and François de Tessan, patron of the *Plan de Réformes* and an undersecretary in all the Popular Front cabinets, were able to do little more than cushion Morocco against the formidable coalition of settlers, financiers, entrepreneurs and career officials who had discovered their happy hunting ground in the Maghreb.

But despite the warnings of Arslan, the antagonism of the S.F.I.O., and the equivocations of the Popular Front, the Moroccans had reason to persist in their optimism. Viénot's conciliatory reception of July and Peyrouton's removal in September seemed to presage a new departure. The achievement of Egyptian independence in August and the signing of the Franco-Syrian Treaty in September opened the prospect of similar treatment for the Tunisians and Moroccans.[13] And even the Socialists of Morocco were not a lost hope, for the official policy of the congress of 1936 was mainly the work of the Rabat section which was composed largely of Residency officials, was more conservative than the others, and prevailed in party caucuses up through 1936. Thereafter, party leadership began to shift to the more liberal sections of Fez and Casablanca, the former of which worked closely with the nationalists while the latter had backed the *Plan de Réformes* and had received Omar Abdeljalil and Mohammed Lyazidi as members.[14]

Thus encouraged, the Zawiya again sent Abdeljalil and al-Ouezzani to Paris in October to remind Viénot of his "promises," but when they waited upon the undersecretary, he refused to see them. Either their request for an audience was a bit peremptory (the reason given by Viénot) or the government's position had hardened since July because it no longer feared a rightist coup in the French zone. Whatever the reason, the delegation returned home empty-handed on October 29th to find that news of their failure had preceded them and that their colleagues had already taken action.[15]

On October 25th, al-Fassi had called a meeting in Rabat of some fifty members of the Kutlat which determined on a double course of action. In view of the government's refusal to consider a broadly construed program of reform based on the 1934 Plan, certain "immediate demands" were to be singled out in hopes that piecemeal concessions would be more palatable. The four-page document which resulted was presented to the sultan and Resident-General Noguès and distributed in the *medinas* during the following weeks. It was little more than a selective condensation of the *Plan de Réformes*, to which was appended a demand for an amnesty for all those imprisoned or transported for political crimes since the establishment of the protectorate. The presentation of the "immediate demands" evoked no response whatever on the part of the authorities.[16]

A ballot was also taken at this meeting which resulted in the election of the following officers: [17]

President:	Allal al-Fassi
Secretary:	Mohammed Hassan al-Ouezzani
Councilor:	Omar Abdeljalil
Treasurer:	Ahmed Mekouar
Vice-treasurer:	Abdelaziz Bendriss

The ambitious al-Ouezzani was furious, and interpreted both the election and the timing of the meeting as moves by al-Fassi to oust him from his rightful place as leader of the party. This was quite possible, because the two were incompatible and worked together with difficulty. Whatever the reason, this meeting opened a rift between the two leaders which grew progressively wider in the following months.

At the same meeting was adopted the proposal of Mohammed Lyazidi to hold mass *réunions* throughout Morocco in order to explain the aims of the Kutlat and to enlist popular support.[18] This was a notable change from the old policy and the first deliberate effort to respond to the charge that the Kutlat was nothing more than a club of elite malcontents. The first of the meetings was held on November 2nd in Fez, where 300 people heard seven speakers elaborate on the reform program. There was no violence, not even a street demonstration, and the second gathering, which drew a crowd of 200 in Salé on November 6th, was equally free of disorder.[19]

By mid-November, however, the authorities were becoming uneasy, and the third *réunion*, scheduled for Casablanca on November 14th, the eve of the *Fête du Trone*, was prohibited for fear that the large number of French journalists present would lead to bad publicity in the metropolitan press.[20] This proved to be poor psychology, for the crowd continued to gather after police blocked the entrance to the hall, and a street demonstration resulted with al-Fassi, Lyazidi and other leaders triumphantly carried off on the shoulders of the crowd to the edification of the assembled newsmen.[21] Despite the restraint of the crowd, the

Residency sought to forestall further *réunions* by decapitating the movement, and al-Fassi, Lyazidi and al-Ouezzani were arrested. In doing so the government misjudged the extent to which the local sections of the Kutlat had been maintained, and as if by prior concert, the arrests of November 14th provoked riots in Fez, Salé, Casablanca, Oujda and Taza on November 16th and 17th, resulting in collisions with the police and additional arrests.[22]

With most of its leadership in confinement, the nationalists were, for the moment, neither willing nor able to press further within Morocco, but Abdeljalil went hastily to Paris where he received a warmer welcome than before from Viénot who was now greatly concerned that an outbreak of violence in Morocco might embarrass the Popular Front. Not only did Abdeljalil on this occasion succeed in arranging for conversations between the resident-general and the nationalists in Rabat, he took the opportunity to establish the first permanent Paris bureau to be maintained by the Moroccan nationalists and put Mohammed al-Kholti in charge.[23]

THE BLANDISHMENTS OF FRANCO: THE SPANISH ZONE IN 1936

Meanwhile, shifts in Spanish politics were causing similar repercussions in the northern protectorate. The nationalists of that zone had been following a more or less independent line since 1931, and it was only the personal contact with Fez and Rabat maintained by the Bennounas and Mohammed Daoud which preserved a semblance of unity. But after Abdesselam Bennouna's death in January 1935, it was neither Daoud nor M'Hammed Bennouna but Abdelkhalek Torrès who assumed leadership in Tetuan. Daoud remained a member of the Zawiya until 1937 when he severed even that tenuous connection with Fez, but after 1935 he ceased to play a leading, or even an active role in the nationalist movement, devoting himself to his literary pursuits and public service. Like other Tetuanis, he came to believe that more could be won by accommodating than by alienating the Spanish authorities, and from 1937 to 1948 he served in various public capacities, principally as director of Islamic education for the Spanish zone from 1942 to 1948.[24]

With Torrès in control, the rift between Tetuan and Fez grew ever wider, for the new leader was even more desirous than his predecessors of operating independently, in hopes of wringing concessions from the Spanish government. And Spanish policy, whether royal, republican or falangist, encouraged such thinking by permitting a "nationalist" press to operate and by taking nationalists like Daoud and Torrès into the administration from time to time. Accordingly, when the government of the Spanish Popular Front was in formation during January and February of 1936, Torrès accepted the post of administrator of *habous* for the Spanish zone. He soon found the ties too binding, however, and resigned in June in order to refashion the old Kutlat into a new party, the *Hizb al-Islah al-Watani* (National Reform Party), which came into existence with the tacit approval of the Spanish authorities.[25]

Islah consisted of Torrès and his followers, a journal or two, and the free school, Mahad al-Horr, founded by Torrès in Tetuan.[26] Its "inner circle" comprised a score or so of the younger men who had chosen to follow the dynamic lead of Torrès rather than the scholarly Daoud; many of them, including Torrès himself, had been Daoud's pupils at the Ahliyah school. Torrès was the party's president. Thami al-Ouezzani was its vice-president and editor of the daily *er-Rif*, which fed propaganda to Radio Seville for beaming into the French zone. The inner circle also included M'Hammed Bennouna, Abdesselam Bennouna's two sons, Taieb, who served as secretary, and Mehdi, today a prominent African newspaperman, as well as Mohammed Tnana, Mohammed and Abdullah al-Khatib, and Ahmed Ghilane, who later edited the party's other journal, the daily *el-Hurriya*.[27]

The members of the inner circle managed the party's bureaus which Torrès set up in Larache, Arzila and Alcazarquivir, and there were even agents at key points in the French zone, notably Casablanca and Kénitra.[28] The bureaus of Islah, however, enjoyed none of the local autonomy exercised by the sections of the French-zone Kutlat but were tightly controlled by the inner circle. Membership was strictly limited, because no need was seen for a mass following in a party whose chief purposes were negotiation and propaganda. Most of the leaders were young Tetuani aristocrats reared in the traditions of their Andalusian forebears, disdainful of the crowd and preferring to operate through personal contacts or at most as a pressure group. Their propaganda was designed to evoke mass agitation, perhaps, but not to recruit mass membership. It was characteristic of Torrès' *modus operandi* that he organized the alumni of the Tetuan scouts into a paramilitary corps of Moroccan Falangists, known as the "Green-shirts," in the autumn of 1936.[29]

The outbreak of Franco's rebellion on July 18th caused the rift between Fez and Tetuan to widen even further, because Torrès thought he saw possibilities of playing off the loyalists and the insurgents against one another. To this end, talks were first initiated in Geneva and Barcelona among Shakib Arslan, the Tetuan nationalists, and the Spanish premier, Francisco Largo Caballero, and his staff.[30] At this development, Léon Blum, fearful of the sympathies which the Franco *movimiento* might evoke in the French zone, hastily dispatched a delegation to Fez in August to explore the possibilities of cooperation with the Kutlat. There it was learned that Omar Abdeljalil and M. H. al-Ouezzani were already in Madrid with Arslan offering President Azaña Moroccan assistance against Franco in return for a grant of independence for the northern zone.[31] Both Azaña and Blum, who were in contact throughout these negotiations, now began to have second thoughts about the long-term repercussions of encouraging nationalist autonomy movements for short-term advantages, and all of the negotiations came to naught.[32] In Madrid the talks ended abruptly after al-Ouezzani flew off the handle when Azaña declared the Moroccan demands unacceptable. In Fez the French emissaries backed off in fear that their position as negotiators would be compromised should the Spanish promise independence for the northern zone, and they thereby missed another opportunity to work out an evolutionary solution.[33]

The net result of these abortive conversations was to give Franco a splendid opportunity to play honest broker to Moroccan nation-alism. Torrès had been imprisoned by the rebels at the outbreak of the revolution for his association with the republicans but was soon released on condition that his party rally to General Franco. The insurgents sought to protect their flank by ensuring the co-operation, or at least the neutrality, of the Moroccans and to this end made many vague promises of reform which the nationalists interpreted as commitments to independence.[34] In October 1936 General Queipo de Llano, speaking from Radio Tangier on be-half of Franco, let it be known that the insurgent government was drafting a law to give the Spanish zone the independence promised but denied it by the republic.[35] Although the exact nature of Franco's promises seems difficult to pin down, Torrès was suffi-ciently sanguine of their realization to assure the delegates attending the A.E.M.N.A. congress in Tetuan in October 1936 that Spain was Morocco's greatest hope in liberating her from the "oppressors of North Africa." [36]

From this moment on, Torrès demonstrated a willingness to abandon the sultan and cooperate with the Falangists for the independence of the Spanish zone.[37] This development drove the final wedge between the nationalists of the two Moroccos, for the French zone nationalists henceforth found it expedient to castigate Franco (and by implication, Torrès) in order to win leftist support in France, while the Spanish zone nationalists found the converse policy to their advantage.[38] From 1936 until 1947, when the Istiqlal established its office in Tetuan, Spanish and French zone nationalism lived in different worlds.

NOGUÈS' INTERLUDE OF INDULGENCE: DECEMBER 1936 TO MARCH 1937

From mid-November 1936 until the eve of the Muslim fete of *Aid al-Seghir* (December 17th), the French zone was relatively quiet, and Noguès judged the moment opportune to inaugurate a policy of indulgence towards European workers in Morocco and to proclaim a general amnesty for the nationalists. The riots and demonstrations of June and November, in which industrial workers took part for the first time, had demonstrated the effectiveness with which Morocco had been assimilated into the French economy, for they were an integral part of the wave of industrial unrest which swept over France and Algeria in the spring and summer of that year.[39] Noguès took cognizance of this fact when he caused a *dahir* to be issued on December 24th authorizing trade-union organization in the protectorate. As it turned out, this act played into the hands of the nationalists, for the *dahir* explicitly denied union membership to Moroccan workers, and while a few of them filtered into the *syndicats*,[40] they were not welcomed by the C.G.T. leadership and began from this moment to take refuge in the nationalist movement.

Noguès' general amnesty released, among others, some thirty-seven nationalist leaders who had been taken into custody in November. The nationalists misinterpreted this as a victory for, and vindication of, their recent efforts to rally support, and they seized upon the opportunity to improve even further on this tactic. From this moment dates the first really effective organization of the Moroccan movement on a national scale, effective in the sense that it henceforth could produce, on demand, an impressive demonstration in any part of Morocco where local branches were established.

In December 1936, the Kutlat appointed Allal al-Fassi and M. H. al-Ouezzani a committee of two to draft procedures for opening new branches and enlisting wider participation, and their suggestions were adopted at a January meeting.[41] The new party apparatus would consist of an executive committee, a higher council, technical committees and local sections. At either this or the next meeting, the membership of the first two committees was constituted as follows: [42]

EXECUTIVE COMMITTEE:	HIGHER COUNCIL: (among others),
Allal al-Fassi, *President*	Ahmed Balafrej
M. H. al-Ouezzani, *Secretary-General*	Mohammed Diouri
Mohammed Lyazidi	Ahmed Cherkaoui
Ahmed Mekouar	Boubker Kadiri
Omar Abdeljalil	Bouchta Jamai
Hassan Bouayad	Hachemi al-Filali
Mohammed Ghazi	Said Hajji
Abdelaziz Bendriss	Mohammed Chemao

It should be noted how closely the membership of the executive committee paralleled that of the old "board of directors," seven of its eight members being held over.

The rivalry and suspicion which underlay the continued collaboration of al-Fassi and al-Ouezzani now broke the surface. For several months, friends of the two, including even Shakib Arslan, had tried to heal the widening rupture, but al-Ouezzani refused to be placated, regarding himself as the better fit for the top position.[43] Now that the leadership of al-Fassi had been confirmed in the new organizational hierarchy, al-Ouezzani objected to being fobbed off with the post of secretary-general, and so stated to his colleagues. His dissatisfaction was the subject of an executive committee meeting of February 6, 1937 at which an effort was made to mollify him by proposing to abolish the presidency should the first general assembly of the party approve.[44] But al-Ouezzani refused to be mollified, resigned his post, and was replaced, more or less informally, by Ahmed Balafrej,[45] who from this moment forward occupied a commanding position in the nationalist movement second only to Allal al-Fassi.

At the same meeting, resolutions were adopted to democratize the organization by opening its doors to all who would prove capable of working for the nationalist cause and of being faithful to its principles. Emissaries of the movement were to canvas the country appealing to the peasants and workers alike in an effort to flesh out the skeletal network of local sections.[46] Discipline would be tightened by the use of membership cards and the administration of an oath of loyalty, and full advantage was to be taken of the resident-general's liberal press policy and of the new law which legalized Muslim private schools.

Under Balafrej's vigorous command much of this program was actually accomplished. In the cities, where depressed economic conditions played into their hands, the nationalists won a large following among the artisans and unemployed country folk, newly arrived in town, by reminding them that they were discriminated against in the trade unions and by stressing the welfare proposals first enunciated in *Maghreb*, *L'Action du Peuple* and the *Plan de Réformes* a few years earlier.[47] In the tribal areas, where traditionalism persisted and the masses understood religious organizations better than secular ones, the nationalists invoked Salafiyya once again and permitted the peasants to regard them as the lay priests of a reformed religion.[48] It is still uncertain whether Allal al-Fassi paraded himself as the "Shaykh Allal," head of the *Zawiya al-Wataniya* (National Brotherhood), or that his followers called themselves *Allaliyin* (Disciples of Allal), as claimed in an article which appeared in *La France Méditérranéenne et Africaine* in 1938,[49] but it is quite clear that traditional religious sentiments and associations were exploited in the tribal areas and that this resulted, for the first time, in the successful recruitment of the country folk in the nationalist movement.[50] Le Tourneau points out that the Tunisian nationalists lacked the religious zeal of the Moroccans and were separated to that extent from their followers, whereas in Morocco the quasi-religious appeal of the Kutlat made great headway wherever tradition still rendered communities socially cohesive, notably in the countryside around Fez and in the cities of Fez, Meknes, Salé and Taza.[51] With this development, the religious brotherhoods began to lose their appeal proportionately, and from 1937 onward, each time the nationalist movement made an advance, the brotherhoods lost.[52]

The recruiting campaign was a notable success, for just before the party's dissolution in March 1937, card-carrying membership totaled somewhat over 6,500, excluding the Spanish zone, and in addition to the twelve sections which had existed since 1935 in the north (in Casablanca, Rabat-Salé, Kénitra and Fez), there were twenty new sections widely distributed throughout the country.[53] The leadership had gone far to refute the old charge that their movement did not represent the people, for even though Le Tourneau may assert that the nationalists of 1937 did not speak for the nation and that many Moroccans did not understand or were affronted by their brashness, he concedes that the nation could not help but approve the way the nationalists spoke out against the protectorate in the name of Islam and for a "revival" of Moroccan patriotism.[54]

The reorganized party also took advantage of the *dahir* of April 1, 1935 which officially recognized the existence of private Muslim schools and authorized their foundation and regulation by the Residency.[55] Thereafter the number of free schools directly or indirectly controlled by the Kutlat increased steadily, slowly at first, until after World War II, then quite rapidly. Similar efforts were made at Qarawiyin, where nationalist pressure was exerted to modernize and rationalize the curriculum and where the students were considerably aroused by nationalist harangues.[56]

The party activity most visible to the public as well as to the authorities was its periodical press. Noguès' relaxed policy had also resulted, on January 19, 1937, in the authorization of the first unofficial Arabic-language newspaper to be published in the French zone, the weekly *el-Atlas*, which was edited by Mohammed Lyazidi and whose first issue hit the streets of Rabat on February 12th. Shortly afterward, on the 27th, its French-language counterpart, *L'Action Populaire*, made its debut in the same city, edited by Mme. Khadidja Diouri and financed by her husband, Mohammed Diouri, who was a member of the old Zawiya. Both journals were organs of the Kutlat and both carried on their mastheads the legend, "Organe Hebdomadaire du Parti d'Action Marocaine," the first time the word "party" had officially replaced "committee" or *kutlat* and an indication of the increasing emphasis being placed on organization and recruitment.[57] Approximately the same people wrote for *L'Action Populaire* as had written for *L'Action du Peuple* in 1933–34, the names of Lyazidi, Abdeljalil "A.B." (Ahmed Balafrej) and Mohammed al-Kholti figuring prominently among the by-lines. And the articles which it carried dealt with the same concerns as before, except that the persistence of drought and depression caused greater attention to be paid to the plight of the fellah and the unemployed artisan.

The party also controlled a more moderate Arabic-language journal, *el-Maghreb*, an evening paper of Salé edited by Said Hajji who was a member of the old Taifa, of the Kutlat's *conseil supérieur*, and was elected to the equivalent council of the National Party late in 1937. Mohammed Chemao, also a member of the Kutlat's *conseil supérieur* and later head of the Moroccan Socialist Party, collaborated with Hajji on this paper. Finally, the party disposed of a monthly journal in Paris, *La Voix du Maroc*, edited by Mohammed al-Kholti who had worked with al-Ouezzani on *L'Action du Peuple* and was now the party's bureau chief in the capital. *La Voix du Maroc* was aimed chiefly at the growing number of Moroccan workers in France.[58]

Nationalists of other hues were no less backward in exploiting the indulgent press policy. Mohammed Hassan al-Ouezzani, partly to air his differences with Allal al-Fassi, obtained authorization on January 21, 1937 to revive the old *L'Action du Peuple*, although the first number did not appear until April. On January 20th Mohammed Chamao was authorized to publish a weekly journal, *el-Widad*, which was so moderate as to arouse suspicions of official subsidization, and on the day before that, January 19th, approval for the daily *el-Amal* was granted to Abdellatif Sbihi who had been a militant nationalist at the time of the Berber *dahir* but thereafter had gone his own way. The first number of *el-Amal* also appeared in April.[59]

DISSOLUTION AND SUPPRESSION: MARCH–NOVEMBER 1937

So successful were the recruiting efforts of the nationalists in the winter of 1937, that Viénot and Noguès, who had hoped to channel such activity into manageable rivulets, decided to put a stop to the proliferation of sections, and the Kutlat was dissolved by a vizierial decree of March 18, 1937 which charged it with violating the law against organizations requiring membership cards and dues payments.[60] The decree added, somewhat pontifically, that the swearing of an oath by party members was a grave affront to the authority of the sultan and the traditions of Islam, although Mohammed V had shown no signs of being offended.[61] The dissolution of the Kutlat was in part an indication of the growing sensitivity of the French authorities to the developments in North Africa and Spain and was paralleled in Algeria by the dissolution of the Étoile Nord-Africain and by Messali Hadj's trial and imprisonment which also took place in 1937.[62] Repeated articles in *L'Afrique Française* throughout these prewar years reveal how jumpy the authorities had become about German, Italian and even Communist influence in North Africa.[63]

The dissolution of the Kutlat did not apply to its journals, nor, apparently, did it much effect its organization, for the first issue of *L'Action Populaire* which appeared thereafter (March 27th) announced that it had become the organ of the Mouvement Populaire pour le Plan de Réformes.[64] To avoid further attention by the authorities, the party was secretly reconstituted, at a meeting held in Rabat in April, as the National Party for the Realization of the Plan of Reforms (*al-Hizb al-Watani li Tahqiq al-Matalib*).[65] The executive committee of the dissolved Kutlat was now slightly reduced in size by the demotion of Hassan Bouayad and Abdelaziz Bendriss to the *conseil supérieur*, leaving al-Fassi, Balafrej, Lyazidi, Abdeljalil, Mekouar and Ghazi, thus equalizing the influence of the French-educated with the Muslim-educated for the first time. Only M. H. al-Ouezzani of the original inner circle was missing.

The rift between al-Fassi and al-Ouezzani had widened after the executive committee meeting of February 6th, but while the latter had resigned his post, he had not withdrawn completely. The final breach took place at the first national congress of the party held in Rabat in April.[66] Eighteen of the twenty-three delegates voted for al-Fassi's proposal to elaborate and expand the party hierarchy, while only five supported al-Ouezzani in his effort to retain the old form of an elite pressure group.[67] Rézette places great emphasis on this structural disagreement between the two leaders,[68] and from this premise some commentators have argued that Noguès' policy of indulging moderate nationalist activity was a factor in widening the rift between the two, because such a policy made possible for the first time the open recruitment campaign that al-Fassi advocated and al-Ouezzani resisted. This logic might have applied before the Kutlat was suppressed in March, but thereafter al-Fassi was forced to limit himself to a clandestine recruitment policy not unlike that which his rival had been recommending. It is unlikely that the final breach would have occurred at this moment over a difference of strategy which had become academic.

Al-Ouezzani himself claims that the breach occurred over his insistence, which the al-Fassi clique rejected, on the development of a full-fledged doctrine or party program along the lines of the "Declaration of the Rights of Man and of the Citizen." [69] But an examination of their respective newspapers does not bring to light any significant differences on this score. If anything, the al-Fassi faction could boast the more complete party program, for as the lineal descendant of the Kutlat, it had inherited the *Plan de Réformes* which it now republished in *L'Action Populaire*. The most al-Ouezzani had to offer was a "Minimum Program," four columns in length, which was little more than a rearranged abstract of the *Plan de Réformes*,[70] although even al-Ouezzani could claim authorship of the Plan and in fact had urged its adoption in July 1937 as the best basis for a general reform and the return to a true protectorate.[71] This should suggest that the doctrinal differences between the two men were no more significant than the strategic differences.

In discussing the rupture with the participants, one concludes that the chief factor was temperamental incompatibility. Al-Ouezzani is candid enough to admit that his own personality tended to be domineering and sometimes caused friction,[72] and while al-Fassi could be equally domineering, he was, perhaps, more diplomatic. Each was a man of strong convictions and forceful expression. The National Party of 1937 was simply not large enough to contain two such ambitious aspirants to leadership.

Whatever his motives, al-Ouezzani's decision to form a rival party, the Action Nationale, terminated his influence in the mainstream of the nationalist movement. In April he revived his old newspaper, *L'Action du Peuple*, subtitling it the *Hebdomadaire d'Action Nationale Marocaine*. Under the direction of Abdelhadi Chraibi, former member of the National Party who had sided with al-Ouezzani in April, an Arabic-language journal, *ed-Difaa*, began to appear in Fez in June.[73] Not to be outdone by al-Fassi, al-Ouezzani also formed a clandestine counterpart to Action Nationale which he entitled the Mouvement Populaire, but despite the implied hope of its name, its membership was limited largely to the editorial boards of the two journals and a few dozen other intellectuals who had defected from the National Party where they felt their talents were not fully appreciated.[74]

Undeterred by the dissolution of the Kutlat and the defection of the al-Ouezzani faction, the nationalist leadership clung to the hope that reform was still possible with the cooperation of the French authorities, and following the Kutlat's dissolution somewhat forlornly began to serialize the old *Plan de Réformes* in its new journal, *L'Action Populaire*.[75] In the same issue the leadership also reiterated its fundamental objectives: to persuade the authorities to lift the ban against the party and to continue to use "all legal means to realize the ideal of Moroccan nationalism and to secure the implementation of its just demands."[76] The leadership wanted it clearly understood that it recognized the legality of the protectorate and wished to secure its reform, not its termination, and this policy was stated once more as clearly as possible in the next issue of *L'Action Populaire*.[77] Even *L'Afrique Française*, as it congratulated itself for its part in the dissolution of the Kutlat, felt constrained to admit one month later that the nationalists were not seeking immediate independence but only a return to the spirit of the Treaty of Fez.[78] It is important to note that, as of mid-1937, Moroccan nationalism was not only desperately trying to regain its legality but had no intentions, despite the greatest provocation, of becoming separatist.

Operating clandestinely, the party was necessarily hampered in the scope of its activities, but acting on instructions from the party headquarters in Fez, local sections managed to busy themselves with the dispatch of congratulatory telegrams to the sultan and denunciatory telegrams to the French authorities, and with some perfunctory recruiting. There was no other marked activity until the return of Balafrej and Abdeljalil from France in July.[79] The two had been sent to Paris to present to their former patron, François de Tessan, now undersecretary of state for foreign affairs, a memorandum in the name of the National Party condemning the policies of Resident-General Noguès during the previous year. It was thus that on July 23, 1937 the National Party first became known to the authorities. The undersecretary could do no more than promise to take up the charges with the resident-general and see what could be done.[80]

On their way home the pair paused at Marseille to lobby for their cause at the S.F.I.O. annual congress. The congress had already received a telegram from al-Fassi and Lyazidi urging it to reverse its stand of the previous year,[81] and the Moroccans knew they had support for the first time from the Fédération Socialiste du Maroc. The Casablanca delegate, Paul Chaignaud, holding quite different views from his more conservative colleagues from

Rabat, argued the case so eloquently for collaboration with the Moroccan nationalists [82] that the party decided officially (in December) to come out in their support.[83] December was a bit late, however, for the National Party had been effectively suppressed in November, and the Socialists lost what official influence they had the next month when they deserted the Popular Front.

As of July, however, the nationalists had nothing to show for their previous year's efforts save their organization, which remained intact. Taken less than seriously by both the French government and the Socialists, they then decided to employ that organization in direct action.[84]

Morocco was in a state of acute distress in the summer of 1937. Unemployment had become chronic among the growing urban populations of the north, and the problem was aggravated many times over in May and June by the arrival of refugees from the south where the third drought in three years had ruined the crops. It was estimated by the Residency in June that there were 1,400,000 natives (about 20 per cent of the population) either starving or without adequate means of subsistence until the next harvest.[85] Around this powder keg the nationalists heaped their journalistic tinder, until only an incident was needed to touch off an explosion.

The incident occurred in Meknes, where it was learned that the authorities planned to divert water from the city's main supply, the Bou Fekrane River, for the benefit of four *colons*. On September 1st, crowds which gathered in the streets crying "Water or death!" and "Not a drop for the *colons*!" were dispersed only after considerable effort and restraint on the part of the police. The following day the authorities decided to make an example of the leaders by arresting several and announcing that they were sentenced to three months in prison. The crowds which assembled on the evening of September 2nd were in an ugly mood, and their confrontation by the police resulted in about a dozen deaths among the demonstrators and thirty or forty wounded on both sides. Numerous arrests followed the tragic "evening of Bou Fekrane." [86]

Justifiably aroused, *L'Action Populaire* published on September 4th a virulent attack which began: "Meknes, lair of Fascism, takes its revenge on the allies of the Popular Front . . . dozens of dead, hundreds of wounded," and for its temerity was immediately suspended.[87] The National Party now called for demonstrations throughout Morocco to protest the brutal suppression in Meknes, and on September 6th Casablanca, Fez, Rabat, Oujda, Marrakesh and Meknes responded, all of them without serious disorders. On September 11th a final issue of *L'Action Populaire* which appeared on the stands under the title *L'Action* was immediately confiscated, and on the 15th the annual congress of the A.É.M.N.A. scheduled for Rabat was postponed by the authorities in order to preclude any incident. On the 24th, the Marrakesh visit of undersecretary of state for public works, Paul Ramadier, was turned into a riotous stone-throwing demonstration in which 3,000 people invaded the *Djemaa al-Fna*, caused the *cortège* of the minister to alter its course, and resulted in the arrest of about fifty demonstrators. The dozen or so who were regarded as the leaders were quickly sentenced to three months' forced residence in the Sahara. This first round of unrest culminated rather peaceably on October 4th when demonstrations were organized throughout Morocco to show solidarity with the Arabs of Palestine on the occasion of the Pan-Arab congress then being held in Bludan, Syria.[88]

In Meknes, where the rash of riots had first erupted, an investigation proved that the real grievance was not so much the diversion of water per se as an error in timing on the part of the authorities. The four *colons* would have diverted about twenty litres per second from a total flow of about 250 litres per second, in normal times. The error was made in taking care to divert the full twenty liters for the *colons* in a dry period when the rest of the city would not receive its quota.[89] The Meknes riots were thus part of the more profound problem caused by the continued immigration of French colonists during these years when depression and drought jointly afflicted Morocco.

Throughout September and October, the National Party had labored diligently in the towns and among the tribes to arouse the people to defend their liberties and to preserve their religion from the infidel, with the result that the agitation was not for long permitted to die out.[90] Early in October the executive committee had drawn up a petition of grievances to be sent to the resident-general, and on the evening of October 13th delegates from some twenty sections of the party met in the home of Ahmed Cherkaoui in Fez to decide what further action to take.[91] The minutes of this meeting were printed and distributed to the crowd which assembled in Meknes several days later for the annual pilgrimage to the tomb of Moulay Idriss. The tract proclaimed that the

National Party would struggle energetically for an end to the "regime of martyrs" imposed by France, would continue to send telegrams of protest, and that its members would press on to action and, if need be, sacrifice themselves to provide an example.[92]

The results were not long in coming. On October 16th *el-Atlas* was suspended for an article inciting to riot in its issue of October 14th. On Friday, October 22nd, four students from Fez exploited the announcement of the previous Sunday, that a Catholic pilgrimage would be made to the church of Sainte-Thérèse in Khemisset, to urge the worshipers assembled there in the mosque to defend their religion and their town against this infidel incursion. On leaving the mosque the crowd attacked the office of the *contrôleur civil*, and the inevitable clash with the police resulted in a number of casualties on both sides. The police managed to make the *agents provocateurs* confess that they had instigated the riot on orders from Allal al-Fassi who, accordingly, was arrested in Fez on October 25th along with Mekouar and Abdeljalil. The three were conducted to the military prison at Ksar al-Souk where they joined Mohammed Lyazidi.[93]

Until now the Chautemps government had been reluctant to act in spite of Noguès' urgings, but the riots of Meknes and Khemisset demonstrated that the situation was indeed critical. This time, measures were taken to prevent the spread of disorders which the arrest of the leaders had precipitated the year before. On October 26th troops were moved into Fez, the journal *ed-Difaa* was shut down by the pasha, a vizierial decree outlawed the National Party as an illegal reconstitution of the Kutlat, and three more leaders were arrested, although M. H. al-Ouezzani escaped for the moment by taking refuge in a foreign consulate.[94] Despite the precautions, there were demonstrations in Casablanca on October 26th, in Marrakesh and Oujda on the 28th, and in Rabat on the 30th, all relatively peaceful, as well as a riot in Kénitra where the police fired into the crowd, killing four, and where Mohammed Diouri was apprehended and sentenced to two years in prison.[95]

On the night of October 27th the authorities moved to seal off the source of the trouble by occupying the Fez *medina* for the first time since 1912. The grand vizier instructed all *caids* and pashas to arrest immediately anyone caught making a political speech, and Boubker Kadiri was apprehended for this crime the next day in Salé and sentenced by the pasha to a year in prison.

Nothing untoward occurred in Fez until the night of the 29th when several hundred students who had gathered in the Qarawiyin heard a "veritable appeal to civil war," delivered perhaps by Mohammed Hassan al-Ouezzani who was still at liberty. Native troops surrounded the mosque and arrested some 650 people as they left, including al-Ouezzani. Later in the evening Hassan Bouayad was apprehended elsewhere in town.[96] By midnight of October 29th the entire executive committee and many other ranking leaders of the National Party were in custody.

According to official figures, 444 prison terms were meted out, of which forty-five were for two years, six for eighteen months, thirty-three for one year, and the rest presumably for less than a year.[97] On November 3rd, Allal al-Fassi was flown to Libreville in the Gabon to begin an exile which was to last nine years. Al-Ouezzani, Lyazidi and Mekouar were exiled to the Sahara, Mekouar returning in 1940, Lyazidi in 1941, al-Ouezzani not until 1946.[98] Balafrej happened to be in Paris when the arrests were made and remained in voluntary exile until 1943, traveling between Tetuan and Berlin during the war. Omar Abdeljalil was soon liberated and joined Balafrej in the Spanish zone, while Hassan Bouayad, as a British protégé, was expelled, rather than imprisoned, and took himself to Cairo.[99] After November 1937, only Mohammed Ghazi of the National Party's executive committee and Ahmed Cherkaoui, Said Hajji and possibly Bouchta Jamai of the *conseil supérieur* remained at liberty within Morocco, and none of these can be said to have exercised dynamic leadership.

The arrest of the leaders had accomplished the purpose of the Residency to destroy the effectiveness of the National Party by decapitating it.[100] The membership of the party had steadily declined after the dissolution of the Kutlat in March and probably totaled no more than 4,000 in October. Thereafter, with its leaders in prison, its membership certainly declined further, although no reliable statistics are available.[101]

During the months when its leadership was intact, however, the new organization had proved, by the events of September and October, that it could operate with great effect. These events constituted a conscious attempt to make force prevail where persuasion had not. The attempt failed because the authorities were thorough in their suppression and because neither the people of Morocco nor of France were as yet morally prepared for

Moroccan independence. The resort to force had failed once before when Abd al-Krim surrendered in 1926. The third time the Moroccans tried it, in 1953–54, it would succeed.

The events of 1935–37 showed clearly that doctrine had come to play a subordinate role in the nationalist movement. Much of the activity of these years was guided by political expediency; that is, not what program to present but how to get reforms, any reforms, accepted by the authorities. The elaborate proposals of the *Plan de Réformes*, while not superseded, receded somewhat into the background as the demands of the nationalists changed both in substance and in emphasis. Thus, in 1935 they were chiefly concerned with the flood of colonization and its attendant problems; in 1936, with removing an egregious resident-general and the relaxation of the press and associations laws; in 1937 with raising the ban on the party and counteracting the demand of the settlers, illegal under the terms of the Treaty of Fez, for a voice in the administration of the protectorate. This did not mean that the broad program of reform had been wholly abandoned, for repeated efforts were made during this period to resuscitate the *Plan de Réformes*, but it did mean that the ideological influences, occidental as well as oriental, which had shaped the nationalist movement in former years, had lost some of their force as the nationalists discovered that tactics or organization were far more important than they had formerly thought.

Hence, after 1934, Moroccan nationalist doctrine developed very little, if at all, while method and organization, largely Western in origin, took precedence. We have seen this in the formation of Torrès' "Greenshirts" and in the increasing use of telegrams of protest, of delegations, of street demonstrations and of the propaganda press. The influence of French political parties, especially the S.F.I.O., is quite evident in the proliferation of the Kutlat's sections and in the later formation of its *comité exécutif* and *conseil supérieur*. The nationalists had learned the lesson of organization the hard way during the fruitless years between the Berber *dahir* and the *Plan de Réformes*, and they sought thereafter to put it to use, initially to persuade, finally to constrain, with about equal lack of success. Their failure was not essentially owing to faulty organization but chiefly to the fact that their power to intimidate the authorities was not, in 1937, equal to the authorities' power to intimidate them. But if the nationalists had failed with France, they had succeeded in spreading the word to the Moroccan people, and this foundation of popular sympathy would stand the nationalists in good stead when the time came to revive their organization in 1943.

While noting that organization had taken precedence over doctrine by 1937, it should be pointed out that the third major factor in shaping Moroccan nationalism, i.e., the French presence, became more important in 1935 as the Depression reached its nadir in Morocco. This can be seen not only in the nature of the appeals made to the French government during the worst of the crisis, wherein much greater concern is shown, for example, for trade unionism and unemployment; it is also reflected in the stress placed on social welfare in the speeches and articles which appeared in the nationalist journals and in the disturbances of 1936 and 1937, especially those of Casablanca, Fez and Meknes, whose excesses were unquestionably a function of the economic malaise.

Finally, modern as it was becoming, Moroccan nationalism still found it expedient to bow to tradition by affecting the trappings of a religious brotherhood (the *Zawiya al-Wataniya*) in order to make effective its recruiting among the tribes.

The year 1937 had proved to the nationalists that reforms of the type they sought would not be forthcoming under the protectorate, and while they remained loyal to France as Hitler's war approached, they began now to explore avenues which might lead to independence.

XIV

REFORMISM TO SEPARATISM: 1937–1944

Noguès had no intention of permitting the nationalist movement to revive in the riotous form it had taken in 1936–37. His policy was to mollify rather than repress. The arrests of 1937 had been made quietly and, with the exception of October 29th, selectively. Immediately thereafter, the resident-general proceeded to contact responsible Muslim leaders in order to demonstrate his good faith. On the evening of October 30th he arrived in Fez where his local deputy, General Blanc, had already assured a conclave of notables that Residency policy was not to reestablish order at any price, but to ameliorate economic conditions, to expand educational facilities and to give Moroccans an increasing voice in the government. On the following day, Noguès himself received the notables and toured the city, stopping periodically to talk to the people and reassure them of his good intentions.[1] On November 22nd, he issued a circular which acknowledged the contribution to Morocco's problems made by official irresponsibility and pledged a better use of governmental resources for the benefit of the Moroccan people.[2] Conditions soon returned to normal, and the troops were withdrawn from Fez without further incident.[3]

Official policy now became flexible enough to permit the release of Omar Abdeljalil, the continued operation of National Party offices in Fez and Rabat, and the publication of several "moderate" native periodicals. After *L'Action du Peuple* and *L'Action Populaire* were closed down, the only paper in circulation which could possibly be construed as "nationalist" was Said Hajji's *el-Maghreb*. It limped along on a limited budget as a two-page bi-weekly until 1939 when it was finally suspended for expressing pro-Axis sentiments. The weekly *et-Tagaddum*, published from October 22nd onward by Ahmed ben Mohammed Nejjar, former National Party member, was so moderate in its editorial policy as to constitute collaboration with the authorities. The French-language *La Voix Nationale* was another weekly which first appeared on February 15, 1938. Edited by Abdellatif Sbihi, it was even more moderate than his earlier journal, *el-Amal*, its stated editorial policy being to act as a connecting link between Frenchmen and Moroccans of good will. Two other journals tolerated during the war were Mohammed Ghazi's *el-Risala el-Maghrib*, a monthly literary and scientific review founded in 1942, which, despite its editor's eminence in the nationalist movement, carefully avoided political topics until 1944 when it was taken over by the Istiqlal, and *el-Thaqafa el-Maghribiya*, founded by Ahmed ben Ghabrit in 1941, the political complexion of which can be judged from the fact that Allal al-Fassi regarded Ghabrit as a French agent.[4]

These journals can hardly be compared with the vituperative *L'Action Populaire* and *L'Action du Peuple*, but they did furnish an outlet for reformers who were willing to employ restraint, for Noguès' purpose was not to eradicate nationalism but to guide it into constructive channels in accord with his pledge of November 22nd to institute reforms. The resident-general was willing to compromise with the nationalists if they did not systematically oppose every act of the Residency and if they refrained from agitation, and to this end, he tried to reorient official native policy along lines more responsive to native welfare.

He began by attaching to his staff as advisors two former members of the editorial board of *L'Action du Peuple*, Mohammed Tazi and Mohammed Omar al-Hajoui. Tazi was a graduate of the Collège Moulay Idriss in Fez, al-Hajoui of the Lycée Janson-de-Sailly and the École des Sciences Politiques in Paris.[5] Both came from eminent Moroccan families and personified Noguès' return to Lyautey's practice of partnership with the country's elite. In the same vein, the resident-general maintained close ties with the alumni of the *collèges* in Fez, Rabat and Marrakesh, asking their advice on the budget and other policy matters and reserving seats for them in the Moroccan section of the *Conseil de Gouvernement*.[6]

In early 1937 Noguès had already accomplished the feat of reducing the salaries of French functionaries and military personnel in the face of considerable bureaucratic resistance. And it was partly on Noguès' behest that the Conference for the Coordination of North Africa met in Paris on November 7–12, 1937, under the presidency of Albert Sarraut, and recommended economic reforms (famine relief, aid to native artisans, irrigation projects and public works to relieve unemployment), the reform of native justice, the extension of general and professional education, and the admission of greater numbers of the native elite into administrative and representative bodies. Noguès' circular of November 22nd was the direct result of this meeting, and honest efforts were made thereafter to institute some of these reforms with the limited funds available. New schools were opened for Moroccan children, scholarships were provided for study in France, and the selection of *cadis* for the Sharia courts was regularized. A climate of mutual confidence, however tenuous, began to be established between the resident-general and the sultan.[7] On July 2, 1938 Noguès was able to summarize his achievements of the previous six months in a speech before the Moroccan section of the *Conseil de Gouvernement*, to such effect that even Shakib Arslan acknowledged that substantial progress had been made.[8]

The astute combination of suppression and gestures of reconciliation and reform seemed to bode well for French rule in Morocco. The years 1938 and 1939 were possibly the most tranquil the protectorate had known. The economy was recovering in a fair way, unemployment was down, agricultural and mineral production and exports were on the rise. Even May 16, 1939, the anniversary of the Berber *dahir*, passed by without incident, the nationalists having enjoined calm upon their friends.[9] On August 29th a delegation of nationalists consisting of Mohammed Ghazi, Ahmed Cherkaoui, Boubker Kadiri and Ahmed ben Ghabrit called on the resident-general and pledged the loyalty of the nationalists to France in the event of war.[10] Morocco appeared to have accepted the benevolent despotism of her rulers.

THE RECONCILIATION DESTROYED

After the fall of France, however, a number of things occurred which revealed that the tranquillity was superficial. The Spanish occupation of Tangier (June 14, 1940), the Atlantic Charter (August 14th), the Japanese occupation of French Indo-China (September), the Lebanese declaration of independence (November 26th), the arrival of German armistice commissions, the discrepancies between clothing and food ration allowances for Europeans and Moroccans, the emergence of French nationalist organizations in Morocco, and the Allied landings of November 1942 assuredly heightened a Moroccan yearning for independence. But in the minds of the Moroccan leaders languishing in jail or in exile, that yearning had already taken shape.

Despite the apparent aura of good will and common sympathies which characterized Morocco before the Second World War, the hard-core nationalists had no intention of devitalizing their movement by collaborating with the French authorities. The years of futile effort following 1934 had finally convinced them that it was vain "to seek cooperation with a regime which had withheld its hand from them and had flouted even the provisions of the 1912 agreement." [11]

It had become obvious since 1937 that an irrevocable divorce had occurred between the people on the one hand and the protectorate regime on the other . . . It is futile to deny the impact of the war . . . [but] it must be said that the real driving force behind the new approach had been the bitter experiences of the nationalist movement . . . There was [already] a general agreement on the need for . . . a forthright and unequivocal policy of independence, independence before all else.[12]

Thus wrote Allal al-Fassi. To fix the moment at which he and his lieutenants abandoned the reform of the protectorate for its dissolution would be artificial, but it surely occurred sometime between November 1937 and the capitulation of France.[13]

A defeated France, moreover, presented new strategic possibilities. The structure of the National Party, though greatly shaken, had not completely disintegrated after 1937. Sections lay dormant here and there throughout the country, somewhat less dormant perhaps in the three leading centers of Fez, Rabat and Casablanca.[14] After the return of Ahmed Mekouar from his Saharan exile in 1940 and that of Mohammed Lyazidi in April 1941, the *conseil supérieur* of the National Party was reconstituted and began to meet twice a month in Rabat. Comprising as many as forty people, these meetings initially concerned themselves with forecasting the outcome of the war, for having determined on independence, it seemed to the nationalists a good strategy to exert leverage on a stricken and divided France through whichever powers might dominate the future Europe.[15] This policy prevailed from the capitulation of June 1940 until July 1943, when the United States reneged on Roosevelt's airy promises and threw the nationalists upon the mercy of the resurrected French authorities.[16]

THE ILLUSION OF GERMAN LEVERAGE

Exerting pressure on France through Germany, which the nationalists sought to do until the end of 1942, was not without precedent. Morocco had never forgotten the visit of the Kaiser to Tangier in 1905 and his spirited, if self-serving, defense of Moroccan independence on that occasion. And from the time of the Riff War onward, Germany had been strident in her condemnation of French oppression in North Africa.

The rise of Hitler changed nothing, and among the eminent Arabs welcomed in Berlin were the Grand Mufti of Jerusalem and the Amir Shakib Arslan who had opted for the Axis as early as September 1939. Hitler employed the Moroccan physician Takki eddin al-Hilali, originally from Tafilelt, as a propagandist on Radio Berlin and later as an agent in Tetuan where, among his other activities, he wrote for *el-Hurriya*. The Nazis also sought to exploit the traditional anti-Semitism of Islam as a bond of brotherhood, but while it may have appealed to some of the more reactionary Moroccans, there is no indication that it attracted widespread approval. The Moroccans who welcomed German collaboration were, in fact, occasionally embarrassed by the identification of their avowed anti-Zionism with the repugnant creed of anti-Semitism.[17] The projected collaboration, moreover, produced nothing concrete in the way of German commitments to Moroccan independence. The Moroccans soon found that the Nazi regime would make concessions only so far as these served German strategy, and this proved to be a very short distance indeed, for the Wehrmacht had apparently discounted the possibility of an Allied landing in the Maghreb and was too preoccupied elsewhere to cater to tiresome Moroccan nationalists.

Meanwhile, developments in the Spanish zone followed a similar course. The Tetuani nationalists had also been beguiled by promises of reform in 1936–37, had become disillusioned, and sought to collaborate with the Germans. Torrès might have suspected that Franco was playing a deeper game. The Generalissimo may have been partly sincere in his vague pledges, but he did not intend to permit the Moroccan tail to wag the Spanish dog. It was necessary to keep the Moroccans happy and hopeful, but it was just as necessary to keep them divided, and Franco's adjutant, Colonel Juan Beigbeder, pursued with great success this policy of conciliation and division during his term as high commissioner for the Spanish zone from December 15, 1936 to August 10, 1939.

Conciliation was achieved by the promises already mentioned and by the granting of limited concessions which in no way diluted Spanish authority: autonomy for the *habous* administration, augmentation of the education budget and the use of Arabic in the modern course of studies, curtailment of land acquisition by Europeans, and qualified freedom of speech and press. These were all the more beguiling because similar concessions had been denied in the French zone two years before. On March 1, 1937 the Islah journal, *el-Hurriya*, was licensed, less than three weeks before the Kutlat was suppressed in the French zone. And on March 17th, Torrès was named vizier of the department of *habous*, whose new autonomy returned to native hands the greater part of the landed property of the Spanish zone. Torrès once again found that his official position compromised his nationalist leadership and resigned the post in April, but he remained for a while in the good graces of the astute high commissioner who saw in him a useful pawn against Noguès' strategy and who, moreover, entertained a genuine personal respect for the Tetuani aristocrat.[18]

But even Beigbeder's diplomacy could not for long disguise the true intentions of the new Spanish regime. In March 1938, the assurance by Thomas Borras, editor of the review *Vertice*, that Morocco was already incorporated into the Spanish state and would be integrated even more closely in the future, considerably upset Mekki Naciri who took the opportunity to remind Franco of his debt to his Moroccan troops.[19] But in June 1939, when Beigbeder announced a general amnesty for political prisoners, loans for public works and education, and the autonomy of Islamic justice, nothing was said about the earlier promises of independence.[20] By the eve of World War II, it had become painfully clear that Madrid had no intentions of honoring them.

It had become equally clear that the wily high commissioner had split the Spanish zone nationalists into rival factions led by Torrès and Naciri. Naciri had been expelled from the French zone again in 1936 and had taken refuge in Tetuan, where for a while he edited *Maghreb el-Djedid* in collaboration with the Islah. By that autumn he had acquired a certain journalistic and oratorical reputation among the Tetuanis and was beginning to find Torrès' preeminence irksome. Moreover, there was a genuine difference of opinion between the two, for Torrès, owing perhaps to his ancestral ties with Andalusia, could conceive of an independent northern zone, whose khalifa would become sultan, working in harmony with Spain, while Naciri remained steadfast in his loyalty to the Sharifian dynasty and to the old ideal of a unified Morocco, thereby identifying himself with the goals of the French zone nationalists.[21]

The rupture took place in the fall of 1936, and Naciri immediately found himself deprived of financial support. Here was a circumstance tailored to the plans of Beigbeder, and in December the high commissioner offered the desperate Naciri financial backing for a new party Thus it was that in February 1937, *el-Wahda el-Maghribiya* (Moroccan Unity Party) came into existence along with a new journal of the same name. A Spanish-language supplement, *Unidad Marroqui*, was soon in circulation,[22] and it was in this journal that Naciri's own plan of reforms appeared in December 1937 under the heading *Declaración*. These proposals, adopted at a party meeting on December 11th, borrowed much from the *Plan de Réformes* of 1934, although they were cut to fit the special conditions prevailing in the northern zone. They praised the liberal protectorate policy of Spain, condemned the oppressive colonial policy of France, and demanded a unified and independent Morocco.[23] The favorable attention which the *Declaración* received in the Spanish press leaves no doubt that it had the approval, perhaps even the backing, of the Spanish authorities.[24]

With the help of official subsidies, Moroccan Unity acquired all the trappings of a real party, including branches in Alcazarquivir, Chechaouen, Larache, Tangier and Arzila. By the end of 1937, Naciri had attracted a not insignificant following, and much to Beigbeder's satisfaction, many of them were renegades from Torrès' party. Having achieved his aim, the high commissioner now began to withhold funds periodically from Naciri in order once again to favor Torrès.[25]

Three years of such tactics finally convinced Torrès that the Spanish were not to be trusted, and after the fall of France, he, too, thought he saw possibilities in an understanding with the Germans. He allowed his elation over the French capitulation to get the better of his reason, however, for he now assumed that the end of the French protectorate was a *fait accompli* and that the Germans would help him take vengeance on the pettifogging Spanish, to which end he began to woo the German consul in Tetuan, Dr. Richter. This simply demonstrated his political naiveté, for he ignored the sympathies which united Spain and Germany, forgot that Spain was far more important than Morocco to Germany, and failed to observe that it suited Germany to have Spain extend her control over Morocco, which had already been demonstrated concretely by the Spanish occupation of Tangier with Hitler's blessing on the morrow of the German entry into Paris.

In the context of this grander strategy, it is hardly surprising that Torrès' attempt to extend his party activity to Tangier was resisted by the Spanish authorities and that even in Tetuan the party was somewhat circumscribed. Torrès had so far abandoned discretion that his articles in *el-Hurriya* became openly antagonistic to Spain, with the result that the indulgent high commissioner, General Ascencio, was replaced in May 1941 by General Orgaz who had instructions to cut Torrès down to size. The Islah, subsidized by the Spanish government since 1936, was now subjected to the harassment of fines, suspensions and prohibitions such that it could no longer operate effectively, and in December 1941 Orgaz terminated its official subsidy. Thereafter, Torrès had to step warily to avoid further repression.[26] His effort to employ Germany as leverage on Spain had been no more successful than the parallel tactic in the French zone.

Naciri and the leadership of the Moroccan Unity Party, while rejoicing equally over France's defeat, never actively sought Nazi collaboration. Naciri, indeed, demonstrated his fidelity to Spain when on July 5, 1940 he addressed a quite respectful open letter to Franco reminding him again of his 1936 promises. Both nationalist parties in the Spanish zone had to proceed with caution after the arrival of Orgaz, for the only nationalist activity the new high commissioner regarded as permissible was anti-French propaganda.[27]

THE ILLUSION OF AMERICAN LEVERAGE

Following the Allied landings in North Africa, the prestige which Germany had won from France passed to the Americans, and the Moroccans sought now to realign themselves with the new victors.[28] American agents had, in fact, led the Moroccans to believe even before the invasion that they had much to expect from the United States after the war, expectations which President Roosevelt made no effort to dispel during his dinner meeting with the sultan in Casablanca-Anfa in January 1943.[29]

But such was not to be. The cooperation of the Free French, much as Roosevelt and Churchill distrusted de Gaulle, was a factor which the Americans could not afford to ignore. Thus, when French officials returning to Morocco systematically discouraged contact between their allies and the Moroccans and put the Americans off with half truths about nationalist collaboration with the Axis and the plausible sounding threat of a flanking attack from the Spanish zone, the American authorities, innocent of the true position of the nationalists and intent on the primary objectives of an Axis defeat, obliged their French allies by backing away from commitments which the nationalists thought had been made in the euphoric post-invasion days. In July, only a month after the Anfa conference, Cordell Hull made American nonintervention official by warning that independence for former colonial peoples depended on their ability to assume the responsibilities of self-government.[30]

Although the American landings did not directly touch the Spanish zone, Torrès found it wise, despite his predilection for Germany, to hedge his future by entering a "national pact" with Naciri. Should the Allies win, Torrès and the Islah would be sheltered by Naciri who was less compromised by Axis connections; should the Axis win, Naciri would find Torrès' patronage useful. In pursuit of this new alliance, the so-called "National Front" began to cultivate relations with the British consul in Tetuan through Naciri's friend, the English protégé, Mohammed R'Zini, and with the United States chargé d'affaires in Tangier, through Torrès' brother, Ahmed, whose father-in-law was also a British protégé. These efforts were no more fruitful than those pursued in the southern zone.[31] By mid-1943, the Moroccans of both zones had come to realize the futility of outside leverage, and, clinging to their determination to abolish the protectorate, they now took matters into their own hands.

ISTIQLAL

French-Moroccan relations continued to deteriorate during 1943. Noguès finally resigned (June 4, 1943) and fled to Spain to avoid imminent arrest, and Ambassador Gabriel Puaux, who was wholly uninformed about Moroccan conditions, took charge under unusually difficult circumstances. The presence of the Americans, whose military might in contrast to the poorly equipped French was eye-popping and whose anti-colonialism was outspoken, was a most disconcerting influence. The publication of the Algerian Manifesto in February and the Algerian Reform Program in May, and the stalling of French authority in the face of Lebanese nationalist opposition in November left the Moroccans on the fence, waiting to see which way to jump.[32]

Their decision was simplified by the return of Ahmed Balafrej from exile in January 1943. During the ensuing year he contacted the dormant sections of the National Party, rallied some of the followers of M. H. al-Ouezzani, and won over the alumni associations which had formerly collaborated with Noguès.[33] By the year's end, Morocco was as ripe for a revival of nationalism as it had been in 1937,[34] and in December Balafrej founded a new party, Istiqlal, whose title (Independence) denoted its main objective. On January 11, 1944 the party issued its manifesto whose fifty-eight signatures, each opposite a section of the party, indicated the success which Balafrej had had in reviving the old party organization as well as the overwhelmingly bourgeois composition of the new party at its inception, for not a single signer could be classed as an artisan or worker.[35] (See Appendix E.)

The Istiqlal Manifesto was a thoroughly secular document, paying only the briefest formal attention to the earlier preoccupations of the Salafiyyist reformers. It began with a summary of the situation in Morocco and the responsibilities of the Allies, and terminated with demands for the immediate implementation of democratic and constitutional reforms and for independence in the very near future. As a declaration of independence, it was qualified by not asserting independence to be a *fait accompli*. It stated simply that the party had decided "to ask for independence" and "to request His Majesty to undertake with the interested nations negotiations whose object would be the recognition and guarantee of that independence. . . ." The party leadership further explained on January 19th that the manifesto aimed at "obtaining, within legal bounds, the independence of our country," and that the party had "no intention of achieving our goal by employing violence . . ." or by "fomenting . . . a seditious movement. . . ." [36]

The manifesto documented and formalized the transformation which had taken place in Moroccan nationalism since 1937. The program of reform had changed very little in those years, and on the rare occasions when a program was discussed, it was the old *Plan de Réformes* which was referred to and which remained the ideological foundation of Moroccan nationalism until independence. After 1937, however, reform was thrust into the background as the nationalists became preoccupied with party organization, mass support and independence.[37]

XV

SUMMARY AND CONCLUSIONS

METAMORPHOSIS

The origins of Moroccan nationalism were rooted in the concern of select individuals that the revered values of Muslim society were being subverted by France. At the outset these individuals were wholly unorganized and can hardly be said to have represented a national consensus, but they represented something more than the parochialism of the Berber tribesmen who were vainly fighting a rearguard action under Abd al-Krim; they stood for reform. And because their chrysaloid reformism was shaped largely by the Salafiyya movement, it took a strongly religious and cultural bent and first materialized as an educational effort designed to defend the young Muslim mind from the infidel society which threatened it.

The fledgling reformers were soon jolted out of their naive optimism by the Riffian defeat and the rapid consolidation of French hegemony, and in their first rudimentary organizations of the late 1920's began to discuss political affairs and the dislocations caused by alien rule. They were still a tiny elite, and they still lacked cohesive ideas, but they were beginning to search. Their first attack against the Berber *dahir* in 1930 was not a success. As a result, they were obliged to reflect on the importance of organization and a more broadly appealing program, although for several years thereafter, the former was subordinated to the latter. The hard knocks of 1930 had dashed their remaining hopes for a religious and cultural rejuvenation on the rocks of political reality, and while the basic tenets of Salafiyya were never quite abandoned, the drift towards secular nationalism became even more pronounced.

By 1934 the program of reform was well articulated, and the nationalists vainly devoted most of their efforts until 1937 to its adoption. The movement was thoroughly political by this time and the connection with Salafiyya almost wholly obscured. The importance of organization was now better understood, and while the movement was still closely held by the original elite and can hardly be called a mass party, it had become "national" to the extent that it could command mass demonstrations at will and could boast a skeletal organization which covered the important cities and which later proved itself sufficiently hardy to outlast suppression and global war. As of 1937, the nationalist organization was a well-oiled propaganda machine whose operators were still intent on reform.

All such hopes were prostrated by the suppression of 1937 and the events of the wartime era, which demonstrated that it was illusory to expect significant reforms under French rule, that for nearly a decade their French masters had beguiled them with false promises, and that the reforms they sought could be achieved only by a free Morocco. Thereafter, doctrine and program became more or less irrelevant, and the truly "national" organization of Istiqlal was conceived for the sole purpose of marshaling a massive popular demand, at home and abroad, for independence. By the end of the war, Moroccan nationalism had sublimated its elaborate reformist program and had become a separatist movement, although it still relied on peaceful means. Another decade of frustration would be necessary to drive it to revolution.[1]

DOCTRINAL STEW

In noting that the Moroccans abandoned reform for independence, Rézette concludes that ideology was of less account to them than practical results and that what there was of Moroccan nationalism was structure.[2] The doctrinal sincerity of colonial nationalist leaders is always suspect, to be sure, and after the bloom of Salafiyya wore off, one cannot discount the charge made by the Socialists in 1936 that the Moroccan nationalist movement was primarily a power struggle on the part of a diminutive bourgeoisie to replace the French by themselves, and that the mumbo jumbo of propaganda and reform was simply a device to win popular support. The manner in which they organized their party, secretly and from the top down, and their efforts to maintain secrecy and authoritarian control throughout the Istiqlal period and even after independence would seem to reveal them as a clique which sought power, above all. But it is this author's opinion that Rézette underrates the rationality of the *Plan de Réformes* and passes off too lightly the years when the main intent was to convert, first the authorities, then the masses, to the new rationale. During the period which primarily concerns Rézette — that of Istiqlal from 1944 to 1955 — his assessment is probably valid, if one interprets "structure" broadly, but Moroccan nationalism was three times as old as that, and during its first two decades the Moroccans were far less concerned with structure, or power — to their detriment — than they were with their plans for reform which they naively assumed the French would take seriously.

French observers who depreciate Moroccan nationalist doctrine, however, can certainly claim that it was anything but doctrinaire. One of its foremost characteristics, in fact, which ought by now to be apparent, was its eclecticism. We have seen that the Egyptian influence, in the form of Salafiyya, was profound, while the pan-Islamic ideal, also propagated at al-Azhar, appealed very little to the Moroccans. Moroccans were inspired by the revival of Arab self-esteem and the sense of dignity which emanated from the Arab renaissance, but they were quite uninterested in the practical applications of pan-Arabism. They sought to reform the Sharia, but they refused to separate religion and the state, as Turkey and Egypt had done. From Egypt they accepted the idea of extending popular sovereignty gradually downward through provincial and local councils, but they rejected, for the time being, the notion of ministerial responsibility. They may have dreamed of national independence — what nationalist could avoid it? — but unlike the Syrians and Egyptians, they viewed it as a long-range goal rather than a prerequisite for reform, at least until 1937 or even later. They adopted the organization of the Communist Party but rejected its dogma. And while they drew largely from France both the structure and ideological content of the educational and judicial systems sketched out in the *Plan de Réformes*, they were nonetheless determined to avoid the typically French secularization of these two institutions.

Commentators on the French left have found this doctrinal stew extremely distasteful. They complain that it is impossible to classify Moroccan political parties as "right" or "left," "socialist" or "conservative," "proletarian" or "bourgeois," because they were politically immature, their platforms had not sufficiently evolved, and their leaders did not take doctrine seriously enough to allow it to become a cause of dissension.[3] This was partly true. The leaders were young and untried, their program had never stood the test of administrative responsibility, and pragmatic as Moroccans are, in comparison with their coreligionists to the east, they were quite unperturbed about doctrinal contradictions and less concerned with finely-spun ideologies than with specific reforms. But despite the French complaint that Moroccan nationalism is unclassifiable, the movement was distinctly "bourgeois" during at least two-thirds of its career, and if the *Plan de Réformes* smacks of anything, it smacks of socialism. It was a bourgeois socialism of an exceedingly opportunistic and selective variety, to be sure, but this fact should have rendered it all the more feasible as a basis for reform had the authorities been so disposed. Thus, doctrine — or doctrines — did play an important role in Moroccan nationalism, but the resulting program bore less resemblance to the political ideologies of Europe than to that little understood and much derided phenomenon sometimes called "African socialism," and has tended to be disparaged equally by European observers.

THE SPELL OF EUROPE

The opening chapters of this book described the complex of forces, internal and external, which shaped Moroccan nationalism. That movement itself was complex, comprising several phases or aspects: 1) its awakening and reformist spirit, 2) its inspiration and the courage to persist, 3) its general philosophy, 4) its *raison d'être* and subject matter, 5) its proposed remedies, 6) its methods of organization and operation, and 7) its terminology and style. When the first complexity is applied to the second, the possible combinations of cause and effect are enormous. The author has tried to explore the most significant, or perhaps just the most noticeable, of these combinations in order to understand why Moroccan nationalism arose and why it expressed itself as it did at various times in its early history.

Its awakening was caused, not by the imposition of alien political control — all *that* had produced was tribal rebellion — but by the threat of cultural assimilation. To the sense of foreboding with which Muslims viewed the secularization of Morocco by France, Salafiyya provided the antidote. But Salafiyya was more than religious revivalism. Its political aspects, along with the excitement of the Riff War, were responsible for the first stirrings of a political consciousness which can be called "nationalist." Salafiyya was the dominant positive influence on the movement until 1930, and while other factors superseded it thereafter, it continued to color the basic reformist spirit of the nationalists, although on an increasingly personal basis, up to and even after independence. This was more true of the older leaders who were active in the 1920's than of the younger men who later joined them, and some of the older men today deplore the later dilution of Salafiyyist influence.[4]

Once awakened, the young reformers were inspired with the courage to resist and to persist in their efforts by the doctrines and actions of both Arab and European nationalists and by the exhortations of the French left. Before 1930 they were affected in a general way by the atmosphere of the Arab renaissance and, more particularly, by the deeds of Egyptian, Syrian and Turkish nationalists who served as a kind of pantheon of Islamic heroes, and throughout the next decade and the Second World War, the resistance of Middle Eastern nationalists to their Western masters continued periodically to resuscitate flagging Moroccan nationalism. The Moroccans who attended French schools and universities were inspired by what they learned of the Mazzinis and Kossuths and were animated with a sense of mission and of personal importance by the attentions of French Socialists and Communists with whom they associated, but the words and deeds of Christian Europeans, historic or contemporary, did not impress their imaginations as forceably as the doings of their coreligionists in the Arab world. Accordingly, the inspiration and the mettle of Moroccan nationalism came principally from the Middle East.

The general philosophy of the movement stemmed in nearly equal proportions from Salafiyya, Middle Eastern secular nationalism and European liberalism. This is hardly surprising, since such general concepts as constitutional government, national sovereignty, basic civil rights, the importance of education, and even religious reform were common to all. While these ideas originated in the West, they had been assimilated into Middle Eastern philosophies before any of the Moroccan nationalists were born, and by the time the Moroccans began to encounter them in the mid-1920's, it is no longer possible to distinguish one source from another.

The grievances, real or imagined, of which the nationalists complained, furnished the *raison d'être* and subject matter of the movement. They first became pressing after 1925 when the new secret societies began to take a first, hard, self-conscious look at the colonial regime, and they formed the grist of the propaganda mill from 1932 onward in the nationalist journals and the *Plan de Réformes*. French example and French education compounded these grievances by whetting desires and expectations which inevitably were thwarted. Fundamentally, it was not so much the injustices and abuses themselves which gave the movement its *raison d'être*, for comparable afflictions had been the lot of Moroccans from time immemorial; what made them seem unbearable now was the discovery, thanks to the impressive example set by France's rehabilitation of the country, that they were not ordained by God.

In searching for solutions, then, to these man-made afflictions, Moroccans were guided by Salafiyya prior to 1930 and somewhat by Middle Eastern secular nationalist doctrines thereafter, but neither of these offered the specific remedies to specific problems which ultimately had to be faced, and the debility of Middle Eastern governments attested to this shortcoming. The superior organization and efficiency of European society was quite apparent to all Moroccans, not only those who sojourned in France but those who witnessed only its attenuated effect on Morocco's *risorgimento*. Hence, the Moroccans derived their most concrete reform proposals principally from the West — from their French education, from hobnobbing with French politicos and engineers and doctors, and from watching French institutions operate both at home and abroad. The ideological, organizational and technological content of the European revolution was the fountainhead of the Moroccan nationalist program as materialized in the *Plan de Réformes*.

Methods of organization and operation were also derived primarily from Europe. The manifest ineffectiveness in the late 1920's of the Wafd, the Destour, and other Middle Eastern parties, whatever their romantic appeal, caused the Moroccans to seek their tactics elsewhere, and such tactical influence as came from the Middle East is discernible chiefly in Arslan's guidance during the early 1930's. Internal political conditions, alternately repressive and indulgent, determined to some extent what kind of organization and tactics could be employed. But after 1933, when recruitment and propaganda began in earnest, it was what the Moroccans had learned in the French schools, from French Republicans and Socialists, and from the structure of the Parti Communiste Français which shaped party organization and guided their campaigns.

Finally, the dissection of the literary output of the nationalists has shown that their terminology or vocabulary and their literary style are clearly traceable to French education and the influence of French liberal thought. Thus, the idiom in which Moroccan nationalist doctrine was expressed also came preeminently from the West.

Our conclusions up to this point have dealt only with doctrines and methods. But from the observations made about the selective character of Moroccan nationalism and the tardy development of its structure, it would appear that its leadership was more important than its doctrines, methods and structure combined. One must keep in mind that the same ten to twenty men directed the movement from 1925 until World War II and after. It was they who rose to authority in the first discussion groups founded in Fez and Rabat. It was they, or rather their French-educated complement, who founded the A.E.M.N.A. It was they who launched the campaign against the Berber *dahir* and who sent the Fez delegation to see the sultan that same summer. They, too, founded the Zawiya and Taifa, financed and edited *Maghreb*, and *L'Action du Peuple*, formed the committee to draft the *Plan de Réformes*, and organized the *Kutlat al-Amal al-Watani*, Morocco's first political "party." It was the same group which reorganized the Kutlat in 1936, instigated the demonstrations of 1936 and 1937, founded the National Party in the latter year, and finally, with the addition of new recruits, formed the executive committee and *conseil supérieur* of Istiqlal after 1944.

It has been demonstrated that a majority of this inner circle, the dynamic element, was French-educated. Unlike the situation in Syria, where competing French and Russian education, politically inspired, debilitated an already functioning national movement by dividing the country's elite against itself,[5] in Morocco the European-educated were all French-educated, and they fortified the nationalist movement by providing modern organizational leadership and a rationalized plan of reform where neither had previously existed. Deprived of this contingent, Moroccan nationalism would either have halted at the tribal stage under the leadership of a latter-day Abd al-Krim or have become affiliated with, perhaps even the subordinate appendage of, one of the movements emanating from the Middle East. Whatever it might have been, its doctrinal content, its modes of action and its structure would surely have been quite different.

Doctrines, methods, structure, leadership — all were increasingly shaped to Western designs as the nationalists grew more sophisticated. The Arab renaissance had served well enough at the outset when the reformers sought only to negate the assimilative tendencies of their protectors, and the emotional and inspirational links with the East thereby established were never completely severed. But the European revolution clearly overshadowed the Arab renaissance in the later stages. When the nationalists began to search in earnest for a constructive program of national reform, they were compelled to abandon the frustrating impracticalities of modern Islamic institutions and philosophies for the manifest utility of their European counterparts. European political institutions and ideas enjoyed prestige in Morocco because even the renascent Arab world had nowhere contrived to establish effective, modern, representative government; European economic and financial institutions also did, because Islam had not effectively assimilated the rational, scientific method upon which Western commerce and industry were built. And European justice, education, medicine and welfare, which were unmatched by anything the Middle East had to offer, had an obvious appeal to the modern Moroccan leader. Moroccans recognized the Arab world for what it was: a transitional society stumbling over its medieval traces as it crossed the threshold of the modern world. How much wiser for Morocco — although an "Arab" country endowed with an Arab culture but customarily holding aloof from the Arab world, yet at times rising to cultural and imperial heights hardly dreamed of in most of that world — to forego the pallid Arab facsimile of Europe's revolution for the real thing, when the real thing was closer at hand and hers for the asking. Moroccans chose to emulate the prototype because the facsimile was unprepossessing.

Their movement had begun as an effort to resist assimilation by France. They found they could do so only by assimilating nearly everything France had to offer. The spell of Europe once again mesmerized these latter-day Moors, the Pyrenees once more beckoned, and the reborn Moorish nation responded as of old, by leaving one foot firmly embedded in the East while planting the other, no longer in Andalusia, but in France.

APPENDICES A–E

APPENDIX A

TRAITÉ CONCLU ENTRE LA FRANCE ET LE MAROC LE 30 MARS 1912, POUR
L'ORGANISATION DU PROTECTORAT FRANÇAIS DANS L'EMPIRE CHÉRIFIEN.

Le Gouvernement de la République française et le Gouvernement de
Sa Majesté chérifienne, soucieux d'établir au Maroc un régime régulier
fondé sur l'ordre intérieur et la sécurité générale qui permettra l'introduction des réformes et assurera le développement économique du pays, sont
convenus des dispositions suivantes:

ARTICLE PREMIER. Le Gouvernement de la République française et Sa
Majesté le Sultan sont d'accord pour instituer au Maroc un nouveau régime comportant les réformes administratives, judiciaires, scolaires, économiques, financières et militaires que le Gouvernement français jugera utile
d'introduire sur le territoire marocain.

Ce régime sauvegardera la situation religieuse, le respect et le prestige
traditionnel du Sultan, l'exercice de la religion musulmane et des institutions
religieuses, notamment de celles des habous. Il comportera l'organisation
d'un Makhzen chérifien réformé.

Le Gouvernement de la République se concertera avec le Gouvernement
espagnol au sujet des intérêts que ce Gouvernement tient de sa disposition
géographique et de ses possessions territoriales sur la côte marocaine.

De même, la ville de Tanger gardera le caractère spécial qui lui a été
reconnu et qui déterminera son organisation municipale.

ART. 2. Sa Majesté le Sultan admet dès maintenant que le Gouvernement
français procède, après avoir prévenu le Makhzen, aux occupations militaires
du territoire marocain qu'il jugerait nécessaires au maintien de l'ordre et
de la sécurité des transactions commerciales et à ce qu'il exerce toute
action de police sur terre et dans les eaux marocaines.

ART. 3. Le Gouvernement de la République prend l'engagement de
prêter un constant appui à Sa Majesté chérifienne contre tout danger qui
menacerait sa personne ou son trône ou qui compromettrait la tranquillité
de ses États. Le même appui sera prêté à l'héritier du trône et à ses
successeurs.

ART. 4. Les mesures que nécessitera le nouveau régime de protectorat
seront édictées, sur la proposition du Gouvernement français, par Sa
Majesté chérifienne ou par les autorités auxquelles elle en aura délégué
le pouvoir. Il en sera de même des règlements nouveaux et des modifica-
tions aux règlements existants.

ART. 5. Le Gouvernement français sera représenté auprès de Sa Majesté
chérifienne par un Commissaire résident général, dépositaire de tous les

pouvoirs de la République au Maroc, qui veillera à l'exécution du présent accord.

Le Commissaire résident général sera le seul intermédiare du Sultan auprès des Représentants étrangers et dans les rapports que ces Représentants entretiennent avec le Gouvernement marocain. Il sera, notamment, chargé de toutes les questions intéressant les étrangers dans l'Empire chérifien.

Il aura le pouvoir d'approuver et de promulguer, au nom du Gouvernement français, tous les décrets rendus par Sa Majesté chérifienne.

ART. 6. Les Agents diplomatiques et consulaires de la France seront chargés de la représentation et de la protection des sujets et des intérêts marocains à l'étranger.

Sa Majesté le Sultan s'engage à ne conclure aucun acte ayant un caractère international sans l'assentiment préalable du Gouvernement de la République française.

ART. 7. Le Gouvernement de la République française et le Gouvernement de Sa Majesté chérifienne se réservent de fixer d'un commun accord les bases d'une réorganisation financière qui, en respectant les droits conférés au porteur des titres des emprunts publics marocains, permette de garantir les engagements du trésor chérifien et de percevoir régulièrement les revenus de l'Empire.

ART. 8. Sa Majesté chérifienne s'interdit de contracter à l'avenir, directement ou indirectement, aucun emprunt public ou privé et d'accorder, sous une forme quelconque, aucune concession sans l'autorisation du Gouvernement français.

ART. 9. La présente convention sera soumise à la ratification du Gouvernement de la République française et l'instrument de ladite ratification sera remis à Sa Majesté le Sultan dans le plus bref délai possible.

En foi de quoi les soussignés ont dressé le présent acte et l'ont revêtu de leurs cachets.

Fait à Fez, le 30 mars 1912.

Signé: REGNAULT.   Signé: MOULAY ABD EL HAFID.

APPENDIX B

Marshal Lyautey	April 28, 1912—September 26, 1925
Théodore Steeg	September 27, 1925—December 30, 1928
Lucien Saint	January 1, 1929—July, 1933
Henri Ponsot	July, 1933—March 21, 1936
Marcel Peyrouton	March 21—September 17, 1936
General H. Noguès	September 17, 1936—June 4, 1943
Gabriel Puaux	June 7, 1943—March 15, 1946
Eirik Labonne	March 30, 1946—May 13, 1947
General A.-P. Juin	May 14, 1947—August 28, 1951
General A. Guillaume	August 28, 1951—May 20, 1954
Francis Lacoste	May 20, 1954—June 20, 1955
Gilbert Grandval	June 20—August 30, 1955
General P. G. Boyer de La Tour	August 30—November 11, 1955
André Dubois *	November 11, 1955—March 2, 1956

* Dubois became high commissioner on March 2, 1956 and French ambassador on June 15, 1956.

APPENDIX C

Louange à Dieu!

Que l'on sache par la présente, — que Dieu en élève et en fortifie la teneur, — que notre Majesté chérifienne,

Considérant que le *dahir* de notre Auguste père, S. M. le Sultan Moulay Youssef, en date du 11 septembre 1914 a prescrit dans l'intérêt du bien de nos sujets et de la tranquillité de l'Etat de respecter le statut coutumier des tribus berbères pacifiées, que dans ce même but le *dahir* du 15 mai 1922 a institué des règles spéciales en ce qui concerne les aliénations immobilières qui seraient consenties à des étrangers dans les tribus de coutume berbère non pourvues de *Mahakmas* pour l'application du *Chrâa*; que de nombreuses tribus ont été depuis lors régulièrement classées parmi celles dont le statut coutumier doit être respecté, qu'il devient opportun de préciser aujourd'hui les conditions particulières dans lesquelles la justice sera rendue dans les mêmes tribus;

A décrété ce qui suit:

ART. I. Dans les tribus de notre Empire reconnues comme étant de coutumes berbères, la répression des infractions commises par des sujets marocains que serait de la compétence des caïds dans les autres parties de l'Empire est de la compétence des chefs de tribus.

Pour les autres infractions, la compétence et la répression sont réglées par les articles IV et VI du présent *dahir*.

ART. II. Sous réserve des règles de compétence qui régissent les tribunaux français de notre Empire, les actions civiles ou commerciales, mobilières ou immobilières, sont jugées en premier ou dernier ressort, suivant le taux qui sera fixé par arrêté viziriel, par les juridictions spéciales appelées *tribunaux coutumiers*; ces tribunaux sont également compétents en toute matière du statut personnel et successoral.

Ils appliquent en tous cas la coutume locale.

ART. III. L'appel des jugements rendus par les tribunaux coutumiers dans les cas où il sera recevable est porté devant les juridictions appelées tribunaux d'appel coutumier.

ART. IV. En matière pénale, les tribunaux d'appel sont également compétents en premier et dernier ressort pour la répression des infractions prévues à l'alinéa 2 de l'article I ci-dessus et en outre de toutes infractions commises par des membres des tribunaux coutumiers dont la compétence normale est attribuée au chef de la tribu.

ART. V. Auprès de chaque tribunal coutumier de première instance ou d'appel est placé un commissaire du gouvernement délégué par l'autorité régionale de contrôle de laquelle il dépend. Près de chacune de ces juridictions est également placé un secrétaire-greffier, lequel remplit en outre la fonction de notaire.

ART. VI. Les juridictions françaises statuant en matière pénale suivant les règles qui leur sont propres sont compétentes pour la répression des crimes commis en pays berbère quelle que soit la condition de l'auteur du crime.

ART. VII. Les actions immobilières auxquelles seraient parties soit comme demandeur soit comme défendeur des ressortissants des juridictions françaises, sont de la compétence de ces juridictions.

ART. VIII. Toutes les règles d'organisation, de composition et de fonctionnement des tribunaux coutumiers seront fixées par arrêtés viziriels successifs, selon les cas et suivant les besoins.

Fait à Rabat, le 17 hija 1348 (16 mai 1930).

Vu pour promulgation et mise à exécution, Rabat, le 23 mai 1930.

Le Commissaire résident général,

Signé: Lucien Saint.

APPENDIX D

NAME	WHERE EDUCATED,* AND DEGREE (IF AVAILABLE)
Omar Abdeljalil	Franco-Muslim School (Fez), to 1917 Collège Moulay Idriss (Fez), 1917–23 École Nationale d'Agriculture (Montpellier) 1923–25, *diplôme* École Nationale d'Agriculture (Grignon), *stagiaire* 1925–26
Ahmed Balafrej	École des fils de notables (Rabat), to 1920 Lycée Gouraud (Rabat), 1920–26 Lycée Henri Quatre (Paris), 1926–27 Fuad University (Cairo), 1927–28 University of Paris (Sorbonne), 1928–32, *licence* and *diplôme d'études supérieures*
Abdelaziz Bendriss	Free school (Fez) Qarawiyin University, c. 1921–31, *diplôme*
Abdelkader Benjelloun	Collège Moulay Idriss (Fez), to 1926 Lycée Louis le Grand (Paris), c. 1926–27 University of Paris (Faculty of Law), 1927–1930, *licence* École Libre des Sciences Politiques (Paris), –1930?
Abdesselam Bennouna	Qarawiyin University
M'Hammed Bennouna	Tutored by Tetuani *ulama*, c. 1912–20 Qarawiyin University, c. 1920–22 Fuad University (Cairo), 1925–c. 1927
Ahmed Bouayad	Koranic school, only
Hassan Bouayad	Free school Qarawiyin University, to 1929, 1933–34, *diplôme* al-Azhar University (Cairo), 1929–33
Larbi Bouayad	Koranic school, only

* Nearly every Muslim child, whatever his later educational career, begins in a Koranic school, not listed here.
Note. The above information is not complete, but is compiled from whatever sources were available to the author.

Name	Where Educated, and Degree (if Available)
Ahmed Cherkaoui	Franco-Muslim school (Rabat) Thereafter, attended lectures by visiting Qarawiyin professors in Rabat
Messaoud Chiguer	Franco-Muslim school Collège Moulay Youssef (Rabat), 1918–24 Institut des Hautes Études Marocaines, 1924–27, *certificat d'études juridiques*
Mohammed Daoud	Tutored by Tetuani *ulama*, 1912–20 Qarawiyin University, 1920–22
Mohammed Diouri	Collège Moulay Idriss (Fez), to *c.* 1930, no *diplôme*
Abdelkebir al-Fassi	Collège Moulay Idriss (Fez), to 1923 Qarawiyin University, to 1923 Institut des Hautes Études Marocaines, 1923–26, *certificat d'études juridiques*
Allal al-Fassi	Qarawiyin University, 1920–30, *diplôme*
Mohammed al-Fassi	Collège Moulay Idriss (Fez), 1919–26 Qarawiyin University, 1919–26 Lycée Henri Quatre (Paris), 1926–28 University of Paris (Sorbonne), 1928–34, *licence* and *diplôme d'études supérieures* École des Langues Vivantes Orientales, 1930, *diplôme*
Hachemi al-Filali	Free school (Fez) Qarawiyin University, to *c.* 1928, no *diplôme*
Mohammed Ghazi	Qarawiyin University, *c.* 1918–27, *diplôme*
Ahmed Ghilane	Koranic school, only
Abdullah Guennoun	Qarawiyin University
Said Hajji	Najah National School (Nablus, Palestine), *c.* 1930–33 Syrian College (Damascus)
Mohammed Hassar	Franco-Muslim school (Salé) Collège Moulay Youssef (Rabat)
Bouchta Jamai	Qarawiyin University, to *c.* 1930, *diplôme*
Mohammed ben Abbès Kabbaj	Tutored by Rabati *ulama*
Boubker Kadiri	Attended lectures by visiting Qarawiyin professors in Rabat and Salé
Mohammed al-Kholti	Collège Moulay Idriss (Fez), to 1926 Lycée Charlemagne (Paris), 1926–27? University of Paris (Sorbonne and Faculty of Law), *c.* 1927 ff., *licences*
Ibrahim al-Kittani	Qarawiyin University, to 1930, *diplôme*

Name	Where Educated, and Degree (if Available)
Mohammed al-Korri	Qarawiyin University, *c.* 1918–28, *diplôme*
Mohammed Lyazidi	Franco-Muslim school (Rabat), to 1917 Collège Moulay Youssef (Rabat), 1917–23 Institut des Hautes Études Marocaines, 1926–28, *diplôme d'Arabe*
Ahmed Mekouar	Koranic school, only
Mekki Naciri	Free schools (Rabat), to 1927 Fuad University (Cairo), 1927–30 University of Paris (Sorbonne), 1930–31, no *diplôme* Institut des Études Islamiques (Paris), 1930–31, no *diplôme* University of Geneva, 1931–32, no *diplôme*
Mohammed Naciri	Koranic school, only
Ibrahim al-Ouezzani	Qarawiyin University, no *diplôme*
Mohammed Hassan al-Ouezzani	Franco-Muslim school (Fez), to 1920 Collège Moulay Idriss (Fez), 1920–24 Lycée Gouraud (Rabat), 1924–26 Lycée Charlemagne (Paris), 1926–27 École des Langues Vivantes Orientales (Paris), 1927–29 University of Paris (Sorbonne), 1927–29 École des Hautes Études Sociales (Paris), 1927–30, *diplôme* École Libre des Sciences Politiques (Paris), 1927–30, *diplôme*
Thami al-Ouezzani	Collège Moulay Idriss (Fez), to 1926 Lycée Pierre le Grand (Paris), 1926–?
Abdellatif Sbihi	École des fils de notables (Salé) Collège Moulay Youssef (Rabat), graduated before 1920
Lghali Sebti	Koranic school, only
Mohammed Sebti	Collège Moulay Idriss (Fez)
Omar Sebti	Collège Moulay Idriss (Fez)
Abdelkader Tazi	Franco-Muslim school Collège Moulay Idriss (Fez) Qarawiyin University, *c.* 1920–22
Abdelkhalek Torrès	Qarawiyin University Fuad University (Cairo), *c.* 1930–31 University of Paris (Sorbonne), *c.* 1931–32

APPENDIX E

Présenté le 11 janvier 1944 à S.M. le Sultan du Maroc, au Résident Général de France au Maroc et aux représentants des principaux gouvernements alliés.

Rabat, le 11 janvier 1944.

Monsieur l'Ambassadeur Gabriel Puaux,
Résident Général de la République Française au Maroc. Rabat.

Monsieur l'Ambassadeur,

En vertu du mandat dont nous sommes investis, nous avons l'honneur de porter à votre connaissance que nous venons de déposer entre les mains de Sa Majesté bien-aimée Sidi Mohammed, les motions dont ci-joint copie.

Nous prions Votre Excellence de bien vouloir transmettre à M. le Président du Comité de la Libération Nationale la dite copie et de porter à sa connaissance l'appel que nous faisons à l'esprit libéral et compréhensif qui anime tous les Français de la Résistance afin que la question marocaine soit réglée conformément aux principes de bonne foi qui président à toutes les relations internationales.

Nous avons la conviction que notre vœu trouvera auprès du Général de Gaulle, ainsi qu'auprès de Votre Excellence, un bienveillant accueil.

Nous vous prions également de noter que notre mouvement, qui tend à l'émancipation de notre pays, dans le cadre de la légalité, n'a rien de contraire aux intérêts légitimes de la France au Maroc.

Nous pensons que le moment est venu pour la France de tenir compte aux Marocains du sang qu'ils ont versé, versent et verseront encore s'il est nécessaire, pour le triomphe de son idéal et de sa propre liberté.

Nous vous prions, Excellence, de bien vouloir agréer l'hommage de notre profond respect.

Pour le Conseil supérieur du Parti de l'Indépendance:

Omar ABDELJALIL.
M'hamed ZEGHARI.
Mohamed GHAZI.

TEXTE DU MANIFESTE DU PARTI DE L'ISTIQLAL

Le Parti de l'Istiqlal (Parti de l'Indépendance) qui englobe les membres de l'ex-Parti National et des personnalités indépendantes;

Considérant que le Maroc a toujours constitué un Etat libre et souverain et qu'il a conservé son indépendance pendant treize siècles jusqu'au moment où, dans des circonstances particulières, un régime de protectorat lui a été imposé;

Considérant que ce régime avait pour fin et pour raison d'être de doter le Maroc d'un ensemble de réformes administratives judiciaires, culturelles, économiques, financières et militaires, sans toucher à la souveraineté traditionnelle du Peuple Marocain sous l'égide de son Roi;

Considérant qu'à ce régime les Autorités du Protectorat ont substitué un régime d'administration directe et d'arbitraire au profit de la colonie française dont un fonctionnariat pléthorique est en grande partie superflu et qu'elles n'ont pas tenté de concilier les divers intérêts en présence;

Considérant que c'est grâce à ce système que la Colonie française a pu accaparer tous les pouvoirs et se rendre maîtresse des ressources vives du pays au détriment des autochtones;

Considérant que le régime ainsi établi a tenté de briser par des moyens divers l'unité du Peuple Marocain, a empêché les Marocains de participer de façon effective au gouvernement de leur pays et les a privés de toutes les libertés publiques et individuelles;

Considérant que le monde traverse actuellement des circonstances autres que celles dans lesquelles le Protectorat a été institué;

Considérant que le Maroc a participé de façon effective aux guerres mondiales aux côtés des Alliés; que ses troupes viennent d'accomplir des exploits qui ont suscité l'admiration de tous aussi bien en France qu'en Tunisie, en Corse, en Sicile et en Italie et qu'on attend d'elles une participation encore plus étendue sur d'autres champs de bataille, notamment pour aider à la libération de la France;

Considérant que les Alliés, qui versent leur sang pour la cause de la liberté, ont reconnu dans la Charte de l'Atlantique le droit des peuples à disposer d'eux-mêmes et qu'ils ont récemment, à la Conférence de Téhéran, proclamé leur réprobation de la doctrine qui prétend que le fort doit dominer le faible;

Considérant que les Alliés ont manifesté, à différentes reprises, leur sympathie à l'égard des peuples dont le patrimoine historique est moins riche que le nôtre et dont le degré de civilisation est d'un niveau inférieur à celui du Maroc;

Considérant enfin que le Maroc constitue une unité homogène que, sous la haute direction de son Souverain, prend conscience de ses droits et de ses devoirs tant dans le domaine interne que dans le domaine international et sait apprécier les bienfaits des libertés démocratiques qui sont conformes aux principes de notre religion et qui ont servi de fondement à la constitution de tous les pays musulmans.

DECIDE:

A. En ce qui concerne la politique générale

1° Le demander l'indépendance du Maroc dans son intégrité territoriale sous l'égide de Sa Majesté Sidi Mohammed Ben Youss que Dieu le glorifie;

2° De solliciter de Sa Majesté d'entreprendre avec les Nations intéressées des négociations ayant pour objet la reconnaissance et la garantie de cette indépendance, ainsi que la détermination, dans le cadre de la souveraineté nationale, des intérêts légitimes des étrangers résidant au Maroc;

3° De demander l'adhésion du Maroc à la Charte de l'Atlantique et sa participation à la Conférence de la Paix.

B. En ce qui concerne la politique intérieure

De solliciter de Sa Majesté de prendre sous sa haute direction le mouvement de réforme qui s'impose pour assurer la bonne marche du Pays et laisse à Sa Majesté le soin d'établir un régime démocratique comparable au régime de gouvernement adopté dans les pays musulmans d'Orient, garantissant les droits de tous les éléments et de toutes les classes de la société marocaine et définissant les devoirs de chacun.

Fait à Rabat, le 14 Moharem 1363 (11 janvier 1944).

Pour toutes les sections du Parti de l'Istiqlal dans toutes les régions du Maroc,

Signé:

Mohammed Lyazidi, membre du Comité Exécutif de l'ex-Parti National;

Hadj Ahmed Cherkaoui, membre du Conseil Supérieur de l'ex-Parti National, directeur d'école à Rabat;

Hadj Ahmed Balafrej, membre du Comité Exécutif de l'ex-Parti National, licencié ès-lettres, diplômé des Hautes Etudes de la Sorbonne, directeur de l'Institution Mohamed Guessous;

Mohamed Ghazi, membre du Comité Exécutif de l'ex-Parti National, Alem, directeur de la Revue "Rissalat el Maghreb";

Abdelkrim Benjelloun Touimi, licencié ès-lettres, licencié en droit, juge au Haut Tribunal Chérifien;

Abdelkebir El-Fihri El-Fassi, juge au Haut Tribunal Chérifien;

Abdeljalil El-Kabbaj, inspecteur des Habous, président honoraire de l'Association des Anciens Elèves du Collège Moulay Youssef de Rabat;

Abdellah Erragragui, secrétaire à la Bibliothèque Générale;

Messoud Chiguer, secrétaire au Makhzen Central;

El-Mehdi Ben Barka, président de l'Association des Anciens Elèves du Collège Moulay Youssef de Rabat, membre du Conseil du Gouvernement, professeur au Collège Impérial et au Lycée Gouraud;

Mohamed El-Jazouli, ancien membre du Conseil du Gouvernement, membre de la Commission Municipale de Rabat, commerçant;

Haj Mohamed Riffaî, Alem, ex-Cadi suppléant de Rabat;

Boubker Kadiri, membre du Conseil Supérieur de l'ex-Parti National, directeur d'école à Salé;

Mohammed El-Bakkali, directeur d'école à Salé;

Saddik Ben Larbi, journaliste;

Abderrahim Bouabid, vice-président de l'Association des Anciens Elèves de Salé, instituteur à l'école des Fils de Notables;

Boubker Sbihi, président honoraire de l'Association des Anciens Elèves de Salé, secrétaire au Makhzen Central;

Tahar Zniber, licencié ès-lettres, secrétaire au Makhzen Central;

Mohamed Diouri, membre du Conseil Supérieur de l'ex-Parti National, ancien membre du Conseil du Gouvernement, président honoraire des œuvres sociales de Kénitra, commerçant;

Mohamed El-Fersioui, Alem à Ouezzan;

Driss Mhammedi, chef du Mouvement Scout Hassanien, membre de la Commission Municipale de Meknès, avocat;

Ahmed Ben Chekroun, Alem, membre du Comité-directeur de l'Enseignement religieux à Meknès;

Mohamed Ben Azzou, agriculteur de la région de Meknès;

Mohamed Aïssaoui Mastassi, secrétaire près du Mohtasseb de Meknès;

Omar Ben Chamsi, vice-président de l'Association des Anciens Elèves de Meknès, agriculteur de la région de Meknès;

Abdelhadi Skalli, interprète près du Tribunal du Pacha de Fès;

Ahmed Mekouar, membre du Comité Exécutif de l'ex-Parti National, commerçant à Fès;

Haj Omar Abdeljalil, membre du Comité Exécutif de l'ex-Parti National, ingénieur agricole, gérant d'exploitation agricole à Boulhaut;

Hachmi El-Filali, membre du Conseil Supérieur de l'ex-Parti National, directeur d'école à Fès;

Abdelaziz Ben Driss Amraoui, membre du Conseil Supérieur de l'ex-Parti National, Alem, directeur d'école;

Haj Hassan Bouayad, membre du Conseil Supérieur de l'ex-Parti National, Alem;

M'hamed Zeghari, président de l'Association des Anciens Elèves du Collège Moulay Driss de Fès, membre du Conseil du Gouvernement, et de la Commission du Budget, industriel, ancien directeur de la Cie Algérienne à Fès;

Ahmed Bahnini, vice-président de l'Association des Anciens Elèves du Collège Moulay Idriss de Fès, membre du Conseil du Gouvernement, diplômé d'Etudes Supérieurs en Droit, avocat à Fès, défenseur agréé;

Ahmed Khatat El Hamiani, secrétaire de l'Association des Anciens Elèves du Collège Moulay Idriss de Fès, avocat, défenseur agréé;

Ahmed Ben Bouchta, défenseur agréé près des Tribunaux Chérifiens, ancien juge au Haut Tribunal Chérifien;

Mhamed Soudi, membre du Comité de l'Association des Anciens Elèves du Collège Musulman de Fès, propriétaire, agriculteur dans la région de Fès;

Abdelkébir Ben Mehdi El-Fassi, professeur de mathématiques au Collège Moulay Idriss et à l'Université de Karaouiène, diplômé d'Etudes Supérieures de mathématiques;

Abdelouhab El-Fassi, Alem, professeur à l'Université de Karaouiène;

Mohamed ben Abderrahman Sâadani, instituteur;

Kacem Ben Abdeljalil, professeur au Collège Moulay Idriss de Fès;

Docteur El-Fatmi El-Fassi, à l'hôpital Cocard;

Bennacer Ben El-Haj Larbi, propriétaire à Oujda;

Abdelhamid Ben Moulay Ahmed, président de l'Association de Anciens Elèves du Collège berbère d'Azrou, instituteur à Taza;

Abdellah Ben Omar, secrétaire de l'Association des Anciens Elèves du Collège berbère d'Azrou, instituteur à Ifrane;

Ameur Ben Bennacer, instituteur à l'école de Khemisset;

Bouchta Jamai, membre du Conseil Supérieur de l'ex-Parti National, Alem;

Mhamed Ben Jilali Bennani, commerçant à Casablanca;

Ahmed Ben Ottmane Ben Della, commerçant à Casablanca;

Hassane Ben Jelloun, commerçant à Casablanca;

Mohamed El-Hamdaoui, directeur d'école à Casablanca;

Mohamed Larbi El-Alami, diplômé de l'Ecole Normale du Caire, directeur
   d'école libre à Casablanca;
Mhamed Ben El-Khadir, instituteur à Mazagan;
Abdeslam El Mastari, Alem de Safi;
Abdellah Ben Brahim, membre du Conseil Supérieur de l'ex-Parti National,
   Alem à Marrakech;
Abdelkader Hassane, Oukil judiciaire à Marrakech;
El-Houssain Ben Abdellah El-Ourzazi, instituteur à Marrakech;
M'barek Ben Ahmed, directeur d'école libre à Marrakech;
Ahmed El-Manjra, commerçant à Marrakech.

BIBLIOGRAPHY

NOTES

KEY TO INTERVIEWS

M.b.A.	Mehdi ben Aboud	1. 10/14/58	2. 10/15/58	3. 7/8/63
A.alA.	Ahmed al-Alaoui	1. 5/20/59		
M.A.alA.	Mohammed bel-Arabi al-Alaoui	1. 7/17/63	2. 7/18/63	
O.A.	Omar Abdeljalil	1. 5/19/59	2. 5/26/59	
		3. 6/10/59	4. 6/23/59	
A.B.	Ahmed Bennani	1. 5/20/59		
M.B.	Mehdi Bennouna	1. 5/4/59	2. 5/11/59	
		3. 7/16/63	4. 8/13/63	
M.b.B.	Mehdi ben Barka	1. 4/7/59		
M.C.	Messaoud Chiguer	1. 5/25/59		
M.D.	Mohammed Daoud	1. 7/30/63	2. 7/31/63	3. 7/31/63
A.alF.	Allal al-Fassi	1. 5/6/59	2. 6/20/59	3. 6/21/59
		4. 6/22/59	5. 6/23/59	6. 8/7/63
M.alF.	Mohammed al-Fassi	1. 3/23/59	2. 8/9/63	
A.alH.	Ahmed al-Hamiani	1. 6/2/59		
I.alK.	Ibrahim al-Kittani	1. 6/12/59	2. 6/15/59	
		3. 6/19/59	4. 7/3/63	
M.alK.	Mohammed al-Khatib	1. 5/18/59		
M.L.	Mohammed Lyazidi	1. 5/20/59	2. 5/27/59	3. 6/19/59
		4. 6/23/59	5. 6/30/59	6. 8/7/63
A.M.	Ahmed Mekouar	1. 5/30/59	2. 7/19/63	
		3. 7/19/63	4. 7/20/63	
M.N.	Mekki Naciri	1. 6/28/59		
M.H.O.	Mohammed Hassan al-Ouezzani	1. 5/29/59	2. 5/30/59	3. 5/31/59

BIBLIOGRAPHY

I have made no effort to compile an exhaustive bibliography. A number of books and journals from which isolated references were taken appear in the footnotes but not in the bibliography. On the other hand, if a work provided helpful background, it may appear here but not in the footnotes. The two criteria adopted for the inclusion of a source in the bibliography were its specific utility for this study or its general interest to the reader.

Documents, Public and Private

Daoud, Mohammed, Miscellaneous private papers relating to Moroccan nationalism, covering events from 1924 to 1947, especially on Salafiyya and the Berber *dahir*. Microfilmed in Rabat, July 1963, and on file at Lockwood Library, State University of New York at Buffalo.

Gooch, G. P. and Harold Temperley, eds. *British Documents on the Origins of the War, 1898–1914*, vol. II, London, H.M.S.O., 1927.

France. Ministère des Affaires Étrangères. *Documents Diplomatiques Français, 1871–1914*, Paris, 1929–1936. Published in three series covering 1871–1901, 1901–1911, 1911–1914. Cited as *Doc. Dipl. Fr. 1871–1914*.

—————— *Documents Diplomatiques. Affaires du Maroc, 1901–1912*, 6 vols., Paris, 1905–1912.

—————— *Documents Diplomatiques. Question de la protection diplomatique et consulaire au Maroc*, Paris, 1880.

—————— Direction de la Documentation. "L'Enseignement au Maroc," *Notes et Études Documentaires*, no. 1986, Feb. 24, 1955. A recapitulation of the development since 1912.

Lyautey, Maréchal Louis Hubert, *Rapport générale sur la situation du protectorat du Maroc au 31 juillet, 1914*, Rabat, 1916. Published in *Documents Diplomatiques. Affaires du Maroc*, vol. IV. The basic source for the early years of the protectorate. Cited as Lyautey, *Rapport . . . 1914*.

—————— *La Renaissance du Maroc, 1912–1922*. See Maroc. Résidence-Générale . . . etc.

Maroc. Direction de l'Instruction Publique. *Bilan 1945–1950*, Rabat, 1950. A kind of sequel to *Historique*, leaving a gap of fifteen years. Cited as *Bilan*.

—————— Direction-Générale de l'Instruction Publique . . . au Maroc. "L'État présent des enseignements primaires . . . ," prepared by Roger Thabault, *Chef de l'Instruction Primaire*, Rabat, Jan, 1939. Cited as *Thabault Report*.

—————— Protectorat de la République Française au Maroc. *Graphiques 1912–1938*, Rabat, 1939. A series of eight graphs on educational progress prepared to supplement the *Thabault Report*.

—————— Protectorat de la République Française au Maroc. *Direction-Générale de l'Instruction Publique, des Beaux-Arts et des Antiquités-Historique: 1912–1930*, Rabat, 1931. Recapitulation of the French educational effort prepared as an information piece for the International Colonial Exposition held in Paris in 1931. Many statistics, but must be used with discretion. Cited as *Historique*.

—— Résidence-Générale de la République Française au Maroc. *La Renaissance du Maroc: dix ans de protectorat, 1912–1922*, Rabat, 1922. Cited in notes as Lyautey, *Renaissance . . . 1912–1922*. A kind of sequel to Lyautey's *Rapport . . . 1914*.

—— "Situation politique et économique: mois de mai, 1939," Rabat, 1939. These were confidential reports prepared monthly for the resident-general.

Mekouar, Ahmed. Miscellaneous private papers dealing with various aspects of the nationalist movement from 1921 to 1937. Microfilmed in Rabat, July 1963, and on file at Lockwood Library, State University of New York at Buffalo.

PERIODICALS, PUBLIC AND PRIVATE

L'Action du Peuple, Fez, Aug. 4, 1933–May 16, 1934 and April 8, 1937–October 28, 1937. Weekly paper of the Kutlat in 1933–34. Affiliated with the al-Ouezzani splinter group in 1937.

L'Action Populaire, Rabat, Feb. 27, 1937–Sept. 6, 1937. Weekly paper of the National Party.

L'Afrique Française, Paris, 1891 ff. Monthly bulletin of the Comité de l'Afrique Française, the colonial lobby. The single most authoritative and valuable source of information on current events in the French African empire. Consulted by the author for the years 1923–1939. Cited in notes as *A.F.*

Annuaire Économique et Financière, Casablanca, periodically (there are volumes extant for 1917, 1918–19, 1920–21, 1924, 1929), by the Sharifian government. The predecessor of the *Bulletin Économique, q.v.*

Bulletin de l'Enseignement Public du Maroc, Paris, quarterly 1914–20, monthly thereafter, by the Direction de l'Instruction Publique. Contains enabling legislation, reports, statistics, commentaries and articles relating to all aspects of education in Morocco. Cited as *Bull. Ens.*

Bulletin Économique et Social du Maroc, Rabat, quarterly July 1933–39; monthly 1945 ff. Not published 1939–45. A continuation of the *Annuaire Économique et Financière, q.v.* Cited as *Bull. Econ. et Soc.*

Bulletin Officiel du Protectorat de la République Française au Maroc, Rabat, 1912–56, weekly, by the Protectorat de la République Française au Maroc. The official publication for all legislation, administrative notices and the like. Cited as *Bull. Off.* Abstracted in Rivière, *Traités, codes et lois . . .*, q.v.

El-Hayat, Tetuan, Feb. (?) 1934–Aug. 22, 1935, (in Arabic). Weekly paper of Torrès' Islah Party.

Journal Officiel de la République Française, Annales de la Chambre des Députés, Paris, annually. Cited as *Journal Official, Députés*.

Maghreb, Paris, July 1932–April, 1934. Monthly review of the Kutlat.

Es-Salam, Tetuan, Oct., 1933–Nov. 1934, (in Arabic). A putative monthly published by Mohammed Daoud, but only ten numbers actually appeared.

Survey of International Affairs, London, 1925 ff., annually. Documented accounts of the events of the year since 1925, arranged by geographical areas. Volume I, *The Middle East*, covers 1920–25. See especially the two extensive reports on North Africa: "North-West Africa (1920–26)," 1925, vol. I, pp. 92–188, cited as *S.I.A.1925*, and "Unrest in the North-West African Territories under French Rule (1927–37)," 1937, vol. I, pp. 486–543, cited as *S.I.A.1937*.

La Volonté du Peuple, Fez. Replaced *L'Action du Peuple* from Dec. 8, 1933 to Mar. 2, 1934. Weekly paper of the Kutlat.

OTHER WORKS

Abun-Nasr, Jamil. "The Salafiyya Movement in Morocco: The Religious Bases of the Moroccan Nationalist Movement," *St. Antony's Papers, No. 16, Middle Eastern Affairs, Number Three*, London, 1963, pp. 90–105.

Adams, Charles C. *Islam and Modernism in Egypt: A Study of the Reform Movement Inaugurated by Muhammed Abduh*, London, 1933. Authoritative and scholarly examination of the Salafiyya movement, based on Arabic sources.

Ahmed, Jamal M. *The Intellectual Origins of Egyptian Nationalism*, London, 1960.

André, P. G. (Général). *Contribution à l'étude des confréries réligieuses musulmanes*, Algiers, 1956. A good substitute for Depont and Coppolani.

Annuaire Général du Maroc, 1957. Tome I, *Annuaire politique, parlementaire et administratif*, Tangier, 1957. Privately printed. No equivalent official publication as of 1959. Helpful but uneven.

Antonius, George. *The Arab Awakening: The Story of the Arab National Movement*, London, 1938.

Ashford, Douglas E. *Political Change in Morocco*, Princeton, N.J., 1961.

Aubin, Eugène. *Morocco of Today*, London, 1906. One of the best descriptions of pre-protectorate Morocco; especially good on governmental institutions.

Ayache, Albert. *Le Maroc: bilan d'une colonisation*, Paris, 1956. Scholarly analysis of the institutions of the protectorate but with a Marxist bias.

Barbari, Mouslim (pseud.), *Tempête sur le Maroc, ou les erreurs d'une "politique berbère,"* Paris, 1931.

Barthou, Louis. *La Bataille du Maroc*, Paris, 1919.

de la Bastide, Henri. *Guide des carrières à l'usage des jeunes marocains*, Paris, 1952.

Benabdallah, Abdelaziz. *Les grands courants de la civilisation du Maghreb*, Casablanca, 1958.

Bennouna, Hadj M'Hammed. "The History of What is Ignored by History: The Silver Anniversary of the First Nationalist Movement" (in Arabic), *el-Alam*, August 3–19, 1951.

Bennouna, Mehdi A. *Our Morocco:The Story of a Just Cause*, Tangier, 1951. Hastily compiled for the 1951 U.N. session. Nationalist propaganda.

Bernard, Augustin. *Le Maroc*, 8th ed., Paris, 1932. Good general description of Moroccan life and social institutions both before and after 1912. Inferior to Surdon on political and judicial institutions.

Betts, Raymond F. *Assimilation and Association in French Colonial Theory: 1890–1914*, New York, 1961.

Borny. "Au Maroc — organisations nationalistes — émissions de propagande," *Dépêche de Toulouse*, April 26, 1937.

Caillé, Jacques. "Les Marocains à l'école du génie de Montpellier, 1885–1888," *Hespéris* (Rabat), XLI (1954), pp. 131–145.

Célérier, Jean. *Le Maroc*, 2nd ed., Paris, 1954.

Chaignaud, Paul. *La Question marocaine*, Paris, 1937. Report of the Casablanca delegate to the S.F.I.O. Marseille congress in July 1937.

Comité d'Action Marocaine. *Plan de Réformes Marocaines*, Paris, 1934.

Crocker, Walter R. *On Governing Colonies: Being an Outline of the Real Issues and a Comparison of the British, French and Belgian Approach to Them*, London, 1947. Covers only Black Africa.

—— *Self-Government for the Colonies*, London, 1949.

Daoud, Mohammed. *Tarikh Tatwan* (History of Tetuan), vol. I, Tetuan, 1959.

Delphin, Gaetan. *Fas, son université et l'enseignement supérieur musulman*, Paris, 1889. Especially informative on course offerings.

Depont, Octave and Xavier Coppolani. *Les Confréries réligieuses musulmanes*, Algiers, 1897. The most comprehensive work on the Sufi orders of North Africa.

Despois, Jean. *L'Afrique du Nord*, 2nd ed., Paris, 1958 (vol. I of the *Géographie de l'union française*).

Djamal al-Din al-Afghani. *Réfutation des matérialistes*, Paris, 1942. Trans. by A. M. Goichon of the 3rd Arabic edition of Djamal al-Din's *al-Radd ala al-Dahriyyin*, Cairo, 1925.

al-Fassi, Allal. *The Independence Movements in Arab North Africa*, Washington, 1954. Reflects the author's personal experience, with emphasis on Morocco. Useful, but unreliable on controversial matters.

Friedlander, Robert A. "Holy Crusade or Unholy Alliance? Franco's 'National Revolution' and the Moors," *The Southwestern Social Science Quarterly*, March 1964, pp. 346–356.

Gaillard, Henri. *Une Ville de l'Islam: Fès*, Paris, 1905.

Gaudefroy-Demombynes, Roger, *L'Oeuvre française en matière d'enseignement au Maroc*, Paris, 1928. The only thorough "non-official" study of French education in Morocco until Paye's unpublished dissertation (1957). Strong colonialist and assimilationist bias.

Gibb, Hamilton A. R. "The Islamic Conference at Jerusalem in December, 1931," *Survey of International Affairs*, 1934, vol. I, pp. 99–109.

—— *Modern Trends in Islam*, Chicago, 1947.

—— *Mohammedanism: An Historical Survey*, 2nd ed., New York, 1953.

—— "Studies in Contemporary Arabic Literature," *Bulletin of the School of Oriental Studies*, IV (1928), pp. 745–760; V (1929), pp. 311–322 and 445–466; VII (1933), pp. 1–22. (Cited as *B.S.O.S.*)

Girardière, E. "L'École coranique et la politique nationaliste au Maroc" (d'après une étude par M. E. Girardière), *La France Méditérranéenne et Africaine*, 1938, no. 1, pp. 99–109.

Goulven, Joseph. *La France au Maroc: vingt-cinq ans du protectorat, 1912–1937*, Paris, 1937.

Guernier, Eugène. *La Berbérie, l'Islam et la France: le destin de l'Afrique du Nord*, 2 vols., Paris, 1950.

Halstead, John P. "The Changing Character of Moroccan Reformism, 1921–1934," *Journal of African History*, V (1964), no. 3, pp. 435–447.

Hérauté, S. "L'Alerte marocaine," *L'Afrique Française*, January 1937, pp. 9–16.

Hertz-Wolfram, Georges. "Naissance du nationalisme marocain," *L'Age Nouveau*, June 1938, pp. 340–345.

Hourani, Albert H. *Arabic Thought in the Liberal Age, 1798–1939*, London and New York, 1962.

Jalabert, Louis. "Dans le Maghreb qui bouge." I. "Tendances réligieuses et politiques," *Études*, April 20, 1938, pp. 164–178; II. "Les réactions réligieuses et politiques," *Études*, May 5, 1938, pp. 342–360.

———— "Le Nationalisme marocain," *Études*, Aug. 20, 1934, pp. 433–448; Sept. 5, 1934, pp. 625–637; Sept. 20, 1934, pp. 758–767. Sympathetic and discerning.

Jomier, Jean. *Le Commentaire coranique du Manâr: tendances modernes de l'exégèse coranique en Égypt*, Paris, 1954.

Julien, Charles-André. *L'Afrique du Nord en marche: nationalismes musulmans et souveraineté française*, Paris, 1952. The most complete treatment of the subject in French. Stresses the postwar years.

———— "France and Islam," *Foreign Affairs*, July 1940, pp. 680–699. Good summary of North African nationalism before World War II.

———— *Histoire de l'Afrique du Nord: Tunisie, Algérie, Maroc*, 2nd ed., 2 vols., Paris, 1956. Vols. I and II cover the period 647–1830. Vol. III has not yet been published. The best history of North Africa extant.

Kamil, Ali Bek Fahmi. *Mustafa Kamil Pasha: His Biography and Actions, Including Political Speeches, Articles and Letters*, 6 vols. Cairo, 1908.

Kamil, Mustafa. *Lettres égyptiennes-françaises, adressées à Mme. Juliette Adam, 1895–1908*, Cairo, 1909.

Al-Kittani, Ibrahim. "My Recollections of the Moroccan Revival" (in Arabic), *el-Alam*, Nov. 3, 1956.

———— "Recollections of the First Phase of the Rise of the Moroccan Nationalist Struggle" (in Arabic), unpub. MS, Rabat.

Knight, Melvin M. *Morocco as a French Economic Venture: A Study of Open Door Imperialism*, New York, 1937.

de Lacger, L. "Le Mouvement nationaliste au Maroc," *En Terre d'Islam* (Lyon), appearing serially, November 1934 to April 1935.

Ladreit de Lacharrière, Jacques. "Autour du 'nationalisme' marocain," *L'Afrique Française*, January 1938, pp. 11–19.

Lahbabi, Mohammed. *Le Gouvernement marocain à l'aube du XXᵉ siècle*, Rabat, 1958.

Landau, Rom. *Moroccan Drama, 1900–1955*, San Francisco, 1956. The only acceptable history of twentieth-century Morocco in English. Strong anti-French bias.

Laoust, Henri. "Le Réformisme orthodoxe des 'Salafiya' et les caractères généraux de son orientation actuelle," *Revue des Études Islamiques*, VI (1932), pp. 175–224.

Lepp, Ignace. *Midi sonne au Maroc*, Paris, 1954. Treats the period since 1865. One of the least tendentious and most perceptive works in French on Moroccan nationalism. Unfortunately, not documented.

Le Tourneau, Roger. *Évolution politique de l'Afrique du Nord musulmane*

1920–1961. Paris, 1962. An objective survey, drawn almost entirely from secondary sources.

Lévi-Provençal, E. "L'Émir Shakib Arslan, 1869–1946," *Cahiers de l'Orient Contemporain*, 1947, nos. 9–10, pp. 5–19.

Liebesny, Herbert J. *The Government of French North Africa*, African Handbooks, No. 1, Philadelphia, 1943.

Lyautey, Maréchal Louis Hubert. "Les Origines du conflit," *Les Cahiers des Droits de l'Homme*, June 10, 1926, pp. 267–273. On the Riff War.

Maroc, voici tes maîtres, Rabat, *ca.* 1937.

Martinot, A. *Les Délires de l'impérialisme et les folies marocaines*, Paris, 1925.

Marty, Paul. *Le Maroc de demain*, Paris, 1925.

Mellor, Capt. F. H. *Morocco Awakes*, London, 1939. Emphasis on military affairs. Strongly pro-French.

Ménard, A. "La Crise méditerranéenne vue de Tanger," *L'Afrique Française*, February 1937, pp. 64–69.

Miège, Jean-Louis. *Le Maroc et l'Europe (1830–1894)*, Paris, vols. I and II, 1961; vol. III, 1962. Vol. I is an exhaustive classification of MSS and printed sources in the archives of Europe and North Africa. Vols. II and III, over 500 pp. each, are an economic history of European-Moroccan relations from 1830 to about 1884. Vols. IV and V are to appear.

Montagne, Robert. *Révolution au Maroc*, Paris, 1953. A presentation by a competent sociologist and Moroccan expert of the problems faced by France in Morocco owing to the convergence of two cultures. Sympathetic to Moroccan youth but not to the nationalist "fringe."

Morel, E. D. *Morocco in Diplomacy*, London, 1912.

Morocco 54. Special edition of the *Encyclopédie Mensuelle d'Outre-Mer*, Paris, 1954. Although issued for propaganda purposes, a most informative introduction in English to the political, social and cultural institutions of Morocco during the protectorate.

Naciri, Mekki. *France and Its Berber Policy in Morocco* (in Arabic), Cairo, 1931.

Nicolson, Harold. *Sir Arthur Nicolson, Bart., First Lord Carnock: A Study in the Old Diplomacy*, London, 1930.

Nuseibeh, Hazam Z. *The Ideas of Arab Nationalism*, Ithaca, N.Y. 1956.

Parti de l'Istiqlal. Bureau de Documentation. *Documents 1944–1946*, Paris, September 1946.

Paye, Lucien. "Enseignement et société musulmane: introduction et évolution de l'enseignement moderne au Maroc," unpub. dissertation, 3 vols., University of Paris, 1957. Covers 1883–1952. Thoroughly assimilationist.

Pérétié, A. "Les Medrasas de Fez," *Archives Marocaines* (Tangier), XVIII (1912), pp. 257–372.

Porter, Charles W. *The Career of Théophile Delcassé*, Philadelphia, 1936.

Redjai, Omer. *L'Évolution constitutionnelle en Turquie et l'organisation politique actuelle*, Strasbourg, 1934.

Rézette, Robert. *Les Partis politiques marocains*, Paris, 1955. The evolution of Moroccan political parties from 1925 to 1950, with the emphasis on the postwar years. Objective and detailed.

Rida, Mohammed Rashid. *Le Caliphate dans la doctrine de Rachid Rida,*

Beirut, 1938. Trans. by Henri Laoust of Rida's *al-Khilafah, aw al-Imama al-Uzma* (The Caliphate, or the Great Imam), Cairo, 1922.

Rivière, Paul-Louis, ed. *Traités, codes et lois du Maroc*, 3 vols., Paris, 1924–25.

——— *Traités, codes, . . . etc. Suppléments*. Published annually 1926–1939. These two works comprise a most valuable compendium of treaties concerning Morocco (1797–1923), legislation reorganizing the protectorate (1912 ff.), and customary law (1912 ff.). Contains texts of laws and footnote commentaries.

Rivlin, Benjamin. "The Tunisian Nationalist Movement," *Middle East Journal*, Spring 1952, pp. 166–193. A good summary, covering forty years.

Roberts, Stephen H. *The History of French Colonial Policy, 1870–1925*, 2nd ed., Hamden, Conn., 1963. An immense and scholarly undertaking, based on original sources. Clamors for a sequel.

Safran, Nadav. *Egypt in Search of Political Community: An Analysis of the Intellectual and Political Evolution of Egypt, 1804–1952*, Cambridge, Mass. 1961.

Stewart, Charles F. *The Economy of Morocco 1912–1962*, Cambridge, Mass., 1964.

Stuart, Graham H. *French Foreign Policy from Fashoda to Serajevo: 1898–1914*, New York, 1921.

——— *The International City of Tangier*, 2nd ed., Stanford, Calif. 1955.

Surdon, Georges. *La France en Afrique du Nord*, Algiers, 1945. By far the most thorough and authoritative work on the governmental institutions of North Africa, French as well as indigenous, from 1830 to World War I.

Taillard, Fulbert. *Le Nationalisme marocain*, Paris, 1947. Deals largely with the period after 1945. A relatively objective analysis, suggesting a moderate but non-pan-Arab solution. Based on some false premises.

Terrasse, Henri. *Histoire du Maroc dès origines à l'établissement du protectorat français*, 2 vols., Casablanca, 1950. The best and most scholarly history extant, but somewhat marred by its "official" viewpoint. The English edition, an abridgement of 225 pp., is deplorable propaganda.

Thomasset, René. "Les Problèmes marocaines," *Revue Politique et Parlementaire*, CLXVII, April 1936, pp. 50–65.

Vidal, Federico S. "Religious Brotherhoods in Moroccan Politics," *Middle East Journal*, October 1950, pp. 427–446.

NOTES

1. Much of the material in this chapter is general information for the student of North Africa and requires no documentation. I have relied primarily on five sources: Stephen H. Roberts, *The History of French Colonial Policy, 1870–1925*, 2nd ed. (*Hamden, Conn., 1963*); Harold Nicolson, *Sir Arthur Nicolson, Bart., First Lord Carnock: A Study in the Old Diplomacy* (London, 1930); Graham H. Stuart, *The International City of Tangier*, 2nd ed. (Stanford, Calif., 1955) and *French Foreign Policy from Fashoda to Serajevo: 1898–1914* (New York, 1921); and Rom Landau, *Moroccan Drama, 1900–1955* (San Francisco, 1956).

2. Nicolson, p. 112.

3. See table in Roberts, p. 556.

4. Landau, p. 68, citing a letter in the Archives of the British Legation, Tangier.

5. Charles W. Porter, *The Career of Théophile Delcassé* (Philadelphia, 1936), p. 26.

6. See the analysis of the Madrid Convention in E. D. Morel, *Morocco in Diplomacy* (London, 1912), pp. 221–227. Text of the Convention will be found in *Documents Diplomatiques Français. Question de la protection diplomatique et consulaire au Maroc* (Paris, 1880), pp. 271ff.

7. Instructions to Saint-René Taillandier, *Documents Diplomatiques Français, 1871–1914* (Paris, 1929–36), 2nd ser., vol. 1, no. 337. Cited as *Doc. Dipl. Fr. 1871–1914.*

8. *Ibid.*, 1st ser., vol. 15, no. 122.

9. *Ibid.*, 2nd ser., vol. 1, no. 17.

10. Nicolson, p. 147.

11. Jean Jaurès charged in 1911 that the French bankers withheld 12,500,000 francs of this loan as commission, but that the sultan was obligated for interest charges on the full 62½ million (*Journal Officiel de la République Française, Annales de la Chambre des Députés, 2ᵉ séance du 24 mars 1911*, p. 1434). Cited hereafter as *Journal Officiel, Députés.*

12. "Morocco — The Financial Interests Involved — The Squeezing of the Sultan," *Manchester Guardian*, May 8, 1911, p. 7. For a fascinating cross-listing of the directorates of these companies, see *Maroc, voici tes maîtres* (Rabat, c. 1937).

13. *Journal Officiel, Députés, 2ᵉ séance du 10 nov. 1904*, p. 2387; Roberts, p. 551.

14. G. P. Gooch and Harold Temperley, *British Documents on the Origins of the War, 1898–1914*, II (London, 1927), pp. 386–387.

15. *Ibid.*, pp. 393–394, Secret Article III.

16. *Doc. Dipl. Fr. 1871–1914*, 2nd ser., vol. 5, no. 358.

17. *Ibid.*, vol. 4, no. 368.

18. *Ibid.*

19. *Ibid.*, no. 384.

20. *Ibid.*, vol. 5, no. 17.

21. See summary of the Act in Nicolson, pp. 443–447. For official text, *Doc. Dipl. Fr. 1871–1914*, 2nd ser., vol. 9 (II), no. 631.

22. *Doc. Dipl. Fr. 1871–1914*, 2nd ser., vol. 11, no. 220. All French translations are the author's unless otherwise stated.

23. Landau, p. 73.

24. Roberts, p. 553.

25. *Ibid.*, pp. 553–555, citing report in *Documents Diplomatiques. Affaires du Maroc*, vol. 4, pp. 215–228. The French intention ultimately to withdraw is made clear in the instructions to General d'Amade which appear on pp. 253–254.

26. See *Doc. Dipl. Fr. 1871–1914*, 2nd ser., vol. 12, nos. 449, 457, 466, 521, 544, 545, 547, 548, 551.

27. Roberts, p. 555.

28. The softening of the German position is partly explained by the adverse decision of the Hague Court of Arbitration in the Casablanca deserters' case, by the Young Turk revolution and by the Austrian annexation of Bosnia and Herzegovina, all of which placed German foreign policy on a shaky footing. But the role played by powerful German business interests has not been thoroughly ventilated. As much as 25 per cent of the capital, perhaps more, in the cartels, which comprised the Comité du Maroc, was German, so that the German members of the Comité had everything to gain by a peaceful penetration of Morocco under the Algeciras guarantees. And the erratic nature of Germany's response to French ambitions in Morocco throughout the period 1904–1911 may have been caused by a tension which existed between ambitious German politicians with territorial aims and influential German businessmen who preferred not to upset the work of the Comité du Maroc. This is conjecture, however, or at best an educated guess, and the whole matter needs further investigation. Also see Stuart, pp. 261–262, and the *Manchester Guardian*, May 8, 1911, p. 7.

29. Text in *Doc. Dipl. Fr. 1871–1914* , 3rd ser., vol. 1, no. 19.

30. *Ibid.*, no. 20.

31. From *Doc. Dipl. Fr. 1871–1914*, vol. 2, no. 278.

32. Article I of the Treaty.

33. *Ibid.*

CHAPTER II. ORDER AND TUTELAGE

1. *L'Afrique Française* (Sept. 1933), p. 490. Hereafter cited as *A.F.*

2. See Robert Montagne, *Révolution au Maroc* (Paris, 1953).

3. Louis Jalabert, "Le Nationalisme marocain," *Études* (Paris), Sept. 5, 1934, pp. 625 and 627. A good example is the crusading anti-militarism of A. Martinot, *Les Délires de l'impérialisme et les folies marocaines* (Paris, 1925).

4. Roberts, p 572.

5. Primo de Rivero arrived in Casablanca on August 22, 1925 to coordinate the counteroffensive with Pétain.

6. Joseph Goulven, *La France au Maroc: vingt-cinq ans du protectorat, 1912–1937*, (Paris, 1937), p. 35.

7. Paul-Louis Rivière (ed.), *Traités, codes et lois du Maroc* (Paris, 1924–25), II, p. 467.

8. See the summary of the early Berber policy by Lt.-Col. Huot, *Directeur des Affaires Indigènes*, in Maroc, Résidence-Générale de la République Française au Maroc, *La Renaissance du Maroc: dix ans de protectorat, 1912–1922* (Rabat, 1922), pp. 175–184. Hereafter cited as Lyautey, *Renaissance . . . 1912–1922.*

9. Montagne, p. 152.

10. *Survey of International Affairs, 1937,* I, p. 500. Cited as *S.I.A. 1937.*

11. Ignace Lepp, *Midi sonne au Maroc* (Paris, 1954), p. 157. Also see Montagne's discussion of the tribes in *Révolution*, pp. 41–61.

12. For the displacement of "assimilation" by "association," see Raymond F. Betts, *Assimilation and Association in French Colonial Theory: 1890–1914* (New York, 1961).

13. Lyautey, *Renaissance . . . 1912–1922*, p. 113.

14. Roberts, pp. 565–566.

15. *Ibid.,* pp. 574–576.

16. Mohammed Lahbabi, *Le Gouvernement marocain à l'aube du XX* siècle (Rabat, 1958), pp. 140–147.

17. *Ibid.,* pp. 151–153.

18. *Ibid.,* pp. 157, 158, 162.

19. *Ibid.,* pp. 164–181.

20. *Ibid.,* p. 169.

21. Georges Surdon, *La France en Afrique du Nord* (Algiers, 1945), p. 233.

22. *Bulletin Officiel du Protectorat de la République Française au Maroc* (Rabat), no. 3 (Nov. 15, 1912), p. 17. Cited hereafter as *Bull. Off.*

23. Goulven, p. 26; *Bull. Off.,* no. 96 (Aug. 31, 1914), p. 690.

24. Rivière, *Traités,* II, p. 2.

25. The two principal reforms of the Makhzen between World War II and independence occurred in 1947 and 1953. The first, initiated by Marshal Juin, enlarged the Makhzen by the appointment of nine *délégués* who were to serve as undersecretaries (*sous-directeurs*) in each of the major administrative departments which comprised the Residency: finance, education, public works, etc. This was intended to provide high-level experience for Moroccans but also had the effect of assimilating the native government more closely into the French colonial system. In 1953, the so-called "grandes réformes" of the interim sultan, Moulay ben Arafa, resulted in further assimilation by the creation of a *Conseil Restreint* and the transformation of the *Conseil des Vizirs et des Directeurs.* The former was designed to lighten the burdens of the grand vizier by the appointment of two deputy viziers for administrative and economic affairs, who would be associated, respectively, with two French officials, the counsellor of the Sharifian government and the director of the interior. This body formed a kind of privy council under the chairmanship of the grand vizier. The second council consisted of Moroccan viziers and French directors of the departments of the Residency, in equal numbers, to a total of twenty, and performed a proto-legislative function, having to pass on *dahirs* for the sultan's signature, and empowered, should the sultan prove recalcitrant, to force through such legislation by a two-thirds vote at the second reading Both bodies passed out of existence after independence.

26. *Bull. Off.*, no. 1 (Nov. 1, 1912), p. 2.

27. Goulven, p. 17.

28. *Ibid.*, decree of June 6, 1925.

29. Goulven, pp. 30–31.

30. *Ibid., p. 18; Bull. Off.*, no. 1 (Nov. 1, 1912), pp. 3–5.

31. *Bull. Off.*, no. 13 (Jan. 24, 1913), p. 66.

32. *Bull. Off.*, no. 1 (Nov. 1, 1912), pp. 3–5; Goulven, pp 19–20, 31; Jean Célérier, *Le Maroc* (Paris, 1954), p. 115.

33. Goulven, pp. 19, 21.

34. Decrees of Jan. 15, 1912 (*Bull Off.*, no. 13 [Jan. 24, 1913], p. 66) and of May 19, 1917 (*Bull. Off.*, no. 241 [June 4, 1917], p. 611). Until 1917 the counsellor was called secretary-general of the Sharifian government.

35. *Bull. Off.*, no. 407 (Aug. 10, 1926), p. 1365.

36. *Dahir* of June 2, 1917 and Residential circular of June 10, 1917 (*Bull. Off.*, no. 242 [June 11, 1917], p. 631).

37. Lyautey, *Renaissance . . . 1912–1922*, pp. 126, 130.

38. Decree of July 31, 1913 (*Bull. Off.*, no. 45 [Sept. 5, 1913] p. 343).

39. Landau, pp. 105–106.

40. Goulven, pp. 34–35.

41. Lyautey, *Renaissance . . . 1912–1922*, pp. 130–131.

42. Goulven, pp. 21, 35.

43. Residential orders of June 29, 1913 and June 1, 1919 (Albert Ayache, *Le Maroc: bilan d'une colonisation* [Paris, 1956] p. 95).

44. *Ibid., dahir* of Jan. 20, 1919.

45. Roberts, p. 572.

46. Residential decrees of Mar. 18, 1919 and May 10, 1923 (Ayache, p. 95); Charles-André Julien, *L'Afrique du Nord en marche: nationalismes musulmans et souveraineté française* (Paris, 1952), p. 162.

47. Ayache, pp. 95–96.

48. *Ibid.*, pp. 94–95.

49. *Ibid.*, p. 94, *dahir* of Sept. 2, 1912.

50. *Ibid.*, p. 95; Julien, *Afrique du Nord*, p. 162.

51. Marcel Peyrouton also served as minister of interior in the Vichy government. General Noguès served as resident-general and military commander in Morocco throughout the Vichy period. For Lyautey's warning, see his circular of Nov. 18, 1920, cited in "Le Drame marocain devant la conscience chrétienne," *Cahiers de Témoignage Chrétien* (Paris), 1953, p. 60; Landau, p. 133.

52. Goulven, pp. 31–37.

53. *Ibid.*, p. 101.

54. Paul-Louis Rivière (ed.), *Traités, codes et lois du Maroc. Supplément pour 1937*, pp. 116–118.

55. Lucien Paye, "Enseignement et société musulmane," unpubl. dissertation, Faculty of Letters, University of Paris (1957), vol. II, pp. 241–242.

56. *Dahir* of Oct. 13, 1947 and Residential decree of Dec. 20, 1947. For the immensely complicated methods of representation and election for the *Conseil*, see Robert Rézette, *Les partis politiques marocains* (Paris, 1955), pp. 41–44.

After the Second World War, the same self-canceling combination of administrative assimilation and wider native representation was pursued with even greater determination. On the one hand, the Makhzen was more tightly linked to the Residency by the creation of the Limited Council and the Council of Viziers and Directors, both of which had French and Moroccan members, and by the appointment of Moroccan undersecretaries to serve in each of the "technical services." While the remnants of indirect rule were thus being destroyed, greater representation was being accorded Moroccans in the *Conseil de Gouvernement*, where a third college, partly elective, was created for Moroccans in 1947. At the same time, the French and Moroccan sections of the *Conseil* became numerically equal and began to deliberate jointly, and committee organization was authorized in 1953. The chief duty of the *Conseil* was still to advise the resident-general, and its chief privilege was to discuss the budget. But in spite of its non-legislative character, it provided a forum where Moroccans could express their views and witness the consideration of problems at a national level.

CHAPTER III. DISILLUSION

1. *S.I.A. 1937*, p. 133.
2. Allal al-Fassi, *The Independence Movements in Arab North Africa* (Washington, 1954), pp. 141–142.
3. *A.F.* (Sept. 1933), p. 490.
4. Goulven, p. 23.
5. M.H. al-Ouezzani, "Le Protectorat," *Maghreb* (Paris) (Aug. 1933), pp. 21–26.
6. *Cahiers de Témoignage Chrétien* (1953), p. 60.
7. Omar Abdeljalil, "Le Hakem," *Maghreb* (Nov. 1932), p. 5.
8. Montagne, pp. 135–136.
9. Goulven, p. 43.
10. O. Abdeljalil, "Les Biens *habous*," *Maghreb* (Apr. 1934), pp. 20–28.
11. *S.I.A. 1937*, p. 491.
12. Goulven, p. 33.
13. M.H. al-Ouezzani, "Protectorat et Colonie," *Maghreb* (Apr. 1934) pp. 4–12.
14. Goulven, p. 33.
15. *S.I.A. 1937*, p. 492.
16. The most celebrated and disgraceful case being that of Gilbert Grandval in 1955.
17. Ponsot and Peyrouton.
18. Rézette, p. 41.
19. *Ibid.*, p. 44.
20. Ayache, p. 96.
21. Kadour (pseud. A. Benjelloun), "La Crise économique au Maroc," *Maghreb* (Sept. 1932), pp. 30–35.
22. O. Abdeljalil, "Défense marocaine," *L'Action du Peuple* (Fez), April 6, 1934, p. 1. The figure of 130,000 French settlers may be low, for Goulven, p. 95, cites 177,000 for 1936.
23. Rézette, p. 29.
24. *Ibid.*, p. 30.
25. *Dahir* of Oct. 24, 1953.
26. Rézette, p. 31.
27. These events are treated fully in Chapters IX, X, XIII and XIV.
28. See Chapter IV for details.

29. *A.F.* (Sept. 1932), p. 518.

30. M.C. 1:2. (See Note on Method, p. vi and Key to Interviews, p. 288.)

31. Permanent, that is, until mid-1956 when all three belatedly received their diplomas.

32. Letter from the three protesting the administrative action, dated Jan. 30, 1933 (I.alK.1:1).

33. The basic laws were the *dahirs* of April 27, 1914 and Jan. 12, 1918 (Rézette, p. 33).

34. *Ibid.*, p. 34.

35. *A.F.* (Jan. 1928) p. 14.

36. Rézette, p. 34.

37. A.alF.3:3.

38. I.alK.

39. After the founder of Qarawiyin University. (A.alF.)

40. A.alF.

41. *A.F.* (Jan. 1928), pp. 16-17; (Sept. 1932), pp. 516-517. The author was unable to find comparable references to press suppressions in *L'Afrique Française* for later years.

42. M.H.O.1:5; *A.F.* (Aug. 1929). p. 366.

43. Kadour, "Les Libertés politiques au Maroc," *Maghreb* (Dec. 1932) p. 36.

44. Rézette, p. 37.

45. *Ibid.*, p. 275.

46. The name of the Moroccan nationalist organization in the French zone from 1934 to 1937.

47. Rézette, p. 33.

48. M. H. al-Ouezzani, "L'Interdiction du troisième congrès," *L'Action du Peuple*, Sept. 22, 1933, p. 1.

49. Rézette, p. 60.

50. *Ibid.*, p. 64.

51. "La Jeunesse marocaine," *A.F.* (Jan. 1930), pp. 24-27.

52. Rézette, p. 65.

53. *A.F.* (Aug. 1933), p. 444.

54. Lepp, p. 144.

55. M. Lyazidi, "Propos d'un jeune," *L'Action du Peuple*, May 4, 1934, p. 2.

56. Lepp, pp. 146-148.

57. *A.F.* (Aug. 1930), p. 444.

58. *A.F.* (Feb. 1935), p. 92.

59. See the analysis of the Plan in Chapter XII.

60. For another unsympathetic study of Moroccan nationalism in the same period, see L. de Lacger, "Le Mouvement nationaliste au Maroc," *En terre d'Islam* (Lyon) appearing serially, November 1934 to April 1935.

61. Jalabert, "Le Nationalisme marocain," *Études* (Aug. and Sept. 1934), one of the most dispassionate and incisive essays on the subject by a Frenchman.

CHAPTER IV. MACHIAVELLIAN JUSTICE

1. E.g., see Lyautey, *Renaissance . . . 1912-1922*, pp. 191-192, 194.

2. The fullest discussion of the judicial aspects of Moroccan government on the eve of the protectorate appears in Lahbabi, *passim.*

3. H. A. R. Gibb, *Modern Trends in Islam* (Chicago, 1947), p. 89, and Roberts, pp. 576-577.

4. *Morocco 54*, spec. issue, *Encyclopédie Mensuelle d'Outre-Mer* (Paris, 1954), p. 51 (a document which must be used with discretion); Goulven, p. 90; Herbert J. Liebesny, *The Government of French North Africa* (Philadelphia, 1943), p. 30.

5. *Morocco 54*, p. 51.

6. *Dahir* of Nov. 5, 1937 and vizierial order of June 23, 1938 (Liebesny, p. 45).

7. *Morocco 54*, p. 51.

8. Maréchal Louis Hubert Lyautey, *Rapport général sur la situation du protectorat du Maroc au 31 juillet 1914* (Rabat, 1916), pp. 268-269. Hereafter cited as Lyautey, *Rapport . . . 1914*.

9. Liebesny, p. 45.

10. Roberts, p. 577.

11. Liebesny, pp. 45-46; *Morocco 54*, p. 52.

12. *Morocco 54*, p. 51.

13. *Ibid.*

14. By the *dahir* of Feb. 7, 1921 (Lyautey, *Renaissance . . . 1912-1922*, p. 194). *Chraa* is the French transliteration of the Moroccan dialect for Sharia.

15. *Morocco 54*, p. 52. A *dahir* of Sept. 7, 1939 permitted suits in first instance to be heard directly by the *Tribunal* (Liebesny, p. 46).

16. Liebesny, pp. 46-47; Goulven, p. 91.

17. Liebesny, pp. 47-48.

18. Lyautey, *Rapport . . . 1914*, p. 269; Liebesny, p. 46.

19. *Dahir* of July 7, 1914 (Liebesny, pp. 45-46).

20. *Ibid.*, p. 46.

21. *Ibid.*, p. 47.

22. Goulven, p. 91.

23. Landau, pp. 106, 237.

24. Jean Despois, *L'Afrique du Nord* (Paris, 1958), p. 140; Landau, p. 88.

25. *S.I.A. 1937*, pp. 525-526.

26. Julien, *Afrique du Nord*, p. 146; Mouslim Barbari (pseud.), *Tempête sur le Maroc* (Paris, 1931), pp. 20-21.

27. Julien, *Afrique du Nord*, p. 146; Goulven, p. 97.

28. See *A.F.* (Dec. 1928), pp. 783-786.

29. M. Lyazidi, "Divers aspects de la politique berbère au Maroc," *Maghreb* (May-June 1933), pp. 15-16.

30. Paul Marty, *Le Maroc de demain* (Paris, 1925), p. 216.

31. *Ibid.*, p. 219.

32. Quoted in *Maghreb* (May-June 1933), p. 14.

33. Marty, p. 228. (Italics added.)

34. English text in *S.I.A. 1937*, p. 525.

35. See Chapter X.

36. See Barbari, *Tempête*, and Lyazidi in *Maghreb* (May-June 1933). Hardly an issue of *Maghreb* lacked a diatribe against the egregious *dahir*.

37. Julien, *Afrique du Nord*, p. 146.

38. R. Gaudefroy-Demombynes, *L'Oeuvre française en matière d'enseignement au Maroc* (Paris, 1928), p. 119.

39. Protectorat de la République Française au Maroc, *Direction Gén-*

érale de l'Instruction Publique . . . Historique: *1912–1930* (Rabat, 1931), pp. 63–64. Hereafter cited as *Historique.*

40. *Maghreb* (May–June 1933), p. 37.

41. Marty, pp. 241–252.

42. E.g., Barbari, *Tempête,* and Mekki Naciri, *France and Its Berber Policy in Morocco* (in Arabic) (Cairo, 1931).

43. E.g., *al-Fath* (Cairo), one of the most influential reformist weeklies of the Muslim world in the 1930's.

44. *Maghreb* (May–June 1933), p. 18.

45. Montagne, pp. 180–181.

46. Quoted in al-Fassi, p. 120.

47. Julien, *Afrique du Nord,* p. 147; Roger Le Tourneau, *Évolution politique de l'Afrique du Nord musulmane, 1920–1961* (Paris, 1962), pp. 183–184.

48. Julien, *Afrique du Nord,* p. 146.

49. Liebesny, pp. 49–50; Montagne, p. 186.

50. Surdon, p. 744.

51. *Time Magazine,* April 22, 1957, p. 35.

CHAPTER V. THE PARTIAL CORNUCOPIA

1. *Maroc, voici tes maîtres,* pp. 5–6.

2. Roberts, pp. 567–568.

3. Goulven, pp. 45–46.

4. *Dahir* of Aug. 28, 1915 (*Bull. Off.* [Aug. 30, 1915], p. 537).

5. *Dahir* of Feb. 28, 1921 (*Bull. Off.,* no. 437 [Mar. 8, 1921], p. 395).

6. *Dahir* of Jan. 15, 1921 (*Bull. Off.,* no. 433 [Feb. 8, 1921], p. 206).

7. *Dahir* of Jan. 4, 1926 (*Bull. Off.,* no. 693 [Feb. 2, 1926], p. 186).

8. Melvin M. Knight, *Morocco as a French Economic Venture: A Study of Open Door Imperialism* (New York, 1937), p. 40.

9. *Ibid.,* pp. 43–44. Knight points out that what the French called "loans" were often parliamentary authorizations.

10. *Ibid.,* pp. 40, 42.

11. For details, see Goulven, pp. 60–61.

12. Knight, p. 51.

13. *Firman* of Oct. 31, 1912 (*Bull. Off.,* no. 3 [Nov. 15, 1912], p. 17).

14. *Dahir* of Apr. 18, 1913 (*Bull. Off.,* no. 26 [Apr. 22, 1913], pp. 103–105).

15. Roberts, p. 582; Knight, p. 47.

16. Walter R. Crocker, *Self-Government for the Colonies* (London, 1949) pp. 36–37.

17. Goulven, p. 67.

18. Knight, pp. 70, 102–103, 130–131.

19. M. H. al-Ouezzani, "Le Maroc en face de l'emprunt," *Maghreb* (Aug. 1932), pp. 23–29; and see *Plan de Réformes,* p. 120.

20. Goulven, p. 21.

21. Roberts, pp. 572, 580.

22. Agadir, Mogador, Safi, Mazagan, Fedala, Rabat and Port Lyautey (Kénitra).

23. Goulven, p. 71.

24. Roberts, p. 580; Goulven, pp. 69–70.

25. *Ibid.*

26. Charles F. Stewart, *The Economy of Morocco 1912–1962* (Cambridge [Mass.], 1964), p. 112.

27. Knight, p. 104; Stewart, p. 112.

28. E.g., Roberts, p. 582.

29. *Ibid.*, pp. 583–584.

30. *Bull. Off.*, no. 1 (Nov. 1, 1912), pp. 6–7.

31. Roberts, p. 584.

32. *Ibid.*, p. 585; Goulven, p. 47.

33. Goulven, p. 47; Roberts, p. 585.

34. *Dahir* of June 15, 1922 (*Bull. Off.*, no. 505 [June 27, 1922], pp. 1034–1035.

35. Roberts, pp. 569–586. Authorities differ on the number of actual *colons* in Morocco as of 1925. Roberts himself quotes figures of 180 and 400 on different pages. Landau (p. 135) cites the figure 1,000, and *S.I.A.1937* (p. 491) uses the figure 2,000. Official statistics are quite unreliable.

36. Roberts, p. 586.

37. *S.I.A.1937*, pp. 491–493; Landau, p. 223; Goulven, p. 48.

38. Arable land in Morocco totals about 7,500,000 hectares (1957) of which some 4,100,000 ha. were under cultivation before World War II (*Bulletin Économique et Social du Maroc* (Rabat), vol. XXI, no. 74 [Oct. 1957], p. 180). The 1919 figure is given in Stewart, p. 86.

39. *Bull. Écon. et Soc.* (Oct. 1957), p. 183; *Annuaire Économique et Financière: 1929* (Rabat), p. 207. The *Annuaire* was the predecessor of the *Bull. Écon. et Soc.* which was first published in July 1933. The *Annuaire* was published irregularly, one volume each for 1917, 1918–19, 1920–21 (available in bound volumes at Harvard University), 1924 and 1929 (available on microfilm at the State University of New York at Buffalo).

40. *Bull. Écon. et Soc.* (October 1957), p. 180.

41. Eugène Guernier, *La Berbérie, l'Islam et la France* (Paris, 1950), vol. II, p. 106.

42. *Dahir* of Jan. 15, 1919 (*Bull. Off.*, no. 328 [Feb. 3, 1919], p. 89).

43. *Dahirs* of May 26, 1917 (*Bull. Off.*, no. 242 [June 11, 1917], pp. 633–636) and Jan. 28, 1922 (*Bull. Off.*, no. 488 [Feb. 28, 1922], pp. 346–350).

44. Goulven, pp. 49–64.

45. O. Abdeljalil, "Le Patrimoine immobilier de la colonisation officielle et les expropriations," *La Volonté du Peuple*, Mar. 2, 1934, p. 3.

46. Goulven, p. 48.

47. Augustin Bernard, *Le Maroc* (Paris, 1932), pp. 457, 460.

48. A.B.1:2; Landau, p. 240. See *Bull. Off.* for late 1927 and early 1928.

49. Abdeljalil, *La Volonté du Peuple*, Mar. 2, 1934, p. 3; al-Ouezzani, *Maghreb* (Aug. 1933), p. 23.

50. *S.I.A.1937*, p. 491.

51. René Thomasset, "Les Problèmes marocains," *Revue Politique et Parlementaire* (Paris), vol. CLXVII (Apr. 1936), p. 55.

52. *S.I.A.1937*, pp. 493–494.

53. O. Abdeljalil, "Caisses indigènes de crédit agricole et sociétés indigènes de prévoyance — première partie," *L'Action du Peuple*, Sept. 1, 1933, p. 3 and "Les Marocains et la crise," *Maghreb* (Mar. 1933) p. 16–17.

54. Stewart, p. 89.

55. Stewart, p. 90. Abdeljalil, *Maghreb* (Mar. 1933), p. 17, cites somewhat different figures.

56. O. Abdeljalil, "Bilan et parallèle," *La Volonté du Peuple*, Feb. 2, 1934, p. 1. The figure 765 million seems rather large, and certainly must include the sums charged to the 1931 and later budgets.

57. Abdeljalil, *L'Action du Peuple*, Sept. 1, 1933, p. 3.

58. Knight, pp. 49–50.

59. Stewart, p. 179.

60. O. Abdeljalil, "Le cultivateur et l'impôt," *L'Action du Peuple*, April 27, 1934, pp. 2–3.

61. Abdeljalil, *Maghreb* (Mar. 1933), pp. 17–19.

62. *Morocco 54*, p. 155.

63. Knight, p. 94.

64. *Ibid.*, p. 100.

65. Stewart, pp. 116–117.

66. Knight, pp. 51–52.

67. *Morocco 54*, p. 159.

68. Stewart, pp. 119–122.

69. *Morocco 54*, p. 158; Stewart, p. 123.

70. *Ibid.*

71. *Morocco 54*, p. 177.

72. *Ibid.*, pp. 178–179; Stewart, p. 134; Goulven, pp. 77.

73. Landau, p. 226.

74. Stewart, pp. 128–130.

75. *Ibid.*, p. 127.

76. *Ibid.*, p. 126; Landau, p. 226.

77. Roberts, p. 578.

78. Knight, p. 146.

79. Roberts, p. 579.

80. Knight, p. 127.

81. Goulven, pp. 60–61.

82. Knight, p. 53.

83. Stewart, pp. 124–125.

84. *S.I.A.1937*, pp. 507–508.

85. Montagne, pp. 82–84.

86. Stewart, pp. 137–138.

87. O. Abdeljalil, "Tribune du Fellah," *La Volonté du Peuple*, Feb. 2, 1934, pp. 1–2.

88. Stewart, p. 129.

CHAPTER VI. RISING EXPECTATIONS, OR EDUCATING NATIVES TO BE FRENCHMEN

1. *Bulletin de l'Enseignement Public du Maroc* (Paris), no. 102 (Feb. 1930), p. 84. Hereafter cited as *Bull. Ens.*

2. Henri Gaillard, *Une Ville de l'Islam: Fès* (Paris, 1905), p. 162.

3. Eugène Aubin, *Morocco of Today* (London, 1906), p. 222.

4. Gaillard, p. 164. The *medersa* Ben Youssef still existed in 1959 in Marrakesh, but in a state of such dilapidation that it could hardly be ranked as an institution of higher learning.

5. A. Pérétié, "Les Medrasas de Fez," *Archives Marocaines* (Tangier),

vol. XVIII (1912), pp. 335–344. For a comprehensive study see G. Delphin, *Fas, son université et l'enseignement supérieur musulman* (Paris, 1889).

6. Gaillard, pp. 167–168; *Historique*, p. 50.

7. For curriculum details, see *A.F.* (Oct. 1933), pp. 604–605.

8. Henri de la Bastide, *Guide des carrières à l'usage des jeunes marocains* (Paris, 1952), pp. 105–107.

9. *Bull. Ens.*, no. 1 (June 1914), p. 11.

10. Georges Hardy in *Bull. Ens.*, no. 24 (Oct. 1920), p. 418.

11. There is a good, brief summary of French colonial objectives in W. R. Crocker, *On Governing Colonies* (London, 1947), pp. 59–63.

12. *A.F.* (Feb. 1924), p. 112.

13. *Bull. Ens.*, no. 25 (Nov. 1920), p. 454.

14. Direction Générale de l'Instruction Publique . . . au Maroc, *L'État: présent des enseignements primaires* . . . , prepared by Roger Thabault, *Chef de l'Instruction Primaire* (Rabat, Jan. 27, 1939), pp. 43–44. Hereafter cited as *Thabault Report.*

15. *Historique*, Annex II, Table 3; *Thabault Report*, p. 44, and accompanying graphs, *Graphiques 1912–1938*, p. 1. Statistics on education in Morocco are extremely scarce for the years 1933–1945, before and after which there are official publications of doubtful reliability. Whether or not this was a reaction to the spurt of nationalist criticism in the early 1930's is hard to say, but after May 1933, the "Administrative Part" of the *Bulletin de l'Enseignement Public*, along with its statistical content and its listing of educational legislation, was suppressed. Thereafter the *Bulletin* became a literary outlet for French personnel, on subjects often wholly unrelated to Morocco, rather than a professional journal addressed to the educational needs of the protectorate.

16. *Historique*, Annex II, Table 2.

17. *Thabault Report: Graphiques*, p. 6, and from lists of baccalaureates granted to Moroccans 1917–1958 furnished the author by the Bureau of Examinations, Ministry of Education, Rabat. Statistics derived therefrom must be considered no more than approximate.

18. *Bull. Off.*, no. 4 (Nov. 23, 1912), p. 22; *Historique*, pp. 16–17.

19. *Historique*, pp. 18–20, 210; Bastide, pp. 109–110.

20. *Bull. Ens.*, no. 24 (Oct. 1920), pp. 394–395.

21. *Historique*, pp. 58–59.

22. *Bull. Ens.*, no. 24 (Oct. 1920), pp. 394–407.

23. *Ibid.*, no. 8 (July–Sept. 1917), pp. 35–37; no. 24 (Oct. 1920), p. 394; *Bull. Off.*, no. 345 (June 2, 1919), pp. 532–542.

24. *Bull. Ens.*, no. 8 (July–Sept. 1917), p. 36.

25. *Ibid.*, p. 37 and no. 33 (July 1921), p. 312.

26. *Bull. Off.*, no. 345 (June 2, 1919), pp. 532–542.

27. *Historique*, p. 245. Official statistics fail to differentiate between the two.

28. *Bull. Ens.*, no. 8 (July–Sept. 1917), p. 37.

29. Paye, vol. II, p. 234.

30. *Historique*, p. 226.

31. *Bull. Ens.*, no. 24 (Oct. 1920), pp. 394, 407.

32. *Historique*, p. 60; Capt. F. H. Mellor, *Morocco Awakes* (London, 1939), p. 210.

33. *Bull. Ens.*, no. 24 (Oct. 1920), p. 394.

34. *Historique*, pp. 62–63.

35. *Ibid.*, p. 70.

36. Mellor, p. 210.

37. *Bull. Ens.*, no. 24 (Oct. 1920), pp. 394, 413–416.

38. *Historique*, p. 60–62.

39. *Bull. Ens.*, no. 24 (Oct. 1920), pp. 417–418.

40. Mellor, p. 210.

41. *Bull. Ens.*, no. 8 (July–Sept. 1917), p. 56.

42. O. Abdeljalil, "L'Enseignement secondaire musulman," *La Volonté du Peuple*, Jan. 12, 1934, p. 4.

43. M. Lyazidi, "À propos d'un discours du Résident," *Maghreb* (Feb. 1933), p. 24.

44. Abdeljalil, *La Volonté du Peuple*, Jan. 12, 1934, p. 1.

45. *Ibid.*

46. Al-Ouezzani, *Maghreb* (Aug. 1933), p. 22.

47. By the *dahir* of April 1, 1935, *Bull. Off.*, no. 1181 (June 14, 1935), p. 642–643.

48. *Historique*, p. 60.

49. *Bull. Off.*, no. 467 (Oct. 4, 1921), p. 1545.

50. *Bull. Off.*, no. 916 (May 16, 1930), p. 601.

51. *Bull. Off.*, no. 1322 (Feb. 25, 1938), p. 266.

52. Lyazidi, *Maghreb* (Feb. 1933), p. 22.

53. Hadj Mohammed al-Mokri, made grand vizier by Lyautey in 1912, still occupied the post when Morocco became independent in 1956, and died near Rabat in September 1957 at the reputed age of 105.

54. Gaudefroy-Demombynes, p. 131.

55. Bastide, pp. 12–13.

56. Abdeljalil, *La Volonté du Peuple*, Jan. 12, 1934, p. 1.

57. It was affiliated with the University of Bordeaux which furnished instruction and supervised examinations.

58. M.H. al-Ouezzani, "Les Iniquités de la politique scolaire," *L'Action du Peuple*, Jan. 9, 1933, pp. 1–2.

59. M.L.5:3.

60. Abdeljalil, *La Volonté du Peuple*, Jan. 12, 1934, p. 1.

61. France. Direction de la Documentation, "L'Enseignement au Maroc," *Notes et Études Documentaires* (Paris), no. 1986 (Feb. 1955), p. 15; *Historique*, p. 250; Ayache, p. 317.

62. Jalabert, *Études*, Sept. 20, 1934, p. 764.

CHAPTER VII. THE IMPACT OF THE ARAB AWAKENING

1. Summaries of Djamal al-Din's career and his philosophical influence in the Arab world may be found in Charles C. Adams, *Islam and Modernism in Egypt* (London, 1933); Hazam Z. Nuseibeh, *The Ideas of Arab Nationalism* (Ithaca, 1956); and Albert H. Hourani, *Arabic Thought in the Liberal Age, 1798–1939* (London, 1962).

2. For further details of Abduh's career, his thought and his collaboration with Djamal al-Din, see Adams, especially pp. 68–82 for his educational

and judicial reforms, and the opening chapter of Jean Jomier, *Le Commentaire coranique du Manâr* (Paris, 1954).

3. Rida's *curriculum vitae* will be found in the above-mentioned works by Adams, Nuseibeh and Hourani, as well as in Nadav Safran, *Egypt in Search of Political Community* (Cambridge [Mass.], 1961). For his conception of the revived Caliphate, see Henri Laoust, *Le Caliphat dans la doctrine de Rachid Rida* (Beirut, 1938), a translation of Rida's *al-Khilafa, aw al-Imama al-Uzma* (The Caliphate, or the Great Imam).

4. For additional data on Abduh's educational and judicial reforms, see Adams, pp. 68–82.

5. Henri Laoust, "Le Réformisme orthodoxe des 'Salafiya'," *Revue des Études Islamiques*, VI (1932), pp. 175–224; and reprinted in *L'Action du Peuple*, serially, beginning in November 1933.

6. Jamil Abun-Nasr, "The Salafiyya Movement in Morocco," *St. Antony's Papers, No. 16, Middle Eastern Affairs, Number Three* (London, 1963), pp. 96–97.

7. P. J. André, *Contribution à l'étude des confréries réligieuses musulmanes* (Algiers, 1956), pp. 140, 161.

8. *Ibid.*, p. 138.

9. *Ibid.*, pp. 162, 172–175. The chief exception is the Tijaniyya of Tetuan, whose Arabist character and hostility to French rule often led it into active collaboration with the nationalists.

10. *Ibid.*, p. 177.

11. See Chapter IV for the Berber controversy.

12. Although the Association of Algerian Muslim Men (*al-Jamiyyat al-Ulama al-Muslimin al-Jaziriyyin*) was founded in 1931, presumably the Salafiyyist influence had been felt long before. See Abun-Nasr, p. 103, and Julien, *Afrique du Nord*, p. 16.

13. A.alF.3:1; O.A.3:5; A.M.1:5; I.alK.1:1–2.

14. A.alF:3:1; M.L.4:1; O.A.1:1; A.M.1:5; I.alK.2:1; A.B.1:1–2.

15. Omar Abdeljalil and Abdelkebir al-Fassi. O.A.1:1–2; M.L.1:4; I.alK.3:3.

16. *Al-Urwa al-Wuthqa* (The Indissoluble Bond), published in Paris during 1884, eighteen numbers. Reprinted by the Tawfiq Press, Beirut, 2 vols., 1910.

17. M.b.A.alA.1:1.

18. *A.F.* (April 1937), p. 215.

19. M.H.O.2:1; I.alK.1:4; O.A.3:5; M.L.1:1; A.alF.4:1; A.M.1:5; A.B.1:1.

20. A.alF3:3; M.L.2:7; M.H.O.2:1; I.alK.1:4; M.N.1:8.

21. A.alF.3:3; M.H.O.2:1; M.N.1:8; A.B.1:1.

22. Louis Jalabert, "Dans le Maghreb qui bouge," *Études*, May 5, 1938, p. 352.

23. Julien, *Afrique du Nord*, pp. 144–145.

24. A.alF.3:2–3; M.L.1:1, 2:4; I.alK.1:4; A.B.1:1; M.N.1:8.

25. *Al-Furkan bain Awliya al-Rahman wa-Awliya al-Shaitan.* (*Encycl. of Islam*, vol. II, Leiden, 1927, p. 423.)

26. M.b.A.alA.1:1.

27. A.alF.3:5; M.H.O.2:1; O.A.3:5.

28. Especially *The Refuge* (*Kittab al-Itisam bi al-Kittab wa al-Sunna*), 2 vols. (Cairo, 1913–14).

29. *Revelation of the Truth* (*Izhar el-Haqiqa*) (Tunis, 1925).

30. *A.F.* (July 1928), p. 492.

31. A.alF.3:4; M.L.2:3; I.alK.3:3.

32. Farid Oujdi (ed.), *Daira al-Maarif*, 10 vols. (Cairo, 1910–18). Oujdi and Allal al-Fassi were apparently in correspondence before 1930. A.alF.3:4; M.L.2:3; I.alK.3:3.

33. See note 3, above.

34. *Tarikh al-Ustadh al-Imam al-Shaykh Muhammad Abduh*, 3 vols. (Cairo, 1908–31).

35. Julien, *Afrique du Nord*, p. 20.

36. The author admits to fragmentary information on this point, but he is reasonably sure that the generalization is valid. The six who definitely studied in the Middle East were Ahmed Balafrej, M'Hammed Bennouna, Hassan Bouayad, Said Hajji, Mekki Naciri and Abdelkhalek Torrès. (See Appendix D for details.)

37. The total exceeds forty-one because some received both types of education.

38. Adams, p. 212, quoting Hifni Bey Nacif (1856–1919), Egyptian teacher and public servant, and student of both Djamal al-Din and Abduh.

39. For most of the descriptive summaries of Middle Eastern secular reformism, I am indebted to the works of Adams, Hourani, Nuseibeh and Safran already cited, as well as H.A.R. Gibb, "Studies in Contemporary Arabic Literature," *Bulletin of the School of Oriental Studies*, vols. IV, V and VII (1926–35).

40. *Tabai al-Istibdad* (Cairo, n.d.).

41. *Umm al-Qura* (Cairo, n.d.).

42. M.H.O.2:5; A.alF.3:1; M.L.1:2; I.alK.2:1; M.N.1:7.

43. *Hadir al-Alam al-Islami*, ed. by Adjadj Nuwaihad (Cairo, 1933).

44. For an account of Arslan's life and activities, see E. Lévi-Provençal, "L'Émir Shakib Arslan, 1869–1946," *Cahiers de l'Orient Contemporain*, nos. 9–10 (1947), pp. 5–19.

45. I.alK.3:1; M.H.O.2:4; M.L.2:7; M.C.1:3. The decree of proscription appears in *Bull. Off.* (Aug. 6, 1930), p. 977.

46. Charles-André Julien, "France and Islam," *Foreign Affairs* (July 1940), p. 684; Rézette, pp. 6, 14–19, 68–79.

47. M.L.1:2; A.B.1:3.

48. Julien, *Afrique du Nord*, p. 22.

49. Nuseibeh, p. 94.

50. O.A.2:2; M.alF.1:1; M.B.2:4.

51. M.H.O.2:4. By 1937 a personality conflict between al-Ouezzani and Allal al-Fassi had caused a schism in the nationalist leadership.

52. *L'Action du Peuple*, July 1, 1937.

53. A.alF.3:3; M.L.1:2; M.B.2:2; M.D.3:1.

54. A.M.4.1; M.L.2:7; O.A.2:2;3:3; M.C.1:3; A.alF.4:1; M.alF.1:1; I.alK.2:1; M.D.3:1.

55. Published in Paris, 1906.

56. *Lettres égyptiennes-françaises, adressées à Mme. Juliette Adam, 1895–1908* (Cairo, 1909), alternate pages in French and Arabic.

57. *Mustafa Kamil Pasha: His Biography and Actions, including Political Speeches, Articles and Letters*, 6 vols. (Cairo, 1908).

58. Shawqi (1868–1932) was a conservative nationalist who rebelled against

all Western influences on Arab literature and whose poetic works are collected under the title *Diwan* (vol. 1, Cairo, n.d.). Ibrahim (1871–1932) was endowed with an active social conscience which had been profoundly stirred by the translations of Ahmed Fathi Zaghlul. See his work on social reform entitled *Layali Satih* (Cairo, 1906–07); Gibb, *B.S.O.S.*, V, p. 461, and VII, p. 6; Jamal M. Ahmed, *The Intellectual Origins of Egyptian Nationalism* (London, 1960), p. 46.

59. M.L.1:2, 2:4; O.A.1:2; A.alF.3:3.

60. I.alK.1:4; M.N.1:7; A.alF.3:1–2; A.M.1:5. Of course the Organic Law of 1883 had provided the first concrete model for general, provincial and local representative councils.

61. For a brief summary of Zaghlul's career, see Adams, pp. 226–229.

62. *Al-Siyasa al-Usbuiya*. Gibb, *B.S.O.S.*, V, p. 447.

63. M.H.O.2:3; I.alK.1:4; M.C.1:3; A.alF.3:3; O.A.3:5–6; M.N.1:8.

64. Mehdi A. Bennouna, *Our Morocco: The Story of a Just Cause* (Tangier, 1951), p 34; M.L.1:2–3, 5:2.

65. See note 36, above.

66. *Tahrir al-Marah* (Cairo, 1899) and *al-Marah al-Jadidah* (Cairo, 1901).

67. Lepp, pp. 178–79; M.L.1:1; O.A.3:5; I.alK.

68. A.alF.3:2–3; M.H.O.2:2–3; O.A.3:7; M.L.1:2; M.N.1:5.

69. M.H.O.3:1; M.L.1:2–3; A.B.1:3.

70. For the programs of the first three congresses, see *L'Action du Peuple*, Sept. 22, 1933, p. 1; Rézette, p. 258; A.alF.3:2; M.H.O.3:1; I.alK.3:4; M.C.1:3; O.A.

71. A.alF.3:3; M.H.O.2:3; M.L.2:5; I.alK.1:4; M.N.1:8.

72. *A.F.* (Oct. 1928), p. 635; also M.H.O. and M.L.

73. *Kittab al-Jazaiar* (Algiers, 1926); A.alF.; M.L.; A.B.1:1; O.A.3:6; I.alK.1:5.

74. A.B.1:1; M.B.2:1; M.alK.1:1; M.D.1:1.

75. A.alF.3:1; M.H.O.2:2; I.alK.1:5; M.N.1:5; O.A.1:2; A.B.1:1.

CHAPTER VIII. THE IMPACT OF THE EUROPEAN REVOLUTION

1. For a list of the Moroccan nationalist leaders and their education, see Appendix D.

2. I.alK.3:3; A.alH.1:1; *S.I.A.1937*, p. 511.

3. Ministère de l'Éducation Nationale, Bureau Universitaire de Statistique, "Étudiants Marocains en France," Jan. 13, 1959 (MS list provided the author by the Bureau), lists the numbers of Moroccans enrolled in French universities each year, 1919–39 and 1949–57. There is no indication of the number of individuals involved, however, because each student is counted once for each year spent in France. Accordingly, I have estimated as follows:

Nine of the prewar nationalist leaders were educated in France during 1923–32. They attended a total of 26 school years, or an average of three years per student.

According to the figures of the Bureau all Moroccans in French universities in 1923–32 attended a total of 91 school years. Assuming an average attendance of three years, there must have been about thirty Moroccans in French universities in 1923–32. This more or less agrees with other observations of the author.

4. There were thirteen Moroccans in French universities in 1933, according to Le Tourneau, p. 194.

5. A.alF.5:2.

6. M.L.4:1–2.

7. A.alF.4:1 and elsewhere.

8. M.alF.1:1; A.alH.1:1; M.H.O.3:4; O.A.4:1–2; I.alK.3:2. Also see Lepp, p. 159; E. Girardière, "L'École coranique et la politique nationaliste," *La France Méditérranéenne et Africaine* (1938), no. 1.

9. M.b.A.1:4; Rézette, p. 65.

10. L. Brunot in *Bull. Ens.* (Jan. 1928), no. 85, pp. 11–13.

11. Lepp, p. 157.

12. Rézette, pp. 29–37; Jalabert, *Études*, May 5, 1938, pp. 357–358; M.L.3:3; M.C.1:4.

13. A.alF.4:1, 5:2; M.L.4:3; O.A.4:2; I.alK.3:2; M.C.1:5; M.alK.1:2.

14. Jalabert, *Études*, May 5, 1938, pp. 357–358.

15. M.L.1:1; O.A.1:1; M.B.2:4; M.H.O.

16. I.alK.3:4; M.b.A.2:1; M.L.1:2; also A.alF., M.H.O., O.A.

17. O. Abdeljalil, "Le troisième Congrès des étudiants musulmans nord-africains," *L'Action du Peuple*, Sept. 29, 1933, p. 2; O.A.3:6; M.L.1:2; M.H.O.3:4; M.N.1:6.

18. M.L.3:3; O.A.3:7; M.H.O.2:5; M.b.A.1:3; also A.alF., I.alK.

19. A.alF.3:2; M.alF.1:1.

20. Quoted in *Annuaire Général du Maroc* (Tangier, 1957), p. 14.

21. Rézette, pp. 40–44; M.H.O.2:5; 3:2; O.A.3:7; A.alF.4:1; M.N.1:3.

22. *A.F.* (Feb. 1935), pp. 69–70.

23. M.b.B.1:2; Jalabert, *Études*, May 5, 1938, p. 355; Julien, *Foreign Affairs* (July 1940), p. 692.

24. M.H.O.3:2; O.A.4:2; M.L.3:2; M.C.1:2, 1:4; M.N.1:6; A.alA.1:3; Rézette, pp. 37–39.

25. *S.I.A.1937*, p. 501; Paye, vol. II, p. 235.

26. Rézette, p. 69; Jalabert, *Études*, May 5, 1938, p. 355; M.H.O.3:2; A.alF.4:1; M.L.4:3; O.A.4:2; M.alF.1:1; M.N.1:6.

27. *A.F.* (Dec. 1932), p. 710. The editorial board of *Maghreb* was as follows (no Moroccans were listed on it for tactical reasons):

François-Albert, president (retired Feb. 1933), president of the Chamber of Deputies' Commission on Foreign Affairs.

Robert-Jean Longuet, editor-in-chief, militant Socialist.

Jean Longuet, S.F.I.O. deputy from Seine, vice-president of the Chamber of Deputies' Commission on Foreign Affairs.

Pierre Renaudel, deputy from Var, president of the Socialist Party of France.

Gaston Bergery, former Radical deputy, member of Central Committee of the League of the Rights of Man.

Anatole Sixte-Quenin (Nov. 1932 ff.), deputy from Bouches-du-Rhône.

Georges Monnet (Mar. 1933 ff.), deputy from Aisne.

Étienne Antonelli, *professeur agrégé* of law.

There were also four Spanish members:

Fernando de Los Rios (retired Mar. 1933), Spanish minister of instruction.

Gim Argila, Communist writer.

Edouard Ortega y Gasset (Jan. 1933 ff.), deputy.

28. A.M.1:3.

29. O.A.2:2, 3:6; A.M.1:4; A.alA.1:3; M.H.O.3:2; A.B.1:3; I.alK.3:2; also A.alF.

30. Rézette, pp. 69–71; *L'Action du Peuple*, Sept. 8, 1933 ff.

31. Julien, *Afrique du Nord*, p. 24; O.A.3:6, 4:2; A.M.1:4; M.L.2:5; M.C.1:3; M.H.O.3:2; M.alF.1:1; also I.alK., A.alF.

32. Julien, *Afrique du Nord*, p. 149; M.L.1:2; O.A.3:7; M.C.1:3; I.alK., A.alF.

33. E.g., *The Spirit of Socialism* (Cairo, n.d.), *The Spirit of Society* (Cairo, 1909), *The Progress of the Emancipation of Nations* (Cairo, 1913).

34. I.alK.3:3.

35. *A.F.* (Feb. 1935), p. 70, (June 1936), pp. 361–362; Rézette, pp. 70–71; Julien, *Afrique du Nord*, pp. 161–162.

36. *Maghreb* (Dec. 1932), no. 6, pp. 20–21.

37. M.H. al-Ouezzani, "Regrets inopportunes," *L'Action du Peuple*, Sept. 8, 1933, pp. 1–2; A. Balafrej in *Maghreb* (Aug. 1933), p. 3; M.N.1:6.

38. M.H. al-Ouezzani, "Le Problème marocain et le socialisme espagnol," *Maghreb* (Nov. 1932), pp. 9–14, and "Le Problème marocain et le parti radical-socialiste espagnol," *Maghreb* (Dec. 1932), pp. 9–15.

39. M.B. 2:1.

40. For examples which span the period, the reader might refer to: Louis Barthou, *La Bataille du Maroc* (Paris, 1919) and Borny, "Au Maroc-organizations nationalistes-émissions de propagande," *Dépêche de Toulouse*, Apr. 26, 1937, both of which beleaguer the Germans; as well as Georges Hertz-Wolfram, "Naissance du nationalisme marocain," *L'Age Nouveau* (June 1938), pp. 340–345, and J. Ladreit de Lacharrière, "Autour du 'nationalisme' marocain," *A.F.* (Jan. 1938), pp. 11–19.

41. See *A.F.* (Sept. 1932), pp. 516 ff. and *passim*.

42. *A.F.* (Oct. 1934), pp. 574 ff. and *passim*; Jalabert, *Études*, May 5, 1938, p. 355.

43. See for example: Maréchal Lyautey, "Les Origines du conflit," *Les Cahiers des Droits de l'Homme*, June 10, 1926, pp. 267–273; Résidence-Générale . . . , "Situation politique et économique: mois de mai, 1939" (Rabat). Both thoroughly cover Axis intrigue but neither makes any mention whatsoever of Communism.

44. M.L.3:1, 4:3; M.H.O.3:2; A.alF.4:1; I.alK.; O.A.

45. *S.I.A.1937*, p. 503; Lepp, pp. 171–173; M.L.3:1.

46. *La Nation Arabe* (Mar.–Apr. 1932), p. 58.

47. Lyautey, *Cahiers des Droits de l'Homme*, June 10, 1926, p. 269.

48. *S.I.A.1937*, p. 502; Julien, *Afrique du Nord*, p. 158.

49. Formal title: *Jamiya al-Taqafa al-Islamiya (Trait d'Union des Intellectuels de l'Islam)*.

50. *A.F.* (Dec. 1934), pp. 699 ff.

51. Rézette, pp. 126–127.

52. Allal al-Fassi, Mohammed Hassan al-Ouezzani, Mohammed Lyazidi and Ahmed Mekouar were either in jail or in exile, although Balafrej and Abdeljalil were at liberty in Tangier at this time.

53. Résidence-Générale, "Situation politique," pp. 2, 5.

54. Rézette, p. 132.

55. A. Balafrej, "First Anniversary of Hitler's Rule" (in Arabic), *el-Hayat*, no. 5 (Apr. 1934), p. 6.

56. Résidence-Générale, "Situation politique," pp. 1–2.

57. M.L.3:2.

58. *A.F.* (Nov. 1933), pp. 665–667.

59. *S.I.A.1937*, pp. 502–540.

60. A.alF.3:2; I.alK.3:4; M.L.3:2.

61. For examples, see *A.F.*, especially from 1927 to 1930.

62. Julien, *Afrique du Nord*, pp. 158–159.

63. *S.I.A.1937*, p. 503; Julien, *Foreign Affairs* (July 1940), p. 692.

64. A. Balafrej, "Le Danger italien," *Maghreb* (Mar. 1933), p. 9.

65. Julien, *Afrique du Nord*, p. 157.

CHAPTER IX. THE DECADE OF GESTATION: 1921–1930

1. Record book of the Sidi Bennani school, p. 4, provides the earliest documented date for the existence of a free school in Fez, *Chaoual* 1339 (June/July 1921), at which time parents owed varying amounts of tuition. Accordingly, it must have been founded early in 1921 or late in 1920. Girardière, p. 100, gives the opening date of Mohammed Lahlou's school as *Chabaan* 1339 (April/May 1921), but the source of this information is not cited, and those interviewed by the author seemed to think it was founded later in the year.

2. Girardière, p. 100. The article lists in addition, the Diouane, Baral, Derb ed-Drouj and as-Seffah schools. Most of the data on the foundation of the earliest schools which appear in this study were obtained in interviews with the nationalist leaders closely identified with them, especially Ahmed Mekouar, Ibrahim al-Kittani, Allal al-Fassi and Mohammed Daoud.

3. M.N.1:1; M.H.O.1:1; M.L.2:3; A.alF.6:1.

4. I.alK.1:2. There may have been another, named al-Akkour, founded by a Casablanca merchant of that name (A.alF.6:1).

5. Ledger of the Ahliyah school, pp. 6–7, 27; Rézette, p. 83; Girardière, p. 100; interview with Allal al-Fassi and Abdesselam al-Fassi, *Chef du Bureau des Recherches et d'Orientation*, Palais Royal, Aug. 14, 1963.

6. *Bull. Off.*, no. 368 (Nov. 10, 1919), pp. 1282–1284; *Bull. Ens.*, no. 20 (Apr. 1920), pp. 82–83.

7. Le Tourneau, p. 193.

8. Rivière, *Traités . . . Supplément, 1936*, pp. 41–42.

9. In addition to those already listed, were the Derb al-Taouil, Sidi Bou ar-Ramadan, Ben Ghazi, and Kakkliyyin schools. (Interviews with Allal al-Fassi and Abdesselam al-Fassi, August 14, 1963 and with Mohammed al-Fassi, Aug. 9, 1963.)

10. Girardière, p. 107.

11. M.L.2:3; A.M.1:1; also see John P. Halstead, "The Changing Character of Moroccan Reformism, 1921–1934," *Journal of African History*, vol. V, no. 3 (1964), p. 438. Arabic journals appeared ephemerally in Morocco throughout the nineteenth and early twentieth centuries, but they were without exception published by foreign consulates or by Lebanese expatriates. A small beginning to a native Arabic press was made when Ahmed Mekouar established the Imprimerie Moulay Hafid and started

publishing books in 1923, but for many years thereafter most of the free-school texts were supplied from abroad. (Letters from Ahmed Mekouar, May 10, 1966 and Mohammed Lyazidi, May 9, 1967.)

12. For a good example of this myth, see M.H. al-Ouezzani, *Maghreb* (July 1933), pp. 16–23.

13. M.A.alA.1:1; A.alF.1:1.

14. I.alK.1:2.

15. M.D.2:1.

16. The nationalists, who were interviewed, gave dates for its foundation from 1924 to 1926, but the most reliable on this point seemed to be Ibrahim al-Kittani, whose unpublished MS (in Arabic), *Recollections of the First Phase of the Rise of the Moroccan Nationalist Struggle,* gives the date as "either Rebia II or Joumada I, 1344," A.H., which corresponds roughly to November 1925, A.D.

17. I.alK.1:2, 2:1; A.alF.2:1; M.H.O.1:2; A.B.1:1.

18. M.H.O.1:3; I.alK.1:2, 2:1.

19. Hadj M'Hammed Bennouna, "The History of What is Ignored by History: The Silver Anniversary of the First Nationalist Movement" (in Arabic), *el-Alam,* Aug. 3, 1951, p. 1; Aug. 4, 1951, p. 1.

20. O.A.2:5; M.L.2:3; A.alF.2:2; M.H.O.1:2.

21. M.L.3:1. M'Hammed Bennouna, *el-Alam,* Aug. 7, 1951, p. 1, has it that the group was known publicly as the Supporters of Truth, a study and reform society, but that it also had a clandestine counterpart, *ar-Rabita al-Maghrebia* (The Moroccan League), whose aim was independence. This contention, which reappears in Landau, Ashford and elsewhere, may well be apocryphal, for none of the leading nationalists interviewed by the author could recollect such names.

22. M.H.O.1:2–3.

23. Arabic title: *Darbu Nitaq el-Hissar ala Ashab Nihayat al-Inkisar* (The Encirclement of the Authors of the Book, "The Defeat") (Rabat, 1926).

24. Listed as sponsors:

[Members of the Rabat society]	[Members of the Fez Society]
Mohammed Naciri, author	Allal al-Fassi
Abdelkebir al-Fassi, Introduction	
Mohammed Lyazidi	Ibrahim al-Kittani
Omar Abdeljalil	Mokhtar Soussi
Mohammed ben Abbès Kabbaj	Mohammed al-Fassi
M.H. al-Ouezzani	
Ahmed al-Moudden	
Ahmed Balafrej	

[Five others who did not become active nationalists]

25. M.L.2:1, 2:5; O.A.2:5.

26. M.H.O.1:2; A.alF.2:2; M.alK.1:1; M.B.2:2.

27. M.D.1:1.

28. M'Hammed Bennouna, *el-Alam,* Aug. 4, 1951, p. 1; Mehdi Bennouna, p. 34; M.alK.1:2; A.B.1:1; M.H.O.1:2; O.A.2:5.

29. A.alF.2:2; M.H.O.1:3; M'H. Bennouna, *el-Alam,* Aug. 9, 1951, p. 1.

30. M.H.O.1:3; I.alK.1:2.
31. M.D.1:1, 2:2.
32. Letter from Mekki Naciri to Mohammed Daoud, 5 *Chabaan* 1345 (Feb. 8, 1927), defending the Salafiyyist position of the Rabati nationalists. A.M.4:1.
33. Letter from M. H. al-Ouezzani to Mohammed Dauod, n.d. [early 1927] explaining the philosophy behind the activities of the Rabat society.
34. See Ibrahim al-Kittani, "Min Dhikriyati an al-Yaqtha al-Maghribiya" (My Recollections of the Moroccan Revival), *el-Alam*, Nov. 3, 1956, pp. 1–2, wherein the author lists nineteen works characteristic of their interests at that time. Approximately equal representation is given to Salafiyyist works by Djamal, Abduh, *et al.*, to "secular" works by Kawakibi, Zaydan, *et al.*, and to classical Arabic literature. Also see Mehdi Bennouna, p. 40.
35. A.alF.3:4; I.alK.1:2–3; M.H.O.1:3; O.A.2:5–6; M.L.2:3, 5:1.
36. A.alF.2:1; I.alK.3:1. See Chapter X for the reaction to the *dahir*.
37. M.L.2:4; Paye, vol. II, pp. 239–240.
38. A.alF.3:3; M.L.1:2, 2:4, 3:3.
39. M.H.O.1:4.
40. *Ibid.*; A.M.2:1; M.alF.2:1; Rézette, p. 258.
41. Rézette, pp. 76–77; M.H.O.3:1.
42. Rézette, p. 258; M.H.O.1:4; O.A.3:7; M.b.A.1:3;M.alF.2:1.
43. Julien, *Afrique du Nord*, p. 23.
44. I.alK.3:4.
45. Especially the letters addressed to Mohammed Daoud from Rabat by Mekki Naciri (Feb. 8, 1927), Mohammed Lyazidi (Apr. 17, 1927), Abdelkebir al-Fassi (Feb. 8, 1927) and Ahmed al-Moudden (Feb. 11, 1927); also M.alF.2:1; A.alF.6:1.
46. *Izhar el-Haqiqa* (Revelation of the Truth) (Tunis, 1925).
47. I.alK.3:3; M.L.2:1–2, 5:1; M.N.1:5; M.H.O.3:2.
48. Rabat, the capital, ranks as the "first" city for its political importance, although it is exceeded in population by Fez, Casablanca and Marrakesh.
49. M.A.alA.1:1.
50. A.B.1:1; M.N.1:5.
51. A.alF.1:2, 5:1; I.alK.1:3; *S.I.A.1937*, p. 489.
52. Letters to Mohammed Daoud from Mekki Naciri (Feb. 8, 1927) and Omar Abdeljalil (Feb. 9, 1927).
53. I.alK.1:3; M.H.O.1:3; O.A.1:2; M.L.2:5, 6:1.
54. A.M.1:1; M.H.O.1:3; O.A.2:5; M.L.3:1.
55. M.D.2:2.
56. M.alK.1:1. Also see the correspondence of early 1927 mentioned above.
57. Mehdi Bennouna, p. 41.

CHAPTER X. THE CAMPAIGN AGAINST THE BERBER POLICY: 1930–1931

1. See Barbari, pp. 8–9.
2. *S.I.A.1937*, p. 509.
3. Girardière, p. 103. The catalytic nature of the *dahir* has been clearly recognized by most commentators on Moroccan nationalism. The *dahir* has also been regarded, customarily, though erroneously, as the event which launched that movement.

316 REBIRTH OF A NATION

4. Barbari, p. 39.

5. *Ibid.*, pp. 39, 43; Le Tourneau, p. 184; M.L.2:6.

6. The information in this paragraph was taken from Ahmed Mekouar's ledger ("Agenda, 1930"), for the following dates: July 4, 18, 25, 29–30, August 2 ff., 11, 13.

7. M.L.2:6; Julien, *Afrique du Nord*, p. 148.

8. The delegation: Mohammed ben Abdesselam Lahlou, Abdel Rahman ben al-Korchi, Mohammed Acherki, Mohammed ben M'Fedel Benjelloun, Mohammed Diouri, Driss al-Ouezzani, Abdelwahad al-Fassi, and Hadi ben al-Mouaz (Mekouar's ledger, Aug. 22–23, 1930; Barbari, p. 47).

9. The memorandum (in Arabic) is reproduced in *Maghreb* (May–June 1933), opp. p. 36. A French translation will be found in the microfilmed papers of Mohammed Daoud located at the State University of New York at Buffalo.

10. Mekouar's ledger, August 23, 1930.

11. The other four members, less prominent in nationalist circles, were Hamza Tahiri, Ahmed Bouayad, Larbi Bouayad, and Driss Berrada.

12. Mekouar's ledger for 1930: Aug. 26–31, Sept. 2 and Oct. 27; A.M.3:4.

13. *A.F.* (Sept. 1930), p. 517.

14. Lévi-Provençal, *Cahiers de l'Orient Contemporain* (1947), nos. 9–10, pp. 11–12.

15. Barbari, pp. 49–58.

16. *Ibid.*, pp. 67–72.

17. M.L.5:1; M.N.1:3; M.H.O.3:3.

18. Text of the protest in *La Nation Arabe*, nos. 5–6 (May–June 1932), pp. 33–34.

19. M.H.O.3:3; M.N.1:3; al-Fassi, p. 124; *L'Action du Peuple*, Sept. 15, 1933, p. 2. *France and Its Berber Policy in Morocco* was summarized in 32 pages in May 1932 and published (in Arabic) by the Comité d'Action Marocaine under the title *Colonial Policy in the Maghreb*. Copies of both are on microfilm at the State University of New York at Buffalo.

20. Naciri, p. 1.

21. Barbari, p. 55.

22. Julien, *Afrique du Nord*, p. 149.

23. *Maghreb* (May–June 1933), p. 38.

24. Toynbee noted in 1937 that the replacement of the Berber dialects by French was far more noticeable in Tunisia and Algeria than in Morocco (*S.I.A.1937*, p. 498).

25. Julien, *Afrique du Nord*, pp. 142, 148.

26. *Ibid.*, pp. 149–150, citing especially Georges Hardy, a long-time observer of Moroccan affairs, who at that time was director of the École Coloniale.

27. Barbari, pp. 65–66.

28. M.H.O.2:2.

29. M.L.4:1.

CHAPTER XI. BUILDING AN ORGANIZATION: 1931–1934

1. Ahmed Mekouar's ledger for 1930 (A.M.2:1); A.alF.2:2; O.A.2:7.

2. Mekouar's ledger.

3. A.alF.2:3; M.L.2:8; M.H.O.1:8; O.A.2:7.

4. A.alF.2:3; M.L.2:9.

5. Mohammed Daoud has in his possession a draft of articles for the foundation of a secret society drawn up in Fez in 1930 by Mohammed Hassan al-Ouezzani, with the help of Allal al-Fassi and Daoud. While M. Daoud was unwilling to make its contents public, enough is known about its provisions to identify it with the Zawiya, founded about that time.

6. O.A.2:7, 3:1; M.L.2:7–8; M.H.O.1:5–6; A.M.1:3; A.alF.2:2. The list given here may not be exhaustive, but it certainly contains all the important members.

7. M.L.5:2; A.M.1:2.

8. A.M.2:1.

9. O.A.3:1–2; M.L.2:7; A.M.2:1.

10. M.L.2:7, 2:9, 3:1, 4:3; A.alF.2:3; M.H.O.1:8; O.A.2:7.

11. M.L.2:8–9; A.M.1:3; M.H.O.1:8; O.A.3:1; A.alF.2:3.

12. Rézette, pp. 264, 279.

13. M.L.4:4–5; O.A.1:3, 4:3–4; A.alF.5:2; M.H.O.3:4; I.alK.3:1–2; M.alF. 1:1; M.N.1:7; A.M.4:2

14. M.H.O.1:5; M.L.2:7.

15. M.H.O.1:5.

16. A.M.3:5; M.H.O.1:7; *A.F.* (Dec. 1932), p. 709.

17. M.D.2:4.

18. Rézette, p. 259.

19. *Ibid.*, p. 77.

20. *Ibid.*, p. 80.

21. *S.I.A.1937*, p. 531.

22. Rézette, p. 82.

23. *Ibid.*, pp. 78–79.

24. M. Bennouna, pp. 47–48.

25. *La Voix du Tunisien*, May 22, 1932, as reprinted in *A.F.* (Sept. 1932), p. 518.

26. Rézette, pp. 80–81; Julien, *Afrique du Nord*, p. 157.

27. M.D.2:3.

28. *La Volonté du Peuple*, Dec. 22, 1933, p. 1. The article names only Ahmed Ghilane, vice-president of the delegation, Abdesselam Hajjaj and Ahmed Lahbabi, but Mehdi Bennouna was certain that his father had led it. If he did not lead it, he certainly sent it.

29. From the "Biography of Mohammed Daoud" appearing in volume I of Daoud's multi-volume, unfinished *History of Tetuan* (*Tarikh Tatwan*) (Tetuan, 1959).

30. Nearly complete collections of each are on microfilm at Lockwood Library, State University of New York at Buffalo.

31. M.H.O.1:7–8; M. Bennouna, pp. 52–53.

32. I.alK.2:2; O.A.2:4. Jean Lacouture, *Cinq hommes et la France* (Paris, 1961), which includes a biography of Mohammed V, offers no new information on his role in the movement during the period covered by this book.

CHAPTER XII. FRAMING A PROGRAM: 1932–1934

1. Rézette, p. 69.

2. *A.F.* (Dec. 1932), p. 710. See Chapter VIII, note 27, for other members.

3. *A.F.* (Oct. 1928), p. 655.

4. A.M.1:3; O.A.3:3. For the membership of this committee, see Chapter VIII.
5. M.H.O.1:5; M.L.1:4, 2:7.
6. *A.F.* (Dec. 1932), p. 710.
7. *Ibid.*, p. 708.
8. O.A.3:3.
9. Rézette, p. 75.
10. M.H.O.1:8; A.M.1:4; M.L.2:7.
11. O.A.2:2.
12. M.H.O.1:8; O.A.2:2.
13. Rézette, p. 76.
14. O.A.2:2. See list of nationalists classified by function in Chapter XI.
15. O.A.2:1; A.M.1:5.
16. O.A.1:4–5, 2:1, 3:3–4; A.M.1:4–5; M.L.1:3, 2:9; A.alF.2:4; M.N.1:2.
17. A.alF.2:4.
18. *Plan de Réformes*, p. III.
   Eight Deputies:
   Pierre Renaudel, president of the Parti Socialiste de France (Neo-Socialist Party).
   Jean Longuet, vice-president of the Chamber's Commission on Foreign Affairs and deputy from Seine.
   François de Tessan, vice-president of the Chamber's Commision on Foreign Affairs and deputy from Seine-et-Marne.
   Jean Piot, member of the Chamber's Commission on Foreign Affairs and deputy from Seine.
   Henry Clerc, deputy from Haute-Savoie.
   C. Campinchi, deputy from Corsica and vice-president of the Radical Socialist Party.
   Gabriel Gudenet, president of the Radical Socialist Party.
   Georges Monnet, deputy from Aisne.
   Two Former Deputies:
   Gaston Bergery, Radical and member of the Central Committee of the League of the Rights of Man.
   André Berthon, a Communist lawyer.
   Four Writers:
   Robert-Jean Longuet, Louis Roubaud, Magdelaine Paz, and Andrée Viollis.
   One Professor:
   Felicien Challaye, *agrégé de philosophie.*
19. *Plan*, pp. IV–V.
20. Rézette, pp. 76, 87, 89.
21. O.A.1:4, 2:1, 3:3; M.L.1:3, 2:10; M.C.1:1, 1:4; A.M.1:4; M.H.O.1:9; A.alF.1:2.
22. *Ibid.*
23. Rézette, p. 89; *Plan*, p. 33.
24. *La Volonté du Peuple*, Feb. 9, 1934, pp. 1–2.
25. M.H.O.3:3; M.L.1:3.
26. Benjamin Rivlin, "The Tunisian Nationalist Movement," *Middle East Journal* (Spring 1952), p. 169.
27. M.L.1:3.

28. Text of the Egyptian Constitution appears in *L'Afrique Française*, "Renseignements coloniaux et documents" (May 1923), pp. 168–176.

29. *Maghreb*, no. 3 (Sept. 1932), pp. 5–11; *La Volonté du Peuple*, Dec. 22, 1933, p. 1.

30. Rézette, p. 85; M.L.1:3.

31. *Plan*, pp. VIII–XVI.

32. M.H.O.2:6; O.A.3:5.

33. Julien, *Afrique du Nord*, p. 22.

34. M.H.O.2:6; M.L.4:2.

35. The regional councils were to consist of the old Chambers of Agriculture and of Commerce and Industry, reformed so as to include Moroccans.

36. M.L.4:1, 5:2; M.C.1:4; M.N.1.2.

37. O.A.2:1, 3:4; M.L.1:3; M.C.1:4.

38. Julien, *Afrique du Nord*, p. 154.

39. M.L.5:2; O.A.3:4.

40. O.A.1:5; M.L.1:3.

41. O.A.2:2, 3:4; M.C.1:4.

42. M.L.5:2; M.N.1:1.

43. O.A.3:4; M.L.1:3; M.N.1:2.

44. M.L.1:3; M.N.1:2.

45. O.A.2:2, M.N.1:6; M.C.1:4; A.alA.1:3.

46. *Plan*, p. 34.

47. Julien, *Afrique du Nord*, p. 154.

48. Al-Fassi, p. 139.

49. From the essay on "Self-Reliance."

50. Al-Fassi, p. 140.

51. *Ibid.*, pp. 140–141.

CHAPTER XIII. SPREADING THE WORD: 1935–1937

1. Rézette, p. 270.

2. *Ibid.*, pp. 269–270.

3. See Thomasset, pp. 50–65, for a discussion of the problems caused by the settlers' demands.

4. Douglas E. Ashford, *Political Change in Morocco* (Princeton, 1961), p. 39.

5. *S.I.A.1937*, p. 535.

6. Julien, *Afrique du Nord*, p. 156; Rézette, p. 98.

7. M.H.O.3:5; Rézette, p. 97.

8. Al-Fassi, p. 155, and interview with Omar Abdeljalil.

9. Julien, *Afrique du Nord*, p. 163.

10. *A.F.* (April 1937), p. 220.

11. *Ibid.*

12. M.H.O.3:5.

13. *S.I.A.1937*, p. 501.

14. Julien, *Afrique du Nord*, p. 164.

15. Al-Fassi, p. 155; Julien, *Afrique du Nord*, p. 160; Rézette, p. 97.

16. M.L.2:10; Julien, *Afrique du Nord*, p. 153. The "immediate demands" are summarized in al-Fassi, pp. 156–157.

17. A.M.3:5; these ballots, from Mekouar's private papers, are on microfilm at the State University of New York at Buffalo.

18. Al-Fassi, p. 156; O.Á.2:3.

19. Rézette, p. 98.

20. Ashford, p. 40.

21. M.L.6:1.

22. Rézette, p. 99.

23. Ashford, p. 40.

24. From "Biography of Mohammed Daoud" in Daoud, *History of Tetuan*, vol. I.

25. Al-Fassi, pp. 154–155.

26. Rézette, p. 117.

27. Interview with Mehdi Bennouna.

28. *Ibid.*

29. Rézette, pp. 117, 362–363.

30. Robert A. Friedlander, "Holy Crusade or Unholy Alliance? Franco's 'National Revolution' and the Moors," *The Southwestern Social Science Quarterly* (March 1964), p. 351.

31. A.M.4:2.

32. Friedlander, p. 352.

33. Al-Fassi, pp. 150–152; A.M.4:2.

34. Rézette, pp. 114–115.

35. *A.F.* (Oct. 1937), p. 456.

36. Rézette, p. 117.

37. *A.F.* (Apr. 1937), pp. 214–215. The astonishing willingness of Moroccan tribesmen to enlist in Franco's army (50–60,000 of them ultimately did) was a matter quite distinct from the collaboration between Franco and the nationalists, as Robert Friedlander has so well demonstrated. The tribesmen were paid off in guns, ammunition and silver. The nationalists had to be paid off in higher coin.

38. Rézette, p. 100.

39. *S.I.A.1937*, p. 533.

40. Julien, *Afrique du Nord*, p. 161.

41. Al-Fassi, p. 163.

42. *Ibid.*, pp. 163–164; A.alF.2:4–5.

43. M.L.5:2.

44. Mekouar papers: Minutes of the meeting held on 25 *Kaada* (Feb. 6) on microfilm.

45. M.L.5:2; A.alF.2:4.

46. Julien, *Afrique du Nord*, p. 155.

47. *Ibid.*

48. Le Tourneau, p. 199; M.L.6:2; M.D.1:1.

49. No. 1 (1938), p. 103.

50. *Ibid.*; A.alF.6:1; A.M.4:1.

51. Le Tourneau, p. 203.

52. M.N.1:5.

53. Rézette, pp. 270–271, 279.

54. Le Tourneau, p. 203.

55. Rivière, *Traités . . . Supplément, 1936*, pp. 41–42, for text.

56. Julien, *Afrique du Nord*, p. 155.

57. *El-Atlas*, no. 1 (Feb. 12, 1937), p. 1; *L'Action Populaire*, no. 1 (Feb. 27, 1937), p. 1.

58. Rézette, p. 102.

59. *Ibid.*

60. The reference is to the *dahir* of May 24, 1914 (*Bull. Off.*, no. 1273 [Mar. 19, 1937], p. 386).

61. Rézette, p. 103.

62. *S.I.A.1937*, p. 535.

63. See especially S. Hérauté, "L'Alerte marocaine," *A.F.* (Jan. 1937), pp. 9–16; A. Ménard, "La Crise méditérranéenne vue de Tanger," *A.F.* (Feb. 1937), pp. 64–69; and the two series entitled "L'Afrique et l'Espagne" and "L'Afrique et l'Italie" which appeared during 1937–40.

64. Rézette, p. 104.

65. *Ibid.*, p. 105; al-Fassi, p. 166.

66. Rézette, p. 105.

67. Mehdi Bennouna, who furnished the names and how they voted, believes that this *congrès* was held in Fez in March or April 1937, rather than in Rabat in April, as Rézette has it. It is quite likely that two such meetings were held. (M.B.2:5.)

68. Rézette, p. 103.

69. M.H.O.1:9, 3:5.

70. *L'Action du Peuple*, Apr. 8, 1937, pp. 2 and 5.

72. M.H.O.3:6.

73. Rézette, p. 106.

74. *Ibid.*, p. 107. The most prominent members were Chraibi, Ibrahim al-Ouezzani, Mohammed al-Korri, Ali Laraki, Ibrahim al-Kittani and Rachid Derkaoui, all of whom, interestingly enough, with the sole exception of their leader, had received a thoroughly traditional Muslim education.

75. The first installment appeared in issue no. 4 (Mar. 27, 1937), p. 3. It was probably no more than coincidence that Mekki Naciri, now forming a splinter group from the Torrès party in Tetuan, began two days later to serialize the *Plan de Réformes* in his own party journal, *Unidad Marroqui* (Tetuan).

76. *L'Action Populaire*, no. 4 (Mar. 27, 1937), p. 1.

77. *Ibid.*, no. 5 (Apr. 3, 1937), p. 1.

78. *A.F.* (Apr. 1937), p. 215.

79. Julien, *Afrique du Nord*, p. 167 and al-Fassi, pp. 165–169.

80. *Ibid.*, Rézette, p. 105. Text of the memoire in *L'Action Populaire*, no. 18 (July 24, 1937), pp. 1 and 4.

81. Al-Fassi, pp. 178–179.

82. See Chaignaud's report to the Marseille congress, *La Question marocaine* (Paris, July 1937), on microfilm.

83. Julien, *Afrique du Nord*, p. 164.

84. *Ibid.*, p. 167; Rézette, p. 108.

85. *S.I.A. 1937*, p. 508.

86. Mekouar's ledger for 1937, page for Sept. 2nd, on microfilm; *A.F.* (Oct. 1937), p. 453; Julien, *Afrique du Nord*, p. 168.

87. *L'Action Populaire*, no. 21 (Sept. 4, 1937), p. 2.

88. *A.F.* (Oct. 1937), pp. 453–454; Julien, *Afrique du Nord*, p. 169.

89. *A.F.* (Oct. 1937), p. 455.

90. Rézette, pp 108–109.

91. Al-Fassi, pp. 187–190. The sections represented, according to *L'Afrique Française*, were: Oujda, Berkane, Taza, Fez, Meknes, Ouezzane, Sidi-Kacem, El Gharb, Kénitra, Salé, Rabat, Casablanca, Marrakesh, Mazagan, Safi, Mogador, Moulay Bou Chaib, Settat, Oued Zem and Boujad.

92. *A.F.* (Nov. 1937), pp. 518–519.

93. *Ibid.*, p. 519; Rézette, p. 109; Julien, *Afrique du Nord*, p. 170; Mehouar's ledger for 1937, page for October 25, on microfilm.

94. Rézette, p. 110.

95. *A.F.* (Nov. 1937), p. 520; Julien, *Afrique du Nord*, p. 171.

96. *Ibid.*

97. Julien, *Afrique du Nord*, p. 172. *S.I.A. 1937*, pp. 538–539, lists 300 arrested, 62 sentenced to terms ranging from 3 months to 2 years, 85 sentenced to 30 days' *corvée* on the roads.

98. A.M.3:7.

99. Rézette, p. 111. It was fortunate for Bouayad that these events took place before 1938, for after many years of trying, the Quai d'Orsay had finally persuaded His Majesty's Government to sign a treaty on July 27, 1937, abolishing British capitulations in Morocco, to go into effect on Jan 1, 1938. (*A.F.* [Aug.-Sept. 1937], p. 434). The British Post Offices, which for so long had served the nationalists, were in fact closed down during the month of August 1937. (*A.F.* [Nov. 1937], p. 538.)

100. Rézette, p. 111; *A.F.* (Nov. 1937), p. 522.

101. Rézette, p. 279.

CHAPTER XIV. REFORMISM TO SEPARATISM: 1937–1944

1. Le Tourneau, pp. 201–202.

2. Julien, *Afrique du Nord*, p. 172.

3. Le Tourneau, p. 202.

4. Rézette, pp. 111, 112, 131.

5. *Ibid.*, p. 112.

6. Paye, vol. II, pp. 241–242.

7. Le Tourneau, p. 204.

8. Noguès' speech is quoted verbatim in *La Nation Arabe* (May-Aug. 1938), pp. 1009–1024. Arslan's favorable comments appear on pp. 1024–1025.

9. Résidence-Générale . . . , "Situation politique . . . mai 1939," p. 1.

10. Rézette, p. 113.

11. Al-Fassi, p. 198.

12. *Ibid.*, pp. 213–214.

13. Rézette, p. 136.

14. *Ibid.*, p. 288.

15. A.M.4:2.

16. Rézette, p. 130.

17. *Ibid.*, pp. 130–131.

18. *Ibid.*, pp. 115, 118, 119.

19. *A.F.* (Apr. 1938), p. 182.

20. Rézette, p. 115.

21. M.N.1:4; *L'Afrique Française, Renseignements Coloniaux et Documents*, no. 1 (Jan. 1938), p. 2; Rézette, p. 125.

22. Rézette, p. 121.

23. For text, see *A.F., Renseignements* . . . *etc.*, pp. 1-7.

24. Rézette, pp. 122-123.

25. *Ibid.*, p. 123-124.

26. *Ibid.*, pp. 132-134.

27. *Ibid.*, p. 135.

28. *Ibid.*, p. 136.

29. On the Casablanca meeting, Elliott Roosevelt, *As He Saw It* (New York, 1946), pp. 109-112.

30. *Ibid.*, p. 137.

31. *Ibid.*, pp. 138-139.

32. Le Tourneau, p. 207.

33. M. H. al-Ouezzani returned from exile in 1946 and revived his Mouvement Populaire as the politically unimportant Parti Democratique d'Indépendance.

34. Le Tourneau, p. 208; Rézette, p. 139.

35. Le Tourneau, pp. 209-210; Rézette, p. 301. Text and signers in Parti de l'Istiqlal, Bureau de Documentation . . ., *Documents 1944-1946* (Paris, Sept. 1946), pp. 2-4. Text is also in Le Tourneau, pp. 208-209.

36. *Documents 1944-1946*, p. 7.

37. The career of Istiqlal from 1944 to 1956 is the chief burden of Rézette, *Partis Politiques* and Ashford, *Political Change*, although both works are studies in political science rather in history.

CHAPTER XV. SUMMARY AND CONCLUSIONS

1. For a more complete summary of this transformation, see the author's article in the *Journal of African History*.

2. Rézette, pp. 245-246.

3. *Ibid.*, pp. 250-251.

4. Mohammed al-Fassi, Rector of the University of Morocco, in a conversation with the author on August 9, 1963, expressed his concern over the forsaking of Salafiyya by the nation's leaders, who perhaps reasoned that once it had achieved its goal (i.e., independence), they could now ignore it. M. al-Fassi believes this to be a grave mistake for which Morocco will suffer.

5. George Antonius, *Arab Awakening*, (London, 1938), pp. 92-93.